WALES AND WAR

This poster was printed by the Parliamentary Recruiting Committee during the Great War and depicts Lord Roberts of Kandahar (1832–1914) with his Victoria Cross (awarded in 1858). Its Welsh title reads 'He did his duty – Will you do yours?'

WALES AND WAR

*Society, Politics and Religion in
the Nineteenth and Twentieth Centuries*

Edited by

MATTHEW CRAGOE and CHRIS WILLIAMS

UNIVERSITY OF WALES PRESS
CARDIFF
2007

British Library Cataloguing in Publication Data
A catalogue record for this book is available from the British Library.

ISBN 978-0-7083-1901-7

Printed in Great Britain by Antony Rowe Ltd, Wiltshire

For
Desmond Cragoe
and in memory of
John Wood (1928–2001)

Contents

Acknowledgements   ix
Editors and contributors   x
Maps and tables   xiii

Introduction   1
   MATTHEW CRAGOE AND CHRIS WILLIAMS

1. A pacific people – a martial race: pacifism, militarism and
   Welsh national identity   15
   JOHN S. ELLIS

2. Loyalties: state, nation, community and military recruiting in
   Wales, 1840–1918   38
   NEIL EVANS

3. Arming the citizens: the Volunteer Force in nineteenth-century
   Wales   63
   PAUL O'LEARY

4. Garibaldi and the Welsh political imagination   82
   KEES WINDLAND

5. 'Brimful of patriotism': Welsh Conservatives, the South
   African War and the 'Khaki' election of 1900   101
   MATTHEW CRAGOE

6. Taffs in the trenches: Welsh national identity and
   military service, 1914–1918   126
   CHRIS WILLIAMS

7. Christ and Caesar? Welsh Nonconformists and the State,
   1914–1918   165
   ROBERT POPE

Contents

8. 'The second Armageddon': remembering the Second
   World War in Wales   184
   ANGELA GAFFNEY

9. Don't mention the war? Interpreting and contextualizing
   the 1982 Falklands/Malvinas War   204
   GERWYN WILIAMS

Selected further reading   230

Index   234

Acknowledgements

This collection of essays began life, as so many collections of essays do, in the context of an academic conference. In July 2000, three papers were presented to the annual Anglo-American Conference of Historians held at the Institute of Historical Research in London, the broad theme of which was 'War and Peace'. This, however, proved to be only the starting point. We soon discovered that this brief session in no way exhausted the possibilities of the topic, and a year later, this time under the auspices of Llafur: The Welsh People's History Society, and the Centre for Modern and Contemporary Wales at the University of Glamorgan, a one-day conference took place, with the theme 'Wales and War; Wales and Peace, 1861–1939', at which several new papers were delivered. In the wake of the conference, it emerged that there was yet more to be said about the attitude of the Welsh to war, that individual scholars had been puzzling over aspects of the topic in isolation, had things they wanted to say and articles they wished to write. This volume accordingly grew to accommodate such deep-seated interest in the historical responses of Welsh men and women to war in the last one hundred and fifty years.

As editors, our pleasant duty is to acknowledge all those who have helped the process along. We must begin with a vote of thanks to the organizers of the Anglo-American Conference of Historians of 2000 and the Llafur Conference of 2001, and to all those who presented papers at these two investigations of Wales's martial past. Next, we would like to thank the contributors for the dispatch with which they turned round their articles, the patience with which they responded to our editorial queries, and the good humour which they maintained throughout. We wish, too, to acknowledge the helpfulness of all those we have worked with at the University of Wales Press. Lastly, we would like to thank those gathered on our respective 'home fronts' – Carol in London, and Sara, Samuel and Owen in Pontypridd – for their love and support.

Matthew Cragoe
Chris Williams

Editors and contributors

Matthew Cragoe is Professor of Modern British History at the University of Hertfordshire. He is the author of *An Anglican Aristocracy: The Moral Economy of the Landed Estate in Carmarthenshire, 1832–1895* (Oxford University Press, 1996), and *Culture, Politics and National Identity in Wales, 1832–1886* (OUP, 2004). He is editor of an edition of Henry Richard's *Letters on the Social and Political Condition of Wales* (British Heritage Database, 2003), (with Nigel Aston) *Anticlericalism in Britain 1500–1900* (Sutton, 2000) and (with Antony Taylor) *London Politics, 1760–1914* (Macmillan, 2005).

John S. Ellis is Assistant Professor of History at the University of Michigan, Flint. A former Fulbright scholar, he received his MA from the University of Wales Aberystwyth, and his Ph.D. from Boston College. Dr Ellis is Secretary/Treasurer of the North American Association for the Study of Welsh Culture and History (NAASWCH) and is the founding editor of the *North American Journal of Welsh Studies*. He is currently working on a book for the University of Wales Press on Welsh national identity, politics and the investitures of the Prince of Wales in 1911 and 1969.

Neil Evans is an Honorary Lecturer in the School of History and Welsh History, University of Wales Bangor, and an editor of *Llafur: Journal of the Welsh People's History Society*. He has published widely on the urban, labour, ethnic and women's history of Wales. Most recently he has edited (with Charlotte Williams and Paul O'Leary), *A Tolerant Nation? Exploring Ethnic Diversity in Wales* (University of Wales Press, 2003). He is currently writing a book on Cardiff's multi-ethnic community, *Darker Cardiff: The Underside of the City, 1840–1960*.

Angela Gaffney worked in the National Health Service for fifteen years before studying History at University of Wales College of Cardiff. She remained at Cardiff for postgraduate research and gained her Ph.D. in 1996. She held two Research Fellowships at the Centre for Advanced Welsh and Celtic Studies, University of Wales, working on the Visual Culture of Wales and Public Sculpture projects. Her monograph, *Aftermath: Remembering the Great War in Wales*, was published by the University of Wales Press in 1998, and she continues to research and publish on the commemoration of war. She is an Honorary Research Fellow in the Department of Modern History at the University of Birmingham.

Paul O'Leary is Senior Lecturer in the Department of History and Welsh History at the University of Wales Aberystwyth. He is the author of *Immigration and Integration: The Irish in Wales, 1798–2002* (UWP, 2000), and has written the introduction to a new edition of Joseph Keating's autobiography, *My Struggle for Life* (University College Dublin Press, 2005 [1916]) for the 'Classics in Irish History' series. He is the editor of *Irish Migrants in Modern Wales* (Liverpool University Press, 2004) and (with Charlotte Williams and Neil Evans) of *A Tolerant Nation? Ethnic Diversity in Modern Wales* (UWP, 2003).

Robert Pope is Senior Lecturer in the Department of Theology and Religious Studies at the University of Wales Bangor. He is the author of *Building Jerusalem: Nonconformity, Labour and the Social Question in Wales, 1906–1939* (UWP, 1998) and *Seeking God's Kingdom: The Nonconformist Social Gospel in Wales, 1906–1939* (UWP, 1999). He is the editor of *Religion and National Identity: Scotland and Wales, c.1700–2000* (UWP, 2001).

Gerwyn Wiliams is Professor in the School of Welsh at the University of Wales Bangor, and former Dean of the Faculty of Arts and Social Sciences. He is the author of *Y Rhwyg: Arolwg o Farddoniaeth Gymraeg ynghylch y Rhyfel Byd Cyntaf* ('The Rupture: A Survey of Welsh Poetry regarding the First World War') (Gomer Press, 1993), *Tir Neb: Rhyddiaith Gymraeg a'r Rhyfel Byd Cyntaf* ('No Man's Land: Welsh Prose and the First World War') (UWP, 1996) and *Tir Newydd: Agweddau ar Lenyddiaeth Gymraeg a'r Ail Ryfel Byd* ('New Ground: Aspects of Welsh Literature and the Second World War') (UWP, 2005).

Chris Williams is Professor of Welsh History at the University of Wales Swansea. He is the author of *Democratic Rhondda: Politics and Society, 1885–1951* (UWP, 1996), *Capitalism, Community and Conflict: The South Wales Coalfield, 1898–1947* (UWP, 1998) and (with Bill Jones) *B. L. Coombes* (UWP, 1999). He is the editor of *A Companion to Nineteenth Century Britain* (Blackwell, 2004), (with Bill Jones) *With Dust Still in His Throat: A B. L. Coombes Anthology* (UWP, 1999), (with Bill Jones) *B. L. Coombes, These Poor Hands: The Autobiography of a Miner Working in South*

Wales (UWP, new edition 2002), (with Duncan Tanner and Deian Hopkin) *The Labour Party in Wales, 1900–2000* (UWP, 2000) and (with Jane Aaron) *Postcolonial Wales* (UWP, 2005).

Kees Windland taught history, music and literature for many years at Rudolf Steiner schools in north Wales and California. Since completing his doctoral thesis, 'Garibaldi in Britain: reflections of a liberal hero' (University of Oxford, 2002) he has lectured in modern British and European history at Oxford Brookes University, and conducts summer seminars in Victorian culture and society for the University of Oxford, Department of Continuing Education.

Maps and tables

Map 6.1 Counties of birth, Welsh-born soldiers,
Welsh regiments (based on Table 6.2).   133

Map 6.2 Counties of birth, English-born soldiers,
Welsh regiments (based on Table 6.3).   136

Map 6.3 Towns sampled.   147

Table 3.1 Volunteers as a proportion of the male population
aged 15–49, 1862–99.   71

Table 3.2 Strength of the Volunteer Force in Wales, 1881.   72

Table 6.1 Availability of data on residence, Welsh regiments.   130

Table 6.2 Counties of birth, Welsh-born soldiers, Welsh regiments.   134

Table 6.3 Counties of birth, Welsh-born soldiers, Welsh regiments,
and counties of enumeration, males 15–44, Wales, 1911 census.   134

Table 6.4 Counties of birth, English-born soldiers, Welsh regiments.   137

Table 6.5 Birthplaces, by battalion type, Welsh regiments.   139

Table 6.6 Birthplaces, by regiment, Welsh regiments.   140

Table 6.7 Soldiers born in Welsh counties (percentages),
Welsh regiments, by regiment.   141

Table 6.8 Soldiers born in English counties
(percentages), Welsh regiments, by regiment.   142

Table 6.9 Soldiers born in Wales (percentages), Welsh battalions.   143

Table 6.10 Distribution by unit type, from towns sampled. 148

Table 6.11 Regiments with highest representation, from towns sampled. 150

Introduction

MATTHEW CRAGOE AND CHRIS WILLIAMS

War is an evil and a preventible evil.
Free Press of Monmouthshire, 31 July 1914.

In the second half of the nineteenth century, the cause of peace came to hold a special place in the rhetoric of Welsh politics. Men like Henry Richard and Lloyd George, inspired by the precepts of their Nonconformist faith, and spurred on by the moral imperatives of the doctrine of Free Trade, urged the world's powerful nations to eschew armed conflict and seek the resolution of their differences in a system of international arbitration. Even in the twentieth century, though it flickered in the face of the huge moral challenges posed by the two World Wars, the flame of pacifism did not die out. Writing in 1939, the social reformer Edgar Leyshon Chappell could argue that 'the genius of Modern Wales lies in the arts of peace'.[1] Conscientious objection remained a distinctively Welsh option during the Second World War – embraced by many members of Plaid Cymru, for example – and beyond.

The enduring relationship between the Welsh people and the desire for peace has been examined in some detail, and given definitive form in Goronwy Jones's standard text, *Wales and the Quest for Peace*, published in 1969. However, subsequent research has suggested that pacifism was always a minority belief in the Principality.[2] It now seems that the Welsh people at large differed very little in their attitudes to war from their English or Scottish contemporaries. The great drama of Empire was followed as closely in the principality as elsewhere (Lloyd George's campaign against the Boer War notwithstanding), and the twentieth century saw the Welsh rally repeatedly to the British flag. During the Great War, Welshmen flocked to the colours in numbers which closely matched the contributions of England and Scotland, while the particular contribution of the Welsh regiments to recent conflicts such as the Falklands War is recorded in the fate of the *Sir Galahad*.[3]

1

In this volume, a group of scholars set out to re-examine the reaction of the Welsh to war by focusing on a series of conflicts spanning the nineteenth and twentieth centuries. Their contributions suggest that the Welsh people responded in a wide variety of ways to war and the threat of war. The purpose of this chapter is to introduce the essays that follow and to suggest further areas of research that might profitably be explored.

The collection opens with John Ellis's scene-setting overview of the Welsh people's reaction to war from the time of the Romans on. In stark contrast to the picture of the Welsh as a naturally pacific people, painted by nineteenth-century Nonconformist intellectuals and twentieth-century nationalists, Ellis demonstrates that the Welsh were celebrated for their warlike qualities. He argues that, during the nineteenth century, both versions of Welsh national identity were still current. In one, the Welsh were acknowledged as a nation of ancient warriors, 'rough heroes of Crecy and Agincourt', who often displayed high levels of enthusiasm for particular conflicts and for the British Empire generally.[4] The other image, taking its cue from contemporary Nonconformist ideals, presented the Welsh as defiantly unmilitaristic, an impression borne out by low levels of recruitment to the regular army in Victorian Wales. The First and Second World Wars were to demonstrate that the former was the more accurate.

During the 1914–18 war, as David Lloyd George accommodated Non-conformist objections by stressing the need to defend Christianity and the rights of small nations, the Welsh flocked to the nation's colours; the moral case for fighting the Second World War appeared as overwhelming to the inhabitants of the Principality as anywhere else in Britain. Yet a strain of pacifism lingered at the margins of Welsh life. The self-conscious champions of Wales's national identity, notably Plaid Cymru, retained an adherence to a more exclusively pacifist construction of Welshness. Since 1945 this has been contested by minorities, even within the nationalist movement, such as the Free Wales Army. Wales, argues Ellis, has suffered from a process of 'selective national amnesia' regarding its military and imperial pasts, and he concludes with the thought that 'Welshness and its relationship to war is not a static concept with unchanging traits, but a fluid construction, constantly contested, negotiated and revised in relation to changing historical circumstances.'

Ellis's chapter provides a broad context for the remaining essays in the book, highlighting as it does the competing traditions of militarism and pacifism within modern Wales. In the second chapter, Neil Evans explores more closely the relationship between nineteenth-century Wales and the British Army. He suggests that while the appeals of Nonconformity and of pacifism are part of the explanation for the low levels of recruitment from the Principality noted by Ellis, the low pay available to soldiers and the competing economic opportunities of industrializing Wales must also form part of the equation. Moreover, there was a cultural dimension. Evans also points out that the army itself made little effort to accommodate Welsh sensibilities in the areas of religion and language until the recruiting exigencies of the Great War forced the War Office's hand. Even then, as his case study of Ruthin between 1914 and 1918 demonstrates, there remained important cultural obstacles to recruitment in the rural areas of Wales.

Paul O'Leary's essay investigates another side of the recruitment problem in Wales, but focuses on the Volunteer Movement rather than on the regular army. Delving beneath the superficial rhetoric of pacifism, he reveals that its hold on Welsh political culture was more tenuous than might have been appreciated. The relatively enthusiastic response of Welshmen to the inauguration of the Volunteer Movement in 1859 indicates that a readiness to take up arms in defence of one's country (however defined) was not lacking across much of nineteenth-century Wales. Such an attitude was reconcilable with the Liberal party's reluctance to engage in imperialist adventures or acts of military aggression through the discourse of defencism.[5] However, it also drew on an identifiable appetite within Wales for stories of military heroes, past and present, and for news of the Crimean War. Furthermore, the Volunteer Movement's significance extended beyond those who enlisted in its ranks: through its bands, parades and reviews it attracted widespread public attention and approval. O'Leary argues that, in some important respects, the Volunteer Movement reveals a Welsh society increasingly reconciled to its place within the British state, and progressively more ready to share in the common identity of Britishness.

The wider appetite within Welsh culture for heroic military exploits was nowhere more dramatically evidenced than in support for the figure of Giuseppe Garibaldi. Good Nonconformist Welshmen, like John Griffith (Gohebydd), the leading Welsh-language journalist of his day, flocked to meet Garibaldi in person when he visited London in 1864, as Kees Windland relates. To such men, the Italian nationalist and military hero embodied a resistance to alien cultural oppression that suggested parallels between the plight of Italy and that of Wales itself. However, as Windland also notes, responses were 'complex, multivalent and contingent on a range of social, cultural and political factors'. As with the Volunteer Movement, so with Garibaldi: it is impossible to identify a single, united public response from Wales. Other prominent public figures, such as the Reverend Thomas Price, were quite prepared to ignore any supposed Welsh dimension, preferring instead to exploit Garibaldi's significance as an icon for British Liberalism. And men like Henry Richard, secretary of the Peace Society, remained adamantly opposed to Garibaldi because of his open resort to war. In the first flush of their ideological potency the Nonconformist, middle-class

Liberal leaders of mid-Victorian Wales were unable to settle on a common interpretation of the Italian example.

As the century wore on, of course, the hegemony of the Nonconformist middle-class was to become established and one consequence of this, as Ellis also points out, was that other social and political groups within the Principality became marginalized. One such group was the Conservative party, and in his essay, Matthew Cragoe examines their role during the period of the Boer War. Welsh Tories embraced the language of a unitary British state and of the British Empire, as well as manifesting strong links with the military establishment, and many of the bodies that served the party well in England, such as the Primrose League and Conservative working-men's clubs, also had a wide popular appeal in Wales. Cragoe examines the importance of these institutions through a study of the 'Khaki' election of 1900 in south-east Wales. His analysis confirms the picture drawn by Kenneth O. Morgan of Wales as a region in which 'pro-Boer' feelings were held only by a minority.[6] The Welsh public, as they had done during the Crimean campaign, thirsted for news of the conflict, and celebrated with unrestrained enthusiasm the relief of Mafeking in the spring of 1900. But, as Cragoe demonstrates, support for the cause of Empire did not necessarily translate unproblematically into support for the Conservative party. As the electoral contests of October 1900 in Cardiff and Monmouth Boroughs reveal, a variety of factors, some intensely local, some clearly material, influenced popular responses both to the Boer War and to the appeals made by rival candidates at the polls.

The Boer War seemed to many of its participants the last gentleman's war. The new century saw the development of a new style of conflict, which made much greater demands on the human capital of participant nations. In Britain, the mass volunteering for 'Kitchener's Army' during 1914 and 1915 was finally superseded in 1916 by conscription. Chris Williams's analysis of enlistment in Welsh regiments during the Great War offers a pioneering analysis of Welsh soldiering in this new environment. It explores particularly the links between Welsh soldiers and those from elsewhere in Britain, and thus returns to the issue of Britishness and British identities raised by Paul O'Leary earlier in the volume.[7] It also suggests that the deployment of Welsh martial rhetoric by Lloyd George and other recruiters during the early stages of the Great War did not result in a homogeneous, all-Welsh Army Corps. The 38th Welsh Division included many soldiers born outside Wales, and, by the same token, a significant minority of Welsh-born soldiers served with units other than the Welsh infantry regiments. The experience of recruitment and military service appears to have been diverse indeed: there was no single 'Welsh' truth to either.

Robert Pope takes up another of the themes identified by John Ellis: the Nonconformist suspicion of the British state and their predilection for pacifism. Such attitudes did not, as we know, long withstand the pressures of the Great War, and most Nonconformist ministers were recruited to the official cause, as they had been during the Boer War. Rather than war itself, to which the majority were able to reconcile themselves as being fought in a just cause, it was the introduction of conscription in 1916 which troubled the Nonconformist conscience most. As Pope shows, the trauma suffered over this issue by both Nonconformist intellectuals and the Welsh Liberal party was to prove extraordinarily destructive of the cultural and political hegemony both had enjoyed in Wales prior to 1914. Pope suggests that, 'this one move, more than any other, marked the end of both political Nonconformity and the Liberal party'; the vacuum that resulted from the collapse of these linked institutions provided the opportunity for a rather more marginal grouping of intellectuals associated with Plaid Genedlaethol Cymru to hoist their standard in the 1920s.

The last two essays in the volume examine different ways in which more modern conflicts have been remembered by those who survived them. The dominant theme with respect to the First and Second World Wars has been commemoration of the dead. The soldiers who fell in the these conflicts were not, in the main, professional soldiers, but conscripts, and society demanded that their sacrifice be recorded in a tangible form. Sigmund Freud suggested in 1917 that memorials played an important part in making bereavement more bearable by establishing limits to a sense of loss.[8] Mourners engage with the memorial, grieve, and then disengage, returning to ordinary life. Angela Gaffney has already made a major contribution to the understanding of the Great War in Wales through her study of the campaign to erect war memorials after 1918.[9] Her essay in this collection is a preliminary exploration of these themes – loss, grieving and collective memory – in the context of the Second World War.

The Second World War remains something of a paradox in the history of Wales. Though quite evidently a conflict of enormous significance, it has yet to draw substantial attention from professional historians. In some respects this might reflect the absence of a clear 'Welsh' dimension to the conflict, once one has exhausted the contortions of the leadership of Plaid Cymru over whether or not the German occupations of Czechoslovakia or of Norway were qualitatively different from the English 'occupation' of Wales,[10] or of the leadership of the Communist party over whether it was an 'imperialist' or 'anti-fascist' struggle.[11] Important work has been done on the *Luftwaffe*'s bombing of Welsh ports,[12] and on the entry in large numbers of women into the munitions factories,[13] but much remains unpublished or unwritten.[14] Angela Gaffney's essay is both a poignant evocation of the human cost of conflict – the story of the Baker family of Cardiff brings home forcefully the personal tragedies that lie behind every name on each war memorial – and an important new development in modern Welsh historiography.

If the first half of the twentieth century saw conflicts fought out by huge civilian armies, the second witnessed a return to engagements contested by smaller, professional military forces. The final essay in this collection forms another attempt to break new ground by studying one such conflict, the Falklands War of 1982. Gerwyn Wiliams, a recognized expert on the Welsh-language literature of both World Wars,[15] here explores responses to the war in the South Atlantic. In keeping with the other essays in the volume he discovers not a single Welsh reaction, but many diverse ones. There were many Welsh soldiers, and at least a part of the Welsh public, who had no particular problem with the conflict as *Welsh* men or *Welsh* women. Likewise, there were many who interpreted the tragic loss of Welsh soldiers on board the *Sir Galahad* not as an event with special resonance for Wales, but in more general terms, symbolic of 'the perennial slaughter and sorrow of war', in Wiliams's own phrase. There were many who sympathized with the need to retake the islands, seized in an act of unprovoked aggression by a fascist dictatorship desperate to distract attention from its appalling domestic record through an act of military aggrandizement, who simultaneously resented the political capital Margaret Thatcher made from the conflict.

Yet there was also a pronounced strand of hostility to the conflict, notably among the minority nationalist element identified by Ellis. Plaid Cymru, as Wiliams reminds us, was the only party officially to oppose the war. In his chapter, Wiliams explores the range of literary and artistic responses to the war, and demonstrates the extent to which opposition to the conflict came to be symbolized by the potential for internecine strife afforded by the connection of Wales and Patagonia. However, Wiliams goes further and compares these analyses with the memories of soldiers who actually served in the war itself. There was, he discovers, a different conception of 'Welshness' among the soldiers and the artists: those who fought found little resonance in the notion of the Patagonians as fellow 'Welshmen'. It may be that Wiliams, in his comments on the experience of Simon Weston, the soldier who survived being so badly burned on the *Sir Galahad*, provides a fitting summary of this volume's chief finding concerning the Welsh people and the wars in which Britain has been involved over the last two centuries. 'Simon Weston', he says, 'has not for a second suggested any inconsistency between his patriotism and his membership of the army . . . In terms of identity and nationhood, he too considered himself a Welshman, a Briton and a monarchist.' In times of war, the evidence adduced in this volume suggests that a vast majority of men and women in Wales would have said the same.

The essays in this book thus offer a series of new perspectives on an important but underexplored area of the Welsh past.[16] However, *Wales and War* makes no claim to present more than an initial reconnaissance of the terrain. Much remains to be done, and we conclude here by laying out some avenues worthy of further exploration. For the sake of convenience, the period has been divided into two broad sections, either side of 1914. Prior to the outbreak of the Great War, wars were fought by professional armies and had a minimal impact on the home front; the assassination in Sarajevo of Archduke Franz Ferdinand, however, heralded a new era of 'total war' which left no aspect of society untouched. The consideration of future research offered here obeys this implicit chronology and begins by examining the nineteenth century, before moving on to examine potential topics in the post-1914 period.

The attitude of people to the affairs of the world at the start of the period covered by this volume was heavily influenced by the outlook of the Nonconformist chapels. Our want of knowledge of the chapels is perhaps the most significant lacuna in current accounts of nineteenth-century Welsh society.[17] The chapels were the central institutions governing the local culture of Welsh community life, and the preachers were men of enormous influence in their local milieux.[18] Any research regarding the internal mechanics of chapel life would be welcome, and the dilemmas occasioned by wars offer fascinating insights for those interested in the mid-Victorian period. John Ellis's essay in this volume points out that many leading figures at this time 'combined support for Welsh cultural, religious and political issues with vigorous campaigning for the pacifist cause', but how widely were such ideas really held at the grass-roots of the chapel community?

The years between 1850 and 1870 offer an especially propitious window for such a study. Alongside the Italian wars discussed by Kees Windland, the period also witnessed the Crimean War (1854–6) and the American Civil War (1861–5), both of which captured the public imagination. What is more, they were covered in the newly viable Welsh-language weekly press, which became a platform through which the Nonconformist middle class could make its views known.[19] The *Amserau*, which was run from Liverpool by Revd William Rees, circulated widely during the early 1850s when the Crimean War was raging, and the American Civil War coincided with the first great flush of success for Thomas Gee's Denbighshire-based title, *Baner Ac Amserau Cymru*, founded in 1859.[20] It offered extensive coverage of the conflict, and indeed, John Griffith (Y Gohebydd), the paper's London correspondent, actually travelled around America between 1865 and 1867.[21] The fact that he continued to lecture on his American experiences long afterwards suggests a degree of popular interest in the war and the society it affected that calls out for further research.[22] An examination of how these views were mediated through the local chapel network would enhance our understanding of the relationship between Nonconformity's leading figures and the rank-and-file membership of the chapels, and represent an important addition to our knowledge of chapel culture.

Our ignorance of chapel life and Nonconformist culture is paralleled by the extent to which the aristocracy remain an unknown quantity in Welsh history. For those bent on studying the relationship between war and mid nineteenth-century society this is a serious drawback. The aristocracy had a distinctively martial outlook, actively sought careers in the armed forces and patronized a range of local organizations that were more or less military in intent, from local militias to rifle clubs. Even their recreations carried militaristic overtones, from shooting to fox-hunting, which, as Jorrocks famously remarked, offered 'the image of war without its guilt, and only five-and-twenty per cent of its danger'.[23] How far the feeling of 'difference' fostered by the chapels between the Nonconformist 'people' and the culturally 'alienated' aristocracy affected Welsh attitudes to war would be an interesting study.[24] Whether it affected attitudes to Britain's imperial adventures is not clear. Certainly, considerable excitement was engendered by the discovery that the great explorer Henry Morton Stanley was Welsh, and *Baner* expended a good deal of ink extolling his virtues. But how were other, more distinctively martial heroes of the late nineteenth-century Empire viewed? How, for example, was news of the death of General Gordon at Khartoum in 1885 received?

By extension, it would be fascinating to study the response of the public to the series of imperial conflicts in which the British army became engaged during the last three decades of the century, culminating in the Boer War. That there is more to Wales and the Zulu Wars than a film starring Stanley Baker and Michael Caine is already being demonstrated by the work of M. Paul Bryant-Quinn.[25] With respect to the Boer conflict, as Matthew Cragoe argues, popular sympathy in the industrial areas of Wales quickly fell in behind the British cause; however, the fact that the Conservatives, fighting on an explicitly 'Khaki' ticket, could not be sure of electoral success, even in 1900, suggests a complicated relationship between the Welsh and the imperial cause, worthy of further investigation.

By examining the history of institutions and groups which have hitherto suffered relative neglect – chapels, aristocrats, Conservatives – therefore, there is the potential to deepen considerably our appreciation of what Welsh people thought about war, both as an abstract concept and as a practical manifestation of imperialism. The coming of the Great War, however, necessarily changed popular perceptions of conflict. If most nineteenth-century wars were wars of aggression, the conflict that broke out with Germany in 1914 had much more the air of a defensive struggle, fought on our own doorstep. If this marked one considerable change, another was the totalizing nature of the conflict. The requirement that societies mobilize all their resources in order to maximize their capacity to sustain conflict drove important developments. Governments took unprecedented control of everyday life, and hitherto-marginalized social groups, notably women, came to the fore in a way that had not been experienced before. Given the extent of the literature produced with respect to this conflict, it is extraordinary that no full-length treatment of the war as it affected Wales has yet appeared.[26] By way of contrast, the Great War experiences of both Ireland and Scotland have been the subject of academic volumes, and Ireland has also recently received its own 'military history', in which the conflict figures prominently.[27]

In terms of Welsh attitudes to war, therefore, the Great War offers many possibilities, and the same point could be made concerning the rise of the Fascist parties in Italy and Germany during the inter-war years. How did Welsh people at large, rather than just that portion bound up with the Labour movement, respond to the rise of Hitler, the Spanish Civil War and the famous vote at the Oxford Union when the flower of British youth declared that they would not fight for King and Country?[28] And the Second World War offers a further series of opportunities for fresh enquiry. Research has been done on the experience of women in munitions factories during the Second World War, but how did society respond to the notion of Welsh women, not simply as defenders of the Home Front, but as active participants in the war effort? Another aspect of the conflict that would repay exploration in a Welsh context concerns the reserved occupations. The following letter from a Montgomeryshire serviceman expresses well the simmering tensions that could surround this issue. Writing to his local newspaper after the successful conclusion of the war in Europe, but while the war against Japan still remained to be won, he pondered whether many who had stayed at home until now might now be enlisted? 'Some who "could not be spared" to fight for their country', he wrote, 'could well be spared to get married and take farms of their own. I have even heard of a case where a farm labourer was dismissed so as to strengthen the son's claim for exemption from National Service.'[29] Whilst acknowledging (facetiously) that he could not imagine the hardships the farmers had had to endure from petrol rationing, he went on:

> But they in their turn do not know what it is to spend nights in water-logged gunpits and foxholes, listening to the whine and crack of shells that might at any minute send you into eternity; they have never seen their comrades fall in battle. So perhaps you will grasp that it is not very pleasant for those of us who have experienced these things, and who at this moment are faced with the prospect of a Far Eastern campaign, to come home on a brief leave and find these sons of well-to-do farmers walking about towns on market days as though they owned the place, hardly knowing that there is still a war to be fought and won.

Can you think of any good reason why these people should stay behind with their cars, their dances and good times generally, while less fortunate men have to go out to face the dangers of a war which may well be more horrible and bloody than the one we have just fought in Europe? I can't.

In a country like Wales, where there were many reserved occupations in both agricultural and industrial areas, such tensions might have played an important role both in the war and in the subsequent years of peace. The bitter tone of this letter also goes some way towards explaining the contempt with which many greeted Plaid Cymru after the war. John Pennant, writing in the *Western Mail* in 1945, summed up the feeling thus:

This was the party that saw more peril to Wales from English evacuee children than from Hitler's hordes. They were 'neutral' in the greatest war for human freedom. They, a handful of fanatics, presumed to speak for Wales from their safe jobs and safe hide-holes when 250,000 Welshmen were risking their lives to resist the greatest military despotism the world has ever seen.[30]

As one Caernarfonshire man put it, Plaid Cymru were not 'fit to be a parish council', let alone a government.[31] How were such tensions reconciled during the difficult years after the Second World War, when the soldiers came home and had to take their places in societies where those in reserved occupations had enhanced their social prospects during the war years? And was there a difference between rural and urban areas?

A similar study might interrogate another very controversial aspect of the recent Welsh past. For many men, the war did not simply end in 1945. Memories of what they had suffered as prisoners of war in Japan ensured a lasting degree of hostility in many parts of the Principality to the creation of Japanese car factories from the 1980s onwards. In this, as in many other ways, the Second World War had an enduring impact on the social history of Wales.

If the first half of the twentieth century was haunted by the ravages of total war, the second was lived in the shadow of the Cold War. This sustained period of international tension between the superpowers was punctuated by armed conflicts – notably in Korea and Vietnam – and nerve-stretching stand-offs, such as the Cuban Missile Crisis of 1962. Much of the popular history of the opposition to the Cold War is undoubtedly bound up with the history of the Campaign for Nuclear Disarmament,[32] but it would also be interesting to explore, in the manner adopted by Gerwyn Wiliams in this volume, how Welsh intellectuals and artists responded, and whether the motifs that marked cultural production in England at this time also found expression in Welsh-language culture.[33]

Another theme in the second half of the twentieth century involves the threat of domestic terrorism. The most potent source of conflict was Ireland. The Welsh had long had an equivocal relationship with Ireland. In the nineteenth century, those Liberals who claimed to speak for the Welsh 'nation' were generally at pains to distance themselves from the violence of Irish agitation. Although Paul O'Leary has skilfully documented the history of Irish people in Wales,[34] little work has been done to trace Welsh attitudes to Ireland after partition, and particularly after the onset of 'the Troubles' in the late 1960s. For much of the 1970s, 1980s and 1990s, the IRA were an active force on the British mainland, and the reaction to their activities, in their own right and as a counterpoint to the activities of militant Welsh nationalist groups, such as the Free Wales Army and Meibion Glyndŵr, would constitute a valuable area of investigation.[35] And to bring the catalogue right up to date, it would be interesting to examine the reaction of Welsh people to the attacks of 11 September 2001, the 'war on terror', the invasions of Afghanistan and Iraq, and the terror campaign mounted by radical Islamists against London in 2005.

Finally, one area about which very little is known is the attitude to their task of those who actually did the fighting. Chris Williams's essay in this volume attempts to identify the individuals who fought in 'Welsh' regiments during the Great War, and highlights some of the social resonances of the inevitably mixed fighting force that evolved. Gerwyn Wiliams's account of the Falklands conflict suggests it would be possible to recapture another level of social experience from conflicts dating back to the Boer War at least. For whom and for what did Welsh soldiers fight and die? And what of the Welsh who fought in the other branches of the Armed Forces, notably the RAF and the Navy, or served with bodies like the Territorial Army? These services, with bases in the Principality, testing grounds in locations like Pendine, and extensive training facilities in the Brecon Beacons, Mynydd Epynt and the Black Mountains, have had deep roots in the community and form part of the fabric of the social and economic history of twentieth-century Wales.

It is envisaged that this volume of essays will provide a starting point for a fresh consideration of the reactions of Welsh people to war over the last two centuries. The contributors hope those who read it will feel inspired to incorporate some of the questions set out in these final pages into their own research. It is clear that if we wish to interrogate the relationship between war and society, we must ask new questions, and include groups hitherto marginalized in the story of the Welsh past – notably aristocracy, Conservatives and women – while also looking with fresh eyes at a range of subjects, ranging from religion to masculinity.[36] Similarly, it may be necessary to confront some difficult issues – such as residual social hostility to those in reserved occupations, pacifists and the Japanese. Nevertheless, we believe the result of such activity will be a more rounded picture, not just of Welsh attitudes to war, but of the social history of modern Wales itself.

NOTES

1 Edgar L. Chappell, *Cardiff Street Names* (Cardiff, 1939), p. 7.
2 Kenneth O. Morgan, 'Wales and the Boer War – a reply', *The Welsh History Review* (hereafter *WHR*), 4, 4 (1969); Ryland Wallace, *Organise! Organise! Organise!: A Study of Reform Agitations in Wales, 1840–1886* (Cardiff, 1991), pp. 84–6; D. Densil Morgan, *The Span of the Cross: Religion and Society in Wales 1914–2000* (Cardiff, 1999), pp. 61–4.
3 Deian Hopkin, 'Patriots and pacifists in Wales, 1914–1918: the case of Capt. Lionel Lindsay and the Rev. T. E. Nicholas', *Llafur: Journal of the Society for the Study of Welsh Labour History*, 1, 3 (1974); Kenneth O. Morgan, 'Peace movements in Wales, 1899–1945', *WHR*, 10, 4 (1981); Morgan, *Span of the Cross*, pp. 49, 158–9, 168.
4 On this theme, see Chris Williams, 'Problematizing Wales: an exploration in historiography and postcoloniality', in Jane Aaron and Chris Williams (eds), *Postcolonial Wales* (Cardiff, 2005), pp. 7–8.
5 Paul Laity, *The British Peace Movement, 1870–1914* (Oxford, 2001).
6 Henry Pelling, 'Wales and the Boer War', *WHR*, 4, 4 (1969); Morgan, 'Wales and the Boer War – a reply'.
7 Paul Ward, *Britishness Since 1870* (London, 2004).
8 Sigmund Freud, 'Mourning and melancholia', in Freud, *Collected Papers*, vol. 4, trans. Joan Riviere (New York, 1959), pp. 152–70, especially p. 154.
9 Angela Gaffney, *Aftermath: Remembering the Great War in Wales* (Cardiff, 1998).
10 Dafydd Glyn Jones, 'Aspects of his work: his politics', in Alun R. Jones and Gwyn Thomas (eds), *Presenting Saunders Lewis* (Cardiff, 1983), p. 69; D. Hywel Davies, *The Welsh Nationalist Party, 1925–1945: A Call to Nationhood* (Cardiff, 1983), pp. 229–31.
11 For which, see Chris Williams, *Democratic Rhondda: Politics and Society, 1885–1951* (Cardiff, 1996), pp. 161–2; John Attfield and Stephen Williams (eds), *1939: The Communist Party and the War* (London, 1984).
12 J. R. Alban, *Air Raids on Swansea* (Swansea, 1981); Alban, *The Three Nights' Blitz: Select Contemporary Reports relating to Swansea's Air Raids of February 1941* (Swansea, 1994); June Morris, 'Morale under air attack: Swansea, 1939–41', *WHR*, 11, 3 (1983).
13 Mari A. Williams, *A Forgotten Army: Female Munitions Workers of South Wales, 1939–1945* (Cardiff, 2002).
14 Though see Stuart Broomfield, 'South Wales during the Second World War: the coal industry and its community' (unpublished Ph.D. Thesis, University of Wales, 1979).
15 Most importantly, Gerwyn Wiliams, *Tir Neb: Rhyddiaith Gymraeg a'r Rhyfel Byd Cyntaf* (Cardiff, 1996), and Wiliams, *Tir Newydd: Agweddau ar Lenyddiaeth Gymraeg a'r Ail Ryfel Byd* (Cardiff, 2005).

16 Although note that in 1986, Dai Smith recommended a close examination of 'the experience of different Welsh peoples, home and abroad, in different wars – from the thirteenth century through to the Zulu wars, from the World Wars, to the Spanish Civil War and the Falklands'. 'Back to the future', *Planet: The Welsh Internationalist*, 56 (1986), 20.

17 See Russell Davies, *Hope and Heartbreak: A Social History of Wales and the Welsh, 1776–1871* (Cardiff, 2005), pp. 324–75, for an interesting recent approach.

18 Matthew Cragoe, 'Conscience or coercion? Clerical influence at the general election of 1868 in Wales', *Past and Present*, 149 (1995).

19 Ieuan Gwynedd Jones, 'The dynamics of Welsh politics', in Jones, *Explorations and Explanations: Essays in the Social History of Victorian Wales* (Llandysul, 1981), pp. 294–5; Kenneth O. Morgan, *Wales in British Politics, 1868–1922* (Cardiff, 1980), pp. 8–9; Matthew Cragoe, *Culture, Politics and National Identity in Wales, 1832–1886* (Oxford, 2004), pp. 208–13.

20 Aled Gruffydd Jones, *Press, Politics and Society: A History of Journalism in Wales* (Cardiff, 1993), pp. 2, 204.

21 For Gohebydd, see Matthew Cragoe, 'John Griffith, Y Gohebydd, and the general election of 1868 in Wales', *Transactions of the Honourable Society of Cymmrodorion 1997*, n.s., 4 (1998).

22 Though see Jerry Hunter, *Llwch Cenhedloedd: Y Cymry a Rhyfel Cartref America* (Llanrwst, 2003).

23 Robert Surtees, *Handley Cross or Mr Jorrocks's Hunt* (London, 1901), p. 220.

24 Philip Jenkins, *A History of Modern Wales, 1536–1990* (Harlow, 1992), p. 305.

25 M. Paul Bryant-Quinn, 'Welsh-language reactions to the Anglo-Zulu War', *The Journal of the Anglo Zulu War Historical Society*, 16 (2004); Bryant-Quinn, '25B/312 Private Owen Ellis, C Company, 1st Battalion, 24th Regiment of Foot (2nd Warwickshire Regiment), Killed in Action 22 January 1879, Isandhlwana, Zululand', *British Army Review*, 137 (2005). See also Alan Conway, 'Welsh soldiers in the Zulu War', *National Library of Wales Journal*, 11 (1959).

26 Even some of the major textbooks have little to say: David Williams, *A History of Modern Wales* (London, 1950), although taking his history up to 1939, and claiming (p. 286) that 'Life in Wales in the quarter of a century after 1914 was entirely dominated by the First World War and by its consequences', has nothing to say about the war itself. Gwyn A. Williams, *When Was Wales? A History of the Welsh* (Harmondsworth, 1985), perhaps straddles both the socialist and the nationalist positions. Astonishingly, there is just one paragraph (p. 249) that deals directly with the Great War, and the Second World War receives merely passing references. An important exception is represented by Mari A. Williams, in her chapter covering Wales between 1914 and 1945 in the BBC Millennium History of Wales. See Williams, 'In the wars: Wales 1914–45', in Gareth Elwyn Jones and Dai Smith (eds), *The People of Wales* (Llandysul, 1999). It is hoped that the situation will be rectified by Robin Barlow, *Wales and the First World War* (Cardiff, forthcoming).

27 Keith Jeffery, *Ireland and the Great War* (Cambridge, 2000); Catriona M. M. Macdonald and E. W. McFarland (eds), *Scotland and the Great War* (Tuckwell, 1999); Thomas Bartlett and Keith Jeffery (eds), *A Military History of Ireland* (Cambridge, 1996).

[28] On the importance of the Spanish Civil War to Wales, see Hywel Francis, *Miners Against Fascism: Wales and the Spanish Civil War* (London, 1984), and Robert Stradling, *Wales and the Spanish Civil War: The Dragon's Dearest Cause?* (Cardiff, 2004).

[29] *Montgomery County Times* (hereafter *MCT*), 14 July 1945.

[30] *Western Mail* (hereafter *WM*), 21 April 1945.

[31] Ibid., 24 April 1945.

[32] Gwyn A. Williams, *Peace and Power: Henry Richard – A Radical For Our Time* (Cardiff, 1988).

[33] Tony Shaw (ed.), *Contemporary British History Special Issue: Britain and the Culture of the Cold War*, 19, 2 (2005).

[34] Paul O'Leary, *Immigration and Integration: The Irish in Wales, 1798–1922* (Cardiff, 2000); O'Leary (ed.), *The Irish in Wales* (Liverpool, 2004).

[35] Alan Butt Philip, *The Welsh Question: Nationalism in Welsh Politics, 1945–70* (Cardiff, 1975), pp. 114–15.

[36] Paul O'Leary, 'Masculine histories: gender and the social history of modern Wales', *WHR*, 22, 2 (2004).

1

A pacific people – a martial race: pacifism, militarism and Welsh national identity

JOHN S. ELLIS

It is widely believed that Welsh culture is essentially imbued with the values of pacifism, and that the Welsh nation is rooted in an historical opposition to war, militarism and imperial conquest. Nonconformist Christianity, the advocacy of mid nineteenth-century cultural nationalists and twentieth-century political nationalists, have all helped to construct an image of the Welsh as a Christian people whose antipathy towards war was grounded upon religion and its own melancholy history of English conquest and domination. Wales has a far more complicated relationship with war than this image allows, and the Welsh have at times been enthusiastic supporters of and participants in war and the British imperial enterprise. This periodic failure of the Welsh to live up to the pacifist ideal has often been explained historically in reference to the forces of Anglicization, the level of support for war theoretically corresponding to the degree of decline in Welshness in any given period. Nowhere is this more evident than in discussions of Welsh support for the Great War. Tecwyn Lloyd, for example, condemned the period as one of an 'almost total loss of purpose and national identity', while Gwynfor Evans wrote that 'the Welsh pattern of values and culture was shaken to its foundations' by Welsh participation in the conflict.[1]

Such interpretations, however, ignore the atmosphere of public discourse in which war has been historically conducted and supported by the Welsh. Rather than being in diametric opposition to Welshness, a native military tradition draws upon Welsh history, sentiments and national aspirations. Indeed, on the matter of war, Wales has been Janus-faced. Welsh national identity is contested by two competing images, alternately defining the Welsh as a pacific people and as a martial race. Although these seemingly contradictory images of the Welsh could overlap, percolate and blend together in the rhetoric of Welsh patriotism, it is possible and useful to define the Welsh pacific and martial traditions and to use the characteristics and history of those traditions better to understand the Welsh response to war. In considering these traditions, it is not enough to merely demonstrate that they are constructed or invented. We must also understand their nature, meaning and power through their relationship to the broader historical context in which they occur, and to the developments, conflicts and the changing notions of Welshness that these traditions reflect.

'AN OLD AND HAUGHTY NATION PROUD IN ARMS'[2]

The Welsh martial tradition ultimately rests on images accumulated during the warlike days of the distant past. In truth, in medieval and ancient times, the Welsh and their tribal Celtic forebears were known for their ferocity, tenacity and daring in battle and were reputed to have a natural enthusiasm for war. Both the Romans and the English contrasted their perception of their own orderly, peaceful societies, where military force was largely the prerogative of the state, with that of the chaotic, militarist societies of the west, where war chiefs abounded, seemingly every man was a soldier and endemic war was a way of life.[3] Giraldus Cambrensis wrote famously of the ferocity of the Welsh as a people, claiming that they 'in peace dream of war' and lived by the poetic maxim 'Turn peace away, for honour perishes with peace'.[4]

Indeed, in the poor, largely pastoral society of mountainous medieval Wales, wars and raids were the primary means to fortune, liberty and political power.[5] No wonder, then, that the Welsh should be seen as violent and opportunistic raiders, 'warlike and skilled in arms', whose 'glory is in plunder and theft'.[6] To English eyes, Welsh military ardour was a product of their wildness and the inherent disorder of their society. The Welsh soldier developed a long-lived reputation as a skilled and hardy fighter, but lacking in discipline, ignoring chivalrous conduct and given over to plunder, drink and womanizing.[7] In the English mind, then, the militarism of the Welsh was symptomatic of the poverty, anarchy and barbarism of their society. While admiring their martial spirit, they regarded with horror the 'mutual slaughter', 'universal discord' and 'brutal and bestial behaviour' characteristic of Welsh martial passions.[8]

Another venerable and widely circulated image, however, held that the Welsh fought principally for their crude notions of freedom and patriotism, one man's anarchy being another man's liberty. 'They are passionately devoted to their freedom and to the defence of their country', Giraldus wrote. 'For these they fight, for these they suffer hardships, for these they will take up their weapons and willingly sacrifice their lives.'[9] From the earliest descriptions, then, the Welsh martial tradition was tied to images of resistance to conquest. This was reflected in the construction of a whole pantheon of heroes. Arising in folklore and recounted in popular history, it typically included Buddug, the Celtic queen who took bloody vengeance upon the Romans; the legendary Arthur, Welsh defender against the Saxon invasion; Llewelyn Olaf, the last of the native princes, who died defying the conqueror; and Owain Glyndŵr, whose revolt seemed to confound the forces of English domination at every turn. Defiant and proud, these heroes represented the unbroken Welsh spirit of resistance, but at the same time, their ultimate defeat signified the bitter and conclusive shattering of military opposition itself. The war for independence was not to be forgotten, but it was over and it had been lost. Writing in 1866, Henry Richard recalled that the old heroes of resistance were 'cherished with great tenacity by the popular mind' in Wales and that:

A passionate . . . fierce and vindictive patriotism . . . was constantly fed by stories, half fact and half fable, transmitted from father to son, of the cruelty and perfidy of their Saxon and Norman oppressors, and of the victories and defeats which had marked their long struggle for independence, while fighting under the banner of the Red Dragon.[10]

The war of independence may have been lost, but the historical narrative of the Welsh martial tradition continued, not in resistance to British imperial expansion, but in service to it. Once again, the traditional image of Welsh militarism had foundations in historical fact. Following the English conquest of the late thirteenth century, the surplus population of war-torn, pastoral Wales became a major source of recruits for the forces of the English kings in their campaigns against the Scots and French. Belief in their inherent military prowess and their value as recruits was such that one leading historian has drawn an analogy between the recruitment of the medieval Welsh and that of the modern Gurkhas.[11] So tightly associated were these Welsh recruits with the use of the new and devastating longbow that the claim has often been made that the Welsh invented the weapon, although English leadership is significantly given the credit for its tactical perfection.[12] Welsh military service to the Crown culminated in the Hundred Years War of the fourteenth and fifteenth centuries. Foremost among the symbols of the Welsh martial tradition were the Welsh archers at the battles of Agincourt (1415) and, most especially, Crecy (1346), where 'the Welshmen did good service in a garden where leeks did grow, wearing leeks in their Monmouth caps'.[13] As Shakespeare was to recount in his 1598 play *Henry V*, the wearing of the leek on St David's Day became a traditional means of asserting Welsh patriotic pride. By the eighteenth century, this symbol of military prowess had become so popular as an icon of the Welsh that caricatures of the period commonly depicted the Welshman with an ever-present leek in his hat.[14]

In addition to the earthy heroes of Crecy and Agincourt, there was a markedly royalist and aristocratic element in the images of the medieval Welsh soldier. An important stream of Welsh historical writing subsumed the history of the Welsh people after the conquest into the military history associated with the English Princes of Wales, most particularly with that of the victor of Crecy, Edward the Black Prince.[15] The Prince's badge of ostrich feathers and 'Ich Dien' ('I Serve') motto was adopted on that battlefield and subsequently came to be used, not only as a symbol of Welsh loyalty, but as an icon of Wales itself. Closely tied to the figures of the princes, several Welsh captains of noble blood achieved prominence in the Hundred Years War and came to personify the Welsh martial tradition, through the poetry of the Welsh bards.[16] Such warriors were epitomized in Shakespeare's *Henry V* in the character of Fluellen, a tough and experienced soldier, a fiercely proud Welshman and a loyal confidant to the English king. In developing this character, Shakespeare may have been making direct allusions to Owen Tudor, another prominent Welsh captain of the Hundred Years War and the ancestor of his royal patrons. The royalist and aristocratic strains of the Welsh martial tradition established in the Hundred Years War were certainly reinforced by the assent of the Tudors. The Welshness of Owen's grandson, Henry Tudor, is a matter of debate, but Henry's victory at Bosworth (1485) was fought with a largely Welsh army under the Red Dragon banner, explicitly crystallizing and personifying the Welsh martial tradition and its ties to the English monarchy and aristocracy. In one tradition of historical writing, fostered by the Tudors and continuing through the modern period, Henry's victory at Bosworth represented the fulfilment of prophecy, the undoing of the conquest and the culmination of Welsh history.[17]

The creation of the modern British army and its system of regiments in the seventeenth and eighteenth centuries provided new outlets for the expression of the Welsh martial tradition. The army, after all, was an institution that recognized and celebrated local patriotisms and cultural identities, perhaps most clearly and effectively in the case of the kilted Highland regiments of Scotland. In like manner, the regimental customs of the Royal Welch Fusiliers drew heavily from Welsh history, symbols and tradition. The regiment held its annual banquet on St David's Day, when it performed a colourful ritual, whereby new officers were initiated into the regiment by the eating of a raw leek to the beating of regimental drums.[18] For over two hundred years, the regiment defied the army high command by stubbornly hanging on to the antiquated spelling of the term 'Welch' in its title, which, in their minds, associated the regiment with 'the archaic North Wales of Henry Tudor and Owen Glendower and Lord Herbert of Cherbury, the founder of the regiment'.[19]

The Welsh martial tradition was thus an old and important source of Welsh pride and an integral component of Welsh identity. But, by the nineteenth century, it was a tradition that was rooted in the rapidly receding past. There had been some notable personages and episodes invoking the Welsh martial spirit in the seventeenth and eighteenth centuries (most famously the siege of Harlech castle in 1647 and the publication of 'Rhyfelgyrch Gwŷr Harlech' in 1784), but thereafter the roots of the tradition became dormant. The weakness of military recruitment from Wales in the eighteenth and nineteenth centuries was at significant odds with the experience of the Irish and Scots, who in the same period were heavily recruited and celebrated. Thus, as the Irish and Scots developed a modern martial tradition based equally on the tragic military glories of their history and on their current role in the modern British army, the Welsh martial tradition largely stagnated in its fixation on the past.[20] Although evocations of the warriors of Wales continued throughout the nineteenth century, the martial tradition became increasingly vulnerable to an alternative construction of national character that emphasized the pacific over the warlike qualities of the Welsh.

A PEOPLE LOYAL, PEACEABLE AND ORDERLY

Although religious Nonconformity in Britain as a whole held a dim view of military adventure, the opposition of the 'Nonconformist conscience' to militarism was compounded in nineteenth-century Wales by the strong connection that had developed between ideas of Welsh national character and religious dissent. From its rise in the eighteenth century, Nonconformity had grown to embrace the majority of the faithful in Wales by the time of the religious census of 1851. By mid-century, Wales was commonly considered to be a Nonconformist nation at odds with the established Anglican church and with Anglican landlords in its midst. The greatest catalyst for cementing Nonconformity to Welsh national identity was the controversy over the so-called 'Brad y Llyfrau Gleision' (Treason of the Blue Books) of 1847.[21] Responding to anxiety aroused by the Newport Rising (1839) and the Rebecca Riots (1839–44), reports published by government commissioners on education attributed the supposed violence, disorder and sexual immorality of early nineteenth-century Welsh society to the pernicious influences of religious Nonconformity and the Welsh language. Stung by these accusations, the leaders of Welsh Nonconformity rose to defend the honour of the Welsh nation and, in the process, came to dominate public life and assume the mantle of national leadership.

As Gwyneth Tyson Roberts has argued, the Blue Books provided a host of officially recognized images of the Welsh people that the Welsh 'might wish to reject but could not ignore'.[22] As the Blue Books charged the Welsh with sexual immorality, disorder and violence, so the Welsh were compelled to show themselves to be the most sexually modest, orderly and pacific people in the British Isles. In perhaps the best known of these defences, the Nonconformist minister Henry Richard championed the Welsh as a people 'loyal', 'peaceable' and 'orderly':

> For the last hundred or hundred and fifty years there is probably no part of the United Kingdom that has given the authorities so little trouble or anxiety. Anything like sedition, tumult, or riot is very rare in the Principality . . . the normal condition of the Principality is one of profound calm, rarely ruffled even by a breath of popular discontent. There is no part of the country probably where the hand of authority is so little seen and so little needed.[23]

Richard claimed that the pacific nature of the Welsh was directly attributable to the influence of the Nonconformist chapel and Sunday School.[24] Stung, then, by English accusations of a violent and disorderly character, the Nonconformist Welsh middle class thus recast the Welsh in their own image by cultivating a more peaceful, respectable and orderly model of their people and nation. In doing so, they constructed and tied Welsh national identity to the ideal of the *gwerin*, a pacific and religious peasantry whose opposition to war and violence was based upon deeply rooted Christian principles of peace and goodwill towards fellow men.[25]

While pacifism as an organized movement had limited support in Victorian Wales, prominent Nonconformists and cultural nationalists during the mid nineteenth century cemented the ideal of Welshness to the cause of peace. Influential Welsh leaders and writers like William Williams ('Caledfryn'), William Rees ('Gwilym Hiraethog'), Samuel Roberts ('S.R.') and Henry Richard combined support for Welsh cultural, religious and political issues with vigorous campaigning for the pacifist cause.[26] Perhaps the most celebrated bards of the century, Caledfryn and Gwilym Hiraethog were chiefly known for their verse glorifying 'Heddwch' ('Peace').[27] One of the most prolific writers in the Welsh language during the nineteenth century and the editor of the widely read journal *Y Cronicl*, S.R. gave equal measure to essays championing the cause of the Welsh Nonconformist tenant farmers and columns expounding on the principles of peace. His opposition to imperial conflicts such as the Crimean War was notable.[28]

Known as the 'Member for Wales' and the 'Apostle for Peace', Henry Richard was the single greatest embodiment of the melding of the Welsh national and pacifist causes. As the first Welsh Nonconformist MP he championed the cause of the Welsh tenant farmer in parliament, but it was in his role as the secretary of the Peace Society, working in the fields of international peace and arbitration, that he enjoyed the highest profile.[29] A romantic and widely celebrated figure, a bronze likeness of Richard clutching a scroll reading 'Peace' was erected in the village of Tregaron in 1893. 'The fashion in olden times was to erect monuments to warriors, whose glory was in the destruction of their fellow creatures', noted the *Cambrian News* upon its unveiling. 'Tregaron took the better part and erected a monument to a saviour of life and an advocate of peace among men.'[30] In this and in the subsequent 1912 commemoration of the centenary of his birth, Richard was hailed as a man whose ideals reflected those of the Welsh nation.[31] As far as national identity is concerned, the actual ambiguous embrace of the pacifist movement by the Welsh people is less important than the powerful and enduring image of pacifist commitment that such leaders constructed. As cultural personalities in their own right, the lives, careers and writings of these leaders provided an exemplar of the new and pacific Welshness of Nonconformity.

In the mid nineteenth century, a revolution seemed to occur within the Welsh national character. The Welsh warriors of old were seemingly dethroned by the gods of a new mythology. As Llewelyn Williams later wrote:

> it was a 'merry world' in Wales before Puritanism took hold of the national conscience. Welshmen were roistering blades, ready for deeds of derring-do, living for the moment, careless of the future, handy with sword and pen . . . quick to take affront, generous in forgiveness, the very type and perfection of soldiers of fortunes. With the coming of Puritanism all this was changed. Arms as a profession was forbidden and the Welsh were taught for the first time that 'peace hath her victories no less renowned than war' . . . The great men of Wales henceforward turned their attention to things spiritual . . . They devoted themselves to what they termed the salvation of souls, but they did more than they themselves knew. They transformed and transfigured the Welsh character.[32]

Through countless and widely read Welsh biographies on the 'lives of the preachers', Nonconformist ministers whose gentle lives extolled the principles of Christian peace became the new heroes for the new Wales. If not forgotten, the old medieval heroes of martial resistance and the 'evil feelings accompanying them', according to Henry Richard, 'happily faded, or are fast fading out of the popular mind'.[33] Once boisterous and bloody-minded warriors and raiders, the Welsh increasingly became represented in terms of their piety and quietism. *Punch* recognized the transformation of the Welsh in a congratulatory and ironic revision of an old and slanderous verse associated with the violent days of the past:

> Taffy is a Welshman;
> Taffy's not a thief;
> Taffy's mutton's very good,
> Not so good his beef:
> I went to Taffy's house,
> Several things I saw,
> Cleanliness and godliness
> Obedience to the law.[34]

By 1870, the Nonconformist transformation of the Welsh from warriors and rioters seemed complete.

The racial ideology of the Victorian period lent further support to the notion of the inherent religiosity of the Welsh. According to racial theorists, the Welsh shared with the Irish and Scots a common racial identity as Celts, a belief giving rise equally to abuses of English racial prejudice and to romantic celebrations of Celticism. Fostered by the great English cultural theorist Matthew Arnold, Celtic racial character was defined in terms of emotion, irrationality and enthusiasm, in opposition to Anglo-Saxon materialism, rationality and reserve. In Arnold's estimation, these qualities imbued the Celts with 'spiritual force', making them, in the words of his contemporary Ernest Renan, a 'gentle' and 'naturally Christian' race.[35] Arnold's volume *On Celtic Literature* (1867) was enduringly popular in Wales and helped establish another method of asserting the order, worth and dignity of the pacific Welsh nation.

In keeping with the essential religious and pacific nature of Welsh national identity, the British military came to be defined as an alien institution, antithetical to Nonconformist perceptions of Welshness. In the words of Robert Graves, 'The chapels held soldiering to be sinful and in Merioneth, the chapels had the last word'.[36] Despite its nods to the Welsh martial tradition, the British military was equally uneasy with the modern, Nonconformist culture of this 'new Wales'. Before the Great War, the language of the drill field and billets was English, and the use of the Welsh language by recruits was viewed with suspicion by officers and NCOs. Nonconformist ministers were prohibited from serving as chaplains, and the religion of Welsh Nonconformists was often dismissively recorded by recruiters as 'C of E'.[37] While the Royal Welch Fusiliers were proud of their Welshness, it was not a Welshness that had much to do with the nineteenth-century Welsh. Indeed, the odd spelling of 'Welch' to which the regiment so stubbornly adhered not only identified them with the heroes of the Welsh martial past, but was thought to distance them from the 'modern North Wales of chapels, Liberalism, the dairy and drapery business, slate mines and the tourist trade'.[38]

In comparison with fifteen Scottish and seven Irish regiments, only three line regiments were to be affiliated to Wales in the nineteenth century, and the Welsh associations of these regiments were weak at best. Although named 'The Welsh' Regiment in 1831, the 41st Foot had little to do with Wales until the Cardwell reforms of 1868–74 encouraged it to recruit from the Principality. Previously known as the 2nd Warwickshire Regiment, the 24th Foot did not receive its title of the South Wales Borderers until 1881, and only 19 of the 145 men who famously defended Rorke's Drift in 1879 hailed from Wales.[39] Although the Royal Welch Fusiliers enjoyed a clear and venerable identification with Welsh tradition, at the battle of Waterloo only three out of every ten recruits were actually Welsh, while it has been estimated that only one fusilier in fifty hailed from Wales in the early twentieth century.[40]

With Welshmen making up only 3 per cent of the army on the eve of the First World War, Wales well deserved its reputation as the leanest recruiting ground in the British Isles.[41] The recruiting march of the Royal Welch Fusiliers in 1896 was both notorious and telling. Proceeding from Anglesey to Wrexham by way of Dolgellau and Llangollen, the regiment managed to enlist only a single man. That sole recruit bought his discharge shortly thereafter, significantly, through a collection administered by his chapel.[42] Socio-economic factors certainly must have played a role in the dearth of Welsh recruiting, but such reluctance to enlist was universally attributed to the Nonconformist character of the Welsh nation. As the winning poem of the 1918 Eisteddfod declared, Wales was a land where:

> The rustic youths, sons of the Sabbath School,
> . . . held hot dispute,
> – Deft like their fathers in such argument,
> On warfare and the Sermon on the Mount.[43]

SAINTS AND WARRIORS

By the dawn of the twentieth century, then, there were two well-established and competing Welsh national traditions related to war, traditions contesting the meaning and definition of Welshness through martial and pacific images. Corresponding to the rise of Nonconformity, it seemed that the image of the Welsh as a Christian and peaceful folk had gained the ascendancy during the mid nineteenth century. Although the pacific ideal of the *gwerin* was broadly accepted, it did not embrace or reflect the experience of all Welsh people. Indeed, much of its strength was drawn from its exclusion of and opposition to key groups in Welsh society, groups who were beginning to find their voice in the late nineteenth and early twentieth centuries. At the same time, the confidence of the mid nineteenth-century British Empire gave way to imperial anxiety as the century drew to a close. Growing fears of Britain's declining economic position in the world, rising military tensions and the Social Darwinist rhetoric of racial struggle and the 'survival of the fittest' prompted a new concern with maintaining Britain's imperial glory.

New voices and other images of national identity thus began to emerge in the late nineteenth and early twentieth centuries, modifying or challenging the predominance of the image of the *gwerin* and reinvigorating the Welsh martial tradition. The image of the *gwerin* firmly rooted Welshness in the countryside, yet Welsh society was becoming increasingly urban and industrial. Fuelled by the expansion of the coal industry and embracing the contributions of native Welshman and immigrant newcomer alike, the middle class of south Wales developed a forward-looking, inclusive and distinctively imperial sense of Welshness that equated Welsh patriotism with civic, cultural and commercial achievement.[44] Vested in the fortunes of the Empire, many of these patriotic Welshmen were left with a nagging sense that the Welsh had either neglected their imperial duty in recent years or that their imperial service had been overlooked. While industrial Wales was revising the rural ideal of the *gwerin*, other members of Welsh society were challenging nineteenth-century Welsh national identity by defending their own Welshness. Long the bugbears of Welsh Nonconformity, the landed Anglican establishment reconciled themselves to the new democratic realities of Wales by re-establishing their own Welsh identity: brushing up on the Welsh branches of their family histories, identifying themselves with the social and cultural aspirations of the Welsh nation, and committing themselves to the public service of the Welsh people through a whole series of honorific positions and charitable enterprises.[45] As an alternative to the rural, Nonconformist ideal, such groups could embrace a definition of Welsh nationalism in imperial terms as:

> the determination to bring Wales to the front in the Empire in every way that offers. Welsh nationalism is the spirit which recognises all that Wales has still to make up, in spite of the progress of the last generation, and then stubbornly sets itself to help in bringing Wales at least abreast of the rest, ready to think of helping her to outstrip them, if that be possible. Nationalism believes that Wales has a distinct and definite value to bring to the Empire and to the world, in all things where mere numbers do not count, if once we can but organise and set that value going.[46]

Sentiments such as these rested uneasily with the more pacific element of Welshness and helped revive interest in the Welsh martial tradition. Like the sentiments of Cardiff's elite, the military emphasized the patriotic inclusion of diverse peoples through their contribution and service to nation and empire. For the Welsh upper classes, association with the military as a 'service elite' or with the martial glories of the Welsh past through their ancestry provided traditional and accepted means of inclusion into Welsh national belonging.[47]

Like the pacific tradition, the Welsh martial tradition found further support and elaboration in the increasingly widespread ideology of race. While Arnold extolled their gentle and spiritual virtues, the supposed racial traits of emotion, irrationality and enthusiasm that made the Celts an inherently spiritual race could also inform their qualities as a 'fighting race', hot-headed, brave and naturally given to battle. Reflecting ancient and medieval commentary, many racially minded observers attributed this martial character to the Celt's inherent taste for anarchy, disorder and violence. However, under the cooler-headed, disciplined leadership of the phlegmatic Saxon, the wild, emotion-driven martial talents of the Celt could be constructively controlled and channelled in the service of Empire. The rough heroes of Crecy and Agincourt who served under the English royal standard seemed to provide historical confirmation of this symbiotic racial tendency. The racial melding of religious devotion and martial fervour found in Celticism was an image difficult for the 'Celtic' Welsh to resist. It reconciled the Christian and martial traditions of their national character, and established that Welsh martial ardour was not merely a temporary accident of history, but a matter of blood and race. Medieval heroes like Arthur, Owain Glyndŵr and Llewelyn the Last proved that, like the Irish and the Scots, the Welsh bore the hot blood of a warrior race within their veins. As one school history of Wales instructed, 'No Welsh boy can well read the history of his ancestors – so stirring a record of so stubborn a race, such a good, grim, fighting race – without feeling that it is good to be a Cymro.'[48]

The renewed vigour of the Welsh martial tradition was fully employed by the propagandists of the Great War. Professed war causes and the pressing needs of total war pushed the drive to reconcile Welsh national identity with imperial duty and broadened the appeal of the martial tradition to the ranks of the Nonconformist elite. Very different from previous imperial wars, this was a war nominally fought to defend religion and the rights of small nations, causes consistent with the principles of Welsh patriotism.[49] In response to the unprecedented need for recruits, a new Welsh Army Corps (later the 38th Welsh Division) was created as a Welsh national institution, complete with Red Dragon insignia, Welsh officers, Nonconformist chaplains and a wider toleration of the Welsh language.[50] The task of arousing Welsh support for the war was taken up by a new breed of imperial propagandists, natives of the soil, led by no less a figure than David Lloyd George.[51]

Invoking the names of the warrior heroes of Wales and celebrating the warlike past of the nation, Welsh propagandists attempted to resurrect the Celtic ardour for battle. During a famous speech made to the London Welsh in 1914, Lloyd George set the precedent:

> I should like to see a Welsh army in the Field. I should like to see the race that faced the Norman for hundreds of years in a struggle for freedom, the race that helped to win Crecy, the race that fought for a generation under Glendower against the greatest captain in Europe – I should like to see that race give a good taste of its quality in this struggle . . . and they are going to do it.[52]

As witnesses to the Welsh martial tradition, the pantheon of Welsh heroes were called to testify. One account of the heroic exploits of the Welsh regiments noted that:

> Wales has lost none of its ardour in warfare, though it has had little need to exercise it for generations . . . [but] given cause as good the Principality which kept out the Saxon and the Dane, and provided such warriors as Ivor Bach and Owen Glendower, can show the same spirit of tenacity, of pertinacity, yes, and of courage and heroism as the Cymry of old.[53]

The rising of the martial spirit in the Welsh bosom after its long peaceful slumber was often symbolized by the return of King Arthur, who, according to Welsh legend, lay sleeping with his men underground, awaiting the call of the nation to lead the fight once more against the Teutonic foe.

Rather than opposing the recent history of Welsh religiosity and pacifism, propagandists recognized and incorporated it. Citing the antipathy of the Welsh to military service in the past, David Lloyd George declared that 'The martial spirit has been slumbering for centuries, but only slumbering. It was just waiting for the occasion, and the occasion came. The great warlike spirit that maintained the independence of these mountains for centuries woke up once more'.[54] Propagandists emphasized the mutual compatibility of Celtic martial ardour and inherent spirituality. In the words of one poet, 'Not for the greed of gold, or lust of land, / But for the cause of righteousness and God' were the Welsh passions for battle aroused.[55] Recruiting meetings in Wales began and ended with Welsh hymns, booklets of marching songs distributed to recruits mixed Welsh martial anthems with traditional hymns, and famous Welsh hymn-writers were prevailed upon to write recruiting songs.[56] The ministers of Welsh Nonconformity played their part, too, in propagating a wholesome image of the military and assuring the Welsh of the essentially religious environment of the trenches.[57] Propagandists maintained that the supposed religiosity of the Welsh actually strengthened, rather than weakened, their arm for combat. The press hailed Welsh officers, like Lieutenant-General Owen Thomas, as a new kind of Christian military hero.[58] But this martial religiosity extended to the lower ranks as well. In recounting the exploits of John 'the king of snipers', one war pamphlet emphasized the fact that 'this little Welshman in private life was a Revivalist'.[59] The Welsh soldiers reportedly responded to the heavy fire of German guns by singing the worshipful words of 'Aberystwyth', 'Cwm Rhondda' and 'Beth Sydd i Mi yn y Byd'.[60]

It is extraordinarily difficult to gauge the influence of propaganda on enlistment, but it is clear that propaganda in Wales at least helped to create an environment that reconciled Welsh national patriotism with the war effort. Initially reluctant, the Welsh soon became enthusiastic supporters of the war. Recruitment in Wales approached the levels found in both England and Scotland, drawing heavily on the Welsh-speaking Nonconformist community, once the bastion of resistance to enlistment. 'As much Welsh as English was now talked in the huts', recalled Robert Graves, 'the chapels having put their full manpower at Lloyd George's disposal.'[61] One poem of the 1918 National Eisteddfod is worth quoting at length for its encapsulation of the transformation of the Welsh from a pacific Nonconformist people to a Celtic warrior race:

Blame them not, if for a tensioned hour,
Despite the hot urge of the Celtic blood,
A hesitation brave did stay their hands.
Though Cambria's past be lit with gleaming steel,
And loud with names, to utter low the which
Do make the faintest brave to recklessness, –
Buddug, Llywelyn Olav and Glyndwr.
After the crash of steel came mellow harps;
Came Pantecelyn's hymning petalled ways
Into a nation's heart . . .
And it was for a proverb in the land,
That 'sloth alone is honour in a sword,
And rust its chiefest glory'.
But ere long
Across the Eastern waves came dripping tales
Of martyred countrysides, and whisperings
Tainting the air of hellish infamies;

And then grew faint the sound of harps and fainter;
Again we saw the darkling avenues
Afar, lit up with shining blade and shield,
And Cymru slowly, reverently said,
'Buddug, Llewelyn Olav and Glyndwr',
And lo the sluice was open![62]

The force of Welsh Nonconformity now seemed solidly behind the martial tradition, but such a transition in the nature of Welshness did not go completely unresisted. Although there was little opposition to the war in Wales, there were voices that reasserted the image of the Welsh as a pacific people. In a letter to the Baptist paper *Y Tyst* ('The Witness') in 1914, Thomas Rees, the principal of Bala-Bangor Theological College, objected to the representation of the war as a struggle for Welsh values. Making unfavourable comparisons with the verdict of nineteenth-century Wales, Rees threw the utterances of Henry Richard against those of Prime Minister Asquith, Gwilym Hiraethog against Lord Grey, and Samuel Roberts against Lloyd George.[63] Although widely condemned within the Welsh-language press, Rees's protest did inspire others. The pacifist journal *Y Deyrnas* ('The Kingdom') explained:

> Wales has something very special to say on the subject of war. Amongst all the small nations of Europe, none has been more roused to their national identity than the Welsh . . . but we have discussed the vanity and foolishness of war for centuries. We admire the principles and heroism of Llewelyn and Owain Glyndwr, but we renounced their methods ages ago.[64]

Papers such as this held up the pacifist pantheon of Henry Richard, S.R. and Gwilym Hiraethog for emulation in articles discussing their lives and works. *Y Deyrnas* warned that the Welsh nation, in the throes of enthusiasm for David Lloyd George's wartime leadership, was in danger of being 'bewitched by personal spells' that would lead it to sacrifice the sacred ideals of their forefathers.[65] *Y Wawr* ('The Dawn') argued that the spirit of Wales was bending a knee to English imperialism, renouncing its own 'trivial and inferior ideals' and 'selling its soul'.[66] Pacifists admonished the Welsh that rather than military glory or imperial might, Wales needed to recall that peace and religion were at the heart of Welsh identity and the future existence of Welsh nationhood.

PLAID CYMRU, 'PLAID HEDDWCH'

Divorcing Welshness from martial patriotism was thus an important factor in the propaganda of Welsh pacifists during the Great War. This tactic was unpopular during the war itself, but proved far more important in its influence on subsequent constructions of Welshness. Journals like *Y Deyrnas* and *Y Wawr* defined and solidified the idea of pacifism as a national tradition and further deified its founding heroes. Following the trauma of the war, the general revulsion against war experienced in Britain as a whole was particularly sharp in Wales, where that revulsion could also be linked to notions of national character and patriotism. With the type of Welsh patriotism associated with David Lloyd George in tatters, the renewal of the Welsh pacific tradition found further expression through the emergence of a revised nationalist ideology associated with a new political party.

Formed in 1925, Plaid Genedlaethol Cymru ('The National Party of Wales', later simply Plaid Cymru, 'The Party of Wales') was marginal in terms of electoral power in the inter-war period, but it had a dispro-portionate influence on the construction of Welsh national identity during those decades. The new nationalists of the party sought to break with the past, to recreate Welsh national identity so as to distance Welsh nationalism from British imperial patriotism and re-establish the nation within the context of a wider European civilization. In doing so, they embraced the cause of pacifism. This was done despite the opposition of the party's principal leader and ideologue, Saunders Lewis. A former army officer, who had served with the South Wales Borderers during the Great War, and a convert to Roman Catholicism, Lewis was often critical of the Nonconformist and pacifist strains in the nationalist ideal. That the party overrode his leadership on these issues demonstrates the increasing depth and resonance of the pacific tradition among the new Welsh nationalists.

Many of the other early leaders of Plaid Cymru, including D. J. Williams and the Revd Lewis Valentine, were self-avowed pacifists whose under-standing of Welsh nationality was deeply rooted in their Nonconformist faith. It is of great significance that the defining moment of the new party was just as much a declaration of the old pacifism as an assertion of the new nationalism. In 1935, the government began building a Royal Air Force training base at Penyberth on the Lleyn peninsula. Plaid Cymru was quick to oppose this 'intrusion of militarism', contrasting Lleyn's proposed role as a school for the new and awful weaponry of aerial bombardment with the peninsula's historic associations with Welshness, Christianity and peace. As Lewis Valentine pointed out:

[The bombs] will be trained in cold blood . . . and if one of them is asked, after falling to the earth and completing the destruction of civilisation and carrying out the greatest villainy in the history of God's creation, 'Where were you trained?', the answer will be 'In Porth Neigwl in Lleyn in the vicinity of Bardsey Island and the Path of the Pilgrims and the Saints of Wales'.[67]

In a symbolic act of defiance and protest, Saunders Lewis, D. J. Williams and Lewis Valentine set alight a workmen's hut, surrendered to police and, after a much-publicized and controversial trial, served jail sentences. Upon their release in 1937, a mass meeting of some twelve thousand people in Caernarfon turned out to welcome 'the Three' as new additions to the pantheon of Welsh nationalism . . . and peace.

The party had less national success in its campaign against conscription and the outbreak of war with Germany in 1939. Public opinion in Wales was overwhelmingly supportive of the Second World War. However, pacifists in Wales remained a small but dedicated vocal minority and, unlike public opinion in Wales as a whole, pacifism was a rising tide among the committed nationalists of Plaid Cymru. After the burning of the bombing school, the issue of peace grew in prominence among the party's rank and file, much to the chagrin of Saunders Lewis, who felt compelled to remind them that Plaid Cymru was a nationalist and not a pacifist party.[68] Bolstered by a whole series of pacifist resolutions at the annual party conferences, Plaid's anti-conscription campaign was welcomed by Saunders Lewis as an opportunity for party members to claim objector status on nationalist grounds. He was dismayed when the nationalists who did register justified their objector status with a blend of pacifism, religion and nationalism. Lewis regarded this as a bitter disappointment for the nationalist cause, because he failed to understand that nationalism was indivisible from religion, morality and the cause of peace for most members of his party.[69]

When Lewis retired from public life in 1945, Gwynfor Evans, a prominent Nonconformist and leader of the pacifist wing of the party, was significantly selected as the party's new president. Primarily celebrated today as a national Moses who led his party out of the political wilderness upon his election as the first Plaid Cymru MP in 1966, in 1945 Gwynfor Evans had compelling pacifist credentials as a vocal opponent of the Second World War, credentials that he was to extend with criticisms of subsequent conflicts including those in South East Asia and the South Atlantic.[70] Although grounded in his Nonconformist faith, Gwynfor Evans's pacifism had a far more explicit political component than had the Christian pacifism of his mid-Victorian forebears. In his view, pacifism and Welsh nationalism were functionally the same cause. Through his writing and speeches, Evans argued that empire, militarism and war inevitably drove the state towards centralization, the accumulation of power and the imposition of uniformity, and therefore led to the deterioration of Welsh language, culture and nationhood. Consequently, the struggle for Wales to live as a nation was also a pacifist struggle, for it would break up the centralization of the state and 'finally end the British imperialist and militarist dream'.[71] The principles of nationalism and pacifism were thus mutually supportive, but nationalist methods had also to be consistent with pacifism, for:

> means and ends are structurally inseparable. Though violent means may speed up the rate of change their consequences seem always to be reactionary and authoritarian . . . Even where it 'succeeds' it usually results in a bureaucratic and centralist system which has to be maintained by reliance on institutional violence; and state power is always found to be increased at the expense of personal and communal freedom and initiative . . . Where the national struggle is identified, as it is in Wales, with social justice and personal liberation, violence must be completely renounced.[72]

As a politician, propagandist and popular historian, Gwynfor Evans projected this potent ideological blend of 'nonviolent nationalism' on to the Welsh nation, cultivating the image of Plaid Cymru's pacifism springing 'naturally from the values of Welsh heritage'.[73] In his memoirs, he reflected that:

> It is easy, indeed quite natural, for a Welshman who has put aside all things British to be a pacifist. He knows that Britain never fought a war in the defence of Wales. On the contrary, its wars have done far more harm than good to our Welsh heritage.[74]

In his histories, Evans claimed that every war fought under the Union flag 'defended nothing of great significance to Welsh civilization', 'augmented the power of the British state, centralized its structure, strengthened its grip on Wales, increased its psychological integration of Wales in England and diminished the vitality of the Welsh tradition'.[75] Evans's work as a popular historian and shaper of national identity has perhaps not received the attention it is due. Evans himself regarded the establishment of what he termed a new 'pattern or myth of Welsh history' as his most important contribution to the nationalist cause.[76]

After the Second World War, the pacifist tradition became nearly hegemonic in its constructions of Welsh national identity. With occasional exceptions, like the Welsh enthusiasm for the film *Zulu* (1964), expressions of the martial tradition of Welshness in the context of the British military have become increasingly muted, restrained and awkward. Imperial Welsh nationalism has gone the way of the Empire. A more serious challenge, however, has occasionally been raised within the ranks of the new nationalism itself. As Gwynfor Evans recognized, the pacifist stance of Plaid Cymru has left the party open to accusations of passivity, limited commitment and naivety. Mudiad Amddiffyn Cymru ('Movement for the Defence of Wales') bomber John Jenkins (himself a one-time soldier in the regular army) explained the sense of frustration that the commitment to pacifism engendered in some nationalists, claiming that if the leaders of Plaid Cymru had 'made rather less of Job, I would not have had to make more of David'.[77] Since the Second World War, several groups of nationalists have split with the party over the use of force, including the Welsh Republican Movement in the 1950s, the Free Wales Army, the Patriotic Front and Mudiad Amddiffyn Cymru in the 1960s and Meibion Glyndŵr ('Sons of Glyndŵr') in the 1980s. Attempting to incite an uprising at the Investiture of the Prince of Wales in 1969, a Free Wales Army leaflet called upon Welshmen to:

> organize, train and equip, to arm themselves with guns, bombs, Molotov cocktails, grenades, pikes, bows and arrows, swords, bayonets, clubs . . . eggs filled with sand, flour and smoke bombs, nuts and bolts, sharpened pennies . . . Stock them up and bring them to Caernarfon.[78]

Even if the seriousness of this threat can be questioned, these were hardly the utterances of an inherently pacific people. Although amounting to only a handful of active individuals with varying levels of commitment, such groups seized the headlines, drew upon the names of Llewelyn and Glyndŵr and, for a time, put the martial tradition back on the agenda of Welsh patriotism.

In contemporary Wales, where nationalists often identify themselves and their national history in opposition to British imperialism and power, the pacific construction of Welshness has tremendous appeal. Its popularity has encouraged a process of selective national amnesia, isolating the Welsh from complicity in the British imperial enterprise and presenting the Welsh as an inherently pacific people.[79] More complicated constructions of Welsh national identity are often forgotten, in favour of a clearer dichotomy between the forces of imperial Anglicization and a defiant, anti-imperial Welshness. However, an examination of the history of national imagery reveals that no such clear-cut dichotomy exists. Both proponents of pacifism and militarism draw upon established national traditions in defining their conception of Welsh national identity. Those who present the Welsh as an essentially peaceful people appeal to the Nonconformist conscience and heritage of the nation, and cite the cultural nationalism of the mid nineteenth century and the political nationalism of the twentieth century. However, the image of the Welsh as an inherently martial people is a far older tradition, dating back to ancient encounters between the ancestors of the Welsh and their conquerors and revised during the medieval wars of English expansion. During the imperial high noon of the late nineteenth and early twentieth centuries, those who attempted to reconcile Welshness with British imperial endeavour could point to a native military tradition personified by the warrior heroes of Welsh history. The appeal of the Welsh martial tradition continues to the present, as seen in the continuing cult of the medieval Welsh heroes and in the activities of the more violent fringes of Welsh nationalism. Welshness and its relationship to war is not a static concept with unchanging traits, but a fluid construction, constantly contested, negotiated and revised in relation to changing historical circumstances. In their response to war, are the Welsh best characterized as a peaceful people, or as a martial race? The answer is not to be found inscribed upon the essential nature of Welsh character, but will depend on when, where and of whom you ask the question.

NOTES

[1] Tecwyn Lloyd, 'Welsh public opinion and the First World War', *Planet*, 10 (Feb. 1972), 25; Gwynfor Evans, *Land of My Fathers: 2000 Years of Welsh History* (Talybont, 1992), p. 430.

[2] John Milton, 'Comus' (1634), cited in Meic Stephens (ed.), *A Most Peculiar People: Quotations about Wales and the Welsh* (Cardiff, 1992), p. 20.

[3] R. R. Davies, *The First English Empire: Power and Identities in the British Isles 1093–1343* (Oxford, 2000), pp. 101–3.

[4] Gerald of Wales, *The Journey through Wales: The Description of Wales* (New York, 1978), pp. 233–4.

[5] See Davies, *First English Empire*, pp. 101–3, 131; Glanmor Williams, *Recovery, Reorientation and Reformation: Wales c.1415–1642* (Oxford, 1987), pp. 166–7.

[6] Cited in Davies, *First English Empire*, p. 131.

[7] W. R. Jones, 'England against the Celtic fringe: a study in cultural stereotypes', *Journal of World History*, 13 (1971); Edward D. Snyder, 'The wild Irish: a study of some English satires against the Irish, Scots, and Welsh', *Modern Philology*, 17 (1920); A. D. Carr, 'Welshmen and the Hundred Years' War', *WHR*, 4, 1 (1968), 22–3; Williams, *Recovery, Reorientation and Reformation*, pp. 166–7.

[8] Davies, *First English Empire*, p. 103.

[9] Gerald, *Journey through Wales*, p. 233.

[10] Henry Richard, *Letters and Essays on Wales* (London, 1884), p. 37.

[11] Carr, 'Welshmen and the Hundred Years' War', 23.

[12] For example, see John Miles, *Princes and People of Wales* (Risca, 1977), p. 37.

[13] *The Complete Works of William Shakespeare* (New York, 1936), p. 585.

[14] Peter Lord, *Words with Pictures; Welsh Images and Images of Wales in the Popular Press, 1640–1860* (Aberystwyth, 1995), pp. 33–51.

[15] Prys T. J. Morgan, 'The clouds of witnesses; the Welsh historical tradition', in R. Brinley Jones (ed.), *Anatomy of Wales* (Peterston-super-Ely, 1972), p. 24.

[16] Carr, 'Welshmen and the Hundred Years' War', 29.

[17] Morgan, 'Clouds of witnesses', pp. 26–7; See also Owen Rhoscomyl, *Flame-Bearers of Welsh History* (Merthyr Tydfil, 1905).

[18] See Michael Glover, *That Astonishing Infantry: Three Hundred Years of the History of the Royal Welch Fusiliers (23rd Regiment of Foot) 1689–1989* (London, 1989).

[19] Robert Graves, *Good-Bye To All That* (New York, 1957), p. 80.

[20] For Irish and Scottish martial traditions, see Thomas Bartlett and Keith Jeffrey, 'An Irish military tradition?', in Bartlett and Jeffrey (eds), *A Military History of Ireland* (Cambridge, 1996), pp. 1–25; Linda Colley, *Britons: Forging the Nation, 1707–1837* (New Haven, CT, and London, 1992), pp. 117–32; H. R. Trevor-Roper, 'The invention of tradition: the Highland tradition of Scotland', in Eric Hobsbawm and Terence Ranger (eds), *The Invention of Tradition* (Cambridge, 1983), pp. 15–41; Diana M. Henderson, *Highland Soldier; A Social Study of the Highland Regiments, 1820–1920* (Edinburgh, 1989).

[21] See Gwyneth Tyson Roberts, *The Language of the Blue Books: The Perfect Instrument of Empire* (Cardiff, 1998); Paul O'Leary, 'The languages of patriotism in Wales 1840–1880', in Geraint H. Jenkins (ed.), *The Welsh Language and Its Social Domains 1801–1911* (Cardiff, 2000), pp. 533–60; Prys Morgan, 'The gwerin of Wales – myth and reality', in I. Hume and W. T. R. Pryce (eds), *The Welsh and Their Country* (Llandysul, 1986), pp. 134–50.

[22] Roberts, *Language of the Blue Books*, p. 3.

[23] Richard, *Letters and Essays*, pp. 80–3.

[24] Ibid., pp. 52–61.

[25] Morgan, 'Gwerin of Wales'; O'Leary, 'Languages of patriotism', p. 538.

[26] For pacifism in Wales see Peter Brock, *Freedom from War; Nonsectarian Pacifism 1814–1914* (Toronto, 1991), pp. 153–84; Kenneth O. Morgan, 'Peace movements in Wales, 1899–1845', *WHR*, 10, 3 (1981), 398–9; Goronwy J. Jones, *Wales and the Quest for Peace* (Cardiff, 1969), pp. 1–77; T. H. Lewis, 'Y mudiad heddwch yng Nghymru, 1800–1899', *Transactions of the Honourable Society of Cymmrodorion, Bicentenary Volume, Sessions 1949–1951* (1953); Iorwerth C. Peate, *Y Traddodiad Heddwch yng Nghymru* (Dinbych, 1963).

[27] William Rees (Gwilym Hiraethog), *Caniadau Hiraethog* (Dinbych, 1855), pp. 93–146.

[28] David Benjamin Rees, *Samuel Roberts* (Cardiff, 1987), pp. 50–69; Brock, *Freedom from War*, pp. 164–71.

[29] Brock, *Freedom from War*, pp. 173–84; Morgan, 'Peace movements', 398–9.

[30] *Cambrian News*, 25 Aug. 1893.

[31] *Welsh Gazette* (hereafter *WG*), 5 Sept. 1912; Trevor Jones, 'Henry Richard centenary 1812–1912', *Wales*, 11 (May 1912), 241–2.

[32] *WG*, 5 Sept. 1912.

[33] Richard, *Letters and Essays*, p. 37.

[34] *C.*1870, and cited in Robert Owen, 'Audi alterem partem; a twentieth century message to nineteenth century Wales', *Young Wales*, Mar. 1900, 59–61.

35 Matthew Arnold, *On the Study of Celtic Literature* (London, 1867). For Celticism see John S. Ellis, 'Celt versus Teuton: race, character and British national identity', in *Irish–German Studies* (2001/2); Murray G. H. Pittock, *Celtic Identity and the British Image* (Manchester, 1999); Malcolm Chapman, *The Celts: The Construction of a Myth* (New York, 1992); Hugh MacDougall, *Racial Myth in English History* (Hanover, NH, 1982); Malcolm Chapman, *The Gaelic Vision in Scottish Culture* (London, 1978); L. P. Curtis, *Anglo-Saxons and Celts: A Study of Anti-Irish Prejudice in Victorian England* (Bridgeport, CT, 1968); Frederic E. Faverty, *Matthew Arnold: The Ethnologist* (Evanston, IL, 1951).

36 Graves, *Good-Bye To All That*, p. 80.

37 Gervase Phillips, 'Dai bach y soldiwr: Welsh soldiers in the British Army 1914–1918', *Llafur: Journal of Welsh Labour History*, 6, 2 (1993), 88–9.

38 Graves, *Good-Bye To All That*, pp. 85–6.

39 J. M. Brereton, *A History of the Royal Regiment of Wales (24th/41st Foot) and Its Predecessors, 1689–1989* (Cardiff, 1989), pp. 104, 130, 149; Zulu War expert Ian Knight has provided the statistics of Welsh soldiers at Rorke's Drift from an analysis of regimental rolls. This is mentioned at his website, *www.kwazulu.co.uk/home.html*. From my own research, only two of the eleven Victoria Crosses awarded for Rorke's Drift were given to Welshmen, namely to Pte. Robert Jones from Raglan and Pte. John Williams Fielding from Abergavenny.

40 Glover, *That Astonishing Infantry*, p. 57; Graves, *Good-Bye To All That*, p. 80.

41 H. J. Hanham, 'Religion and nationality in the Victorian army', in M. R. D. Foot (ed.), *War and Society: Historical Essays in Honour and Memory of J. R. Western 1928–1971* (London, 1973), pp. 161–3; Phillips, 'Dai bach y soldiwr', 94; Cyril Parry, 'Gwynedd and the Great War', *WHR*, 14, 1 (1988), 91; Clive Hughes, 'Army recruitment in Gwynedd, 1914–1916' (unpublished MA thesis, University of Wales, 1983), p. 204.

42 Glover, *That Astonishing Infantry*, p. 332; Owen, 'Audi alterem partem', 60.

43 T. J. Thomas, 'Wales in the war', *Cofnodion a Chyfansoddiadau Eisteddfod Genedlaethol 1918* (London, 1919), p. 144.

44 Neil Evans, 'The Welsh Victorian city: middle class and civic and national consciousness in Cardiff, 1850–1914', *WHR*, 12, 3 (1985).

45 This was the Welsh dimension of a broader British trend. See David Cannadine, *The Decline and Fall of the British Aristocracy* (New Haven, CT, and London, 1990), pp. 559–72.

46 *WM*, 13 July 1911.

47 As a 'service elite', the British aristocracy had long cultivated a martial image of their class and of their patriotic contribution to society; see Colley, *Britons*, pp. 147–94.

48 Rhoscomyl, *Flame-Bearers*, cited in Stephens, *A Most Peculiar People*, p. 115.

49 See John S. Ellis, 'The "methods of barbarism" and the "rights of small nations": war propaganda and British pluralism', *Albion*, 30, 1 (1998).

50 See National Library of Wales (hereafter NLW), Welsh Army Corps Papers; Hughes, 'Army recruitment', pp. 188–201.

51 Established by patriotic Welshmen in response to Lloyd George's inspiring Queen's Hall speech, the Welsh National Executive Committee encouraged Welsh-speaking officials and men who were 'conversant with the habits and

customs of the people' to take the matter of propaganda in hand. It took primary responsibility for recruiting in Wales until the advent of conscription in 1916. See NLW, Welsh Army Corps Papers, C11/17.

[52] David Lloyd George, *Through Terror to Triumph: Speeches and Pronouncements since the Beginning of the War* (London, 1915), p. 14.

[53] Anon., *Welsh Regiments in the Great War* (Cardiff, 1915), p. 40.

[54] House of Lords Record Office, David Lloyd George Papers, C/36/2/36, news-paper clipping, 'The Chancellor and the critics. Address at Llandudno'.

[55] Thomas, 'Wales in the war', p. 144.

[56] NLW, Welsh Army Corps Papers, AG/133, correspondence from Miss Gee regarding Welsh songbooks, Dec. 1914; NLW, D. Vaughan Thomas Papers, 22/40, sheet music, D. M. Beddoes and D. Vaughan Thomas, 'Come Along; Can't You Hear? (Dewch Ymlaen; Oni Chlywch?)'; NLW, Welsh Army Corps Papers, AS/61, correspondence regarding recruiting song 'Come Along' by D. M. Beddoes and D. Vaughan Thomas; Hughes, 'Army recruitment', p. 276.

[57] Hughes, 'Army recruitment', p. 263.; R. R. Hughes, *Y Parchedig John Williams, D. D., Brynsiencyn* (Caernarfon, 1929), pp. 226–42; Morgan, 'Peace movements', 406.

[58] Morgan, 'Peace movements', 407.

[59] Anon., *Welsh Regiments*, p. 35.

[60] Ibid., pp. 5, 14, 31.

[61] Graves, *Good-Bye To All That*, p. 222.

[62] Revd William Evans, 'Wales in the war', *Cofnodion a Chyfansoddiadau Eisteddfod Genedlaethol 1918* (London, 1919), p. 149.

[63] *Y Tyst*, 30 Sept., 21 Oct. 1914.

[64] *Y Deyrnas*, Oct. 1916.

[65] Ibid., Mar. 1917.

[66] *Y Wawr*, Summer 1916.

[67] Cited in D. Hywel Davies, *The Welsh Nationalist Party, 1925–1945: A Call to Nationhood* (Cardiff, 1983), p. 159.

[68] *Y Ddraig Goch*, Dec. 1939; cited in Davies, *Welsh Nationalist Party*, p. 226.

[69] Davies, *Welsh Nationalist Party*, pp. 167–244.

[70] Gwynfor Evans, *For the Sake of Wales; The Memoirs of Gwynfor Evans* (Cardiff, 1996), pp. 40–1, 52–4, 154, 231–6; Davies, *Welsh Nationalist Party*, pp. 225–6, 244.

[71] Gwynfor Evans, *Nonviolent Nationalism* (New Malden, 1973), pp. 1–12.

[72] Ibid., pp. 15, 24.

[73] Evans, *For the Sake of Wales*, p. 236. In addition to his political life, Gwynfor Evans communicated the Welsh pacifist ideal through the writing of several widely read and polemic popular histories, including *Aros Mae* (1971) and its English translation, *Land of My Fathers* (first published in 1974).

[74] Evans, *For the Sake of Wales*, p. 232.

[75] Gwynfor Evans, *Land of My Fathers*, (Swansea, 1974), p. 344.

[76] Evans, *For the Sake of Wales*, pp. 200–8, 252–3; Laura McAllister, *Plaid Cymru: The Emergence of a Political Party* (Bridgend, 2001), pp. 30–1.

[77] Cited in Evans, *Nonviolent Nationalism*, p. 15.

[78] Cited in Stephens, *A Most Peculiar People*, p. 141. For the FWA, Patriotic Front and MAC, see Roy Clews, *To Dream of Freedom* (Talybont, 1980); also see manuscripts in NLW, Ty Cenedl MSS, 1 AI/4, and *WM*, 9 May 1969.

[79] An interesting comparison can be made with the Irish, who achieved a similar state of amnesia regarding Irish military service on behalf of the British Empire by reorienting their martial tradition against the British state and dismissing Irish recruits in the British army as 'degenerate'; see John S. Ellis, 'The degenerate and the martyr: nationalist propaganda and the contestation of Irishness, 1914–1918', *Eire-Ireland*, 35, 3–4 (Fall/Winter 2000–1).

2

Loyalties: state, nation, community and military recruiting in Wales, 1840–1918

NEIL EVANS

Armies are central agencies of the State and in some senses are a major component in its definition. The State is frequently defined (following Max Weber) as a territorially bounded organization which claims a monopoly of legitimate violence. Mass armies, from the French Revolution onwards, have used nationality as a key means of recruiting people to the ranks. Nations are, ostensibly, what people die and kill for. Looking at recruitment for the British army in nineteenth-century Wales ought, therefore, to open a window on to national identity. The State was, of course, a British one, and Wales had been comfortably part of this from 1536 onwards, even before the formation of the modern form of the British state in the eighteenth century. Welsh archers had formed a prominent part of the 'English' armies in the Hundred Years War, and Welsh recruits were the backbone of the Royalist army in the Civil Wars of the seventeenth century.

But by the mid nineteenth century the great majority of those who attended a place of worship in Wales were Nonconformists, and Nonconformity had come to be seen as a central element in Welsh nationality. Some Nonconformists in Britain were not great enthusiasts for the current form of the British state. The state was underpinned by an established Church, and the Empire was seen by John Bright as 'a gigantic system of outdoor relief' for the aristocracy, which supported many in sinecures. Commissions in the army were purchased, rather than being awarded on the basis of merit. While Welsh Nonconformity loudly and frequently proclaimed its loyalty to the Crown, there was frequently hostility to military and imperialist adventures. Richard Cobden and John Bright were perhaps the leading exponents of such a position, and envisaged a world united by free trade, rather than divided by exclusive empires. In Wales, Henry Richard was the most prominent advocate of such a creed, but others, like Samuel Roberts,

Llanbrynmair ('S.R.'), were also spokesmen for such a position.[1] Did such views have any impact on attitudes to the military in Victorian Wales?

Military recruiting was at a low level in nineteenth-century Wales and remained so until the outbreak of the Great War. While the statistics for this are infrequent, and on a basis which makes strict comparison difficult, there seems to be little doubt that Wales was under-represented in the army. In 1843–4 only 167 of the 17,450 recruits to the army were Welsh. In 1864 England produced 15,229 recruits, Scotland 3,101, Ireland 8,877 and Wales a mere 393, well below its share of the population of the British Isles.[2] By 1913 the Welsh-born share of the army was only 1.36 per cent, though 2.4 per cent of that year's recruits were born in Wales. Perhaps these figures suggest a slow process of accommodation with the military.[3]

Why was military recruitment at such a low level in nineteenth-century Wales? In some respects this was a general problem faced by the military in the period. Soldiers were badly paid and their conditions of service were harsh until well into the century. They were seen as having a low moral status, perhaps best exemplified in the large numbers who had to be treated for venereal disease each year. In the 1860s this was as high as half the complement, and the Contagious Diseases Acts (often known at the time as the Garrison Towns Acts) were a ham-fisted attempt to deal with the problem.[4] As late as 1875 it was seen as necessary to raise soldiers' moral status, as well as their pay, in order to boost recruiting.[5] The lack of an army reserve had been seen as a problem ever since the Crimean War, when it had not been possible to keep even a small army (25,000 men) in the field.[6] In 1880 the Director General of Recruiting conceded that, until recently, there had been a great difficulty in recruiting an efficient fighting force because of the periods of absence which service entailed, the climate in parts of the British Empire, the dangers of voyages and the nature of punishments: 'all combined to create a horror in the minds of the quiet country folks of England which has hardly yet died out'.[7] But he felt that the short-service enlistment introduced after 1870, which allowed recruits to the infantry to spend just six years with the colours, as opposed to the previous term of twenty-one years, had removed much of the hostility. Since then there had been an adequate annual supply of recruits for the first time, and the desertion rate had fallen. In 1873, for instance, supply was in excess of need and of good quality. But before that the army had never really been popular with the masses and would have been unable to cope with 'arduous concerns'.[8] Another army observer felt that the Volunteer movement had done much to break down the 'strong prejudice' amongst the urban population against military service, but he felt this still existed amongst the peasantry.[9] A recruiting officer at Shrewsbury reported that 'the idea of recruits being kidnapped by the army while in a state of intoxication is a popular delusion', and suggested that the floating population of the large towns was a better field for the recruiter.[10] In such a context, however, not all experts agreed that it was possible to get the necessary number of recruits each year. A report in 1875 found that getting the requisite 18,000 recruits a year was difficult.[11]

This chapter proceeds by examining especially Welsh sources of dis-affection towards service in the regular army and then looks at the process by which this was broken down in the early days of the Great War, when Wales supplied something like the level of recruits that might have been expected in relation to its population. This discussion suggests that local factors were often important, so the chapter concludes with a discussion of the situation in one market town in north Wales during the war.

If Wales was not alone in presenting problems for the army, there is little doubt that these issues were pressing there. In 1861, in one of the few comments from an army source on recruiting in Wales, Colonel D. Russell remarked on the difficulties of recruiting in north Wales, where 'the recruiting parties suffer immensely (which one would hardly believe from their absurdities) from the speeches and pamphlets of the peace society'. He conceded, however, that low pay was also an issue.[12] Ten years later north Wales was singled out as a difficult area by the recruiting officer in Chester. He thought that establishing offices in every county town would aid recruiting. Such a measure would, he suggested,

> necessarily bring forward every lad with an intention to gain the benefits of a soldier's life, a subject much misunderstood in many parts of the kingdom, and more particularly in the Principality of Wales, in the northern division of which a complete ignorance exists as to the treatment given to the soldier, and whereby many men are every year lost to the service.[13]

Explanations of the peculiar position of Wales in nineteenth-century military recruitment would seem to involve a number of factors. Possibly the scale of economic development minimized the appeal of the army, for it was a commonplace that soldiers were recruited from amongst the most disadvantaged sections of the population. That may have limited recruitment from the expanding industrial areas of Wales, apart from during recessions. This leaves the rural areas, which, as in Ireland and the Scottish Highlands, suffered from economic stagnation and depopulation, and were thus potentially fertile recruiting grounds.[14] That they did not become seedbeds for the army may have been the result of political and religious factors. Nonconformity and, later, Liberalism flourished in rural Wales, and were associated with a desire to reform many features of the existing British state, including the army. Peace movements had some political presence in Wales, also, and they may have hindered whatever efforts at recruiting the army made. The religious and political trends of nineteenth-century Wales were frequently summed up as the expression of an enhanced sense of a distinctive national identity. Did the army make any serious efforts to tap this for purposes of recruitment? Possibly, Welsh people would have been more eager to enlist in an army of which they felt part. Such issues can be confronted only by examining evidence from the period.

Throughout the nineteenth century issues of a military nature recurred in political debate in Wales. During the Crimean War there were complaints of dissenting ministers obstructing recruiting in north Wales and south Cardiganshire, 'in fact everywhere where dissent has a preponderance'. In Aberystwyth a man paraded with a placard bearing the cat-o'-nine-tails to advise enlistees of their possible fate in the colours. The result was that many county militias failed to fill their quotas, and the ballot had to be resorted to. Cardiganshire provided 80 out of a quota of 600; several counties had not filled one-tenth of their quota. The Tory press was quick to draw the moral:

> This crusade against recruiting has been going on in Wales for many years; and although the 23rd is called a WELSH Regiment, and was originally Welsh, and many of the officers are still Welsh, and a real Welsh goat marches at the head of it, yet not one in every twenty of the regiment is Welsh. The muster roll will prove this. The names of those killed and wounded at Alma will also show how very few of them are Welsh. Surely the more respectable of Welsh Dissenters ought to wipe this blot from their pulpits. It is no argument at all to say how readily Glamorgan and Carmarthen appeared to the muster roll. Happily in these counties other lights are shining. It is not so in the North. The preachers are the only law and this is the effect of it.[15]

Collections were held in Wales for the patriotic fund raised to help victims of the hostilities. Again, urban or industrial areas were singled out by the Conservative press for their efforts in this respect. The mining district around Aberafan, and the towns of Haverfordwest, Holywell and Flint were mentioned particularly. On the island of Anglesey, Sir Richard Bulkeley took the platform provided by these activities to denounce Nonconformist opposition: 'He reminded the sectarians that Cromwell, though a puritan and a fanatic, had yet the good sense to attend to the defence of his country, the rights of his subjects and the balance of power throughout the world.'[16]

In this discussion a number of issues arose which resonated throughout the period. There were claims, firstly, of Nonconformist anti-war agitation;

secondly, that the provision of recruits in Wales was lacking, explained in part by the nature of the army itself. It was such a moral objection which underpinned vociferous opposition in Aberystwyth in 1872 to the establishment of a barracks in the town.[17] Thirdly, there were suggestions of a rural–urban split in attitudes; and, fourthly, it was claimed that patriotism in Wales was distinctly lacking, at least in the way in which Conservatives defined that value.

Similar concerns surfaced in 1908, when Colonel Howard appealed to Lloyd George to use his influence in aid of Territorial Army recruiting in Wales – it might, he said, stop the Nonconformist ministers' 'ceaseless crusade against the Army, Territorial or other'.[18] His concerns were greeted by uproar in the Welsh press, but his charges were not effectively rebutted. Thomas Levi, Moderator of the Calvinistic Methodists, replied that the true Christian spirit was anti-militarist. Others were concerned about the moral tone of the army, and its corrupting effect on Nonconformist youth. The discussion looked back to the Boer War as a convenient source of ammunition. The first 116 volunteers from Wales to go to South Africa were said to include 82 Church of England members and only 2 Calvinistic Methodists. Out of one Territorial Army Regiment of 406, 275 were Anglican, and of the other, 308 were Anglicans and 33 Roman Catholics, out of a total complement of 448. Such figures have to be treated with caution, as the army always seemed reluctant to register recruits as Nonconformists and to provide appropriate religious services for them. The issue surfaced again in the early stages of the First World War, when the Bishop of St Asaph claimed that 70 per cent of recruits in Wales were Anglicans. Liberal opponents found it easy to rebut what they saw as the absurdity of such charges and claimed it was common knowledge – except to the army – that recruits were mainly from the Free Churches.[19] Disputes over recruitment were always intimately connected with the wider political struggles within Wales in the period.

In this debate, Owen Thomas, the man who had raised the Prince of Wales Light Horse during the Boer War and who was to be such a prominent recruiter during the Great War, came to the defence of Wales. He claimed that his regiment had included Welshmen who had come from the ends of the earth to defend the Empire, and 500 from Wales itself, including many sons of deacons. Yet his defence served mainly to articulate just what was at issue between some Welsh Nonconformists and the army – the Welshness of the military. When he had been asked to raise a corps of volunteers in 1886 he had done it in Anglesey in the space of six weeks. Seventy per cent of his recruits were Nonconformists, and they included five deacons and one minister. He stressed the necessity to understand the men and their religion, and not to insist upon church parade.[20] This raised the issue of the ease with which Nonconformity could be absorbed into the British army.

The army was, of course, closely associated with an Anglican establishment and its regiments had little close contact with Wales, despite the fact that three of them nominally represented the Principality. Before 1881 the Welch Regiment had little connection with Wales and drew the bulk of its officers and men from England and Ireland. The Royal Welch Fusiliers seem to have had more contact; in 1858 the Mayor of Newport observed that the county of Monmouthshire would always feel a deep interest in the regiment, and in 1877 the Mayor of Wrexham felt it appropriate to welcome it 'to this old Welch town'. Yet the RWF saw north-west Wales as a poor recruiting ground and concentrated its efforts in Wales on the more industrialized Flintshire and Denbighshire; the regiment was nicknamed the 'Birmingham Fusiliers', for the Midlands was its real core area.

The army made little or no attempt to use Welsh patriotic devices for its own purposes. The Royal Welch Fusiliers defiantly insisted on an archaic spelling of their homeland so that they might be associated with the Wales of Glyndŵr, Henry Tudor and Lord Herbert of Cherbury (its founder), rather than with the Wales of Nonconformity, Liberalism, industry and commerce. It was seen as a 'regimental characteristic and possession'; in 1919 the War Office finally accepted their desire to be ancient in tone. Even in the Great War, the army could be insensitive to the needs of Welsh troops; Welsh was banned from the parade ground in Wrexham, and a soldier who wrote home in Welsh had the letter returned to him, as the censor could not read it.[21] Neither did heroic actions of ostensibly Welsh regiments receive much recognition as the actions of Welsh soldiers. When the Bishop of St David's dedicated a memorial to the men of the South Wales Borderers who had fallen in South Africa, in the Priory Church at Brecon in 1882, he said that the catastrophe of Isandhlwana and the triumph of Rorke's Drift would be remembered 'as long as the history of England is read'.[22] These events have come to be seen as a key element in modern Welsh identity and in its military tradition. Yet, at the time, the local press received news of those battles with interest, but solely because the regiment was garrisoned there and some of the casualties were known to the area. Otherwise patriotism was seen as a British virtue, and the struggle interpreted in racial terms more than any other. In 1885 a military chronicler did draw the conclusion that it is 'most appropriate that the "24th" will be known in future as a thoroughly Welsh regiment', but it seemed like an afterthought.[23] The admission of these heroes into a Welsh pantheon was a later business, and it owed something to the successful 1964 film *Zulu* which apparently, those knowledgeable judges, the Ninian Park football crowd, once considered the greatest Welsh film.[24] Perhaps it is necessary to point out that the script of the film was written by John Prebble, author of many popular books on Scottish history, who may have been viewing Wales through the lens of the traditions of Highland regiments.[25] There seems to be little in the immediate discussion in the Breconshire press to suggest that it was associated with Welsh patriotism.

In general, regimental histories seem to be sustained by a diet of British and regimental loyalties, and such traditions left little room for a Welsh dimension. At the outbreak of war in 1914 one officer was quite explicit about this attitude: 'the best morale is the result of the esprit de corps which exists in regard to the maintenance of the honour of the regiment to which the men belong'.[26] When the Crimean colours of the Welsh Regiment were deposited at Llandaf Cathedral in 1895, the only reference to Wales in the order of service was to the Prince and Princess of Wales. From the 1880s onwards links perhaps became a little stronger, particularly with industrial south Wales. The 2nd Battalion of the Welsh Regiment ran a newspaper called *Men of Harlech*, from 1893 to 1914, though its first number had to apologise for the absence of a Welsh dragon design! In 1893 the 1st Battalion marched from Pembroke Dock to Plymouth, an event picked out by the regimental historian as 'successful from a recruiting point of view, but still more so from the hearty welcome the Battalion received from its own folks'.[27] It was this march that a newspaper was recalling in 1908 (despite giving it a different date) as 'a triumphal progress all the way, the receptions at Llanelly, Swansea, Merthyr and Cardiff being especially notable'. Yet in that year, after the Regiment had returned from a long absence abroad, and had not been in Wales since its exploits in the Boer War, the War Office declined to allow it to march through south Wales, probably as an economy measure. It was deaf to the press appeals on the grounds of its effects on recruiting.[28]

In the period immediately before the Great War, there is some evidence of hostility to British militarism and Empire, particularly in the rural areas. In so far as the 'pro-Boer' sympathies of Wales are not a myth, they arose from the predominantly Welsh-speaking and rural areas. The Welsh-language press was more likely to identify with a nation of colonist farmers than was the often imperialist press (especially the *Western Mail*) of the south.[29] A. G. Bradley was appalled at the attitude of men and women around Harlech to military recruiting just before the Great War. Despite flying colours, beating drums and playing 'Men of Harlech' there were almost no takers:

Thanks largely to the non-conformist clergy, it had come to pass that enlistment was accounted as a sort of moral obliquity and social crime. The recruit was regarded almost as a lost soul, to be looked at askance by his neighbours when he returned as a soldier on furlough.

In an English-speaking district of mid Wales he found a similar rejection of the military: no local girls would walk out with them. He saw this as a parochial attitude, and one which the Great War would invert into patriotism.[30] Bradley and other evidence suggests that this rejection was not as strong in industrial areas; the army recruited well there, and especially when there was a stoppage or slowdown in industry. It was well pleased with the harvest it took from industrial south Wales during the industrial strife of 1911.[31]

Industrial areas and the larger towns were most closely integrated into the imperial structure, as the distribution of celebrations of the relief of Mafeking and other victories of the Boer War tend to suggest. It was here that Welsh people celebrated as fervently as in many parts of England. The distribution of population changed greatly in nineteenth-century Wales, and by the eve of the Great War over 60 per cent of the people of Wales were located in towns of more than 5,000 persons. It was sometimes claimed that such urbanization produced a more intimate connection with the wider world. Colonel A. O. Vaughan made the general point in 1914, in a manner reminiscent of Georg Simmel:

> In the industrial districts men's minds were sharpened and revivified by the hourly contact and clashing of each other's thoughts, and by the quick change and stress of daily life. It would not be strange if those men were more temperamentally alive to the great issues, and quicker to respond to the call to them, than men whose lives run in slow grooves as in our agricultural districts, where men meet each other seldom and even then are restricted in the topics of their speech.[32]

Such a perspective was not new. In 1854, at a meeting on delinquency in Cardiff, Edward Priest Richards, town clerk, landlord, and by virtue of his office as the Marquis of Bute's agent, leading citizen, argued that it was necessary for a town of upwards of 20,000 people to express an opinion on a general measure such as the control of delinquency. A smaller town could confine itself to local issues and to self government, but Cardiff needed to stand 'in that position . . . to which our wealth, our population, and, I may add, also, our intelligence entitle us'.[33] Two years later the success of the local police in apprehending a criminal from Birkenhead caused the local paper 'to acknowledge and admire the co-operation which not infrequently exists between the police of cities and towns widely separated in opposite portions of our "little Britain" '.[34] It was from this kind of vantage point that another Cardiff newspaper looked out in 1911 to chastise the Town Improvement Association of Prestatyn for calling on the town council to do everything it could to discourage the holding of territorial army camps in the area, for they brought in no trade and only discouraged the 'better class' of visitor. Cosmopolitan disdain was mustered to belabour this 'narrow and unpatriotic attitude'. National defence was more important than the welfare of a district, and '[i]t is regrettable that from time to time a few well-meaning, but misguided, people in some parts of Wales should do their best to hamper the efforts made for the defence of the Kingdom'.[35] This issue arose quite frequently in rural areas of Britain, in fact, whenever there was a war, and opposition was often more politically inspired than that of the burghers of Prestatyn.

In many respects the problems which some in Wales experienced with the British state evaporated during the Great War. There is no space for a full discussion of this issue here, and the focus will be placed on the first months of the war, when there seems to have been a substantial shift in Welsh attitudes towards the military, and before the discussion becomes complicated by conscription and the extent of reserved occupations in Wales. The early wartime recruiting figures are disputed, with some counts deriving from contemporary propaganda suggesting that Wales had the highest rate of recruitment per head of population in the British Isles. Other estimates suggest that by the end of 1915, as voluntary recruitment came to an end, Wales had provided 4.9 per cent of its population for the army, as compared with Scotland's 6.18 per cent and England's 5.56 per cent. This recruitment level was, of course, much closer to those than it was to Ireland's 2.06 per cent, and it marked a major break with Wales's peacetime contribution, but the shortfall is significant.[36] Yet, the gap had closed considerably and this marked a major transformation of the situation prevailing in the past century. Enthusiasm for war was a pan-European phenomenon and it clearly affected Wales to a great extent, without eradicating all the established hostility to the army.

Patriotism was clearly the dominant mood at the outbreak of the war, though this did not mean to say that it was greeted with uniform and uncritical enthusiasm. The South Wales Miners' Federation was keen to put on record its opposition, in principle, to war, and at least one of its leaders, Vernon Hartshorn, looked forward to the day when workers' organizations would have the power to prevent any European war. It was in this spirit that many miners followed the resolution of their Executive to observe their August 1914 holiday, and not return to work early, as the Admiralty asked them to do. They made and observed a distinction between a European crisis and British involvement in the war. But once war was declared and Germany was seen as the aggressor, it was a different matter, as Charles Stanton and many others pointed out. Within weeks of the outbreak of war, many miners worked an extra hour, as the Admiralty requested. Such attitudes were beyond the comprehension of the *Western Mail*, which expected a straightforward response to the Admiralty's appeal.

Its cartoonist, Joseph Morewood Staniforth, depicted Dame Wales appealing for patriotism at the pithead as dark clouds gathered in the background.[37]

According to press reports there was a great deal of patriotic enthusiasm in Wales at the outbreak of the war. But it was a more complex process to convert this into recruits in uniform. At first, recruiting was portrayed as being for national defence, including 'the defence of Wales', rather than for military service in France, and much of the early enthusiasm surrounded the joining-up to the colours of men in the various military and naval reserves, rather than new recruits. Many who joined were apparently ex-soldiers.[38] Enthusiastic public meetings could be full of people who were too old for military service. What was described as a meeting with 'great enthusiasm' and 'filled to overflowing' in Colwyn Bay, nonetheless produced only 'several' enlistees.[39] The enthusiastic town meetings which were reported in Merthyr, Nelson, Abergavenny, Aberafan, Newport and Pontypridd early in August 1914 were directed at organizing the Prince of Wales Relief Fund for the support of recruits' dependants, rather than at recruiting.[40] It soon became apparent that something more than simple patriotic enthusiasm was necessary.

Five aspects became crucial: one was evident community support for recruiting efforts; a second was an appropriate social and demographic structure; the third was organization, without which enthusiasm frequently evaporated; the fourth was the material needs of dependants of the recruits; and fifthly, there were determined efforts to utilize Welsh patriotism for the cause.

Patriotic appeals might have echoed hollowly if they had not been supported by institutions of the local state and by community organizations and leaders, which served to give them resonance. From the beginning of the war, there were attempts to mobilize such support. The efforts to raise a regiment of Welsh Horse were organized by the Mayor of Cardiff, acting almost as if Cardiff had already been declared the national capital. He called on all the Lords Lieutenant in Wales to join him in this, and all who could be contacted quickly joined the cause.[41] Community support was often shown through send-offs for recruits which involved cheering crowds and military bands. A band of forty recruits who had enlisted 'in a body' from the Neath Steel and Galvanising Works found the local station and the town square packed with 'thousands of people' and were accompanied by their works' manager. There were cheers and shouts of 'Are we down-hearted?' followed by the ringing response, 'No!' They included the rugby player Tim Jenkins, who encouraged other players to come forward. In the *Western Mail*, Staniforth's cartoon summed this up as Dame Wales cheering on departing troops.[42] Generally, there was a stress on using football in this way, as another pull on community structures to mobilize and with the belief that the nature of the sport produced at least a rudimentary military training: 'Rugby Internationals are specially invited to enrol in view of their special training in tactics and unselfish support of one another in combined movements of attack and defence.'[43] There was much public discussion of the need to suspend football fixtures, and praise for teams which did so.[44] Very soon after the outbreak of war, financial benefits were given to individuals who engaged in local recruiting. This was seen as a means of capturing community enthusiasm: 'The great advantage of this new arrangement is that it tends to encourage recruiting enthusiasm in the local districts, as in the case of a community or district wishing to furnish a company or companies for Kitchener's Army.'[45] Many promoters of recruiting became enthusiasts for the formation of such 'pals' brigades', which drew on neighbourhood and friendship networks. In the Rhondda valleys the miners' agent David Watts Morgan was an active promoter of such a unit, while in west Wales a recruiter expressed the need for local community leaders, like schoolteachers and ministers, to be drawn into the work.[46] In October, a group of leading Welsh Nonconformist ministers issued a pamphlet supporting the war effort and recruiting, breaking with the older tradition of opposition to war and the army. In industrial south Wales political agents were drawn into the work, as well as prominent miners' leaders like Vernon Hartshorn, Charles Stanton and William Brace.[47] It was important to find the right community leaders for such work. In Bethesda the presence of the quarry manager on the platform was said to have dampened enthusiasm for recruiting, while one wonders how useful Leonard Llewelyn, general manager of the Cambrian Collieries, was as the recruiting officer in the Rhondda, given the bitterness engendered by his authoritarian stance during the Cambrian Combine strike of 1910–11.[48]

The importance of community efforts prompted attempts to stimulate competition between areas for numbers and proportion of recruits. The press was keen to stress enthusiasm in Wales in general, but went beyond this to look at the response within particular communities. Glamorgan was seen as having a fine response, and Monmouthshire dubbed a 'patriotic county', but this soon descended to local levels: 'A notable example to the more populous centres has been set by two villages – Briton Ferry and St Clears where practically all the men eligible for service have joined the ranks.'[49] Tredegar was said to hold the record in Monmouthshire for numbers enlisted, while in the Rhymney Valley, 'it is probable that no village can beat the fine record of Troedrhiwfuwch, where from 96 cottages no fewer than 56 men have left to do their duty to their country'.[50] But once competition of this kind started some communities were singled out as lacking in patriotism, though at the ultimate cost of shaking the very foundations of this argument and pointing out the relevance of social and demographic structures.

By the beginning of September 1914 it was being pointed out that recruiting was slow in Anglesey and rural west Wales, and that there was a disappointing response from the north Wales quarrymen. Later, Montgomeryshire would be added to the list, and Harlech singled out for attack on the grounds of the (alleged) lack of a single recruit coming forward at a hiring fair.[51] Colonel Wynne Edwards pointed out that Llandudno's 472 recruits would become well over 1,000 in a German town of the same size by virtue of conscription.[52] A framework for this kind of discussion had already been established by invoking the idea of the quota – that each county or district should produce a number of volunteers in proportion to its share of the population. On such grounds much of north Wales was found wanting, and this was interpreted in public discussion as a lack of the appropriate patriotic spirit. But defenders of these areas soon found alternative and more convincing explanations, related to local demography. While many outsiders believed that the economic depression in the slate-quarrying areas made them ripe for recruiting, local observers noted that many men in the relevant age-group had already left the area, some enlisting in south Wales or Lancashire. A similar pattern was identified in west Wales.[53]

Successful recruiting demanded a strong organizational base, and it is the presence or absence of this that explains many of the variations in response. Monmouthshire's structure was activated by the indefatigable Sir Ivor Herbert, MP: 'day after day and night after night he has tramped the county and planted the seeds of that enthusiasm which has borne fruit'.[54] But there were frequently tales from across Wales of the number of volunteers exceeding the capacity to deal with them and of men waiting hours to be seen, hungry and neglected. Some threatened to go back home. In Cardiff, the main recruiting centre for Glamorgan, it was almost the end of August before there were said to be enough clerks to deal with the rush, while Swansea experienced similar problems. Some areas of Glamorgan lacked recruiting stations when the war was almost a month old.[55] Only in early September did Caernarfonshire create a fully organized system, being followed a week or so later by Anglesey.[56] There were also suggestions that too much of the activity went on in the English language, with calls for Lloyd George's speeches to be translated into Welsh. Welsh-language recruiting posters appeared only in early 1915. But there does seem to have been at least some Welsh material, and the Welsh press generally gave support, though less enthusiastically than the English-language press.[57] Beyond simple organization it was also necessary to make some impact. It was frequently advocated that military bands should be used and recruits paraded between and through towns in order to influence the local population. Gradually, this was achieved in many areas.[58]

But voluntary enlistment was ultimately a decision made by individuals who had family responsibilities. Understandably, such loyalties were frequently to the fore. It was some time before the exact level of allowances for wives was settled, and there were complaints that the needs of other dependants, like ageing mothers, were not taken into account. There were also concerns expressed about the treatment which the wounded from previous conflicts had received, when individuals were left to shoulder what should have been social costs.[59] Indeed, many voluntary bodies and businesses were left to plug the gaps in the system. The Whitehead Steel and Iron Company in Tredegar offered to pay allowances to any of its employees who volunteered and to give them their jobs back when they returned. In north Wales the Penrhyn Estate paid allowances to wives and dependants of enlistees. Lodges of the South Wales Miners' Federation played a major role in relieving those left destitute by the outbreak of war, and it regarded all recruits as remaining paid-up members on their return. In the recruiting station in Cardiff the waiting volunteers were aided by the Salvation Army and the local Soldiers' and Sailors' Rest Homes organization.[60] The *Western Mail* rather airily proclaimed that the state could not be expected to do everything, while the *Carnarvon and Denbigh Herald* felt that it should show a higher responsibility.[61]

There were also efforts to harness a specifically Welsh patriotism for the cause. Lloyd George, with his usual contempt for established procedures, launched the idea of a Welsh Army Corps, whose recruiting would draw on specifically Welsh notions of patriotism. The *Western Mail*'s irrepressible Staniforth depicted him as the Pied Piper of Criccieth leading recruits away, in an analogy which the cartoonist clearly had not thought through, and which was to become all too relevant. Lloyd George 'set before us the example of Germany', where, he pointed out, the nationality of the Bavarians, Wurtemburgers, Saxons and so forth was recognized in army grouping, and utilized as a factor of fighting value.[62] He found the style from his early days in Cymru Fydd (when he had lectured on medieval Welsh history), and rediscovered the martial spirit of Wales.[63] Such an approach was not entirely the creation of the Chancellor of the Exchequer. A version of this had been prefigured in a Conservative newspaper, which managed to contradict a great deal of previous writing from this position, but tapped into a favourite theme of Welsh Toryism: that there was a good Welsh patriotic tradition, however much it had been 'corrupted' by Liberalism and Nonconformity.

Wales is a county of proud military tradition. Long before the present recruiting system arose the Welsh people were distinguished for their warlike spirit and unquenchable valour . . . Since the destinies of Wales and England were united the people of Wales have borne a prominent and honourable part in the work of national defence. . . . The enthusiastic plaudits of the public which have greeted every stage in the process of mobilisation are expressive of the national gratitude to the men who are serving.[64]

Liberal newspapers could also locate a Welsh military tradition. An army in France evoked a memory of the exploits of Welsh archers in the Hundred Years War, and in particular of the role of Owain Lawgoch, the claimant to the Welsh principality, who was probably assassinated by English agents. Furthermore, the men of Snowdonia were 'descendants of the men who defied the powerful Norman for generations after the Saxon had submitted to his yoke'.[65] A south Wales newspaper reminded its readers of the role of archers from the Caldicot Levels in Henry V's army.[66] An effort to find a military tradition in Welsh Nonconformity was less successful, yielding only Howell Harris, who had been an enthusiastic sergeant in the militia in the Seven Years War, and Morgan Llwyd, who had been a chaplain in Cromwell's army.[67]

Certainly, there was much enthusiasm expressed in the press for appeals to Welsh patriotism as an effective means of recruiting. Its actual significance may have been less direct but, by August 1915, Lloyd George could point out, with satisfaction, that there was then a bigger Welsh army in the field than the British–Dutch army that Wellington had commanded at Waterloo. That might have been true, but it hid a statistically slightly more disappointing response. Some old attitudes lingered. The Welsh Army Corps itself justified its existence in terms of its effectiveness in recruiting and its assertion of the rightful status of Wales. By October 1915, when recruiting for this force stopped, around 50,000 men had been engaged. This, it was claimed, 'placed beyond question the inalienable right of a small nation to a universal recognition of its own separate entity as one of the sister nations that entered the lists in defence of liberties and freedom of other small nations on the Continent of Europe'. This theme formed a link between Wales and the ostensible cause of Britain's involvement. The nature of Welsh nationality and its role in the world was one of the themes of a gift book sold in aid of the war effort; it featured as a frontispiece the painting 'Wales Awakening', by Christopher Williams.[68]

But there was a problem in sustaining recruiting, once the initial intense enthusiasm, which could be very short-lived, had evaporated. In the south Wales coalfield, the Tylorstown Silver Band joined en bloc in those heady days, yet by February 1915 the Welsh Regiment was finding that recruiting was drying up. Press reports that all was well in France, combined with good wages in mining and anti-war sentiments, were blamed for the situation.[69] Many continued to see the rural areas as the most difficult to approach. Sir Henry Jones, the Welsh-born Glasgow philosopher turned recruiter, was well satisfied with his reception from his 'favourite quarrymen' in Blaenau Ffestiniog, but recognized that he was sent only to the 'stiff' parts.[70] Recruiting was not always a straightforward business in the rural areas, and ingenuity was required to find the right appeals and moral pressure. There were complaints that the rural areas of Carmarthenshire were doing very little for the cause, and that elsewhere farmers' sons took to the hills to avoid the recruiters. One recruiter was threatened with a shotgun! In east Denbighshire, the Parliamentary Recruiting Committee found that public meetings had little real impact – there was a great deal of skin-deep patriotism, but few recruits. It decided on 'local actions accompanied by sniping', and enlisted the aid of the parish councils. Local recruiting committees were formed at the parish level, and locally influential speakers procured. The Royal Welch Fusiliers band, complete with regimental goat, marched around the villages, along with local organizations. A census was taken of all men of military age, they were systematically visited by recruiters, and 'if any local influence could be brought to bear, such was appealed to'. The committee drew the final conclusion: 'Had we not recognised their local influence, but proceeded from our headquarters, they would have construed our action as one of mistrust. Trust the local committees and they will respond; mistrust them and they will negative [sic] all the best of efforts.' Here, better organization meant more successful recruiting than in Gwynedd, showing again the salience of this factor.[71]

Much of the preceding discussion has stressed the role of local communities in promoting recruiting in the early part of the war, and it points to the need for microscopic study as a way forward in research. In this final section, a sketch of such a study is offered. Ruthin, in the Vale of Clwyd, was a market town which had stagnated in the Victorian era of rapid expansion, and many of its citizens felt that modernity and its promise had passed them by: the stagnation was expressed in its relatively high death-rate, which was reflection of its ageing population. War was to be a shock here, as it was to the rest of the western world. At the beginning there was much excitement and patriotic feeling, with a crowd gathering on St Peter's Square on 4 August 1914. About thirty people gave in their names for a corps of volunteers for home defence. Moves to boycott German products were soon instituted, but J. Daniels, toy and fancy goods dealer, begged leave to sell his existing stock of toys first. Ninety per cent of his toys were German and he claimed he would be impoverished if a truce were not extended to him. He ended his letter with the words 'God save the King', lest anyone should accuse him of erring patriotism.[72] Soon, tradesmen and farmers were losing their horses to the army, with some resistance from the latter at first.[73] However, the response to recruiting was more measured: 'The number of persons desiring to enlist in Ruthin has, so far, [been] disappointingly small, and an earnest appeal is now made to able-bodied young men to come forward and offer themselves for service.'[74] Neither were there many subscriptions to the Prince of Wales Fund, which was set up to relieve distress caused by the economic dislocations of the war. An enthusiastic recruiting meeting produced just two volunteers. But soon the town was preening itself on the number of volunteers it was providing, and long lists appeared in the press: 'so far as Ruthin is concerned, there is every reason to be proud of the patriotism of the inhabitants'.[75] Yet such enthusiasm was patchy, and not sustainable over the longer term. By 1917, one observer deplored the lack of knowledge amongst the local population of the issues at stake in the conflict, and found unpatriotic activities like hoarding and black-marketeering, a desire to avoid military service and to enjoy life to the full to be the dominant responses to the conflict. Few followed the progress of the war as avidly as he did.[76]

Some occurrences brought the reality of the war closer to home. Belgian refugees attracted some interest at a meeting held to consider taking them into the town. An illustrated lecture promoted their cause, and it was followed by a public meeting and a house-to-house canvass for funds. By mid November 1914, Belgians were arriving in the town, and soon there would be twenty-one of them living in strange surroundings.[77] Yet all was not well from the viewpoint of the strict patriot. By the end of the month the novelist Stanley J. Weyman, who lived at Plas Llanrhydd, near Ruthin, delivered a homily through *The Times*, and his message was picked up by the local press:

Sir – I write to you because I live the year round in the country, and can gauge what my neighbours are thinking, and what they know. They know that there is a war in France or Belgium or some distant part. They know that we are mixed up in it, as we have been mixed up in wars before. They don't doubt that we shall come out of it, as we have come out of wars before. They know that the gentry are keen on it; but the gentry are apt to be keen on wars – they suspect vaguely that the gentry get something out of wars. And that is the sum of their knowledge – a war, dim, distant, somewhere in foreign parts, in which we are engaged. The upshot is that from the three eastward parishes, covering a large spread of hill country, barely one man, if one man, is serving in England or at the front; and of other parishes, up and down the same may be said. The small town to the west has done its part, not unworthily. But the farmers and farmers' sons shrug their shoulders and think 'Wars are for wastrels; it's no business of ours.'

His remedy was to make it known that 'England' could be invaded, and that then corn-stacks could go up in smoke.[78]

Three years later Robert Jones Edwards, a Tory solicitor who had fallen on hard times, would describe local attitudes in almost identical terms:

> there are this day hundreds of folk in this remote town of Ruthin who know no more about the affair than that we are at war with Germany; that all our available men are required; that they are being killed 'by the thousand'; that food is scarce owing to our ships being sunk by submarines, and that things generally have 'all of a sudden' got into a very queer tangle. But the origin of the cataclysm, the motives which drew us into it, the vast issues at stake, the reason why it is absolutely essential that German Militarism must be knocked off its legs, and all the rest of the story, are still to most of the Burgesses of this Ancient Borough unsolved problems.[79]

Edwards thought he saw the issue much more clearly:

> Yet this seems to me essentially a war into which every young man, and also every man of property in our country should have at once thrown all their energies. For, after the openly avowed, and apparently inextinguishable hatred of the Hun towards the English people and everything English, if the enemy were victorious, and obtained possession of our Island, undoubtedly our wealth would be confiscated, on some pretence, and our young men for the remainder of their lives would be merely second fiddles in back rows. But the predominance of present interest over our future possibilities generally obscures our vision.[80]

He was horrified that not everybody responded in this way. One man had said to him that he was glad that they were over the age at which they would be required to fight, and that he had two daughters, rather than sons who could be taken into the firing line.[81] By May 1915 an unnamed woman was moved to make an appeal 'to the young men of north Wales who have not yet enlisted':

> How is it that every man of you who is single is not ashamed to hold his head up when walking the street? In Denbigh and Ruthin alone and the adjoining parishes, how is it that so many wives are drawing separation allowances; it is because many more married men have enlisted than unmarried ones? that means more expense on the country, besides showing decided disloyalty on your part. Of course in the months gone by young men have rallied nobly to the colours, and in both Denbigh and Ruthin the soldiers billeted will testify; a nicer set of young men will be hard to find anywhere. Does the sight of them never move you to join too?
> Think of those 45 coffins for babies and children carried along the streets of Queenstown on Saturday morning. Think again of those 120 victims of the Lusitania outrage buried on Monday in Queenstown, and determine to avenge them, and also to replace those brave men who have

fallen. You must leave your comfortable posts in offices and shops and tell your employers that they must employ older men who are ineligible for service, or else women or girls of whom there are plenty.

Our enemies, the Germans, are most decidedly barbarians, but they are also skilled barbarians and as such we must be prepared. What would you young fellows say if your mothers or wee sister or brother were amongst those lost on the Lusitania, or killed in Belgium, would you not say, up and avenge them?[82]

Mrs 'Patsy' Cornwallis-West opened Ruthin Castle to wounded soldiers and her increasingly dubious ministrations. The castle also became the focus for the organization of the manufacture of soldiers' comforts, an activity which spread out around the whole district.[83]

The issue with recruiting concerned the surrounding rural areas, rather than the town. By mid 1915 there had been 300 volunteers from Ruthin, with a population of 2,800, but under 200 from the surrounding rural areas, with a population of 7,000, according to the chemist and local historian, T. J. Roberts. He tried to put the best gloss on it:

He knew it was neither cowardice or lack of patriotism, but it might well be that farmers were afraid harvesting operations could not be carried on. He was glad to see that arrangements were being made to liberate soldiers for the two harvests, and even boy scouts and scholars of the secondary school might, no doubt, be ready to volunteer their services.

He had come to the conclusion that people residing in the country did not realise the awfulness of the grim tragedy going on in Europe and the urgent need of men and ever more men to ensure certain victory at the earliest possible moment.[84]

Soon it was being claimed that the Ruthin rural area had the worst response to recruiting in the whole of north Wales. It was claimed that farmers were not to blame, as agricultural labour was very scarce and this presented farmers with great difficulties. But attention then fixed upon gamekeepers, beaters and road men, all of whom were seen as less than indispensable.[85] In an attempt to reassure worried Nonconformists, some of the problems with army life for Welsh people were addressed:

Everyone who enlists now will have the opportunity of choosing what unit of the army he would wish to join . . . and this will give them the advantage of joining the Welsh Army, a portion of which is now encamped at Conway and Kinmel Park. Their officers in these places will be Welshmen and those who join will have every fair play to gain positions in the army on their own merits. They will be cared for by Welsh chaplains and ministers, and the Brigadier-General, Owen Thomas, himself an ardent Welshman, will supervise all their movements, both military and social. We think it most important for the parents of Wales, whose sacrifice has been so great, to see that they secure the healthiest and safest place for the bodies and souls of their sons, and we believe they will do this by encouraging enlistment in the army.[86]

If this were not enough, the recruiter Owen Thomas himself was interviewed in the local paper to stress the Welshness of the army – claiming that it was the most Welsh for 400 years, since a Welsh army had won at Bosworth. The special provisions for different brands of religious observance and the comparison with the principled New Model Army of Cromwell were also aimed at attracting Nonconformist support. But complaints continued of the hoarding of labour by farmers, and about the offence of three men being employed at the Royal Golf Club at St Asaph to look after the greens. Other strong, healthy men were allegedly seen on market days, at concerts and at preaching festivals. Farmers complained that the Labour Exchanges failed to provide alternative labour for them, and said that their farms lacked suitable accommodation to allow women to replace men in farm work. One of the problems was the smallness of local farms: amalgamation might have allowed more labour to be released, but small farms retained more of it than larger ones might have done. Farmers' critics felt they were not keen to use female labour, and simply used the lack of accommodation as an excuse. Farmers, in turn, claimed that women refused all their blandishments – even a gift of onions. Undeniably, they knew how to give a girl a good time, as one wag remarked, that was enough to bring tears to the eyes of anyone! By 1917, munitions work in Wrexham was a competing attraction for female labour.[87]

Not until April 1915, when it prepared a list of those who had enlisted and sent its first letter of condolence to a bereaved family, did the borough council take any notice of the war.[88] But changes did begin to appear in daily life. A shortage of shop assistants had led to many shops closing at lunch hour by early 1916. At one meeting in September 1916 the council had to pass eight votes of condolence with bereaved families. Seven months later there were so many letters of condolence to be sent that a standard form of letter was drafted. By 1918, 35 of the 150 men who had joined up locally had been killed.[89]

War may be an occasion for temporary national unity, yet such was the impact of the Great War that there were attempts to make the experience a permanent one. Vast quantities of stone and metal were fashioned into memorials to the fallen. The memorials and the acts of commemoration were highly localized. In the Vale of Clwyd, the hamlet of Llanbedr refused to join in Ruthin's schemes and insisted on its own artefact. In Ruthin, conflicts like this and differences of opinion over the form which a memorial should take were sufficient to delay the matter for some years. Should the community choose a 'work of art' or a swimming bath, which would improve the health of future generations? The one seemed to represent 'pure' patriotism, while the alternative was a new twist to the old theme of social imperialism. In Ruthin art triumphed, but elsewhere more practical concerns came to the fore. In many areas of north and mid Wales memorial halls were constructed, remedying a defect in rural life which Tom Ellis, MP, and a host of others had previously pointed out. In Llanfair in Merioneth it took ten years to collect the necessary funds for 'a place of social intercourse, mutual helpfulness, mental and moral improvement and rational recreation'.[90]

What might explain the difficulties the army encountered in recruiting in Wales, which in the remoter rural areas seemed to persist into the Great War? Was there a widespread hostility to militarism in Wales? In a country whose religious allegiance was overwhelmingly Nonconformist this was likely to have been the case to some extent, but it probably does not take us very far as an explanation. Early in the Great War, it was certainly claimed that this had been the case in the past: 'Fifty or sixty years ago the Army was unpopular in Wales. Our fathers believed that war under any circumstances was unjustifiable and they looked askance at any young man who enlisted. He was regarded as a slacker or worse.'[91]

But this holds little water generally. Peace movements were only sporadically well-supported, and such support as there was tended to evaporate in times of international crisis. If Wales was a Nonconformist nation, it was one that lacked a strong element of Quakerism, the main religious force for pacifism at the time.[92] There was a certain amount of support for movements advocating open diplomacy and negotiation, but they always foundered on the idea of a defensive war (as was the case throughout Europe in 1914). The Welsh enthusiasm for the Volunteer movements in the 1860s shows just how little absolute pacifism there was in reality.[93] In some senses, Nonconformist objections were often more about the nature of the contemporary British state and suspicion of the warlike nature of its ruling aristocratic elite than they were about the absolute refusal of armed conflict. Welsh Liberals were usually Gladstonians, and preferred a small state and low taxes. They rejected military 'adventures', but not national self-defence. If Nonconformity exerted an influence on military recruitment it was much more likely to be through its moral objections to the army and to the way in which the army treated its soldiers. Indeed, as we have seen, most contemporary comment fastened on this aspect, rather than on absolute moral objections to war. Soldiering offended the Protestant ethic, but this did not mean that there was widespread support for pacifism.

Neither did people in Wales forget the armed conflicts that had marked their society. Anyone who wanders the streets of Carmarthen, for instance, will pass the monument to General Thomas Picton, commemorating a hero of the Napoleonic era; carry on past that to Guildhall Square and the monument to all ranks who fell in the Crimean War, in Portland stone with a base twelve feet square and a height of thirty feet, surrounded by iron railings representing muskets with fixed bayonets.[94] Further on again, in Nott Square, there is a statue of General Sir William Nott, hero of the first Afghan War of 1838–42. Carmarthen was a centre of Nonconformity and its press, but at the very least the iconography of its streets reveals that there were other forces existing in nineteenth-century Welsh society.[95]

It must also be remembered that the image of an unpatriotic, anti-militarist, pacifist nation suited two opposed sets of political actors in Wales. The more militant Nonconformists might see their nation in this way and be glad to accept the viewpoint. But it also suited their Tory political opponents, who saw patriotism for the British (though they usually called it English) state as one of the central virtues which Welsh Nonconformity lacked. Their political language revolved around the Empire, Anglicanism and the existing state. Nonconformity stressed the Welsh nation, which was seen as being based upon voluntary religion and at some distance from the existing state, especially from the religious establishment.[96] Nonconformist hostility to the army seemed more resonant when it complained of the moral failings of soldiers, rather than when some ministers advocated pacifism. Clearly, this had a deeper impact on rural areas than on industrial ones. The response to the Great War suggested that while many did respond to the patriotic appeals, their impact could be short-lived and shallow. Everyday concerns often came quickly to the fore, as Tory moralists like Robert Jones Edwards recognized. Interestingly, he did not indict Nonconformity for any role in reducing recruiting in the Ruthin area. The use of Welsh patriotism as a method of recruiting may have had some effect in breaking the logjam of opposition to the army which had marked the nineteenth century. But the main factor was that there was now a need for troops far in excess of that of the nineteenth century, and a situation which was seen as being a defensive war, in line with Nonconformist (and indeed, many socialist) attitudes. The persuasive power of the state was aligned with Welsh patriotism, and with local community identities and structures. In concert, they produced a force which was hard to resist. Patriotism, we may say, paraphrasing Edith Cavell, was not, by itself, enough. However powerful the appeal of an imagined community, it often needed the reinforcement of a real one to become an active force in society.

NOTES

1   The best work on Richard is Ieuan Gwynedd Jones, *Henry Richard: Apostle of Peace, 1812–1888* (Llandysul, 1988); for S.R. see Glanmor Williams, *Samuel Roberts* (Cardiff, 1950).

2   Keith Robbins, *Nineteenth-Century Britain: Integration and Diversity* (Oxford, 1988), p. 177; Parliamentary Papers (hereafter *PP*), 1867, vol. XV, *Report of Commissioners Appointed to Inquire into the Recruiting for the Army*, p. 316, 'Recruits Inspected and Rejected, 1864'.

3   Clive Hughes, 'Army recruitment in Gwynedd, 1914–16' (unpublished MA thesis, University of Wales, 1983), p. 151; see also Cyril Parry, 'Gwynedd and the Great War, 1914–1918', *WHR*, 14, 1 (1988), 80.

4   S. G. Checkland, *The Rise of Industrial Society in England 1815–1885* (London, 1964), p. 320.

5   The National Archives (hereafter *TNA*), War Office Papers, WO33/27, *Report of the Committee on Recruiting, 1875*.

6   TNA, WO33/26, Major-General Wolseley, 'Our Army Reserve'.

7   TNA, WO33/55, *Report of Director General of Recruiting, 1880*, p. 3.

8   Ibid., p. 10; WO33/26, No. 569, Confidential Note, 'On Recruiting' (1874), pp. 587–8.

9   TNA, WO33/22, Memorandum of F. Robertson-Ackman (1870).

10 TNA, WO33/22, *Reports from the Inspecting Officers of the Recruiting Districts, 1871, Captain J. G. McD. Tulloch*, p. 21.

11 TNA, WO33/27, *Report of the Committee on Recruiting, 1875*, p. 11.

12 PP, 1861, vol. XV, *Report of Commissioners Appointed to Inquire into the Present System of Recruiting*, qu. 248, pp. 16–17.

13 TNA, WO33/22, *Reports from Inspecting Officers . . . Capt. John C. Clarke, Chester, 1 May 1871*.

14 H. J. Hanham, 'Religion and nationality in the mid-Victorian Army', in M. R. D. Foot (ed.), *War and Society: Essays in Honour and Memory of J. R. Western, 1928–1971* (London, 1973).

15 *Cardiff and Merthyr Guardian* (hereafter *CMG*), 24 Nov. 1854.

16 *The Times*, 17, 18, 20, 21, 24 Nov. 1854.

17 *CN*, 2, 9 Aug. 1872. I am grateful to Dr Mike Benbough-Jackson for these references.

18 *The Times*, 31 July 1908.

19 *Carnarvonshire and Denbigh Herald* (hereafter *CDH*), 8 Jan. 1915.

20 *South Wales Daily News* (hereafter *SWDN*), 7 Sept. 1908; *The Times*, 31 July, 24 Sept., 1, 2, 3, 6 Oct. 1908.

21 R. Broughton-Mainwaring, *Historical Record of the Royal Welch Fusiliers, Late the Twenty-third Regiment* (London, 1889) pp. 248, 281; A. C. Whitehorne et al., *The History of the Welch Regiment* (Cardiff, 2 vols, 1932 and 1952) pp. iii, 279; Howel Thomas, *A History of the Royal Welsh Fusiliers: Late the Twenty-third Regiment* (London, 1916); Robert Graves, *Good-Bye To All That: An Autobiography* (Oxford, 1995), p. 85; H. Avray Tipping, *The Story of the Royal Welsh Fusiliers* (London, 1915); *CDH*, 30 Oct. 1914.

[22] Edwin Poole, *The Military Annals of the County of Brecknock* (Brecknock, 1885), p. 17.

[23] Poole, *Military Annals*, p. 14; *Brecon County Times*, 1, 15, 29 Mar., 5, 12 Apr. 1879.

[24] Peter Stead, 'Wales in the movies', in Tony Curtis (ed.), *Wales: The Imagined Nation – Studies in Cultural and National Identity* (Bridgend, 1986), p. 176.

[25] Paramount DVD, PHE 8086, *Zulu* (1964; special Collector's Edition, 2004).

[26] Cited in Colin Hughes, *Mametz: Lloyd George's 'Welsh Army' at the Battle of the Somme* (Norwich, 1990), p. 26.

[27] Whitehorne et al., *History of the Welch Regiment* (1932 vol.), p. 221.

[28] Welsh Regiment, *Order of Service on the Occasion of Depositing the Crimean Colours of the 41st Welsh Regiment at Llandaff Cathedral at 4 o'clock p.m. on Friday August 16th 1895*; Whitehorne et al., *History of the Welch Regiment*, pp. 221, 266; *SWDN*, 19 Sept. 1908.

[29] Kenneth O. Morgan, 'Wales and the Boer War – a reply', *WHR*, 4, 4 (1969).

[30] A. G. Bradley, *In Praise of North Wales* (London, 1925), pp. 159–61. I owe this reference to the late Dr Lewis Lloyd. There seems to have been brisk recruiting in Cardiff in 1857, for instance; *CMG*, 19 Sept., 3 Oct. 1857.

[31] *SWDN*, 4 Oct. 1911.

[32] *WM*, 7 Oct. 1914. Georg Simmel, 'The metropolis and mental life', in Richard Sennett (ed.), *Classic Essays on the Culture of Cities* (New York, 1969), p. 48. This essay was first published in 1903.

[33] *CMG*, 4 Feb. 1854.

[34] Ibid., 23 Feb. 1856.

[35] *WM*, 16 Sept. 1911.

[36] W. Lewis Jones (ed.), *The Land of My Fathers: A Welsh Gift Book* (London, 1915); Hughes, 'Army recruitment'; p. 59; NLW MS3556E.

[37] *SWDN*, 8, 24 Aug. 1914; *WM*, 3, 4, 5 Aug. 1914.

[38] *WM*, 6, 7, 8, 20 Aug. 1914.

[39] *CDH*, 27 Aug. 1914.

[40] *SWDN*, 11 Aug. 1914.

[41] *SWDN*, 3 Aug. 1914; *CDH*, 7 Aug. 1914.

[42] *SWDN*, 1 Sept. 1914; *WM*, 14 Aug. 1914.

[43] *SWDN*, 3 Aug. 1914.

[44] For example, *WM*, 7 Sept. 1914.

[45] Ibid., 20 Aug. 1914.

[46] Ibid., 24, 27 Aug., 7 Sept., 7 Oct. 1914.

[47] Ibid., 9 Oct. 1914; *CDH*, 16 Oct. 1914.

[48] Parry, 'Gwynedd and the Great War', 83, n. 24; *SWDN*, 2 Sept. 1914.

[49] *WM*, 27, 31 Aug., 4 Sept. 1914.

[50] *SWDN*, 28 Aug., 2 Sept. 1914; *WM*, 19 Sept. 1914.

[51] *WM*, 9 Sept. 1914; *SWDN*, 26, 28 Aug. 1914; *CDH*, 28 Aug., 13, 27 Nov. 1914.

[52] *CDH*, 13 Nov. 1914.

[53] Ibid., 6 Nov., 4 Dec. 1914; *WM*, 9 Sept., 7 Oct. 1914.

[54] *WM*, 31 Aug. 1914; *SWDN*, 1 Sept. 1914.

[55] *SWDN*, 13, 27 Aug., 1, 2, Sept. 1914; *WM*, 13 Aug., 3, 5 Sept. 1914.

[56] *CDH*, 11, 18, 25 Sept. 1914.

[57] Ibid., 4 Sept. 1914, 8 Jan. 1915; *WM*, 7 Oct. 1914; Parry, 'Gwynedd and the Great War', 86–7.

[58] *WM*, 26 Aug., 7 Sept. 1914; *SWDN*, 2 Sept. 1914; *CDH*, 11, 18, Sept., 20 Nov., 4, 11, Dec. 1914.

[59] *CDH*, 11 Sept. 1914; *WM*, 10, 12, 18 Sept. 1914.

[60] *SWDN*, 8, 15, 27 Aug., 2 Sept. 1914; *CDH*, 11 Sept. 1914.

[61] *WM*, 10 Sept. 1914; *CDH*, 11 Sept. 1914.

[62] *WM*, 5, 23 Oct. 1914.

[63] Kenneth O. Morgan, *Rebirth of a Nation: Wales 1880–1980* (Oxford and Cardiff, 1981), pp. 159–61; NLW MS3556E, 1st galley; David Lloyd George, *Through Terror to Triumph: Speeches and Pronouncements since the Beginning of the War* (London, 1915), p. 185.

[64] *WM*, 7 Aug. 1914.

[65] *CDH*, 11 Sept., 9 Oct. 1914.

[66] *SWDN*, 24 Aug. 1914.

[67] *CDH*, 13 Nov. 1914.

[68] Peter Lord, *The Visual Culture of Wales: Imaging the Nation* (Cardiff, 2000), pp. 333–5.

[69] *WM*, 4, 12 Jan. 1915 (I am grateful to Dr Keith Strange for these references); Denis Winter, *Death's Men: Soldiers of the Great War* (London, 1979), p. 33; Parry, 'Gwynedd and the Great War', 88–92, stresses the increasing difficulties facing recruiters in 1915, as does Hughes, *Mametz*, ch. 1 (and p. 76 for the Tylorstown Band).

[70] NLW MS3556E, 'Welsh Army Corps. Draft Report Presented for Consideration by Executive Committee'; Hughes, 'Army recruitment'; Henry Jones to A. M. Jones, 27 Oct., 20 Nov. 1915, in H. J. W. Hetherington (ed.), *The Life and Letters of Sir Henry Jones* (London, 1924), pp. 275, 277.

[71] NLW MS5448C, 'Minute Book of East Denbighshire Parliamentary Recruiting Committee'; Hughes, 'Army recruitment', p. 274.

[72] *Denbigh Free Press* (hereafter *DFP*), 26 Sept. 1914.

[73] Ibid., 8, 18 Aug. 1914.

[74] Ibid., 29 Aug. 1914.

[75] Ibid., 5, 12 Sept., 3 Oct. 1914.

[76] NLW MS4837D, R. J. Edwards, 'The War: 1914–18 as seen from Ruthin, North Wales'; for a fuller analysis of this material see Neil Evans, 'Social change and the small town: the Ruthin of Robert Jones Edwards, *c.* 1849–1931' (lecture to Denbighshire Historical Society, 1999); Cyril Parry, *The Radical Tradition in Welsh Politics: A Study of Liberal and Labour Politics in Gwynedd, 1900–20* (Hull, 1970), p. 67.

[77] *DFP*, 24, 31 Oct., 21 Nov. 1914, 10 Apr. 1915.

[78] Ibid., 28 Nov. 1914.

[79] NLW MS4837D, pp. 17–18.

[80] Ibid., pp. 12–13.

[81] Ibid., p. 12.

[82] *DFP*, 15 May 1915.

[83] Ibid., 1 May 1915, 14 Oct. 1916. For the Cornwallis-West case, see ibid., 6 Jan. 1916, and Tim Coates, *Patsy: The Story of Mary Cornwallis West* (London, 2003).

[84] *DFP*, 19 June 1915.

[85] Ibid., 14 Dec. 1915.

[86] Letter from James Charles and others, ibid., 4 Dec. 1915.

[87] Ibid., 29 Jan., 18 Mar., 17 June, 24 Aug., 14 Oct., 25 Nov. 1916, 6 Jan., 3 Feb. 1917.

[88] Clwyd Record Office, Ruthin, Ruthin Borough Council Minutes (hereafter RBCM) 7 Apr., 4 Sept. 1915.

[89] RBCM, 4 Sept. 1916, 2 Apr. 1917; NLW MS4837D, p. 392.

[90] Bernard Crick, *Socialism* (Milton Keynes, 1987), p. 100; Clwyd Record Office, MS BD/B/93; Lewis W. Lloyd, *Neuadd Goffa Llanfair, 1928–1978* (Llanfair, Meirionnydd, 1978), pp. 6–7.

[91] 'Notes of the month: the Welsh Army Corps', *Welsh Outlook*, 1 (1914), 417.

[92] Goronwy J. Jones, *Wales and the Quest for Peace, 1815–1939* (Cardiff, 1970), *passim*.

[93] Paul O'Leary, 'Arming the citizens: the Volunteer Force in nineteenth-century Wales', in this volume.

[94] *CMG*, 8 May 1858.

[95] These were, of course, to some extent monuments expressing the influence of the gentry. Parry, 'Gwynedd and the Great War', stresses the class and cultural divides.

[96] For more analysis of this see Neil Evans and Kate Sullivan, ' "Yn llawn o dân Cymreig" (Full of Welsh fire): the language of politics in Wales 1880–1914', in Geraint H. Jenkins (ed.), *The Welsh Language and Its Social Domains 1801–1911* (Cardiff, 2000), pp. 561–85; and Neil Evans, ' "A nation in a nutshell": the Swansea disestablishment demonstration of 1912 and the political culture of Edwardian Wales', in R. R. Davies and Geraint H. Jenkins (eds), *From Medieval to Modern Wales: Historical Essays in Honour of Kenneth O. Morgan and Ralph A. Griffiths* (Cardiff, 2004), pp. 214–29.

3

Arming the citizens: the Volunteer Force in nineteenth-century Wales

PAUL O'LEARY

Speaking at a meeting of the London Welsh after the outbreak of war in 1914, Lloyd George claimed that, 'There was a time when it seemed that the military spirit of Wales had vanished into the mists of the past'. He bemoaned the absence of a military tradition among his people during the previous few centuries, a lack he ascribed to the strength of organized religion. 'Some of us thought', he said, 'that the religious revivals of the eighteenth and nineteenth centuries had broken the fighting spirit of our race.' In the jingoistic atmosphere of 1914 most Nonconformists had now rallied to the flag, and consequently there was little danger of him alienating those he apparently criticized. He went on to say that, 'No real religion ever broke a nation's spirit . . . Such a nation does not dissipate its power in envious anger and rage against its neighbours, but when justice is menaced it becomes more formidable than ever.'[1]

The nature of this appeal is significant because it is based on a claim that the Welsh were not a militaristic people, but, rather, had through the ages exercised restraint and taken up arms only in response to attacks by external aggressors. This view was more common in the nineteenth century than the more intensively studied tradition of pacifism. While pacifism was championed by prominent public figures like Samuel Roberts ('S.R.') of Llanbrynmair and Henry Richard, one-time secretary of the Peace Society, many other writers asserted the claim that the country did have military traditions, albeit of a defensive rather than an aggressive nature. As one commentator succinctly put it, the Welsh 'did not draw their swords from their scabbards until the enemy troubled the peace of their home, and pointed his spear at their wives and children'.[2] This influential strand of thought was not pacifist, because it emphasized the willingness of the people to take up arms when their kith and kin were threatened, but it did allow those who espoused a restrained approach to the use of armed force to see themselves as 'men of peace'. The 1850s and 1860s were formative decades in the cultivation of 'defencism', and provided the cultural and political context within which attitudes to war in the Victorian period were shaped.[3] An examination of the Volunteer movement from 1859 provides a revealing insight into defencism, as well as shedding light on debates about the significance of class and gender relations in this period.

War was a prominent feature of mid nineteenth-century journalism and a significant theme in literary output. In fact, one neglected feature of publishing in mid nineteenth-century Wales is the concern with military heroes. There appears to have been a lively market in books about military leaders, whether British or Welsh, during the 1850s. A new biography of the Duke of Wellington appeared in Welsh in 1850, and two more were published following his death in 1852.[4] The hero of the Napoleonic Wars still had the capacity to inspire interest and admiration. A history of the battle of Waterloo and a biography of Napoleon Bonaparte published in Welsh during the 1850s underline the continuing interest in the earlier conflict.[5] It is possibly the revival of interest in Wellington's military exploits that prompted the poet John Jones (Talhaiarn) to launch a vitriolic attack on Henry Richard and the Peace Society.[6] He wrote of 'gallant' and 'immortal' Wellington, and his verses were dismissive of Napoleon and the French.[7] In his poem 'Cân y milisia' ('The song of the militia'), he described Henry Richard as one of the 'cowards' of peace, a comment that was bitterly denounced by the peace campaigner Samuel Roberts.[8]

Such exchanges were of more than academic interest. The Crimean War of 1854–6 polarized opinion around the question of war and its consequences. That it was a divisive campaign is demonstrated by the claim that the circulation of the leading Welsh-language newspaper of the day, *Yr Amserau*, was halved from 8,000 to 4,000 because of the editor's support for Russia during the conflict; the financial difficulties the newspaper faced as a result of this eventually forced it to merge with *Baner Cymru* in 1859.[9] The conflict also provided a fillip for pacifist Chartist radicals in Merthyr Tydfil, who used the incompetence of the aristocracy during the conflict (epitomized by their bungling during the infamous Charge of the Light Brigade at the battle of Balaclava in 1854) to make the case for democracy.[10]

The Crimean War inspired Talhaiarn to pen two jingoistic poems in English and one in Welsh. In 'Rhyfel-floedd 1854' ('War-cry 1854'), he wrote of his hostility to the Russian Bear and his unquestioning faith in the military cause of Britain, while at the same time recognizing the horrors of war.[11] On the other hand, writers who were otherwise loyal to Britain could make their opposition to war and the army explicit. In 1855 the poet William Williams (Caledfryn) published several poems depicting the purposeless loss of life on the battlefield and extolling the virtues of peace, a theme that dominated the pages of the religious periodicals.[12] For example, through the early months of 1854 the Baptist periodical *Seren Gomer* provided a detailed commentary on the deteriorating international situation. It praised the government for attempting to secure peace through arbitration and accused the 'madman', Tsar Nicholas, of fomenting war. The enormous cost of the preparations for war caused the publication particular alarm.[13]

It became clear that the monthly periodical press was poorly placed to keep up with newspaper reporting of the quickly changing situation on the battlefield. News of warfare achieved a greater immediacy than ever before, because this was the first conflict to be covered by specialist war correspondents. These journalists provided detailed descriptions of the battles, while the use of the electric telegraph to deliver reports quickly both created and fed an appetite for the latest information. *The Times* led the field in this respect, and it is hardly surprising that several compilations of reports from that newspaper were translated into Welsh and published as books and pamphlets.[14] Among the reading public there was a great thirst for information about the war.

Balladeers, who hawked their compositions around fairs and markets, should be seen as having a symbiotic relationship with the newspaper press in the mid nineteenth century. They relied upon news of a wide variety of stories for information that could be exploited to compose ballads. During the Crimean War, the balladeer Ywain Meirion carried with him a picture relating to the war to advertise his compositions, which he sang in public. His ballad on the Allies' successful attack on Sebastopol provided a detailed narrative of the fighting, praising the brave soldiers and apportioning blame for the war to the Russian emperor. The subject matter was highly specific and depended on some pre-existing familiarity on the part of his audience with events in the war. The Crimea must have been of great interest to his public, because during 1854–5 he composed seven ballads on the subject, at least one of which appeared in several different versions.[15] Other balladeers produced compositions denouncing the 'oppressive' Tsar, Nicholas.[16]

The production of literature about British military heroes and the response to the Crimean War in the 1850s can be seen as part of a wider set of developments that encouraged a closer bonding together of the different peoples of Britain. The Chartists had championed an alternative conception of how society might be organized on democratic lines, which had included a vision of how the different peoples of the British Isles might reorder their affairs, but it had failed. During the late 1840s centrifugal forces had begun to provide the dynamic for mobilizing the different nationalities of the

United Kingdom: the Great Famine in Ireland, the 'Disruption' in the Kirk and the creation of proto-nationalist organizations in Scotland, and the controversy over the government's reports on education in Wales. A series of events ensured that these developments did not reach their full disintegrative potential, including the outrage at 'Papal Aggression' of 1850–1 and the Crimean War.[17] Both events mobilized public opinion against an external 'Other' that was personified as an oppressor threatening British interests and lives. In this context, the creation of the Volunteer Force in 1859 can be seen as a contributory factor to the integration of people in British institutions.

The Volunteer Force was established against a background of intense anxiety about the possibility of a French invasion of Britain in the late 1850s and early 1860s.[18] An example of this is a lecture by Henry Austin Bruce, MP, delivered at Merthyr Tydfil in March 1860 on 'The Invasions of Britain, and How to Meet the Next', in which he argued that Britain had been complacent since 1815, while France had armed unobtrusively in recent years. Suddenly Britain found that it was 'outnumbered and out-matched' in military power, and France now presented a military threat to the country.[19] It was this kind of anxiety, coupled with a belief that it was now safe to arm civilians, which led to the creation of the Volunteer Force, an armed civilian body that was intended to act as a home defence force in the case of invasion. The initiative to establish a particular corps came from the localities rather than from the centre – a fact which gave the movement a broad base across the country – although inspections by centrally appointed officers had to take place before a local corps could be recognized and issued with arms. By 1878 membership topped 200,000.[20] While radicals denounced this 'rifle fever' as no more than a pretext for strengthening militarism and the creation of a force for use against the working class during agitation for political reform,[21] there was considerable support for the new body in parts of Wales, with eleven separate corps (all more than one hundred strong) being established or in the course of enrolment in Glamorgan alone by the end of 1859.[22]

By August 1860 it was claimed that the movement's progress in south Wales was 'very satisfactory' and that 'the Volunteer spirit is extending throughout the whole of the Principality'.[23] By November of that year it was confidently predicted that north Wales would 'soon boast a goodly array of Volunteers', and that the counties of Merioneth and Caernarfon had 'answered to the call with praiseworthy alacrity'. Denbighshire, in north-east Wales, already had four companies and two others were in the course of formation.[24] Sir Watkins Williams-Wynn MP was Colonel of the Denbighshire Volunteers and a great champion of the movement; as well as promoting the movement in his own county he chaired a public meeting to launch a London Welsh Volunteer Corps (which went under the title of the 'Welsh Rifles'), in emulation of the much more active London Scottish and London Irish.[25] In cases like this, the sponsorship of a prominent landowner provided a major stimulus to recruitment, as shown by the decision to form a cavalry corps of Volunteers in Pembrokeshire, on the basis that those used to riding to hounds would enlist.[26]

The motivations that lay behind an individual's decision to join the Volunteers are difficult to unpick. They included some degree of British patriotic sentiment, combined with anxiety about invasion, at least at the outset. For members of the middle classes, at whom the movement was initially aimed, it provided an opportunity for sociable fraternizing with men of a similar background. In most cases, however, this was probably dwarfed by a determination to take advantage of the specific recreational activities (especially rifle-shooting[27]) offered by membership. The prospects for self-improvement that mixing with officers drawn from the ranks of local worthies provided was another attraction for some, especially for working-class men, who soon became the mainstay of the movement. These considerations became more significant as the fear of invasion receded. For example, in the summer of 1882 Lloyd George was encouraged to join the Porthmadog corps of the Volunteers by his superior at the legal firm where he worked; his decision appears to have had nothing self-consciously to do with patriotism.[28] Undoubtedly, one of the attractions of the Volunteers was its attachment to a local urban or rural identity, rather than to a more abstract loyalty to Britain.[29]

In the first decades of their existence the Volunteers recruited particularly strongly among the artisans or upper working class, whereas the Regular Army tended to recruit overwhelmingly from the lower reaches of the working class. One indication of this difference was the high levels of illiteracy among the Regulars when compared with the Volunteers. The first rifle corps mustered in Wales was formed at Swansea, and the town remained a strong centre of the movement. At the meeting to form a corps in the town it was unanimously agreed that 'there should be no distinction of class in the formation of this corps'.[30] Major Lewis Llewelyn Dillwyn, MP, who commanded the 3rd Glamorganshire Rifle Volunteers in the town, stated in 1862: 'My corps principally consists of mechanics and shop-keepers and respectable people.'[31] Men employed by one of the town's factories who joined the Volunteers were said to be 'generally speaking, much better conducted and steadier men since they joined', and those young men who previously had spent time at billiard rooms and public houses now went to drill and the rifle ranges.[32] The language of some advocates of the movement suggests that it was seen to be consistent with the movement for cultivating 'rational recreation' among working people.[33]

However, from its early days prominent figures were determined to claim a greater significance for the movement than that of wholesome leisure activity; in a review of the Radnorshire Volunteers in November 1860 the Lord Lieutenant of the county expressed his conviction that the movement had not been taken up as 'a mere holyday pastime, a mere boy's play, or a mere empty pageantry by the men of Radnorshire'.[34]

While class conflict was not a feature of the movement, an awareness of the importance of class distinctions was always present. At a public meeting to establish a rifle corps at Newport the Hon. Godfrey Morgan, MP, believed that 'all classes should join it – the landlord and tenant, the peasant and the peer, the master and the servant, all shooting at their enemies, side by side'.[35] By contrast, one supporter at Merthyr regretted that members of 'the humbler classes' could not be included because the Volunteers had to bear their own expenses.[36] At Cardiff in 1859 the police superintendent, J. Box Stockdale, established the 'Cardiff People's Rifle Corps', which recruited explicitly among respectable working people because this section of the population was not represented among the town's existing corps.[37] At a Volunteer dinner in January 1860 Stockdale stated that working men could be trusted with arms and that the way to 'make men know themselves, to know the position they hold in the world' was to place confidence in them: 'The working classes are now an educated, thinking set of men, and I am certain they will not abuse that confidence (cheers).' In his view, a fine uniform was all very well, but 'to make a soldier there must be the heart to endure toil and a determination to do its duty to the country irrespective of fine clothes'. The men required to defend the country were:

> men with gallant hearts in their bosoms and courage, men who had to get their living by the sweat of their brows (cheers), the horny-handed sons of toil (renewed cheers). Men who, although they could not afford to spend money in dress, were as anxious as the high born to join the rifle corps, and show how willing they were to do their duty to their Queen and country (cheers).[38]

Statements such as this suggest that, while the language of class was supposedly in retreat during the mid Victorian decades, the language of 'the people' can be regarded as a synonym for class in some instances.[39]

The publicity devoted to the Cardiff People's Rifle Corps prompted another corps in the town to try to 'secure the services of persons who possessing every qualification of health, height, and respectability, were yet unable to put down at once the large amount required for clothing, shako, and accoutrements'. One member protested that such individuals should join the People's Corps instead; his suggestion was defeated.[40] Further overt conflict was partly defused by the adoption by the People's Corps of the name of the largest local landowner, the Marquis of Bute, becoming known officially as the 16th Glamorganshire Bute Volunteers.[41]

Even so, the issue of the class composition of the movement did not disappear entirely. When the Artillery Corps was formed at Cardiff in 1860 it was emphasized that their aim was 'to raise a truly popular corps, one intended for respectable, muscular young men, able and willing to tuck up their shirt sleeves and work'.[42] This statement was a clear description of respectable working-class masculinity. At the Gloucester Volunteer Review in September 1860 (at which contingents from south Wales and Radnorshire participated), Major-General Hutchinson commended the mingling of classes in the movement and hinted that the loyalty and discipline of working-class members supported the case for extending the franchise.[43] His comments were strengthened by the fact that initially each member of a corps had a vote in electing their officers, and was thus contributing to the legitimization of the civilian officers' authority over other civilians. The fact that these elections resulted without exception in the election of middle- or upper-class officers was reassuring to the propertied classes that any proposed extension of the franchise to respectable working men would not lead to social revolution.

Thus, although the Volunteers were initially intended to enrol a middle-class membership, they soon became a predominantly working-class organization. In 1878 the Voluntary Artillery at Cardiff was almost exclusively drawn from the ranks of artisans, with 'some few of the better classes'. In fact, by the late 1870s the Force experienced greater difficulty in persuading 'gentlemen' to make the commitment to serving in the Volunteers than it did in persuading working men to join its ranks, largely because of the financial outlay expected of them and the commitment of time.[44] It became a more onerous duty to be a Volunteer officer than it was to be a member of the rank and file, especially as local worthies were frequently willing to provide, or subsidize the cost of, uniforms for working-class Volunteers, whereas members of the middle classes had to fund themselves.

The support of employers was a significant factor in encouraging the spread of the Volunteers. Most members of the seven corps of rifle volunteers raised in Caernarfonshire in March to April 1860 were connected to the slate quarries of the Pennant interest, and by the end of the year Major G. S. G. D. Pennant commanded an amalgamated county battalion.[45] In the same year eighty-three employees of the Steam Packet Depot of the London and North Wales Railway Company at Holyhead and the Dublin Steam Packet Company in the same port submitted their names for member-ship of the Anglesey Rifle Volunteers,[46] while the 3rd Montgomeryshire Rifle

Corps was known as the 'Railway Rifles' because the majority of its members were employees of the Cambrian Railway Company.[47] Evan Evans, proprietor of the Vale of Neath Brewery, was a captain in the 17th Glamorganshire Rifle Corps, which was raised exclusively from among his employees, and he bore the cost of each man's uniform.[48] At the Dowlais Ironworks, the general manager G. T. Clark (who was a captain in the Volunteers) claimed that 'the cordial feeling produced and fostered by the formation of the corps had been of great use in the works', creating as it did a feeling of 'unanimity'.[49]

However, the lead taken by some employers did not always ensure the survival of the corps. Some units of the Anglesey Rifle Volunteers were disbanded in 1862, and the last unit in the county was wound up the following year, a victim of flagging interest and Nonconformist opposition. The Caernarfonshire battalion continued in existence until 1873, when the remaining units were united with the Flintshire Rifles.[50] Although Volunteering was widely believed to have a positive effect on the character and morale of those who joined the force, the support of employers was not necessarily a guarantee of good military discipline.

Because of the prominent lead taken by some employers, the independence of the Rifle Corps at Tredegar in Monmouthshire from the local ironworks was considered worthy of comment.[51] At neighbouring Brynmawr and Ebbw Vale the corps were also established without the patronage of employers. This area had been a centre of physical force Chartism during the 1830s, and the local employers might have judged it an unwise act to supply workers with firearms – in fact, Thomas Brown, the ironmaster at Ebbw Vale, tacitly admitted as much. He had kept aloof from the movement initially but subsequently gave his public support to the Volunteers, once he was convinced that most men were 'more intelligent than they used to be'. He was reassured by the comments of Captain Roden, who maintained that 'men were better men by becoming volunteers, and made better citizens, the discipline did them good'.[52]

It would be misleading to depict the Volunteers as nothing more than the passive instrument of the ruling class. The force embodied certain common ideals about the duties of patriotism in defending the country, but such ideals were also susceptible to different interpretations. The creation of the People's Corps at Cardiff, with its strong overtones of class distinctions, was merely one indicator of this. Furthermore, the movement also fitted a potentially radical agenda. A willingness to arm working-class men was an implicit (and sometimes explicit) indication that they were citizens who deserved full political rights. In this respect, the establishment of the Volunteer Force anticipated the Reform Act of 1867, which would enfranchise certain sections of the male working class.[53]

This ideology was set out in a staunch defence of the Volunteers in a full-page article on the front page of *Baner Cymru* as early as August 1859. It contrasted the 'oppressor' states of the Continent, which boasted large standing armies, with free countries such as Britain, which found it difficult to recruit to the Regular Army. This difficulty was not a consequence of a lack of patriotism, but derived from the successful and comfortable conditions of the country and the superior morals of its people. The Regular Army, it maintained, recruited mainly from the lowest and most immoral class in society, as shown by the fact that until recently the armed forces had such a large proportion of Irishmen in their ranks. By contrast, 'The defence of a free country is its volunteer force; and this force does not endanger the country's freedom: just as freedom calls forth this defensive ability, so also instead of endangering that freedom, it supports it.' In this account, the Volunteer Force was not an aggressive or bloodthirsty body – neither did it increase taxes – and so it was fundamentally different from the armed forces in Continental states, because the latter had no other function but aggression.[54] Such views chimed with prevailing ideas about the small state and the merits of voluntarism in public life more generally, but they were also susceptible to radical interpretations.

The Volunteer movement ensured that in many towns during the 1860s and 1870s uniformed civilians were a presence in public life. Welshmen enrolling in the Volunteer Force accounted for a similar proportion of the adult male population as for Britain as a whole, and for a higher proportion than in many English regions in the 1860s (see Table 3.1).

Table 3.1 Volunteers as a proportion of the male population aged 15–49, 1862–99.[55]

	1862	1881	1899
Wales	3.0	2.6	2.0
Scotland	5.0	5.5	4.3
Britain	3.0	2.8	2.4

There were opportunities to join a Volunteer corps in most Welsh counties, especially in the towns, but the movement failed to make a lasting impact in three counties in north Wales: Anglesey, Merioneth and Montgomery.[56] Furthermore, enthusiasm for it appears to have been patchy in some other places. Whether this was a consequence of the inactivity of the particular Lord Lieutenant, who was responsible for establishing a force in his county, or whether it was a tacit recognition by such individuals that local opinion was unfavourable, is difficult to tell. Religious opposition was clearly a factor in some areas, while in some places enthusiasm subsided once the invasion scare disappeared. Elsewhere there were considerable concentrations of members, particularly in those areas close to existing military depots, such as Cardiff and Pembroke Dock. In fact, by the end of the 1860s it was claimed that Glamorgan had more Volunteers per head of population than any other county in Britain and that Swansea had a greater number of Volunteers than any other town in the country, when calculated on the same basis.[57]

It was only in the years before the Boer War of 1899–1902 that Welsh enrolment in the Volunteers dipped significantly below the British average. From the movement's inception in 1859 until it was wound up in 1908 support for the Volunteers in Scotland remained consistently higher than elsewhere. As the detailed statistics for 1881 demonstrate, a significant minority of the members consisted of 'non-efficients', a group that was usually composed of older local worthies, who occupied honorary positions in the corps (see Table 3.2). The inclusion of such people was one way of attracting medical men, among others, to serve in the force.

Table 3.2 Strength of the Volunteer Force in Wales, 1881.

County	Arm of the force	A	B	C	D	E	F	G	H	I
Cardigan	Rifle†									
Carmarthen	Rifle†									
Denbigh	Rifle	1	807		743	18	761	27	49	670
Flint	Engineer	1	160		116	4	120	2	9	109
Flint and Caernarfon	Rifle	1	1,010		822	73	895	19	43	772
Brecon	Rifle	1	808		690	18	708	13	33	574
Glamorgan	Artillery	1	1,369		1,320	25	1,345	31	72	1,001
	Rifle	1	1,208		899	31	930	25	34	801
		2	2,212		1,588	271	1,859	42	92	1,456
		3	604		392	110	502	14	34	360
Monmouth	Rifle	1	705		705	1	706	19	34	549
		2	605		605	0	605	16	34	459
		3	866		619	29	648	20	33	526
	Artillery*									
Pembroke	Artillery	1	161	50	77	19	96	1	3	79
	Rifle†	2	1,008		864	40	904	17	48	774
Radnor	Rifle‡									

Source: PP, XXXVIII 1882, *Annual Return of the Volunteer Corps of Great Britain for the Year 1881*, pp. 5–12.

Key

A Number of County Corps
B Authorized establishment
C Number of supernumeraries authorized to be enrolled
D Efficients (i.e. active members)
E Non-efficients (i.e. honorary members)
F Total enrolled
G Officers
H Sergeants
I Present at inspection

* The two batteries of Monmouthshire artillery were included in the returns for Worcestershire; the statistics cannot be disaggregated.
†Pembrokeshire Volunteer Rifles includes one company in Cardiganshire, four in Carmarthenshire and three in Haverfordwest.
‡The two companies of Radnorshire Rifles were included in the returns for Herefordshire; the statistics cannot be disaggregated.

Apart from attracting recruits to its ranks, the Volunteer movement performed a public function of drawing the attention and ensuring the co-operation of non-participating members of the public. *The Times* reminded its readers in April 1861 that 'Popularity is the very essence of the Volunteer movement', by which it meant that provision should be made for spectators to view the Volunteer reviews that were held periodically. 'It should never be forgotten', the paper continued, 'that every battalion of enrolled Riflemen represents the patriotism of many besides its own members.'[58]

Among the public activities of the force were weekly parades, church parades and other ceremonial events. Most corps recruited band members, who were able to provide musical diversions for spectators on such occasions, as well as supplying martial music for drill practice. In April 1860, for example, the two rival corps of the Newport Volunteers paraded separately with their bands through streets lined with hundreds of spectators. This prompted a local newspaper to comment: 'Our town has become quite lively since the enrolment of the Volunteers Corps; and whenever they appear in public they attract an immense concourse of spectators.'[59] Similar crowds were attracted by the parades of Volunteers at Brynmawr and Rhymney, while the funeral of a Volunteer at Mountain Ash was marked by a procession of his comrades and their band, which played the 'Dead March in Saul'.[60] Public attention also focused on more exceptional activities, like the grand parade through the streets of Swansea in 1859 to greet the arrival of guns for the Volunteer Artillery, and the lesson in heavy gunnery at Mumbles Fort, near Swansea, in October 1861, which was observed by 200 to 300 people who had congregated at the lighthouse nearby.[61]

The public gaze was an essential element in promoting decorous behaviour among Volunteers. This was particularly true of the gaze of female spectators, who were not to be shocked or scandalized by the actions of Volunteers, as they might have been by the notoriously less restrained behaviour of regular soldiers. Women also aided the movement by supplying, and sometimes presenting, prizes for rifle competitions.[62] Rifle-shooting competitions with attractive prizes, such as those which took place at Cardiff in July and August 1860,[63] performed the important function of publicizing the movement and attracting new recruits, as well as providing an incentive for Volunteers to improve their aim. The patronage bestowed by middle- and upper-class women was one means of emphasizing the movement's respectability.

However, by becoming the object of the public gaze, the Volunteers also exposed themselves to the disdain of people who found the idea of civilians dressing in military uniforms that often had something of a 'Ruritanian' air about them inherently comical. The local corps had a degree of freedom in choosing its uniform, and some opted for antiquated items of dress, like knickerbockers, that were a source of hilarity among some sections of the public. Furthermore, in smaller towns, where the middle class had a less dominating presence, the Volunteers were not respected by all and could be the object of contempt. In some cases young children threw stones at them.[64]

The biggest public event associated with the Volunteers was the review. This impressive military spectacle performed the function of demonstrating to the public that amateur soldiers were capable of discharging their duties efficiently and could be equal to the challenge of defending the country against the threat of an army composed of regular soldiers. At reviews the execution of military manoeuvres and the enactment of mock battles by large numbers of troops proved to be a significant attraction for spectators. When the first major Volunteer review to include troops from south Wales took place at Gloucester in September 1860, excursion trains from Carmarthenshire in the west to Newport in the east carried large numbers of Volunteers and spectators to attend the event.[65] The relatively new railway network was a factor in enabling the local corps to participate in events outside their immediate locality, and made a wider mobilization of the force a possibility.

Probably the largest review in Wales took place at Crumlin Burrows, near Swansea, in the summer of 1867. On that occasion 2,823 of the county's Volunteers – artillery, engineers and riflemen – took part in large-scale manoeuvres and a 'sham fight'. It was regretted that the county's Volunteer cavalry were unable to participate in the event because they were exercising elsewhere that day, but the spectacle included firing from Captain Evan Evans's steamer, which lay offshore. Thousands of spectators, including a sprinkling of the county's aristocracy, enjoyed the day's events, most being ferried to the site by train from Swansea. The Inspector General of Volunteers, who was present to judge the military competence of the participants, expressed his satisfaction at the execution of manoeuvres and the standards attained by the various corps taking part. A striking engraving of the event was published in the *Illustrated London News*.[66] Later claims that the Volunteers initially knew little about real soldiering would seem to be inaccurate.[67]

As might be expected, given the fears of invasion that had brought the movement into existence, international crises and domestic political events had an impact on the Volunteers. Civilian militias had played a part in the events surrounding the 1848 revolution in the German states, while the early months of the force coincided with news of Garibaldi's exploits in trying to liberate the Italian states. Comparisons between the new rifle corps in Britain and Garibaldi's use of citizens to defeat standing armies were not lost on contemporaries. The press reproduced a letter from Garibaldi praising the initiative of the British Volunteers, while a 'sturdy few' at Cardiff sent their names to be enrolled to assist Garibaldi's forces. Both movements were portrayed as defending the liberties of their respective peoples.[68] The Volunteers at Cardiff were particularly responsive to international events: when war seemed imminent in 1878 approximately fifty members of the town's Volunteer Artillery joined the Regular Army.[69]

The one occasion when the Volunteers were mobilized in south Wales was during the Fenian scare of the late 1860s. The Fenians were a group of Irish revolutionaries committed to the establishment of an Irish republic by armed force, and had considerable support among the Irish in Britain and America. An uprising was planned for 1867, and public opinion in Britain was electrified by the audacious attempt to steal arms from Chester Castle in February of that year and the ability of the movement to free a number of Fenians from custody in Manchester. Among the incidents that intensified anxieties in Wales were dawn arrests of Fenians at Merthyr Tydfil and Dowlais in December 1867. Volunteer corps had their own local armouries, and were instructed to place guards on these arms to ensure they did not fall into Fenian hands. In Swansea, several officers from the Volunteers joined the special constabulary in order to defend the town against the Fenian threat.[70] This was the most significant mobilization of the force in a defensive capacity, and it reinforced the belief that working-class Volunteers could be relied upon to defend lives and property against sedition.

Just as class was an issue in debates about the Volunteers, so was gender. Arming citizens had posed searching questions about the role of men in society on both sides of the Atlantic since the American War of Independence, and the connection between full citizenship and the ability to bear arms was well established in many countries that had experienced revolutions by the mid nineteenth century.[71] In a very different context, the Volunteer Force in Britain reinforced a view that 'active citizenship' belonged to men alone. For members of the middle and upper classes the defence of home and hearth was a duty of 'manliness', and as such was an honourable course of action to take.[72] Because of its defensive nature, becoming a Volunteer entailed the exercise of self-control and restraint, and contrasted with expectations of the regular soldier, who was not always 'among the best specimens of orderly citizenship'. Many 'wild and ungovernable spirits' were driven to seek adventure in the armed forces, and required the discipline of military life to put them under 'due regulation and restraint'. By contrast, Volunteers were initially intended to recruit from social classes who already possessed the necessary self-discipline, by virtue of their upbringing and education. The 'manly games and sports' of the middle and upper classes had prepared them for military training: 'The bat and the oar have been no mean preparation for the rifle; the vigilant fielding and hard rowing for the double-quick and forced march.'[73] Exhortations to the increasingly working-class membership of the Volunteers reflected this concern. After an initial hesitation about the movement, the ironmaster Thomas Brown of Ebbw Vale urged his employees to 'throw themselves heartily and manfully into the affair',[74] while a report on the Volunteer review at Tredegar Park, near Newport, in October 1860 praised the 'soldierly and manly bearing' of the men who took part.[75]

One historian has described the movement as providing an opportunity for members of the lower classes 'to express their manliness through military skills under the control of caring officers'.[76] Such a paternalistic view of men's identity was not necessarily shared by working-class members of the movement.[77] Just as working-class members of friendly societies and the temperance movement could filter notions of middle-class respectability and adapt them to their own circumstances, so middle-class ideas of manliness could be reshaped according to different needs. It is not necessarily the case that artisans had more in common with members of the middle class because they comprised an educated and 'respectable' section of the working class. Indeed, as has been seen, the Volunteer movement crystallized ideas about the correct ordering of society according to prevailing ideas of class distinctions, and even though officers were elected by the members of their corps, they were chosen without exception from the middle or upper classes. The language chosen to describe members of the People's Corps at Cardiff makes plain the difference between middle-class ideals of 'manliness' and those associated with working-class masculinity. Working men were 'men who had to get their living by the sweat of their brows . . . the horny-handed sons of toil'.[78] For working men, the version of masculinity promoted by the Volunteers stressed physicality and the strength acquired from the productive effort, rather than honour; it prized exertion as much as duty. The apparently gender-neutral term 'the people' was, in this context, acutely gender-specific.

One central aspect of these conceptions of masculinity was the way the boundary of self-control and restraint was drawn between different sections of the working class, rather than between the working class and the middle classes. In this respect, the regular drill practice – often several times a week – can be seen as inculcating particular forms of ordered and regularized behaviour in a group of young men who otherwise would not have experienced it outside the workplace. Training in the Volunteers meant acquiring a new bearing and range of gestures, especially when performed in a distinctive uniform that served to suppress individuality.[79] Significantly, one of the few personal accounts of life in the Volunteers stresses the benefits of 'getting a good exercise, drilling & skirmishing', when contrasted with the physical passivity of listening to a sermon.[80]

Critics of the movement tried to undermine the image of a disciplined body of men governed by self-control by linking the Volunteers with the unruly and ill-disciplined behaviour of off-duty regular soldiers.[81] There was at least some basis for this accusation.[82] Camp was not always the disciplined experience it was meant to be. When a chaplain visited a camp in Breconshire to hold an open-air Sunday service he found the Builth Rifle Volunteers 'already well drunk', and although they were dismissed from the ranks they fought during the service, scandalizing the other corps who were present.[83] Lloyd George's membership of the movement was associated with a phase of his life when he tried to shake off the constraints of a puritanical home by frequenting pubs.[84] A fear that the Volunteers would bring recruits into contact with drink was undoubtedly one factor in the opposition of some Nonconformists. However, the tactic of identifying the Volunteers with the Regular Army had only limited success in dissuading young men from joining.

This account of the Volunteer Force in Wales has concentrated on the years of its formation and early development, when its reception was most keenly discussed and its purpose and activities were most frequently debated. During the 1870s it settled into a pattern of quiet sociability, becoming an entrenched feature of life in many parts of the country. At first glance, the enthusiasm for the Volunteers on the part of the minority who enrolled in its ranks, and on the part of the larger number of spectators of its activities, is difficult to square with the widespread suspicion of, and even hostility to, the Regular Army in Wales during the same period. However, this is to misunderstand the way in which many contemporaries perceived the Volunteer Force. For supporters of the movement, Volunteering was consistent with the paternalistic view that the duty of the male citizen was to provide for his family and defend them and his country against external attack. The incorporation of a section of the working class in this vision of armed citizenship had enormous ramifications for political reform in the 1860s.

It was the defensive nature of the movement that was contrasted so strongly with the aggressive 'oppressor' states of the Continent, with their large standing armies. The movement undoubtedly made more civilians familiar with military values than otherwise would have been the case, but the context in which those values were promoted changed over time. In this respect, perhaps the Boer War (1899–1902) is the crucial dividing line in the movement's history, because after this event the context for discussing the arming of British civilians was more markedly militaristic.[85] Even so, it is significant that when Lloyd George made his appeal to the Welsh people to support the war effort in 1914 he did so largely in terms that would have been acceptable to his former comrades in the Volunteers in the 1880s.

NOTES

[1] David Lloyd George, *Through Terror to Triumph: Speeches and Pronouncements since the Beginning of the War* (London, 1915), p. 185. I am indebted to Neil Evans for this reference and for several valuable suggestions.

[2] *Seren Gomer*, Dec. 1851, iii.

[3] For a useful taxonomy of attitudes to war, Martin Ceadel, *Semi-Detached Idealists: The British Peace Movement and International Relations, 1854–1945* (Oxford, 2000), pp. 6–8.

[4] Anon., *Hanes Bywyd yr Enwog a'r Gwron Duc Wellington* (Abergele, 1850); anon., *Hanes Bywyd Arthur Wellesley, Duc Wellington* (Caernarfon, 1852); anon., *Cofiant y Duc o Wellington* (Liverpool, 1853?). On medieval Welsh military heroes in fiction, see E. G. Millward, ' "Cenedl o bobl ddewrion": y rhamant hanesyddol yn oes Victoria', in Millward, *Cenedl o Bobl Ddewrion: Agweddau ar Lenyddiaeth Oes Victoria* (Llandysul, 1991).

[5] Anon., *Hanes Brwydr Waterloo* (Bala, 185?); anon., *Hanes Bywyd Napoleon Bonaparte, Diweddar Ymherawdwr Ffrainc* (2nd edn, Caernarfon, 1851).

[6] *CDH*, 19 June 1852.

[7] [John Jones], *Gwaith Talhaiarn: The Works of Talhaiarn, in Welsh and English* (London, 1855), pp. 357–60.

[8] *Y Cymro*, 15 April 1853. Quoted in Dewi M. Lloyd, *Talhaiarn* (Cardiff, 1999), p. 113.

[9] Aled Gruffydd Jones, *Press, Politics and Society: A History of Journalism in Wales* (Cardiff, 1993), p. 43.

[10] Angela V. John, 'The Chartists of industrial South Wales, 1840–68' (unpublished MA thesis, University of Wales, 1970), vol. ii, pp. 194–8.

[11] *Gwaith Talhaiarn*, p. 94.

[12] William Williams, *Caniadau Caledfryn* (Llanrwst, 1855), pp. 241–4, 251–2.

[13] *Seren Gomer*, Apr. 1854, 183–4; May 1854, 230–1, 237–40; June 1854, 279–80.

[14] John Roberts, *Hanes y Rhyfel yn y Crimea* (Caernarfon, 1855); Thomas Levi, *Hanes Rhyfel y Crimea* (Swansea, 1855).

[15] Tegwyn Jones, *Baledi Ywain Meirion* (Bala, 1980), pp. xx, 51–6, 220.

[16] For example, Abel Jones, *Marwolaeth Ymerawdwr Rwsia* (Llangollen, 1855).

[17] Paul O'Leary, 'A tolerant nation? Anti-Catholicism in nineteenth-century Wales', in R. R. Davies and Geraint H. Jenkins (eds), *From Medieval to Modern Wales: Historical Essays in Honour of Kenneth O. Morgan and Ralph A. Griffiths* (Cardiff, 2004).

[18] See, for example, 'Lloegr a'r rhyfel', *Baner Cymru* (hereafter *BC*), 18 May 1859.

[19] *CMG*, 4 Feb. 1860.

[20] Hugh Cunningham, *The Volunteer Force: A Social and Political History, 1859–1908* (London, 1975), p. 2.

[21] 'Rifle gorau gwirfoddol', *Y Diwygiwr*, Jan. 1860, 33–5.

[22] The corps were located at: Swansea and neighbourhood (three), Cardiff (two), Aberdare, Bridgend, Merthyr Tydfil, Mountain Ash, Neath and Dowlais. *The Times*, 29 Dec. 1859.

[23] Ibid., 20 Aug. 1860.

[24] Ibid., 23 Nov. 1860.

[25] Ibid., 9 Nov. 1860. See also ibid., 18 Mar. 1861.

[26] Ibid., 16 Nov. 1860.

[27] In the 1840s rifle practice had been popular among the colliers of Monmouthshire. 'The Scotch Cattle in Monmouthshire', ibid., 2 Mar. 1843.

[28] W. R. P. George, *The Making of Lloyd George* (London, 1976), p. 104.

[29] See the report on Cardiff's 3rd Corps of Artillery, *CMG*, 23 June 1860. It also had the advantage of providing business for local clothiers, who were often contracted to provide uniforms.

[30] *The Times*, 31 May 1859.

[31] PP, 1862 XXVII, *Report of the Commissioners appointed to Enquire into the Condition of the Volunteer Force in Great Britain*, p. 180.

[32] Ibid., p. 182.

[33] See comments of Captain C. W. David, *CMG*, 28 Jan. 1860.

[34] *The Times*, 8 Nov. 1860.

[35] *Star of Gwent* (hereafter *SG*), 4 June 1859.

[36] *CMG*, 3 Dec. 1859.

[37] Ibid., 17 Dec. 1859. The newspaper's editorial preferred to see a corps composed of all classes.

[38] 'Cardiff People's (16th) Rifle Corps', ibid., 28 Jan. 1860.

[39] On this issue, see Patrick Joyce, *Visions of the People: Industrial England and the Question of Class, 1848–1914* (Cambridge, 1991); and Rohan McWilliam, *Popular Politics in Nineteenth-Century England* (London, 1998).

[40] *CMG*, 11 Feb. 1860. A shako is a type of military hat.

[41] Ibid. The marquis provided a drill hall for the Volunteers' use. PP, 1878–9 XV, *Reports to Enquire into the Financial State and Internal Organization of the Volunteer Force in Britain*, p. 73.

[42] 'Cardiff Artillery Corps', *CMG*, 21 Apr. 1860.

[43] *CMG*, 22 Sept. 1860.

[44] PP, 1878–9 XV, pp. 73, 76, 77.

[45] Bryn Owen, *Welsh Militia and Volunteer Corps* (hereafter *WMVC*), *1757–1908: Anglesey and Caernarfonshire* (Caernarfon, 1989), pp. 152–5, 173–5.

[46] Owen, *WMVC, 1757–1908: Anglesey and Caernarfonshire*, pp. 150–1.

[47] Owen, *WMVC, 1757–1908: Montgomeryshire Regiments of Militia, Volunteers and Yeomanry Cavalry* (Wrexham, 2000), p. 111.

[48] *The Times*, 3 Oct. 1860.

[49] *CMG*, 14 Apr. 1860. See also L. J. Williams, 'Clark the ironmaster', in Brian Ll. James (ed.), *G. T. Clark: Scholar Ironmaster in the Victorian Age* (Cardiff, 1998), p. 51; and Donald Moore, 'The Clark family portraits', in James (ed.), *G. T. Clark*, p. 137.

[50] Owen, *WMVC, 1757–1908: Anglesey and Caernarfonshire*, pp. 150–1.

[51] Cunningham, *Volunteer Force*, p. 22.

[52] *SG*, 21 July 1860.

[53] Cf. Ian F. W. Beckett, *The Amateur Military Tradition, 1558–1945* (Manchester, 1991), p. 191.

[54] 'A ydyw Lloegr mewn perygl?', *BC*, 17 Aug. 1859.

[55] Cunningham, *Volunteer Force*, p. 42. Cunningham does not provide separate data for England.

[56] For the hiatus in Montgomeryshire between 1876 and 1897, see Owen, *WMVC, 1757–1908: Montgomeryshire*, pp. 110–27.

[57] *Cambrian*, 2 Aug. 1867.

[58] *The Times*, 3 Apr. 1861.

[59] *SG*, 21 Apr. 1860.

[60] *SG*, 5, 12 May 1860.

[61] Owen, *WMVC, 1757–1908: The Glamorgan Regiments of Militia* (Caernarfon, 1990), p. 165; *The Times*, 21 Oct. 1861.

[62] In Haverfordwest a silver bugle was presented to the Volunteers by 'the ladies of the place'. *The Times*, 12 Oct. 1860.

[63] Ibid., 27 July, 17 Aug. 1860. The annual rifle competition of the Carmarthenshire Volunteers in September 1861 lasted a week. Ibid., 10 Sept. 1861.

[64] Julie Light, ' "Of inestimable value to the town and district"? A study of the urban middle classes in South Wales, with particular reference to Pontypool, Bridgend and Penarth, *c.* 1850–1890' (unpublished Ph.D thesis, University of Wales, 2003), pp. 184–5.

[65] *CMG*, 22 Sept. 1860; *SG*, 22 Sept. 1860.

[66] *Illustrated London News*, 10 Aug. 1867, p. 157, and the report on p. 162. Also, *Cambrian*, 2 Aug. 1867.

[67] See 'Echoes and re-echoes', *Cambria Daily Leader*, 4 May 1887.

[68] *SG*, 11 Feb. 1860; *CMG*, 25 Aug. 1860.

[69] PP, 1878–9 XV, p. 75.

[70] See Paul O'Leary, *Immigration and Integration: The Irish in Wales, 1798–1922* (Cardiff, 2000), pp. 244–55; John Newsinger, *Fenianism in Mid-Victorian Britain* (London, 1994).

[71] Stefan Dudink and Karen Hagemann, 'Masculinity in politics and war in the age of democratic revolutions, 1750–1850', in Dudink, Hagemann and John Tosh (eds), *Masculinities in Politics and War: Gendering Modern History* (Manchester, 2004).

72 On 'manliness', see J. A. Mangan and James Walvin (eds), *Manliness and Morality: Middle-Class Masculinity in Britain and America, 1800–1940* (Manchester, 1987), and Paul O'Leary, 'Masculine histories: gender and the social history of modern Wales', *WHR*, 22, 2 (2004).

73 *SG*, 30 June 1860. At Hay-on-Wye in Radnorshire the Cricket Club was largely composed of Volunteers: John Toman, *Kilvert: The Homeless Heart* (Chippenham, 2001), p. 235.

74 *SG*, 21 July 1860.

75 *SG*, 6 Oct. 1860.

76 Toman, *Kilvert*, p. 236.

77 This discussion reflects wider debates about the hegemony of middle-class values in Victorian society.

78 'Cardiff People's (16th) Rifle Corps', *CMG*, 28 Jan. 1860.

79 The role of special clothing in reinforcing social identities is discussed in Paul O'Leary, 'The cult of respectability and the Irish in mid-nineteenth-century Wales', in O'Leary (ed.), *Irish Migrants in Modern Wales* (Liverpool, 2004).

80 George, *Making of Lloyd George*, pp. 108–9.

81 'Oddi wrth ein gohebydd', *BAC*, 21 Mar. 1860.

82 Light, ' "Of inestimable value" ', pp. 184–5.

83 *Kilvert's Diary, 1870–1879: Selections from the Diary of the Rev. Francis Kilvert*, ed. William Plomer (London, 1999), p. 137.

84 John Grigg, *The Young Lloyd George* (London, 1973), p. 44.

85 Beckett, *Amateur Military Tradition*, pp. 198, 200–7.

4

Garibaldi and the Welsh political imagination

KEES WINDLAND

When Garibaldi arrived in Britain early in April 1864 for a three-week visit he was welcomed as a war hero by a nation confidently at peace with the world.[1] Yet Britain was also experiencing rising social and political tensions, which were inseparable from the growing popular irritation over the stalled condition of constitutional reform during Palmerston's last years in power. Consequently, the appearance of the world's most renowned republican freedom-fighter in London caused ripples of apprehension throughout the British government and establishment, while radicals of every stamp took heart at this 'apparition' of the redoubtable and incorruptible revolutionary.[2] In this respect, Wales was no exception. Many years have now passed since T. Gwynfor Griffith considered the impact of Garibaldi and Mazzini on the development of a politicized Welsh national consciousness, which he found in the influence of Nonconformist leaders of Welsh radical opinion, notably William Rees (Gwilym Hiraethog).[3] However, there is more to be said. Garibaldi's presence in the imperial capital operated on the Welsh political imagination in a wide variety of ways and precipitated a complex range of responses, from poetic effusions to intense calculation. Thus, it provides a useful tool in exploring the character of the Welsh political nation at a crucial moment in its development.

Few of the tensions associated with those years were obvious as Garibaldi's flower-decked train made its way from Southampton to London. People of nearly all political views turned out to cheer its passage, as bands played 'See the Conquering Hero' or martial airs more directly associated with the Italian struggle for unification. Once in London, Garibaldi and his entourage were mounted on horses and paraded through the streets of Lambeth and Westminster, before the largest crowd to have assembled there since the funeral of the Duke of Wellington. His famous red shirt, 'wide-awake' hat and slightly mournful bearded face were reproduced in enormous quantities in prints, porcelain and commemorative medals, helping to establish Garibaldi as a popular icon of righteous struggle against foreign and papal oppression. C. Lewis Hind, an eyewitness to those heady days in London, recalled many years later the impression Garibaldi made on one young boy:

> I remember peering through an upper window of the house, in north London, where we lived, and seeing Garibaldi and his companions swinging down the middle of the road. Where they came from, whither they were going I knew not; but they wore red shirts, they were bearded, and they marched easily like conquerors. My mother (she was of Welsh descent, and had the imagination of the Celt) told me that they stood for Freedom, and being a Unitarian and a Radical (my father took his religion from her, she her politics from him), Freedom, in her mind, was a lovely Vision, partly attainable. What it meant I did not grasp. What Garibaldi had done I did not understand . . . but the idea remained, the idea of Freedom expressed by red-shirted, bearded Garibaldi, and companions, swinging down that road in north London on a morning of sunshine.[4]

It is interesting that Hind stressed his mother's imagination as a formative influence on his own perceptions of the event; especially since he mistakenly remembered it as occurring in 1867, and must have been only two years old on the actual day. The imagined Garibaldi and the stories told about him assumed a peculiar vividness at that time of intense public uncertainty and speculation over the nation's political future.[5]

Another witness to the hero's passage was the London correspondent of the Denbigh radical weekly, *Baner ac Amserau Cymru*. John Griffith (Gohebydd – 'the Correspondent') had lived in the metropolis for most of twenty years and was therefore a typical Londoner, that is, an immigrant. Although the general enthusiasm appeared to be unqualified, at least among British Protestants, Gohebydd insisted that Garibaldi had a special connection with Wales.

> I am quite sure that there is nowhere in the world outside Italy, where the name Garibaldi has been for the last four years better known . . . And I am more than certain that no race of people under the sun feels more genuine respect for the unostentatious good-natured hero of Caprera than our people, the Welsh.[6]

To what extent was Gohebydd's view justified? Was there a specifically Welsh connection with Garibaldi, either as his mission was understood or in the precise terms in which he was celebrated? Clearly, the events in London afforded journalists and other leaders of Welsh opinion opportunities to explore a range of themes concerning the political and cultural condition of Wales, its ancient, vexed relation to England and the moral dimensions of national struggle against oppression. It might be tempting to suppose that these voices – the truly 'Welsh' voices, as many would regard them – were raised in a unanimous condemnation of English political and cultural hegemony over Wales, but this would be inaccurate. Neither may it be judged that Welsh admiration for Garibaldi was always distinguishable from English praise because it arose out of liberal values 'rooted in the Bible rather than in the Enlightenment'.[7] As elsewhere in Britain, responses were complex, multivalent and contingent on a range of social, cultural and political factors. This complexity owed much to the expanding forums for public debate afforded by the burgeoning industry in cheap newspapers, as well as to the growing sense of political opportunity during the years immediately preceding the Second Reform Act. They were also indicative of the extent to which political expression in Wales drew from sources of inspiration common to other parts of Britain: inspiration which looked inward, to a tradition of moral struggle as justified and illuminated by the Scriptures, as well as outward, to the languages of European republicanism and political pragmatism.

Taken as a whole, Welsh newspapers displayed a unanimity of approval of Garibaldi even more pronounced than that in England, an effect that probably owed much to their distance from the political tensions of the capital. Few readers of Welsh-language radical newspapers would have disagreed with the view of the Conservative *North Wales Chronicle* that 'nothing is more admired by the British nation than those qualities of truth and honesty which so eminently distinguish the patriot Garibaldi'.[8] A common subsidiary theme was the idea that England's celebration of the hero reflected her own virtues as a society firmly united behind the liberal values which Garibaldi sought to introduce in Italy. Much reporting of the event was copied from English newspapers, such the account in the *Merionethshire Herald* of the hero's triumphal procession into Westminster on 11 April: 'The welcome was worthy of the man, and England is honoured by the honour she has to-day paid in her metropolis to the embodiment of all that is noble, admirable and loveable in human nature.'[9] It is clear that when people in Wales, English-speakers most of all, referred to England in such a way, they did not suppose that this state of liberal grace was limited to the far side of Offa's Dyke. Their references thus implied a measure of self-congratulation and a tacit acceptance of the political and cultural reality of a British nation.[10]

The work of Gwilym Hiraethog, the Congregational minister, publisher and poet, provides a well-documented starting point in the search for a distinctly Welsh Garibaldi.[11] Gwilym Hiraethog was at the forefront of a generation of Nonconformist political commentators who were instrumental in making the Welsh chapel a focus of resistance to English political and religious hegemony, and he had lectured throughout Wales on the subject of Garibaldi long before this was a popular subject in England.[12] Gwilym Hiraethog also conducted an intermittent correspondence with Giuseppe Mazzini, the chief republican theorist of the Italian Risorgimento, who had become permanently exiled in London following the collapse of the Roman Republic of 1849, and he was known to Mazzini's closest supporters in London, such as the Unitarian radicals Peter Alfred Taylor, junior, and William Shaen.[13] He shared Mazzini's profound antagonism toward the papacy, and on founding the *Amserau* in 1843 promised that it would be dedicated to opposing 'the superstitious, unchristian and papal doctrines and practices of both Oxford and Rome'.[14]

A version of Gwilym Hiraethog's lecture on Garibaldi, published post-humously, gives an idea of his apocalyptic and elliptical use of symbolic imagery and his fusion of epic and scriptural representations of national bondage. He introduced his theme through lines in the first canto of Dante's *Divine Comedy*, intended to impress on his audiences the moral and literary affinities between Wales and Italy.[15] These describe how Dante's way to Paradise was barred by the last and most terrible of three beasts – the 'Wolf of Greed' – which, as Virgil explains, will devour all in its path until the coming of One who feeds only on knowledge, love and virtue.[16]

For Gwilym Hiraethog, this reference to the prophecies of Jeremiah represented more than an interesting footnote. It was the prime frame of reference within which the hero's significance to his nation could be under-stood. Gwilym Hiraethog called Dante 'the Jeremiah of his age', and believed his prophecy referred to Garibaldi.[17] It is unlikely that he needed to remind his audiences of the lines found in Jeremiah:

> Run ye to and fro through the streets of Jerusalem, and see now, and know, and seek in the broad places thereof, if ye can find a man, if there be any that executeth judgment, that seeketh the truth; and I will pardon it . . .

> Lo, I will bring a nation upon you from far . . . it is a mighty nation, it is an ancient nation, a nation whose language thou knowest not . . .

> And they shall eat up thine harvest, and thy bread, which thy sons and thy daughter should eat: they shall eat up thy flocks and thine herds . . .[18]

Gwilym Hiraethog shared with Dante a scriptural understanding of the importance of individual morality to civic virtue. The subjugation of nations resulted from their poor moral condition, and the way from transgression to salvation was to be found in individual repentance. As J. D. Sinclair has noted, the symbolism of the *Divine Comedy* is both personal and public, relating to Dante's moral state and to that of the country as a whole.[19] The public manifestation of the 'Wolf of Greed' referred to the prevailing condition of papal misrule. The papacy was characterized primarily as a civil, rather than a spiritual, evil, since it had been freed only through a lack of virtue in the civic body. However, a messianic figure, a Hero without moral stain, might offer a shortcut on the arduous journey, insofar as the nation as a whole is concerned. Gwilym Hiraethog asserted that it was through the example of such a man that civic virtues might be instilled in the citizen, who, ultimately, held the key to national salvation. Who might accomplish the same miracle for Wales? Gwilym Hiraethog never posed the question, since it was enough, for his purposes, to offer Garibaldi to the attention of his audience in this light. However, the parallels between the political condition of Dante's Italy and the Wales of their own day would have been self-evident to many in his audiences. Very many people had been profoundly offended by the so-called 'Treason of the Blue Books', the condemnation by parliamentary commissioners on education in 1847 of the Welsh language as encouraging 'wide-spread disregard of temperance, wherever there are the means of excess, of chastity, of veracity, and of fair dealing'.[20] Moreover, the Anglican Church served as a continual reminder to chapel congregations of the evils arising from an established and politically active Church.

Gwilym Hiraethog's interest in Dante as an inspirational voice of relevance in nineteenth-century Wales was far from unique, representing one of the more common expressions of 'Italophilia' common in Britain at this time. Translations of and commentaries on the *Divina Commedia* had multiplied in England since the resurgence of interest in Italian literature during the second half of the eighteenth century.[21] Thomas Carlyle had proposed Dante as a hero in his own right, an example of a 'world voice' which could not 'sing the heroic warrior unless he himself were at least a heroic warrior too'.[22] William Ewart Gladstone began translating the *Commedia* in 1836, interpreting it, as did Gwilym Hiraethog, through the perspective of nineteenth-century anti-clericalism in Italy.[23] John Russell's own translation of a portion of the *Inferno* had attracted a somewhat unfavourable critique by Gladstone.[24] As in Wales, English interest in Dante often focused on his importance as a symbol of cultural unity. Carlyle cited him in emphasizing the importance of literature to a sense of nationhood:

> Poor Italy lies dismembered, scattered asunder, not appearing in any protocol or treaty as a unity at all; yet the noble Italy is actually one; Italy produced its Dante; Italy can speak! . . . The nation that has a Dante is bound together as no dumb Russia can be.[25]

Gladstone represented Italy's cultural superiority over that of Austria as an argument in support of its national struggle. 'Could there be in Christendom', he wrote, 'an instance corresponding with the Austrian power in Italy; an instance where a people glaringly inferior in refinement rule, and that by the medium of arbitrary will, without the check of free institutions, over a race much more advanced?'[26] It is an intriguing irony that both the Welsh radical minister and the High Church future leader of the Liberal party first developed their views on the Risorgimento in Liverpool, the Tory centre of British 'Italophilia'.[27]

Gwilym Hiraethog's use of scriptural language in celebrating Garibaldi as a hero of moral regeneration was also characteristic of a far more widespread trend, and it was especially useful to radical Nonconformists in promoting unity of opinion across class and cultural divides. Derek Beales has noted a sermon by a Methodist minister in Bedford that also drew its inspiration from Jeremiah: 'Thou art my battleaxe and weapons of war; for with thee will I break into pieces the nations, and with thee I will destroy kingdoms.'[28] Many in England also experienced a strong sense of menace emanating from Rome, which had intensified considerably since the re-establishment of the Roman Catholic hierarchy in Britain in 1850 and friction resulting from the arrival, in wake of the Great Famine, of large numbers of Irish immigrants in its towns and cities. As in Wales, any purely doctrinal objections to Roman Catholicism were often obscured by issues of political morality, and especially as related to notions of the just regulation of society. The response of the *Liverpool Mercury* to Garibaldi is characteristic in its focus on the proposed political immoralities of papal rule.

> There may be a fractional minority whom ecclesiastical or political part-isanship disables from recognising the moral greatness of the Liberator of Southern Italy, and whose cold and narrow creed forbids them to bestow their sympathies on the man who extinguished 'legitimate' tyranny in Naples and aims at the subversion of priestly misrule in Rome.[29]

This emphasis on the evils of misrule was echoed by the Dean of Canterbury, who further asserted that such sins were blackest when perpetrated by a spiritual power. 'Nothing will ever reform Rome, short of the entire extinction of the temporal power of the priesthood. Better any secular mis-government than the present hideous blasphemy against God and Man.'[30] Such views reinforced the idea of a British unity derived from a common repudiation of the Church of Rome, while stressing that this opposition was the natural reaction of all who were not in its thrall.

Mazzini became the prime exponent of European republicanism in Britain largely because he had fashioned a rhetorical language of enormously wide appeal to those whose radical views had been shaped from the pulpit, and this was instrumental in reconciling both sectarian and social tensions amongst his supporters. Robustly anti-papal, his response to the restoration of the Roman Catholic hierarchy in Britain was to denounce Pius IX as 'the Beast of Apocalypse'.[31] In this address, Mazzini delivered as powerful a rebuke against the Vatican as could ever have been thundered from any Commonwealth pulpit. It is less a polemical work than an affirmation of faith, delivered in short telegraphic phrases full of emotive imagery that demands to be read aloud:

> By your last Encyclical you have flung your Anathema over the civilized world, over its movement, over the life which it inspires it, as if the world, life, and movement were not things of God. As the tempest-tossed mariner, seeing the waves raising higher and higher around him, despoils himself, in desperation . . . so you, maddened by the restless terrors that surround the death-agony of a despairing sinner.[32]

The 1860s saw a flood of Mazzini's publications, both substantial works, such as *The Duties of Man* (1862), and pamphlets, such as his 'Address to Pope Pius IX on His Encyclical Letter' (fourth edition, 1865). In the first, which Mazzini dedicated to 'the sons and daughters of the people', he stressed that emancipation from 'the arbitrary rule and tyranny of man' may be won only through 'rightly adoring God', and that the greatest tyranny was 'all pretended intermediaries between God and the People'.[33]

In England, scriptural language in praise of Garibaldi was drawn frequently from the New Testament, and focused especially on the hero's Christ-like qualities. Gerald Massey dwelt on the theme of sacrifice in a poem concerning Garibaldi's wounding by Italian troops at Aspromonte in 1862. Betrayal here is represented, not as an uncomplicated act of evil, committed by the ungodly, but as an essential element to the salvation that the hero offers through his sacrifice.

> It is not failure to be thus struck down
> By Brothers who obeyed their foe's command,
> And in the darkness lopped the saving hand
> Put forth to reach their country her last crown
> . . .
> I say 'twas God's voice bade him offer up
> Himself for Aspromonte's sacrifice
> So, to that height, his countrymen might rise;
> For them he freely drank his bitter cup.[34]

The hero's daily passage through the streets of London encouraged messianic associations, as witnesses strove to find words and images that adequately expressed their feelings of veneration. 'Thank God', wrote an anonymous contributor to a women's magazine,

> let us all thank God for the rest of our existence – that this has not been denied us; that we have been privileged to look upon so dearly noble a man that we can ask our children or our friends who may have shared the sight to remember the day, and date life afresh from the hour which gave him to our eyes.[35]

The messianic theme was also found in the accounts of journals better known for their shrewd political analyses than for such effusions of hero-worship, such as the *Spectator*:

> The people flocked about him, pressing their children up to him as they might to an apostle, and the great soldier received them like a father. We may laugh at Garibaldi's wild politics and rhapsodical eloquence, and we have never ignored his errors, but in his demeanour to the people, and in the demeanour of the people to him, we suspect there is something nearer to the mutual bearing of the shepherd and the flock that knows his voice than it is given to ordinary mortals, however earnestly they may battle for the people's rights or work for their salvation, to attain.[36]

It is indisputable that Wales had its own unique literary tradition through which praise of Garibaldi could be formulated, the so-called 'Taliesin tradition' of epic poetry, founded on themes of resistance against oppression and contrasting the cultural superiority of an ancient beleaguered nation with the moral corruption of its foes.[37] This was at least as accessible to Welsh readers as Gwilym Hiraethog's apocalyptic meditations, yet echoed key elements of scriptural discourse with its powerful symbolic imagery and emphasis on righteous struggle. Garibaldi was, understandably, a popular theme for Welsh poets during the early 1860s, and their works are often filled with a specifically Celtic heroic imagery.

A poem in *Y Punch Cymraeg* proposed that Garibaldi's liberating mission might be extended from Italy to the 'old White Island', that is, Britain before the Saxon conquest:

> Selfless hero of patriotism
> Restorer of the nations of the world
> Fearsome apparition to tyrants
> Releasing dear Freedom from her chains.[38]

The hero here evoked is not merely a liberator, being a *restorer* of nations, a 'simple child of nature' who 'does not divide the country by lot / But puts peoples and languages in their [rightful] place'.

A bilingual song probably published in 1861 represents Garibaldi's liberation of Naples with his magical powers in the Welsh version:

> Our irons are melted at the touch of his finger
> Oh shout, shout my fellow prisoners!
> Italy our country is surely free.
> The seats are empty in the tyrannical court
> Let us sing, sing songs of Italy
> And thank heaven the day has come
> That Garibaldi has arrived, Italy is free.[39]

The English version, by contrast, offered a translation of the original German text describing a darkly Gothic hunt: 'And if the black trooper's name you'd know, / Lutzow, 'tis Lutzow's wild Jager a-hunting they go.'

Clearly, the choice of language in praising Garibaldi was itself an act of political significance, allowing the fashioning of a distinctly Welsh hero who could be celebrated in cultural exclusivity. Such texts needed to be managed carefully on the rare occasions when they were disseminated in translation to the anglophone population. This was unavoidable on the one occasion when Wales came to England to honour its hero on a public platform.

On Monday 21 April 1864 the Welsh residents in London presented an address to Garibaldi at the Crystal Palace. Among the six-man delegation was Gohebydd, London correspondent for the *Baner ac Amserau Cymru*, who was well connected to the pulse of radical Nonconformist opinion in both Wales and the metropolis.[40] As *The Times* reported it, a contingent of 'Welsh Congregational Dissenters . . . stalked past [in] stern and gloomy incognito' to pay their respects to the hero.[41] It was perhaps an unfair description, although congruent with a common English preconception of the Welsh character. Silent presentations had been prescribed by the organizers – although the rule was not universally observed – as essential to the successful completion of the ceremony within a reasonable period of time. It is also likely that the delegation carried no banner advertising themselves, as did most of the others, neither were they likely to have been dressed in the extravagant costume worn by many working-men's fraternal societies of the day.[42] Certainly, they considered their business to be with Garibaldi rather than with the audience. The address read:

Your name is a household word throughout the Principality of Wales, and your life a favourite theme of our poets and orators for years, and we looked upon you as an instrument raised by God who 'ruleth in the kingdom of men, and giveth it to whomsoever he will' to accomplish the deliverance of your dear native land. As a Bible-reading nation from whose country the idea of the Bible Society first emanated your name became doubly dear to our countrymen on hearing how you have encouraged the circulation of that liberating Power – the word of God among the people, in which they 'shall know the truth and truth shall make them free.'[43]

Such, at least, was the text, as reproduced in a small number of English-language newspapers in Wales. There was little to distinguish the address from countless others presented to Garibaldi during his visit. The reference to his popularity as a subject of song and poetry was only stating the obvious, even to English ears. Garibaldi's closest British friends, knowing of his aversion to organized religion, might have wondered how, precisely, he had helped to spread the 'word of God'. This might be understood as a reference to the land he had donated in Naples, requisitioned from the Church, to build a Protestant chapel.[44] It is more likely to be a general allusion to the opportunities for evangelizing amongst a newly liberated people whose political and religious subjugation were widely regarded as synonymous. In this sense, also, its pious expressions were typical, rather than in any way remarkable, of numerous other addresses presented to Garibaldi during those weeks.

Yet a significantly different Welsh text was reproduced in *Baner ac Amserau Cymru*. Somewhat extended in length, it is worth quoting in translation:

We, London Welsh Independents, take the opportunity to join with a large body of our fellow countrymen to welcome you on your visit to this kingdom. Your name is famous throughout the Principality of Wales, and your life has been a favourite subject for our bards and orators for years, since we look upon you as an instrument raised up by God – 'the One who rules the kingdom of men, and gave unto them his son' – to lead your country in liberation. As a people who delight in reading the Bible, from a country whence came the idea of the Bible Society, your name came to be much dearer to our countrymen when we heard of the support that you gave to spreading that which can liberate – the word of God – amongst the people, in this case the refrain 'know the truth, the truth that is the people's liberation'. We admire your altruistic patriotism and lack of deceit, and wish you a long life to realise the chief aim of your life – LIBERTY AND UNIFICATION OF THE COUNTRY OF YOUR ANCESTORS.[45]

The disparities between the two versions in both length and precise terms of reference are suggestive of more than merely lingual differences.[46] The Welsh address abounds with expressions of particular significance for its intended readers. It is clear from the context that the 'fellow countrymen' is a reference to the Welsh, rather than the British, nation. 'The word of God' as 'that which can liberate' implies a direct and active process, suggestive of the intimate link found in Wales between religious and political discourse through the function of the chapel as 'a school in democratic management'.[47] So, too, the reference to the 'country of your ancestors' reflects a view of nationhood as arising from ancient tenure. The hero's 'lack of deceit' was a quality frequently admired in Wales, where the epic tale of national origin, 'The Treason of the Long Knives', centred on the sixth-century treachery of the Saxon lords.[48] Finally, the boldly printed phrase with which the address closes expresses an enthusiasm for further action on Garibaldi's part, which Liberal English newspapers may have condoned by implication but seldom voiced openly.

Why were there two versions, and was there any reason for the omission of the first and last lines in the English text? A marked level of detachment may be found in Welsh newspapers of both languages when reporting the celebrations in London, and they showed little inclination to engage in the political factionalism that was a conspicuous element in the reporting of papers in the capital. The speeches presented to Garibaldi at Nine Elms station on his arrival, widely analysed and criticized in London, appeared to hold little interest for Welsh editors, neither did the working-men's organization of the procession, a major issue in London, invite more than passing comment. Tensions closer to home were another matter. In Wales the popular liberal ideal of a community united by its shared sense of moral purpose needed to accommodate cultural divisions, as well as those of class. Any direct engagement with the issues raised by a distinct Welsh national identity appeared to be ruled out at some stage, although whether this was by the Welsh delegation itself or newspaper editors is unclear. It is evident that cultural tensions of this sort were expressed more commonly through omission than by direct engagement. The address was altered for consumption by English readers in Wales, probably because it was accepted that they were capable of recognizing and resenting the implications of the original text as a manifesto of cultural nationalism.

At least one Welsh editor engaged in a degree of plain speaking which would most likely have provoked bitter denunciations had it been published in English. This was John Roberts of Llanbrynmair (known as J.R.), who managed the *Cronicl* (of Dolgellau) during his brother Samuel's long sojourn in America.[49] The *Cronicl* was the Welsh-language organ of the Peace Society, which in England had bowed to the public euphoria over

Garibaldi and heaped praise on his 'virtues of citizenship' and pacifist inclinations.[50] However, John Roberts was less willing to sacrifice his principles, publishing an acerbic essay exploring the contradictions inherent in England's hero-worship.[51] Although Roberts (like Gwilym Hiraethog, a Nonconformist minister) had acknowledged the hero as the 'saviour' of his people in 1860, his enthusiasm had diminished somewhat by 1864, when he asserted: 'his aim is good, but the means he used to achieve his aim are suspicious'.[52] However, most of his disapproval was directed at the hypocritical position of England, which had suppressed with considerable savagery a recent rebellion of Indian 'patriots' attempting to expel a foreign oppressor. Roberts asserted: 'the principles of righteousness are the same whether the supporters win or lose'.[53] Such views would have been regarded as deeply provocative in England, where the Indian Mutiny had entered the popular imagination as a savage betrayal of decency and innocence. It is interesting to note that similar charges of hypocrisy were levelled at England's reception of Garibaldi by a number of Irish nationalist newspapers, most notably A. M. Sullivan's *Nation* and the Fenian *Irish People*.[54] Gohebydd expressed similar reservations, although in more moderate terms. His theme in the following passage is 'the Lion of Caprera', that is, Garibaldi:

> Very rarely, if ever, is London without its 'Lion' from some country or other. London is the best place on earth for 'Lions'. We have seen over the last ten or fifteen years many kinds, – some greater and some lesser. Two years ago the ambassadors of Japan were the 'Lions'. A year ago, the Prince of Wales and the young Princess Alexandra of Denmark were the 'Lions'. And great lions they were . . . for a short time, it was Captain Speke and his friend – the two explorers who discovered the source of the Nile.[55]

London, according to Gohebydd, was jaded by the variety of its celebrities, and he leaves the reader to conclude that the sincerity of its enthusiasm for Garibaldi was somewhat questionable. John Roberts was even more dismissive of the discrimination of the London public:

> If [someone] were to stand one moonlit night by Charing Cross, and point to an owl which had landed on the back of the horse of George III, there would be hundreds of people looking at it, and if it were brave enough to say 'hoo, hoo', it would get *tremendous cheers*![56]

There remain to be considered the contributions of Dr Thomas Price of Aberdare, another outspoken supporter of Garibaldi, whose activities bore superficial similarities to those of Gwilym Hiraethog. Ordained at the age of twenty-five at the Baptist college in Pontypool, he was the incumbent at Capel Pen-pound (Aberdare) from 1845 to his death in 1888. Like Gwilym Hiraethog, he was a popular lecturer as well as a preacher, and edited a number of Welsh newspapers, most notably, within the present context, *Seren Cymru* ('The Star of Wales') from 1860 to 1876. Again like Gwilym Hiraethog, he had spoken out with considerable force against the so-called 'Treason of the Blue Books', his anger undoubtedly augmented by the testimony given to the commission by the young vicar of Aberdare regarding the promiscuity of local women.[57]

However, Price was neither a poet nor was he an associate of Mazzini. While he was by family background and inclination an effective leader of working-class opinion, he was also a director in a number of local companies, occupied a spacious villa and associated on an equal basis with local businessmen. Like his Nonconformist colleagues in England, he sought to promote the widest possible base of support within his community for the aims of the Liberation Society, and saw nothing to be gained by using the case of Garibaldi to highlight class or cultural tensions. During the years prior to the Second Reform Act he was primarily a Liberal politician and was engaged, as were his English colleagues, in the difficult task of attempting to reconcile the disparate and fractious elements of the local Liberal constituency.

Consequently, his newspaper did not respond to Garibaldi's visit in a manner distinguishable from that of Liberal newspapers in England, which were confronted with the same potential risks to Liberal unity in the celebration of a revolutionary.[58] Thus, while Price's praise of the hero was unequivocal, it was also curiously anodyne, making no reference to Wales as a distinct cultural or political entity and stressing England's role as the patron of European liberties. 'In honouring him England honours herself', he unimaginatively remarked of the procession on 11 April, which was 'worthy of the world's first city'.[59] Price clearly felt that the hero was in safe hands with his host, the Duke of Sutherland, who was the government's unofficial minder. 'We might as well advertise at once that his visit has no direct political purpose', he insisted, stressing that Garibaldi had come only to thank his many English friends and seek the advice of English doctors.[60] All this was precisely the government view, as published in *The Times* several days earlier, accompanied by dark hints that moves were afoot to invest the occasion with political significance.[61]

Price was in London during Garibaldi's visit and he claimed membership of the committee which was organizing the celebrations, so it might seem surprising that he played no public role in Garibaldi's welcome.[62] Although there were three Garibaldi committees in London, the Italian, the City and the Working Men's Reception Committees, considering Price's social standing it is most likely that he was a member of that of the City, where he would have joined his colleague in the Liberation Society, Edward Miall.[63] The committee consisted largely of Nonconformist professionals and merchants of advanced liberal opinions, who would have found Price an agreeable associate.[64] Furthermore, the uncomplicated analysis of Garibaldi's mission in Britain disseminated by Price in *Seren Cymru* was also promoted by the City Committee, which was engaged in a campaign to divest the celebrations of any radical associations, in the face of Conservative opposition to the granting of the freedom of the city to Garibaldi. The committee was, in theory, a very large organization, calculated to impress upon the public its role as a representative of a greater British liberal consensus, and included the Lord Mayor (William Lawrence), Charles Dickens and twelve Liberal MPs.[65]

However, Price may have become aware at some point of the strategies of the City Committee's inner circle of ultra-radicals. These were Mazzini's oldest English friends, most notably P. A. Taylor, MP for Leicester and a leading figure at the radical Unitarian chapel at Finsbury, his co-religionist William Shaen and Edmund Beales, a revising barrister for Middlesex who went on to lead the Reform League during its public demonstrations in support of substantial franchise reform.[66] This group was engaged in a far more confrontational agenda than the public image of the City Committee suggested. In collaboration with the Working Men's Committee they sought to promote popular discontent over the government's supposed interference with Garibaldi's itinerary during his visit, and to highlight the inertia of Palmerston's ministry generally with regard to reform.[67] The final days of Garibaldi's stay in London were marked by increasingly bitter recriminations between the committees and supporters of the government. Price might have felt he would do well to avoid a more public connection with a committee which had become publicly associated with Mazzini and the taint of republicanism.

Among them, Gwilym Hiraethog, Gohebydd, Roberts and Price illustrated something of the range of strategies available to leaders of opinion in Wales in their efforts to develop a genuinely Welsh popular political voice. Ieuan Gwynedd Jones has noted that language, the 'touchstone of both politics and religion' was used to highlight 'social differences'.[68] However, responses to Garibaldi demonstrate that language was equally effective in reconciling those differences. Scriptural discourse was especially effective in dramatizing and popularizing republican critiques across Britain. Celebrations of the righteous hero drew much of their power, in both England and Wales, from an urge to reanimate the religious foundations of radical political activism through contemporary examples of individual virtue. A further source of unity, especially among republicans, was found in Mazzini's creed of 'duty' to the cause of national salvation, through which struggles at home could be placed in an international context. The universality of such modes of discourse, drawing, above all, on the traditions of Protestant struggle, permitted dissident voices to publicize their views without danger of direct condemnation. English society had developed great tolerance for radical proselytizing, so long as it was couched in scriptural quotation, rather than in Jacobin rhetoric.

There were those in Wales, such as Thomas Price, who found in the celebration of English liberal virtues a political opportunity, rather than a challenge. In the pages of *Seren Cymru*, any sense of a discernibly Welsh perspective of Garibaldi had disappeared because, within the political terrain in which Price was obliged to labour, it offered no advantages. The Whiggish view of Garibaldi as an uncomplicated icon of patriotism and the student of British liberal accomplishments proved a more effective means to unite opinion or – perhaps more important to Price – prevent any potential further division within Liberal opinion in south Wales. It was through this kind of pragmatic engagement with the public affairs of the greater British nation that Welsh Nonconformist opinion was to be forged into one of Gladstone's 'corps d'armée' of 1868.[69]

The rarefied and inherently exclusive form of political expression exemplified by Gwilym Hiraethog's sermon on Garibaldi was becoming obsolete through the opportunities presented by closer and more varied dialogue with England and the wider world. Gohebydd's reporting of the celebrations helped bring England itself, with its political and social institutions, into sharper focus for many Welsh speakers. It emphasized London's leading place within a liberal European community, whose successes against oppressive government offered new hope and inspiration for those who found similar injustices closer to home. Consequently, the celebrations served to highlight the city as a national capital of importance to the ideals and aspirations of radical Wales, as it was to activists elsewhere in Britain. Finally, the celebrations served to remind Wales of its own thriving diaspora in the capital, which had participated in an event widely regarded as premonitory of the winds of change that were soon to blow through their own 'dear native land'.

NOTES

[1] I am grateful for the useful comments made by Kenneth O. Morgan with regard to an earlier draft of this essay, and, more recently, for those of John Stuart. Thanks are also due to David Heaf and Sara Roberts for help with translations.

[2] The best overall analysis of the political undercurrents generated by the event has been provided by Derek Beales in 'Garibaldi in England: the politics of

Italian enthusiasm', in John A. Davis and Paul Ginsborg (eds), *Society and Politics in the Age of the Risorgimento: Essays in Honour of Denis Mack Smith* (Cambridge, 1991).

3   T. Gwynfor Griffith, 'Italy and Wales', *Transactions of the Honourable Society of the Cymmrodorion 1966, Part 2* (1966); Griffith, *Garibaldi, Cymru Fydd a Dante* (Swansea, 1985).

4   C. Lewis Hind, *Naphtali: Being Influences and Adventures While Earning a Living by Writing* (London, 1926), p. 2.

5   In a similar vein, Menotti Garibaldi McAdam of Glasgow noted how in the early years of the twentieth century he encountered an old man who recollected Garibaldi's appearance in Gallowgate, where he was eagerly awaited throughout April 1864 but never came: Janet Fyfe, 'Aid to Garibaldi from John McAdam and the City of Glasgow', in Anthony P. Campanella (ed.), *Pages from the Garibaldian Epic* (Sarasota, FL, 1984).

6   *BAC*, 20 Apr. 1864.

7   Marian Henry Jones, 'Wales and Hungary', *Transactions of the Honourable Society of Cymmrodorion, Session 1968, Part I* (1969), 23.

8   *North Wales Chronicle* (hereafter *NWC*), 16 Apr. 1864.

9   *Merionethshire Herald*, 16 Apr. 1864. Originally published in the *Birmingham Post*, 12 Apr. 1864.

10   Rohan McWilliam, *Popular Politics in Nineteenth Century England* (London, 1998), p. 85. According to Stefan Collini, *Public Moralists: Political Thought and Intellectual Life in Britain, 1850–1930* (Oxford, 1991), p. 7, during the nineteenth century ' "England" was unselfconsciously used to refer to a territory, a polity, and a culture that all contained much that was not, strictly speaking, "English" '.

11   David Williams has written that it is 'probable that [Gwilym Hiraethog] had greater influence than anyone else in the formation of Welsh public opinion in the nineteenth century'. *A History of Modern Wales* (London, 1950), p. 252. In addition to T. Gwynfor Griffith's contributions, cited above (n. 3), see Philip Jenkins, *A History of Modern Wales* (Harlow, 1992), pp. 304–6; E. Rees, *William Rees: A Memoir by His Son* (Liverpool, 1915); H. E. Hughes, *Eminent Men of Denbighshire* (Liverpool, 1946); Piero Rebora, *Civiltà Italiana e Civiltà Inglese* (Firenze, 1936).

12   Williams, *History of Modern Wales*, p. 250; Rebora, *Civiltà Italiana*, p. 245.

13   Rebora, *Civiltà Italiana*, p. 255. Two letters from Mazzini soliciting Gwilym Hiraethog's support for pro-Italian initiatives survive: NLW, MSS 13705C.

14   Williams, *History of Modern Wales*, p. 259. As Paul O'Leary has recently demonstrated, Gwilym Hiraethog's outspoken anti-Catholicism was far from uncommon among Welsh leaders of opinion during the mid nineteenth century: 'A tolerant nation? Anti-Catholicism in nineteenth-century Wales', in R. R. Davies and Geraint H. Jenkins (eds), *From Medieval to Modern Wales: Historical Essays in Honour of Kenneth O. Morgan and Ralph A. Griffiths* (Cardiff, 2004).

15   'Garibaldi', *Darlithau* (Denbigh, 1907), pp. 67–99.

16   Ibid., p. 68.

17   Ibid., p. 67.

18   Jer. 5: 1; 5: 15; 5: 17.

[19] *The Divine Comedy* (Oxford, 1971), p. 32.

[20] *The Reports of the Commissioners of Inquiry into the State of Education in Wales*, cited in John Wolffe, *God and Greater Britain: Religion and National Life in Britain and Ireland 1843–1945* (London, 1994), p. 109.

[21] C. P. Brand, *Italy and the English Romantics: The Italianate Fashion in Early Nineteenth-Century England* (Cambridge, 1957), p. 49.

[22] *On Heroes, Hero-Worship and the Heroic in History* (London, 1841), pp. 127, 164. Gwilym Hiraethog's own meditations on the importance of heroes to society appeared the following year: *Cofiant y diweddar Barch. E. Williams o'r Wern* (Llanelli, 1842), and in English translation, *Memoirs of Williams of Wern*, trans. 'J.R.J.' (London, 1846), p. 1.

[23] Owen Chadwick, 'Young Gladstone in Italy', in Peter J. Jagger (ed.), *Gladstone, Politics and Religion: A Collection of Founder's Day Lectures Delivered at St Deiniol's Library, Hawarden, 1967–83* (London, 1985), pp. 73–4.

[24] *English Review*, 1 (1844), 164–180. The review was published anonymously but Gladstone is named as the author by Chadwick, 'Young Gladstone', p. 74. Gladstone was apparently dismayed to find that Garibaldi had little interest in Dante: Cecil Y. Lang and Edgar F. Shannon (eds), *Letters of Alfred Lord Tennyson* (Oxford, 1987), vol. ii, p. 364, n. 2.

[25] *The Complete Works* (London, 1896), vol. v., p. 114.

[26] 'War in Italy', *Quarterly Review*, 105 (1859), 549–50.

[27] Brand, *Italy and the English Romantics*, p. 50; Rebora, *Civiltà Italiana*, p. 236.

[28] Beales, 'Garibaldi in England', pp. 185–6.

[29] *Liverpool Mercury*, 8 Apr. 1864.

[30] 'Letters from abroad', in *Good Words for 1864* (London, 1864), p. 481.

[31] Giuseppe Mazzini, *The Pope in the Nineteenth Century* (London, 1851), p. 29.

[32] Ibid., p. 1.

[33] *The Duties of Man* (London, 1862), pp. xii, xi.

[34] 'Garibaldi', from *Littel's Living Age*, series 3, 75 (1862), 335.

[35] From 'The book of the month: *Garibaldi and Italian Unity* by Lt. Col. Chambers', in *The Englishwoman's Domestic Magazine*, n. s., 9 (1864), 42.

[36] *Spectator*, 9 Apr. 1864, 408–9.

[37] Emyr Humphreys, *The Taliesin Tradition: A Quest for the Welsh Identity* (Bridgend, 1983), pp. 5–6. As Prys Morgan has noted, the Welsh had been similarly 'defined by their enemies and attackers': 'Keeping the legends alive', in Tony Curtis (ed.), *Wales: The Imagined Nation – Studies in Cultural and National Identity* (Bridgend, 1986), p. 21.

[38] *Y Punch Cymraeg*, 'Croesaw Garibaldi', 16 Apr. 1864.

[39] 'Garibaldi, or Lutzow's Wild Chase' (1861?).

[40] Gohebydd had been appointed to the *BAC* staff on the recommendation of Gwilym Hiraethog. Aled Gruffydd Jones, *Press, Politics and Society: A History of Journalism in Wales* (Cardiff, 1993), p. 24.

[41] *The Times*, 1 Apr. 1864.

[42] An account of the deputation is found in *BAC*, 4 May 1864. The ceremonial trappings worn by many participants in the procession of the previous week were widely ridiculed. See, for example, *Morning Post* and *The Times*, both 12 Apr. 1864.

43 *CDH*, 2 Apr. 1864.

44 *Nonconformist*, 27 Apr. 1864.

45 'I Garibaldi', *BAC*, 4 May 1864.

46 As Aled Jones has noted, a newspaper's choice of language was of far greater significance than 'a simple linguistic choice', being an embodiment of 'geographical, social, religious, cultural and even political difference': *Press, Politics and Society*, p. 6.

47 Williams, *History of Modern Wales*, p. 250.

48 The tale was popularized through *Drych y Prifoesoedd* (*The Mirror of the First Ages*) by Theophilus Evans (1716): Humphreys, *Taliesin Tradition*, p. 76.

49 Williams, *History of Modern Wales*, p. 260. John Roberts was Gohebydd's uncle.

50 *Herald of Peace*, 1 May 1864. This was too much for one reader, who referred the editor to Christ's dictum, as found on the frontispiece of the journal, 'for all they that take the sword shall perish with the sword', and observed that no amnesty was promised for the well-intentioned warrior: ibid., 1 July 1864.

51 'Garibaldi', *Cronicl*, June 1864, 164–5.

52 'Gwareder Garibaldi', *Cronicl*, Nov. 1860, 309; see also 'Cledd Garibaldi a'r Ital', *Cronicl*, Oct. 1862, 305.

53 'Gwareder Garibaldi'.

54 *Nation*, 26 Mar. 1864; *Irish People*, 2 Apr. 1864.

55 *BAC*, 20 Apr. 1864.

56 *Cronicl*, June 1864, 164.

57 Ieuan Gwynedd Jones, 'Dr Thomas Price and the election of 1868 in Merthyr Tydfil: a study in Nonconformist politics – Part I', *WHR*, 2, 2 (1964).

58 Reporting of the visit in the four April editions of *Seren Cymru* filled two and a half columns, far less than the coverage in *BAC*.

59 *Seren Cymru*, 22 Apr. 1864.

60 Ibid., 1 Apr. 1864.

61 *The Times*, 24 Mar. 1864.

62 *Seren Cymru*, 1, 8 Apr. 1864.

63 Ieuan Gwynedd Jones, 'Dr Thomas Price and the election of 1868 in Merthyr Tydfil: a study in Nonconformist politics – Part II', *WHR*, 2, 3 (1965). Edward Miall was the editor of the *Nonconformist*, the organ of the Liberation Society.

64 Jones, 'Dr Thomas Price – Part I', 162.

65 At least five hundred people had been invited to join the committee: *Reynolds's Newspaper*, 27 March 1864.

66 The Mazzinian leadership of the City Committee has not been widely acknowledged by British historians, although it has long been known to historians of the Risorgimento in Italy. See Emilia Morelli, *Mazzini in Inghilterra* (Firenze, 1938), p. 99, and Kees Windland, 'Garibaldi in Britain: reflections of a liberal hero' (unpublished D.Phil. thesis, University of Oxford, 2002).

67 Sources that touch upon the activities of this unofficial group are diffuse, but the reporting of the *City Press*, *Dial* and *Morning Advertiser* (all of which reported City affairs extensively) during those days reveal the essential elements of its strategies.

[68] Ieuan Gwynedd Jones, 'Language and community in nineteenth-century Wales', in Jones, *Mid-Victorian Wales: The Observers and the Observed* (Cardiff, 1992), p. 77.

[69] The expression is Gladstone's: Hugh Kearney, *The British Isles: A History of Four Nations* (Cambridge, 1989), p. 175.

5

'Brimful of patriotism':[1] Welsh Conservatives, the South African War and the 'Khaki' election of 1900

MATTHEW CRAGOE

The general election of 1900 was a triumph for Lord Salisbury's Conservative government. Fought while the memory of British successes in the South African War was still fresh in people's minds, the government was swept back to power with its majority essentially intact, thus defying what Salisbury himself termed 'the great law of the pendulum', which had routinely swung the opposition into office at every election since 1868.[2] Although contemporaries acknowledged, with varying degrees of bitterness, the influence of war-induced jingoism on the outcome of the contest, historians have been much less ready to allow the result of the election to stand as evidence of widespread popular enthusiasm for Empire.[3] Richard Price, for example, in a key text arguing for the indifference of late-Victorian working men to the notion of Empire, has suggested that 'voter apathy' and not 'patriotic concern' was the keynote of the campaign.[4] Both the turnout and the number of contested seats were appreciably lower in 1900 than at the previous general election of 1895, he observes, adding that the response to the Tories' imperial message was particularly muted in working-class areas, such as the East End of London. The absence of 'patriotic symbols', he goes on, 'illustrated how unimportant such concepts as flag and Empire were to working-class life'.[5] Such enthusiasm as there was for the Empire emanated instead from the ranks of the lower middle-class. Although a later generation of historians, including John Mackenzie and Martin Pugh, has done much to suggest that Price's depiction of an un-imperial working class does not withstand scrutiny, his view of the limited role played by the war in the election of 1900 has been much more durable and is still frequently encountered.[6]

Only recently has Price's interpretation of the election been seriously challenged. In an important article, Paul Readman has demonstrated conclusively the importance of the war as a campaign issue to all sides in 1900. Readman points to the fact that some 95 per cent of Conservative election addresses referred to the war, suggesting that there was 'a collective attempt to impose a Khaki agenda on the contest'. The appearance of the war in almost 80 per cent of Liberal addresses is evidence, he argues, that the Unionists' strategy was successful, the Liberals having had to respond.[7] Having established that the war was the inescapable issue of the election, Readman moves on to challenge Price's interpretation of the number of walkovers allowed by the Liberals and the low voter-turnout on polling day, whose extent in any case he disputes: the root cause, he argues, was not 'apathy' (as Price claimed) but a 'deep feeling of hopelessness' among Liberals at their inability to resist Unionist appeals to patriotism.[8] For Readman the result of the 1900 election stands as a ringing endorsement of the government's imperial strategy: 'the platform patriotism of Liberal Unionist and Conservative candidates was the deus ex machina that kept Salisbury's government in power'.[9]

In this chapter, a comparison of the campaigns run by the Conservatives in two south Walian constituencies will be used to explore the point at issue between Readman and Price, namely, the role of the war in determining the outcome of the 1900 election.[10] The only Welsh seat gained by the Conservatives at this contest was Monmouth Boroughs, where an arch imperialist, Dr Rutherfoord Harris, ousted the sitting Liberal member, Albert Spicer. In Cardiff, by contrast, the party lost a seat, as Alderman James Lawrence, another ardent imperialist, was defeated by Sir Edward Reed. The chapter begins by examining the wider tradition within which Welsh Conservatism operated in the late nineteenth century, tracing its principal ideas and agencies, before moving on to consider the response of people in Wales to the advent of conflict in South Africa. Finally, attention is directed to the election campaigns fought by the Conservatives in the Monmouth Boroughs and in Cardiff. As will be seen, while Harris's enthusiasm for the war received an impassioned response from the voters, in Cardiff, a candidate who began the campaign confidently assertive of Britain's imperial destiny was blown off course and came to electoral grief. The general election of 1900, it is concluded, was a campaign of many issues, not one.

THE CONSERVATIVE PARTY AND THE EMPIRE

Nineteenth-century Conservatism, as Martin Pugh has written, was not an 'ideology'. Rather, Conservatives adhered to 'a collection of attitudes and precepts' which dictated that the scope of governmental authority should be small, that the acceptance of authority and hierarchy should be habitual, and that the best guide to the future should be the past.[11] Yet this did not mean that Conservatism was unchanging. In the last three decades of the nineteenth century Conservatives added to their traditional veneration of Church, Crown and Property a fourth element: Empire. So pronounced did this emphasis become that the Conservatives effectively established a monopoly over patriotism in the last years of Victoria's reign.[12] In the first half of this section the extent to which a shared interpretation of the essential value of Empire governed the response of Conservatives across Britain to the developing crisis in South Africa is examined; attention then turns to the means by which such views were disseminated amongst the public at large, through the press, the Primrose League, and workingmen's clubs.

The Tories' imperial vision

To late nineteenth-century Tories, the assertion that the British were an 'Imperial Race' seemed unproblematic.[13] The Empire was Britain's great gift to the world, and Africa its latest – and perhaps greatest – beneficiary. Wherever Conservatives gathered in the closing years of Victoria's long reign, such sentiments found voice. Thus, at a large Conservative meeting in Newport during January 1899, a visiting speaker, Mr Hayes Fisher, MP, Junior Lord of the Treasury, remarked that the 'Anglo-Saxon race' did indeed have a 'manifold destiny' to 'go forward to the dark countries, to be pioneers and lead the way of civilisation (hear, hear)'. 'They went into the Continent to carry forward civilisation and Christianity', he added, concluding: 'Where the British flag flies there is . . . law and order, equal rights for the people, and equal opportunities for all (cheers).'

Again and again, Conservative speakers drew attention to the manner in which Britain's imperial involvement had brought order to the wilder areas of the African continent. Major Wyndham-Quin, MP for South Glamorgan, told a meeting at Tredegar in 1899 how 'British administration and British justice' had been the 'salvation' of Egypt, turning the native army from a 'timid and disorganised mob' into a force embodying 'fine military qualities' equal to those of the Queen's soldiers in India. Egypt, he concluded, 'now formed a splendid connecting link, for the advancement of civilisation and commerce, from Alexandria to Cape Town'.[14] Those viewing affairs from the other end of the continent saw things in a very similar light. Rutherfoord Harris, for example, a long-time resident of Cape Town, frequently addressed this theme. In 1899, for example, he regaled an audience in Swansea with details of the changes that had come across the area formerly occupied by the Matabele since the power of their savage king, Lobengula, had been broken.[15] 'In ten years', as one reporter recorded, the land of unmitigated savagery – of utter despotism tempered by superstition; a land where blood was ever flowing and which within the four corners of its boundaries contained no sign nor vestige of civilization, had become Rhodesia, with its 900 miles of railway, 2000 miles of telegraph, with its fine townships, and a vigorous white population going ahead with surprising celerity.[16]

As both speeches indicate, the purpose of the good order established by the British was to facilitate trade. Indeed, the need to protect existing markets was a major driver of colonial expansion in this period. As Ewen Green has observed, the growth of Empire was largely defensive, 'prompted by fear that rival powers would seize territories and close them to British trade'.[17] To imperialists of Harris's stamp, the survival of Britain as a first-rate power depended on expanding trade with the carefully pacified, orderly white colonies: 'those colonies', as he put it, 'which had been built up by men of our own race, who shared our language, and shared our religion and history; and shared with us our Queen (applause)'.[18] The relationship of the white colonies to the mother country was thus conceived in highly intimate terms: they were imagined almost as offshore fragments of the United Kingdom itself.[19]

A second feature of the Conservatives' imperial outlook was their support, even enthusiasm, for the military. Historians are somewhat divided over the role played by militarism in late-Victorian society. For Anne Summers, militarism was 'an integral part' of the country's political culture; for Martin Pugh, it was an essentially dilettante affair.[20] On the Conservative side, the former appears more accurate: throughout the century, but particularly at its end, the Tories were the party of the armed forces. It has been calculated that between 1880 and 1914 over half the Conservative parliamentary party had some connection with Britain's military establishment, notably the army, the yeomanry or the volunteers.[21] The same connection was also highly visible within Welsh provincial Conservatism. In the affairs of the Carnarvonshire Constitutional Association, for example, Colonels Marshall, Platt and Wynn Finch and Captain N. P. Stewart all took prominent roles at different times, while at Rutherfoord Harris's final meeting before election day in 1900, the speakers at Tredegar Hall included Colonels C. T. Wallis, Lyne, J. F. Justice, Ingram and Major Jones.[22] Few Liberal meetings would have attracted a similar cast.

For such men, the history of Britain's greatness and her liberty seemed bound up with her willingness to bear and use arms. Typical were the sentiments expressed at the Welshpool Conservative Workingmen's Club in 1895. Mr Pryce-Yearsley set the ball rolling with the boast that 'the history of the British Army and Navy was unsurpassed in the annals of the world, especially such victories as Waterloo and Trafalgar and such heroes as Wellington and Nelson (applause)'. He was followed by Robert Williams-Wynn, candidate for the Montgomery County seat, who asked rhetorically whether the 'individual liberties' enjoyed by the English had been secured in a day. 'No', he answered himself, 'it was gradually formed by the wisdom of their forefathers, cemented by the blows of their soldiers and sailors, all of whom had never shrunk from shedding their last spot of blood for old England (cheers).'[23] As the conflict with the Boer Republics neared, views of this kind proliferated. In Penarth, the sitting Tory MP for South Glamorgan, Major Wyndham-Quin, pointed out that India had been conquered by the sword, and asked, 'Did the people of India bear us any malice? Did they hate us? He did not think so.' It was a lesson from which he drew an important lesson regarding the coming conflict with the Boers: they would learn to respect the advantages of British rule once the army had conquered the Transvaal.[24]

A belief in a strong and determined foreign policy thus characterized Conservative utterances throughout the period. Policies such as international arbitration, which was promoted so assiduously before his death in 1887 by the leading Welsh MP of the period, Henry Richard, were openly mocked by rank-and-file Tories, horrified at the implied cuts in defence expenditure involved. J. T. D. Llywelyn, when a candidate for the suffrages of the voters of the Cardiff Boroughs in 1885, told a meeting of farmers at Cowbridge that this was not the right policy to apply to the affairs of nations. 'He believed in being perfectly firm and keeping the fists closed', he said:

> If a man walked through the slums of some of our large towns he would button up his coat, close his fists, and probably he would not have to strike (Applause.) Perhaps the worst thing he could do was to walk along with his hands behind him and say 'I am prepared to arbitrate' (Laughter and applause) . . . He would prefer anything rather than war, if it could possibly be honourably averted (Applause.)[25]

By the 1890s, the Tories could draw on a well-developed picture of the consequences for the Empire if Britain's military responsibilities were shirked. At the centre of their thinking stood the legacy of the first Boer War, which had ended with the defeat of British forces at Majuba Hill on 27 February 1881.[26] Rather than reinforcing the British forces in South Africa and looking to avenge the defeat, the Liberal government signed the Pretoria Convention, granting effective independence to the Boer Republics, though retaining nominal suzerainty over the whole area for the Crown. The Convention was, said Salisbury, 'a device to cover surrender'.[27] To many others, Majuba Hill remained a burning humiliation, a 'shameful surrender

. . . by Mr Gladstone', in the words of Wyndham-Quin, 'as unnecessary as it was foolish and unpatriotic'.[28] The disaster of Majuba Hill, and Gordon's death in the Sudan, interpreted as another major failure of Gladstonian foreign policy, were endlessly contrasted with the success of Lord Salisbury's diplomacy after his return to power in 1895. The editor of the robustly Conservative *Carmarthen Journal* expressed it thus in 1899:

> the high position England now holds in foreign chancelleries, as in the foreign press, is eloquent testimony to the worth of a bold Imperialist attitude. As long as the traditions of humiliation and surrender by Liberal Governments lingered, snarlings and sneers were the portion of England. When it is seen that a Conservative Government will yield none of England's rights, and will fight, if need be, admiration and respect take the place of contempt and aggression.[29]

As this suggests, the fact that Salisbury's government had increased expenditure on the armed forces to strengthen both the army and the navy was seen by Tories as a key factor in the government's diplomatic successes in the later 1890s.[30] If Conservative militarism, which embraced a strong opposition to conscription and promoted instead institutions such as rifle clubs, looked somewhat absurd when set alongside the Prussian traditions still held dear in Germany, it remains the case that the party recognized the advantages of a strong military and were prepared to countenance its use, when necessary.[31] When diplomacy failed to make headway against the obstinacy of the Boers in the summer of 1899, there were very few on the Conservative side who did not feel that the recourse to arms was a legitimate facet of British imperial strategy.

Disseminating imperialism

The Conservatives thus held strong views on the Empire, and they had developed a coherent network through which these views could be shared and new converts to Tory principles made. In this section, the work of local Conservative agencies such as the Primrose League and Conservative workingmen's clubs is examined before attention turns to the press.

The Primrose League, named after Disraeli's favourite flower, was founded in 1883. Ostensibly an apolitical organization, in fact it championed the range of Conservative ideas outlined above. As Martin Pugh, the principal historian of the League, records, members, upon joining, signed a declaration pledging themselves 'to the maintenance of religion, the monarchy, the estates of the realm and the British Empire': it was an agenda which sounded almost like a Conservative party manifesto, and Conservative politicians certainly regarded a visit to a Habitation of the League as an opportunity to preach to the converted. As Alan Tatton Egerton told a Primrose League demonstration at Abergele in 1897: 'meetings of the Primrose League gave Unionists the opportunity of addressing all those who had at heart the great principles the League tried to inculcate – namely the maintenance of their Queen, the Empire, and the Church (applause)'.[32]

Despite the repeated failure of Welsh Toryism at the polls, the Primrose League enjoyed considerable success in the Principality. By 1895, Habitations of the League existed in every Welsh constituency except Rhondda, and there were often several in a single county.[33] Monmouthshire, for example, contained nineteen Habitations, whilst Denbighshire could boast twenty. Equally impressive was the number of people who joined the League. Membership of the various Cardiff Habitations quickly topped 1,300,[34] that at Cardigan claimed a membership of 2,600 in 1886, and, in the same year, the 'Menai' Habitation in Bangor could boast 1,041 members. The Gower branch had exceeded 1,000 by 1891, and Llandeilo in Carmarthenshire claimed 1,048 members ten years later. The Primrose League quickly became a rare bright spot for Welsh Tories, 'proof, if any were wanted, to show that Conservatism is not yet dead', as one optimistic supporter asserted in 1886.[35]

The Habitations enjoyed an active social life, with concerts, social evenings, outings and, of course, the great set-piece events of the Primrose League year, the summer fêtes held in the grounds of one or other of the local great houses.[36] Central to their activities, however, was an educative function. Martin Pugh is undoubtedly right to claim that the League's success derived ultimately from the 'sheer woolly imprecision' of its political outlook, yet it schooled its adherents to accept a very definite view of Britain's place in the world.[37] Evenings of entertainment were always interspersed with political lectures propounding Conservative lines of policy, and even those like the lecture on 'The British Empire' delivered at Dolgellau by R. S. J. Furlong in May 1899, accompanied as it was by Mr H. Jones, 'illustrating the various scenes with his fine lantern slides', elaborated a subtly Tory message.[38] Once the Boer War got underway, the League moved decisively behind the Government's line: lectures on themes such as 'Our Army' became common, and motions of support for Lord Salisbury's policy from Conservative women were often passed.[39] And, of course, the patriotic feelings of the audience were stirred by the convention of singing 'God Save the Queen', often supplemented in Wales by a chorus of 'Hen Wlad Fy Nhadau' ('Land of my Fathers'), at the end of every meeting.

Beyond the enchanted world of the Primrose League Habitations lay other organizations capable of reaching the grass-roots. The constituency associations, whose primary task was to attend to the electoral register, often sponsored events. In March 1899, for example, Barry Conservatives were regaled with a long speech by James Jeffrey, illuminated with sixty limelight views:

> in which he described the imbecility of the Gladstonian policy of 1882–85 with regard to the Soudan, eventuating in the martyr death of the beloved and brave General Gordon, and the sacrifice of 70,000 valuable lives, and the brilliant campaign, instigated by Lord Salisbury, of General Lord Kitchener and his splendid British and Egyptian armies, culminating in the siege and fall of Khartoum, and the establishment of British prestige and supremacy in that part of the world.[40]

Here, all the imperial buttons were firmly pressed.

More often, local entertainment seems to have been provided by the various clubs organized for working men. Establishing precisely how many clubs there were is not straightforward, but the 1880s saw rapid growth and most towns probably possessed some such body by 1900. The clubs appear to have been a provocative presence to Liberals – one Glamorgan Alderman denounced them as dens of 'infamy' and 'boozing'[41] – and the entertainment on offer certainly seems to have been of a slightly less refined kind than that found in the Primrose League. The entertainment at Barry Docks at a meeting in March 1899 was typical: a tripe supper, a recital of the latest music-hall songs on the gramophone, a long speech by a local Conservative on the comparative merits of the British, Spanish and French as empire-builders (an exercise from which the British emerged very well!), and a rendition of 'God Save the Queen' to close proceedings.[42] Another staple of the workingmen's club scene was the smoking concert – or 'smoker' – where, as ever, entertainment was spliced with political speechifying. Other clubs held debates on the issues of the day. Conservative working men in Tredegar, for example, debated the respective merits of 'free' and 'fair' trade in the spring of 1899;[43] by the end of the year, the South African War was the all-consuming topic and the subject of a lively debate among the Conservative working men of Bangor.[44] The clubs certainly got the Conservative message across in an admirably direct manner.

Finally, it is important to note a third agency capable of promulgating the Conservative message: the press. The leading Conservative title was a daily, the *Western Mail*. Founded in 1869 with considerable support from the Bute family, it maintained an intimate relationship with Cardiff Conservatism that extended in the 1890s to its sharing the same building as the local constituency association.[45] Several other titles also promoted Conservative principles, notably the Swansea-based *South Wales Daily Post*, and two time-honoured weeklies, the *North Wales Chronicle* and the *Carmarthen Journal*. The editors of all four titles were heavily involved in local politics and fervently pro-Empire. Lascelles Carr was responsible for what Kenneth O. Morgan has described as the 'patriotic hysteria' emanating from the *Western Mail*; the editor of the *North Wales Chronicle*, David Williams, was heavily involved in Bangor Conservative politics; and David Davies, editor of the *South Wales Daily Post*, laid all his cards on the table when he concluded a long speech on the strength of the British race with the zealous declaration: 'My faith in the Rhodes cult is complete.'[46]

In the late nineteenth century, a new trend became visible in the management of the political press in Wales. For all the partisanship displayed by newspaper editors earlier in the century, active politicians had tended to keep their distance from minute involvement with the press. Faced with the need to get their message across to the vastly increased electorate created by the Third Reform Act (1885), however, parties increasingly bought into titles that promoted their principles.[47] By the 1890s, for example, the North Wales Chronicle Company had taken over the running of this bastion of north Walian Conservatism: it included among its shareholders 'some of the most senior Conservative politicians, industrialists and landowners' of the region, including Sir Hugh Ellis-Nanney, George William Duff Assheton-Smith and Lord Penrhyn.[48] Many candidates acquired their own newspapers. When he started his campaign in Monmouth Boroughs, Rutherfoord Harris simply bought the *South Wales Telegraph*.[49] Similarly, James Lawrence, who contested Cardiff for the Conservatives in 1900, 'the very day he announced his candidature . . . set to work to buy materials, plant and machinery for starting an independent Conservative newspaper of his own'. It was only when he was assured that the *Western Mail* would support 'the freely chosen candidate' of the party in the town that he 'desisted from his intention'.[50] Such activity was not confined to Conservatives, of course. Harris's opponent in the Monmouth Boroughs, Albert Spicer, owned shares worth £400 in the Liberal *South Wales Argus*.[51] However, it is an indication of how important the press was considered to be to the Conservatives that, in 1900, Lascelles Carr felt obliged to deny the damaging accusation made by the Liberal MP, D. A. Thomas, that 'he carried Conservative candidates about in his pockets', and to reassert in the strongest terms that Lawrence was not a *Western Mail* candidate.[52]

In a variety of ways, therefore, the Conservative party was able to commune with its grass-roots supporters, and to celebrate with them a belief that Britain's best interests lay in a promotion of the Crown, the Constitution and, above all, the Empire. It is easy to see how the growing tension between the British government and the Boers persuaded Conservatives of all ranks that a military solution was the only possible outcome. It is to the origins of this conflict and its reception by Conservatives in the Principality that attention now turns.

Matthew Cragoe

THE BOER WAR AND THE GENERAL ELECTION OF 1900

The origins of the second Boer War lay partly in the muddy resolution of the first. The Convention of Pretoria (1881), while effectively conceding self-government to the Boers, retained the Crown's claim to suzerainty over the Transvaal. It was an ambivalent solution to a distant imperial problem, and one that might have remained of minor significance, had not gold been discovered in the region soon afterwards. Gold changed the dynamics of the situation in two ways. First, it promised to make the Transvaal the richest, and thus the most powerful, presence in the region, a position hitherto occupied by the British Cape Colony. The strategic importance of the Cape as the guarantor of its sea route to India ensured that Britain would resist any threat to its position.[53] Second, it attracted a vast influx of migrant workers to the Transvaal, many of them British. These 'Uitlanders', however, were not granted rights of citizenship in their adopted home, notably the right to vote, the Boers fearing that this would lead to their majority in parliament being swamped. As tension in the region grew, the grievances of the Uitlanders became one of the key battlegrounds between the Transvaal and British governments.

In 1895, pro-British elements in Cape Colony, led by Cecil Rhodes, sought to exploit discontent among the Uitlander community by fomenting a rebellion and promising armed support. The expected insurrection failed to materialize, and the abortive 'Jameson Raid' achieved nothing beyond a diplomatic imbroglio. The issues surrounding the status of the Uitlanders, however, did not go away, and by 1897, the British High Commissioner and Governor of Cape Colony, Alfred Milner, had come to adopt a very aggressive policy in relation to the question. A series of negotiations between the British and the Transvaal government in the summer of 1899 failed to reach a satisfactory conclusion, and war broke out when President Kruger sent the British an ultimatum demanding they withdraw their troops from the borders of the Transvaal.

In its early stages, the war went disastrously for the British. Their forces were quickly surrounded and besieged in a series of key positions – notably Kimberley, Mafeking and Ladysmith. It was only when a far larger force, under the command of Lord Roberts, arrived early in 1900 that the tide began to turn in Britain's favour. The besieged towns were relieved, and Pretoria taken in the second week of June 1900. It was against this backdrop that Lord Salisbury's government decided to hold a general election. It turned out to be an inspired piece of timing, for as soon as the Tories had reaped their electoral harvest, it became clear that the war was far from won. The Boer Commando kept Roberts's forces occupied for another two expensive and morale-sapping years on the veld, while the British also became entangled in controversial policies, such as the incarceration of civilians in concentration camps, as they sought to isolate their enemy. Only in 1902, with the Peace of Vereeniging, was the whole sorry affair brought to a conclusion.

There were mixed opinions within Wales as to how desirable or justifiable the conflict might be. On one side was a minority adamantly opposed to the war from the start. One notable centre of anti-war sentiment was Caernarfonshire, where the county's two MPs, Bryn Roberts and David Lloyd George, opposed the conflict. For pro-Boers like Roberts, the 'civil grievances' of the Uitlanders could not 'compare for one moment with the educational and religious disabilities of the Welsh people'.[54] Lloyd George, meanwhile, told electors during the by-election at Carmarthen in December 1899 that he hated the conflict 'because he knew of nothing that arrested progress like war', and he solemnly appealed to Liberals who were 'fascinated with these fireworks' to reflect that they were simply 'cheering a display that was arresting the cause of their country and their religion'.[55] They found support not only in the dissenting press – Nonconformists were often hostile to the war[56] – but from the largest English-language newspaper in north Wales, the *Carnarvon and Denbigh Herald*. The *Herald* resolutely campaigned for the rights of small nations against imperial power-plays, wherever they occurred, condemning the actions of Russia in Finland, America in the Philippines, France in Madagascar, as well as those of the British in South Africa.[57] Similarly, the paper dismissed the Bishop of Bangor's support for the war, saying that he was 'a captain of a fire-brigade turned incendiary', and concluding that the picture of 'a Christian bishop upholding war' was an offensive one.[58]

On the other side stood the Conservatives. Their outlook could be summarized in the famous lines of 'By Jingo' by George W. Hunt (1877):

We don't want to fight, but by jingo if we do,
We've got the ships, we've got the men, we've got the money too.[59]

Though penned twenty years earlier, this accurately reflected the spirit which inspired the series of linked propositions on which the Tories based their resort to arms in the autumn of 1899. First, they sought to underline the justice of their position, notably with regards to the treatment of the Uitlanders.[60] The editor of the *Carmarthen Journal* expressed well the prevailing mood when he suggested that, 'The Boer wants supremacy in the Transvaal; the Briton simply wants equality'.[61] Next, it was important to emphasize that it was the Boers, in their quest for supremacy, who were spoiling for the fight, as J. Davies Allen of the Imperial South African Association assured the *South Wales Telegraph*, in an exclusive interview, was indeed the case.[62] It was an argument that complemented a grander conspiracy theory, outlined by Rutherfoord Harris in January 1900, in which the war emerged as 'a deliberate and long matured scheme, engineered from Pretoria for the overthrow of British supremacy throughout South Africa'.[63] Thus, it could be concluded that, in the words of the Hon. George Kenyon, candidate at the Denbigh Boroughs by-election of 1899, 'the present war was a just one because it was absolutely necessary. It was necessary if this country was to maintain the proud position she had already taken up as a leader of civilisation throughout the civilised world.'[64]

Judging the mood of the Welsh public, caught between these two well-defined positions, is difficult.[65] Nevertheless, considerable evidence exists to suggest that the anti-war line was held by only a minority and that, however unpopular the conflict was ultimately to become, opinion generally rallied in support of British arms in the first instance. Individuals suspected of being hostile to the war, for example, were sometimes attacked by the mob, while the public meetings of those opposed to the conflict were regularly disrupted.[66] During one such gathering in Wrexham's Public Hall, at which Bryn Roberts appeared on the platform, a report in the *North Wales Chronicle* recorded that the speakers were 'frequently interrupted by the singing of the national anthem, "Rule Britannia", cheers for the Queen and Mr Chamberlain, and cries of "You are a traitor" and "Sit down, Kruger" '. Further confusion was added to the scene when a prominent local Liberal, Wynne Evans, coroner for East Denbighshire, then announced that he could not support the anti-war resolution, and asked all those Liberals present who agreed with him to abstain from voting. The pro-war lobby, seeing its chance, then moved a counter-resolution approving the conduct of the government, and the meeting ended amidst scenes of the most terrible confusion.[67] The anti-war party fared equally badly in the Temperance Hall at Newport, where the principal speaker, Mr Statham of the *London Daily Chronicle*, was frequently hissed and interrupted, and the pro-war party managed to carry a resolution asserting that South Africa could not be held unless the whole of the hinterland was subjected to English rule. 'If the Empire was to remain whole and to be handed down to our posterity', argued the chief proponent of the pro-war line, 'we had to see that the outposts of the Empire were retained intact (applause)'.[68] The only way the anti-war party was able to guarantee order was to restrict entry to carefully selected ticket holders, as happened at Caernarfon when John Morley came to speak at the Guildhall.[69]

The pro-war lobby was more successful at holding its public meetings unmolested, and used its advantage to good effect. In Newport, for example, a series of speakers gave lectures during the war in an attempt to rally support for the cause. Lieutenant-Colonel T. O. Drake, JP, from Rhodesia, visited the town in July 1899, and he was followed by three men from Johannesburg: T. R. Dodd, Secretary of the South African League; Mr Strong, an Uitlander, who made a special address to the working men of Newport; and the Reverend J. Harries.[70] In addition, considerable interest was aroused in the summer of 1900 when a soldier from Newport, T. P. Mathias, who had been present at the relief of Mafeking, delivered a public lecture on his adventures.[71] In similar vein, letters from soldiers at the front, recounting their experiences, formed a staple of newspaper coverage throughout the war.[72] Newsreels formed another source of public information, containing as they did the latest pictures from South Africa; in Newport, they were screened at the local music hall, the aptly named New Empire.[73]

The amount of information in circulation about the war was an important element in the development of public interest in the war. This was undoubtedly fostered by movements like the campaign to collect funds to relieve the widows and orphans of the soldiers killed in the conflict, a remarkably bi-partisan movement.[74] There is evidence, however, that many people, whatever they may have felt about the justice of the war (and that is unknowable) were at least enthused by the drama of the conflict. One particularly striking element is the scale of crowd involvement at various stages of the campaign. In areas which could claim a direct military involvement with the war, for example, public enthusiasm was marked. When 300 Wrexham reservists marched off to join the Royal Welsh Fusiliers in October 1899, one local reporter recorded that 'the town was gay with bunting, and the streets were lined with enthusiastic supporters, who lustily cheered the departing soldiers'. Their reception at the station, he continued, 'was the crowning event of all':

> many thousands had assembled to give the men a rousing send-off. Both platforms were packed, whilst every available open space along the line and outside the station was packed with people eager to bid the Royal Welsh good-bye. . . . Before the departure of the special train 'God Save the Queen' was sung.[75]

Similar scenes were witnessed at Monmouth: between 20,000 and 30,000 people turned out to witness the departure of the Fourth Mountain Battery of the Royal Artillery in November 1899.[76]

Even more striking than these events, however, was the collective hysteria – and there is no other word for it – that greeted news of the British victories in South Africa. The Tories, long the champions of war, had greeted the bad news of the winter months with as much stoicism as they could muster, contending that the 'defeats' were in reality a series of 'drawn' encounters.[77] Nevertheless, they recognized that the stakes had been raised immeasurably higher by the Boers' successful defiance of British arms: as Rutherfoord Harris remarked, 'nothing less is now at stake than the very existence of the British Empire'.[78]

Doubtless, the public at large shared some of this anxiety. At all events, large public celebrations followed the relief of Kimberley and Ladysmith,[79] but the biggest was that precipitated by news of the relief of Mafeking in May 1900.[80] According to the *South Wales Telegraph*, the news arrived in Newport at 9.40 p.m., and within minutes had communicated itself around the town. The sky was lit by fireworks and every instrument capable of making a noise was pressed into service, factory hooters, trains with the steam up, even the fog signals on the railway lines: 'The noise was simply deafening', said the *Telegraph*'s man on the spot. The most memorable feature of the evening, however, was the sheer number of people who joined in: 'Practically the whole of the adult, and a considerable portion of the juvenile population turned out and celebrated the joyous news until about 2 o'clock in the morning, and even at that hour there were still scattered parties making their way homeward cheering and singing.' It was a scene repeated in towns and cities the length and breadth of Britain on what universally became known as 'Mafeking night', and in Newport, at least, it clearly embraced a much larger proportion of the population than simply the lower middle-class.

Whatever may be said about the general feelings of the public for Empire at large, therefore, there is little doubt that, in the spring and early summer of 1900, the South African War was the all-consuming topic. It was against this backdrop that the government called a general election, and it is to the conduct of the campaign in Wales that attention now turns.

THE CONSERVATIVE PARTY AND THE GENERAL ELECTION OF 1900 IN WALES

Although, at the general election of 1900, the Conservative government was swept back to power with its majority essentially intact, the party suffered a series of defeats in Wales. The seven MPs with which it began the campaign dwindled to four, and the pro-Tory swing registered by the electorate in England and Scotland failed to materialize: in Wales, it was the Liberals who increased their share of the votes, by some 2.2 per cent.[81] Hostility to the war doubtless played a role in the more rural constituencies of Wales;[82] however, in the industrial belt the war commanded a remarkable consensus, and some other explanation must be found to account for the Conservative defeats. In this section, the battles fought in Monmouth Boroughs, where the Tories were victorious, and Cardiff, where they were not, will be examined.[83]

The 1900 election campaign in the Monmouth Boroughs may be said to have started some two years earlier, when Dr Rutherfoord Harris was introduced to the constituency and declared his candidacy. For the next two years he cultivated it assiduously, even taking up residence at Llangibby Castle near Usk. Harris, though born and educated in Britain, had lived in South Africa since the early 1880s, where he had become private secretary to Cecil Rhodes and a member of the Cape Parliament.[84] He played strongly on this connection throughout his wooing of the Boroughs, and underlined his central message, that the Empire offered great opportunities to the inhabitants of an industrial region like this, by securing for businesses in the constituency an order for the manufacture and shipping of 25,000 tons of steel rails. The advent of war was an entirely happy development for Harris, and his argument that the outcome of the conflict was vital to Britain's commercial interests undoubtedly gained credibility from the large order his connections had secured. In Cardiff, the Conservatives took the interesting step of choosing Alderman James Lawrence of London instead of their sitting MP, John Maclean, who had not been as supportive of the war as his constituents would have wished. Lawrence was a highly successful entrepreneur with wide-ranging business interests, whose devotion to the imperial cause matched that of the Cardiff constituency association.

The Conservatives' electoral campaign revolved around the conjoined issues of the war, the Empire and patriotism. For Rutherfoord Harris, the issue was simple: voters were being asked to give 'a vote for or against the Empire';[85] Lawrence, likewise, described the war as 'the master issue of the election'.[86] To emphasize the point, Harris went even further, dismissing as parochial and irrelevant the traditional concerns of the Welsh Liberals. The issues of the general election, he said:

> were not whether this or that question of domestic reform should take place: it was not a question of Board v. Voluntary Schools, of Church v. Chapel, or Local Veto v. Sunday Closing. The question was the existence of the country – whether she would continue to hold the chief place amongst the equals, the other Great Powers of Europe (cheers).[87]

The Liberals, by contrast, were constantly portrayed as betraying their country. As Harris, again, put it to a crowded meeting at the Tredegar Hall in Newport:

> Are you going to give a vote which will give joy to the heart of every Boer, or are you going to give a vote which will give joy to the loyal subjects of the Queen in South Africa, the friends of our flag?[88]

The unattributed voice which replied 'For England, and for you' captured perfectly the Conservatives' elision of party and nation at this election.

A similar approach was taken by the various external speakers who visited the region to plead the Conservative cause during the campaign – a clear indication of the critical importance attached to the issue by Conservative Central Office. Various speakers visited the constituencies covered in this chapter, including representatives of provincial Conservatism, such as Isaac Lyons of Newcastle, Mr Prescott of Bristol, J. H. Bottomley of Lancaster and S. W. Deacon from Manchester,[89] some of whom, like Bottomley, could speak directly to the working man. There were also those whose glamour stemmed from their role in central government: Lord George Hamilton, Secretary of State for India, and George Wyndham, Under-Secretary of State for War, both visited the industrial areas of south Wales during the campaign.[90] In all cases, however, the burden of their message was the same: as Lawrence put it at the end of a talk by F. C. Vernon Harcourt entitled 'Truth about the Transvaal', in which 'original scenes and incidents of the war were illustrated by limelight': 'What they had to vote for on October 10th was summed up in the phrase "The Queen or Kruger?" '[91]

As this implies, the Conservatives claimed the mantle of patriotism for their own side in this election. The sincerity of any Liberal candidate's profession of support for the Empire was immediately called into question. Lawrence, in a meeting at Cardiff, was typical when he decried the 'death-bed conversions' to the imperial cause of Liberal candidates who had stoutly opposed the war before the election, and throughout the contest crowds happily hooted and whistled the names of leading Liberal opponents of the war, such as Henry Labouchere.[92] The Conservative newspapers naturally stoked the flames, and in a Welsh context the *Western Mail* was predictably to the fore. Of particular interest were the daily cartoons drawn by Joseph Morewood Staniforth, who has been described by Peter Lord as 'the most important visual commentator on Welsh affairs ever to work in the country'.[93] The campaigns in both Cardiff and the Monmouth Boroughs were extensively covered, and in both cases, Staniforth was at pains to point out who the real champions of imperialism were. In a cartoon entitled 'A Poor Copyist', for example, Staniforth portrayed Lawrence and his opponent, Sir Edward Reed, as two artists, each at his respective easel. The Conservative has produced a fine picture of Britannia, whereas his opponent has managed only a spindly, stick-like figure. The cartoonist has Reed saying: 'Hang it all: I wish I could get mine to look like his!'[94] Similarly, in a reference to the contest in Monmouth Boroughs, Staniforth has a picture in which a large, languid lion bearing the moustachioed face of Dr Rutherfoord Harris gazes over his shoulder at a braying ass, over which is crudely draped a lion-skin bearing the word 'IMPERIALISM'. The caption reads: 'The Genuine

Lion: "Surely, nobody will be silly enough to think him one of my race".' The link between the British Lion and the 'imperial race' is nicely made here, and annexed to the Conservative party.[95] The Conservative press went all out to ensure that whatever advantage was to be gained from the imperial theme came the Tories' way.

How effective such propaganda was is difficult to ascertain; however, one noteworthy feature of the 1900 election was the sheer size of the public demonstrations that accompanied the campaign. As during the spring of that year, when tens of thousands took to the streets to celebrate events like the relief of Mafeking, so the comings and goings of the leading figures on the Conservative side in both Cardiff and Newport were attended by huge displays of public interest. At one meeting in Newport for Rutherfoord Harris, held on a Wednesday evening, a crowd of some 20,000 gathered to watch him travel from the railway station to the Tredegar Hall: 'Mountain battery night was great; Pretoria was great; Mafeking was great; but Wednesday night stands in a category of its own, in a class apart', noted one reporter, adding: 'All down the High Street the scene was the same, roaring crowds, flashing fireworks, waving flags, the street lined with people ten or a dozen deep.'[96] When he eventually won the election, Harris's victory procession was estimated to have been one and a half miles long![97] However, it was not only in Newport that the public came out on to the streets. Lawrence was greeted by several very large demonstrations in Cardiff, and the arrival of George Wyndham produced unprecedented scenes in the town, the drama of the scene heightened by its taking place after nightfall.[98] There was apparently a massive procession, with bands playing patriotic airs; crowds 'yards deep' allowing the carriages only just enough room to pass; the carriages themselves bearing bowls of coloured fire, to add to the hundreds of torches being carried by people in the procession itself; and the windows of all the buildings crowded with people. Even allowing for the poetic licence of a partisan reporter, it is clear that there was not in either Cardiff or Newport that 'apathy' described by Richard Price. The Conservative campaign, premised, as Paul Readman has rightly argued, on the war and patriotism, was very effective in engaging the contemporary electorate.

That said, it is clear that the war on its own was not enough to guarantee the Tories success. The great crowds notwithstanding, the Tories did not take both seats. Although Rutherfoord Harris won his contest against Albert Spicer comfortably, securing a majority of 688, James Lawrence was thrashed by Sir Edward Reed in Cardiff. Kenneth O. Morgan, in accounting for the result of the 1900 general election in Wales, has pointed out that the restoration of old Liberal values across the country was supplemented in the southern industrial belt by the emergence of working-class issues. It appears that these were decisive in Cardiff because on imperial matters the two parties were – whatever the Conservatives liked to claim – at one over the importance of the Empire and the war. As Morgan goes on to say, 'to be identified with a "pro-Boer" position in the summer of 1900' could be 'political suicide' for anyone aspiring to a Liberal candidature.[99] Highly respected local men were turned down by their Liberal Associations in both Cardiff and Swansea because their opinions were known to be hostile to the war, and thus unacceptable to the electorate. Indeed, the Cardiff Liberals selected Sir Edward Reed, described by Morgan as 'the most bloodthirsty of imperialists', precisely because he could counter the Tories' imperial appeal.[100]

With honours even on the score of imperialism, it was supplementary issues that made the difference, and in Lawrence's case it is quite clear that his campaign got badly sidetracked on precisely the theme highlighted by Morgan: the emergence of working-class issues. His initial approach to the working men of Cardiff was very confident. He followed the traditional practice of arranging meetings during the lunch hour to allow working men the opportunity of hearing his views, and supplemented the standard Tory line that the Empire brought trade and prosperity to the country with two examples of his own enlightened approach to industrial relations. During the recent strike of engineers in Lancashire, he claimed, his were the only workers not to down tools, because they were well paid and well treated; similarly, when he took over a printing works in London his first move, in conjunction with Mr Drummond, now a labour representative on the Board of Trade, was to create a pay scale based around the eight-hour day.[101] At another meeting, in Cathays ward, attended by several hundred railway-men, he revealed that he had spent a great deal of money to set up the *Railway Herald*, a paper devoted to the interests of those who worked in the industry. He went on to say that he had received a letter from Sir Fortescue Flannery, President of the Railway Clerks' Association, thanking him for his efforts on their behalf. He concluded by expressing a belief that workmen should have 'proper hours and proper payment', which predictably elicited 'cheers' from those who had gathered to hear him.[102]

Yet for all his confidence, and despite the fact that, as Martin Daunton has made clear, the working class in Cardiff was too fragmented to enjoy any concerted political influence at this stage, Lawrence became subject to a running attack concerning the use of new linotype machines in his London printing works.[103] The first challenge came as a heckle from the floor during an evening meeting at the Stacey Hall: 'ask the machine men', cried a voice. Lawrence rounded on his assailant and told him that although the new linotype machines he had imported from America had resulted in an initial decline in the demand for labour, the fact that there were now fewer men dependent on their union for relief than ever before proved this had been a short-term effect.

> I have introduced a new industry to England, an industry that employed thousands of men in a way that they could not have been employed before. The reading public receive 70 per cent more for their money than they did before and the shareholders have been getting good dividends. No man has been robbed by it, no man has been harmed by it, everyone connected with it has been benefited.

This response, which was punctuated with 'Loud Cheers', ought perhaps to have settled the issue, but it did not. The question continued to be agitated at subsequent meetings, even popping up during a gathering at one of the Conservative Clubs four days before the poll.[104] Lawrence's campaign had undeniably been tainted.

In the immediate aftermath of the defeat, Cardiff Tories proffered a variety of different reasons for their reverse. Councillor Yorath claimed that the 'Nonconformist conscience' had been the cause, while the *Western Mail* admitted that the 'superior organisation and harder canvassing' of their Radical opponents had played a crucial role. Alderman James Lawrence, however, addressing a meeting at the Conservative Club, pointed the finger in another direction. In his eyes it was the lies spread about him by Reed's party, notably over the issue of the linotype machines, that had undermined his campaign.[105]

Interestingly, Rutherfoord Harris seems to have experienced no such problems in the Monmouth Boroughs. Doubtless the *South Wales Telegraph* was correct in its surmise that Harris's well-placed pre-election 'bribe', the order for 25,000 tons of steel rails, had its effect in convincing the working men of ' "the doctor's" undoubted capacity for bringing trade to the port'.[106] However, the Conservative campaign was also marked by a clever handling of issues relating to working men as they arose: in effect, Harris and his supporters seem to have adopted a simple policy of telling the working men what they wanted to hear. Sometimes this was done directly, as when Harris met a deputation of members from the Quay Workers' Society and assured them he was favourable to the idea of the Society's members being allowed to work in the government dockyards, that he opposed the importation of 'coolie' labour to South Africa, and that he favoured an extension of the Compensation Act to sailors and dockers.[107] At other times, prominent supporters did the job for him. During a large Unionist demonstration at Llangibby Castle, which illness prevented Harris attending, Lascelles Carr, editor of the *Western Mail*, claimed that the Conservative candidate had authorized him to say he fully approved of a policy of conciliation to end the ongoing Taff Vale Railway strike; moreover, that he, Harris, would, if returned to parliament, support any measure which would refer such disputes to a tribunal, and thus avoid the dreadful stoppages of labour they had recently witnessed.[108] Carr then did his friend an enormous service by going on to say that if he, Carr, were a working man and felt that one of his fellow workmen had been victimized, he would strike, too. Since the railways had been given a monopoly by government, he continued, they should behave better to their employees than other industries. And he ended by stating that he was in favour of trade unions and believed that men should be allowed to join whichever union they chose and to elect their own officials. Without tying Harris's hands in any way, Carr had associated him with the cause of the working man.

The Conservative strategy of appealing to the working man was complemented by a policy of demonizing Albert Spicer. In a series of vicious attacks the Conservatives accused him of closing down a paper-making factory in Walthamstow and taking the business instead to Italy, where he paid his workers just 9d. a day.[109] Spicer later claimed that this false story had been a significant factor in his defeat, and included it in the petition he presented against Harris's return. In Cardiff, Lawrence did not attempt to overturn the result, despite his repeated claims that the opposition had continued to circulate falsehoods concerning the linotype machines, even after he had corrected them in public. Instead, he retreated somewhat bitterly to London.

It is an ironic coda to the story of the 1900 election in these two boroughs that it was Lawrence, and not Harris, who eventually took a seat in parliament. In April 1901, Harris's election was overturned when it was shown that his agent had illegally employed a voter to work on the campaign, paying him 5s. a day.[110] With Harris debarred from politics for seven years as a consequence, it was to Lawrence that the Conservative Association in Monmouth Boroughs turned at the subsequent by-election. On 7 May 1901, he was returned to parliament with a majority of 343.[111]

CONCLUSION

This investigation of the 1900 election in south Wales demonstrates clearly the extent to which the Conservative party prioritized the war as a campaign issue. All Tory candidates led with it in their addresses, and in the two boroughs studied, there was scarcely a meeting at which the war and the future of South Africa was not the main element. Other issues were naturally discussed: at one gigantic meeting in Newport, Rutherford Harris spoke briefly about Fair Trade, penny postage in the colonies, the need to keep religion in education, the desirability of pensions for the aged and infirm poor, and the beneficial impact of various pieces of Tory legislation, including the Workmen's Compensation Act and the Prison-Made Goods Act. However, as he said after running through this extensive list, all were secondary to the great issue of the day, the South African War.[112]

The working classes, to the extent that they had a separate and identifiable political identity at this election, seem to have responded enthusiastically to the imperial message. Certainly, none of the Liberal candidates in this industrial corner of Wales felt that a 'Little Englander' position would aid them. As a consequence, support for the war was a 'given' in this campaign, a conclusion which entirely bears out Paul Readman's criticism of Richard Price.

Yet, precisely because the war was so ubiquitous, the lines between the candidates had to be drawn elsewhere. In his analysis of the 1900 contest in Wales, Kenneth O. Morgan denies that the election was 'monopolized by a tide of anti-war feeling', and suggests instead that the Liberal victories reflected the party's championship of the 'old radical causes' – disestablishment, education, temperance, land reform – and 'a new emphasis on labour questions' in southern constituencies.[113] The evidence of the two contests reviewed in this chapter strongly confirms this analysis. Lawrence's campaign set out to establish the London Alderman as a progressive employer and a friend of the working man; his opponents were able to undermine this happy picture by suggesting that his true character was revealed in his importation of linotype machines from the United States, which threw men out of work. In Monmouth Boroughs, the same tactics were employed – but by the Conservatives. Harris's team, basking in the goodwill generated by the massive order for steel rails placed in the constituency through their candidate's good offices, launched a vituperative attack against the incumbent MP, Albert Spicer, which he, at least, felt seriously compromised his chances. The inescapable conclusion must be that if there was a role for the 'working class' in this election, it was not their 'apathy' that settled the issue, as Price has suggested, but their active engagement with the detailed nuances of the campaign unfolding before them.

NOTES

[1] A phrase used by Lieutenant R. Bellis, formerly of Naval Volunteers: *North Wales Chronicle* (hereafter *NWC*), 18 Nov. 1899.

[2] Quoted in A. N. Porter, *The Origins of the South African War: Joseph Chamberlain and the Diplomacy of Imperialism, 1895–99* (Manchester, 1980), p. 25.

3. E. H. H. Green, *The Crisis of Conservatism: The Politics, Economics and Ideology of the British Conservative Party, 1880–1914* (London, 1995), p. 74.

4. Richard Price, *An Imperial War and the British Working Class* (London, 1972), pp. 98, 105.

5. Price, *Imperial War*, p. 130; see R. Blake, *The Conservative Party from Peel to Churchill* (London, 1970), p. 163, for a similar view.

6. John M. Mackenzie, *Propaganda and Empire: The Manipulation of British Public Opinion, 1880–1960* (Manchester, 1984); Martin Pugh, *The Tories and the People* (Oxford, 1985), pp. 87–8; Richard Shannon, *The Age of Salisbury, 1881–1902* (London, 1996), pp. 511–14.

7. Paul Readman, 'The Conservative Party, patriotism and British politics: the case of the general election of 1900', *Journal of British Studies*, 40 (2001), 112–16.

8. Ibid., 128–31.

9. Ibid., 140.

10. Very little has been written on the Conservative Party in Wales after the Third Reform Act, but see Felix Aubel, 'The Conservatives in Wales, 1880–1935', in Martin Francis and Ina Zweiniger-Bargielowska (eds), *The Conservatives and British Society, 1880–1990* (Cardiff, 1996).

11. Pugh, *Tories and the People*, p. 70.

12. Ibid., pp. 70–92; Green, *Crisis of Conservatism*, p. 59; Hugh Cunningham, 'The language of patriotism, 1750–1914', in Raphael Samuel (ed.), *Patriotism: The Making and Unmaking of British National Identity*, vol. I, *History and Politics* (London, 1989); Richard Williams, *The Contentious Crown: Public Discussion of the British Monarchy in the Reign of Queen Victoria* (Aldershot, 1997), pp. 174–9; Matthew Cragoe, *Culture, Politics and National Identity in Wales, 1832–86* (Oxford, 2004), pp. 26–31.

13. *South Wales Telegraph* (hereafter *SWT*), 27 Jan. 1899.

14. *Barry Dock News* (hereafter *BDN*), 31 Mar. 1899.

15. Lobengula's ferocity could be breathtaking – see the speech of J. Davis-Allen, *SWT*, 3 Mar. 1899, for the actions of this 'fat, filthy savage'. However, equally typical of the ways Tories presented him to domestic audiences was Harris's account of his first meeting with the Matabele king: 'The dread monarch was propitiated . . . by a present of a pot of strawberry jam and a spoon that looked like silver but wasn't', a comment rewarded with the 'loud laughter' it was surely intended to elicit. *South Wales Weekly Post* (hereafter *SWWP*), 20 May 1899; and see *SWT*, 27 Jan. 1899.

16. *SWWP*, 20 May 1899, editorial.

17. Green, *Crisis of Conservatism*, p. 67.

18. *SWT*, 3 Feb. 1899. This idea was endlessly repeated: *Carmarthen Journal* (hereafter *CJ*), 31 Mar. 1899.

19. Catherine Hall, *Civilising Subjects: Metropole and Colony in the English Imagination, 1830–1867* (London, 2002), pp. 267–89.

20. Anne Summers, 'Militarism in Britain before the Great War', *History Workshop Journal*, 2 (1976), 105; Pugh, *Tories and the People*, p. 92.

21. Green, *Crisis of Conservatism*, p. 66. Many had also been employed in the colonial service; Alex Windscheffel, ' "In darkest Lambeth": Henry Morton Stanley and the imperial politics of London Unionism', in Matthew Cragoe and Anthony Taylor (eds), *London Politics, 1760–1914* (London, 2005).

22 *NWC*, 24 June 1900; *SWT*, 17 Oct. 1900.

23 *MCT*, 26 Jan. 1895.

24 *BDN*, 10 Nov. 1899.

25 *WM*, 20 May 1885.

26 Paul Hayes, *Modern British Foreign Policy: The Twentieth Century, 1880–1939* (London, 1978), p. 19; Andrew Roberts, *Salisbury: Victorian Titan* (London, 1999), p. 777.

27 Cited in Green, *Crisis of Conservatism*, p. 61.

28 *BDN*, 13 Nov. 1899; *NWC*, 29 July 1899.

29 *CJ*, 31 Mar. 1899.

30 *NWC*, 29 July 1899; *SWWP*, 20 May 1899; *SWT*, 27 Jan. 1899.

31 *SWT*, 26 Oct. 1900; Pugh, *Tories and the People*, p. 92.

32 *NWC*, 11 Sept. 1897.

33 These figures are taken from Pugh, *Tories and the People*, pp. 249–51. Rhondda did have a rather half-hearted Conservative Association; Chris Williams, *Democratic Rhondda: Politics and Society, 1885–1951* (Cardiff, 1996), pp. 48–9. For more detail on the Primrose League in Wales, see Cragoe, *Culture, Politics and National Identity*, pp. 106–10.

34 *WM*, 4 May 1886.

35 *CJ*, 25 June 1886.

36 *NWC*, 11 Nov. 1899, for a Denbighshire Primrose League entertainment.

37 Pugh, *Tories and the People*, p. 92.

38 *NWC*, 6 May 1899.

39 *CDH*, 10 Nov. 1899; *NWC*, 18 Nov. 1899.

40 *BDN*, 31 Mar. 1899.

41 Ibid., 17 Mar. 1899.

42 Ibid., 17 Mar. 1899; see also ibid., 27 Jan. 1899; *NWC*, 25 Feb. 1899; *MCT*, 19 Jan. 1895.

43 *SWT*, 10 Mar. 1899.

44 *NWC*, 28 Oct. 1899.

45 Aled Gruffydd Jones, *Press, Politics and Society: A History of Journalism in Wales* (Cardiff, 1993), pp. 128–9; Cragoe, *Culture, Politics and National Identity*, p. 238, for the consequences of this.

46 *SWWP*, 20 May 1899.

47 Michael Dawson, 'Money and the real impact of the Fourth Reform Act', *Historical Journal*, 35 (1992), 376, suggests that the straitened circumstances of candidates after the Great War ended this practice.

48 Jones, *Press, Politics and Society*, p. 126.

49 *Monmouthshire Beacon* (hereafter *MB*), 5 Apr. 1901.

50 *WM*, 28 Sept. 1900; *WM*, 9 Oct. 1900.

51 *MB*, 5 Apr. 1901; Jones, *Press, Politics and Society*, pp. 134–6.

52 *WM*, 22 Sept. 1900.

53 *NWC*, 2 Sept. 1899.

54 Ibid., 14 Oct. 1899; the same line was adopted by *CDH*, 6 Oct. 1899.

55 *CDH*, 1 Dec. 1899.

56 Ibid., 6 Oct. 1899; *WM*, 27 Sept. 1900.

57 *CDH*, 29 Sept. 1900.

58 Ibid., 17 Nov. 1899; *NWC*, 25 Nov. 1899.

[59] Cited in Penny Summerfield, 'Patriotism and Empire: music-hall entertainment 1870–1914', in John M. Mackenzie (ed.), *Imperialism and Popular Culture* (Manchester, 1992), p. 25.

[60] *SWT*, 14 July, 11, 29 Sept. 1899; *BDN*, 22 Sept., 10 Nov. 1899; *SWWP*, 2 Sept. 1899; *CJ*, 29 Sept. 1899.

[61] *CJ*, 29 Sept. 1899.

[62] *SWT*, 29 Sept., 10 Nov. 1899.

[63] Ibid., 19 Jan. 1900; *NWC*, 2 Sept. 1899 for similar sentiments.

[64] *NWC*, 25 Nov. 1899.

[65] Andrew Thompson, 'Publicity, philanthropy and commemoration: British society and the war', in David E. Omissi and Andrew S. Thompson (eds), *The Impact of the South African War* (London, 2002), p. 104.

[66] *SWT*, 9 Feb. 1900, for a Newport man rescued from the mob; Stewart J. Brown, ' "Echoes of Midlothian": Scottish Liberalism and the South African War, 1899–1902', *Scottish Historical Review*, 71 (1992), 168–9, for similar attacks in Scotland.

[67] *NWC*, 7 Oct. 1899; ibid., 16 Sept. 1899.

[68] *SWT*, 29 Sept. 1899.

[69] *NWC*, 14 Oct. 1899.

[70] *SWT*, 14 July 1899, 16, 23 Feb., 2 Mar., 4 May, 29 June 1900.

[71] Ibid., 27 July 1900.

[72] *CJ*, 1 Dec. 1899; Kenneth O. Morgan, 'The Boer War and the media, 1899–1902', *Twentieth Century British History*, 13 (2002).

[73] *SWT*, 16, 30 Feb. 1900.

[74] Ibid., 17 Nov. 1899; *NWC*, 11 Nov. 1899.

[75] *NWC*, 21 Oct. 1899.

[76] *SWT*, 17 Nov. 1899; for further scenes of massive popular support, see ibid., 9 Mar., 6 Apr. 1900.

[77] Ibid., 22 Dec. 1899.

[78] Ibid., 19 Jan. 1900.

[79] Ibid., 2, 9 Mar. 1900 for Ladysmith.

[80] Ibid., 25 May 1900. Williams, *Democratic Rhondda*, p. 39, describes as 'spectacular' the celebrations of Mafeking night in the Rhondda.

[81] Readman, 'Conservative Party, patriotism and British politics', 136–9; H. Pelling, 'Wales and the Boer War', *WHR*, 4, 4 (1969), 363–5.

[82] *WM*, 10 Sept. 1900. *NWC*, 22 Apr. 1899, for the Tories' long-standing view that Imperialism was most strongly supported in towns. Price notes that, in general, there was less war-fever in rural areas: Price, *An Imperial War*, p. 113.

[83] Neither contest has been considered in any detail, but see Kenneth O. Morgan, 'Wales and the Boer War – a reply', *WHR*, 4, 4 (1969), *passim*; Ieuan Gwynedd Jones, 'Franchise reform and Glamorgan politics 1869–1921', in Prys Morgan (ed.), *Glamorgan County History Volume VI: Glamorgan Society 1780–1980* (Cardiff, 1988).

[84] *SWT*, 17 Jan. 1899. He was born in 1856 at Leatherhead, educated at the local grammar school and then the University of Edinburgh, and graduated from the Royal College of Surgeons.

[85] Ibid., 5 Oct. 1900.

[86] *WM*, 3 Nov. 1900.

87 *SWT*, 24 Aug. 1900.
88 Ibid., 28 Sept. 1900.
89 Ibid., 29 June, 27 July, 7 Sept. 1900; *WM*, 15, 19 Sept. 1900.
90 *WM*, 5, 10, 19 Oct. 1900.
91 Ibid., 1 Oct. 1900.
92 Ibid., 25 Sept. 1900.
93 Peter Lord, *The Visual Culture of Wales: Industrial Society* (Cardiff, 1998), p. 164.
94 *WM*, 26 Sept. 1900.
95 Ibid., 9 Oct. 1900.
96 *SWT*, 28 Sept. 1900.
97 Ibid., 12 Oct. 1900.
98 *WM*, 5 Oct. 1900.
99 Morgan, 'Wales and the Boer War', 372–3.
100 Ibid., 375.
101 *WM*, 26 Sept. 1900.
102 Ibid., 27 Sept. 1900.
103 M. J. Daunton, *Coal Metropolis: Cardiff, 1870–1914* (Leicester, 1977), pp. 181–96.
104 *WM*, 6 Oct. 1900; the issue of employment spread to embrace his supporters. At a large meeting in the Clarence Bridge Docks, a 'working man' asked how many foreign workers J. Herbert Cory, who was a member of the platform party, employed on his ships. *WM*, 4 Oct. 1900.
105 Ibid., 11 Oct. 1900.
106 *SWT*, 12 Oct. 1900.
107 Ibid., 5 Oct. 1900.
108 *WM*, 7 Sept. 1900. See Daunton, *Coal Metropolis*, p. 188, for the inefficient planning of the strike.
109 *MB*, 5 Apr. 1901; *WM*, 2 Apr. 1901.
110 *MB*, 5 Apr. 1901.
111 Ibid., 10 May 1901.
112 *SWT*, 5 Oct. 1900.
113 Morgan, 'Wales and the Boer War', 378; Goronwy J. Jones, *Wales and the Quest for Peace* (Cardiff, 1969), pp. 82–4.

6

Taffs in the trenches: Welsh national identity and military service 1914–1918

CHRIS WILLIAMS[1]

By suffering alongside Geordies and Brummies, Cockneys and Scousers, Micks, Jocks and Aussies, the Taffs became part of a new brotherhood; to become a soldier was to assume a new nationality.

John Davies, A History of Wales[2]

It is as though formerly we were coins of different provinces; and now we are melted down, and all bear the same stamp.

Erich Maria Remarque, All Quiet on the Western Front[3]

According to the official record, 272,924 men from Wales (including Monmouthshire) served in the British Army during the Great War, representing 21.52 per cent of the male population of the country. This compares with percentages of 24.02 for England, 23.71 for Scotland and 6.14 for Ireland.[4] About 35,000 Welshmen are calculated to have died in the conflict, although this is not only a rough approximation, but one which is stretched as wide as possible to include all those born in Wales, those living in Wales who served with any unit, and all those who died whilst serving with a Welsh regiment.[5] Nonetheless, whatever the method of calculation, Wales made a sizeable contribution to the largest army, the first citizen-army, in British history.[6]

This essay seeks to explore one aspect of the relationship between Welsh national identity and military service during the Great War. Anthony Smith, one of the leading writers on nations and nationalism, has suggested that warfare has a central role in shaping national identity, yet many works that have been written either on British national identity or on the Great War say remarkably little on the relationship between the two.[7] Neither J. M. Winter, in an essay entitled 'British national identity and the First World

War', nor J. H. Grainger, in his three-volume work *Patriotisms: Britain 1900–1939*, mention military service at all.[8] Although Gerard J. De Groot's acclaimed *Blighty* is subtitled *British Society in the Era of the Great War*, at no point does it pause to consider national identity (and thus what being 'British'[9] meant). Generally, whilst there has been some consideration of the extent to which the phenomenon of the 'nation in arms', as the phrase went, helped to reduce social barriers between the classes, there has been scant discussion of the impact of military service on the popular sense of the 'nation' itself.

The most fecund discussion is to be found in Keith Robbins's work on British national identity in the (long) nineteenth century.[10] Robbins sees the Great War as marking the culmination of trends towards greater British national unity and self-identification as 'British', although he observes that 'national and regional loyalties and identities were by no means submerged'.[11] As he puts it, '[m]en from Inverness and Plymouth played, ate, drank, sang and fought alongside each other, but frequently sensed that they were, at one and the same time, comrades and strangers.'[12] Yet, in a subsequent volume on British national identity, Robbins does not repeat these tantalizing suggestions, omitting any discussion of the war in terms of its impact on popular consciousness and national identity.[13]

In the absence of any sustained consideration of these issues by British social historians, it is hardly surprising that this issue has barely been probed by their Welsh equivalents. John Davies's suggestion, with which this chapter opened, that through the war experience 'Taffs' became 'part of a new brotherhood', remains only speculation. Both Angela Gaffney's work on the commemoration of the war in Wales and John S. Ellis's study of the 'pluralist reconstruction of British national identity' before and during the conflict offer further clues, but the main focus of their attention is, understandably, elsewhere.[14] In the Welsh context, only Gervase Phillips has addressed this issue directly, examining 'the extent to which the trauma of service in a mass army and the trenches overwhelmed the distinctively Welsh character of those caught up in the war'.[15] Phillips sought to 'challenge the assumption that the distinctive features of Welsh politics and society were submerged' by the transformation of 'Welsh civilians' into 'British soldiers', but neither his hypothesis nor his methodology was sufficiently sophisticated to yield much insight into the process.[16]

This essay represents the first attempt to explore systematically an important quantitative source for the Welsh experience of military service during the Great War. *Soldiers Died in the Great War 1914–19* (hereinafter *SDGW*) was originally published in 1921, in eighty-one volumes, approximating to one per regiment or corps. The series lists approximately 635,000 soldiers alphabetically, battalion by battalion, together with their service numbers, rank, awards, places of birth, enlistment and residence, and with the date, theatre of war and nature of their death. To give one example, from the 11th Battalion South Wales Borderers (hereinafter SWB): 'Killingback, Henry, b. Llanhilleth, Mon, e. Newport, Mon (Pontymister) 21931, Pte., k. in a., F. & F., 10/7/16'.[17] This shows that Private Henry Killingback, born in Llanhilleth but resident in Pontymister, enlisted at Newport, and was killed in action in 'France and Flanders' on 10 July 1916. Separate sources reveal that Private Killingback was just twenty years old, 'was very much liked by all his comrades who fought with him, side by side, in the trenches', had been a porter at the Pontypool Road railway station before joining the army in April 1915, and was an eldest son whose parents ran the Sir Garnet Hotel, Crane Street, Pontypool.[18] He was killed in the second attack by the 38th (Welsh) Division on German positions in Mametz Wood, and is buried in Flat Iron Copse Cemetery, along with many others from the 11th SWB or '2nd Gwents'.[19]

SDGW is an undeniably rich and poignant source for the historian of the Great War. Each entry offers a glimpse of a life cut short which, when linked with materials available in the registers of the Commonwealth War Graves Commission, and perhaps with information in battalion war diaries, newspapers and letters, reveals much of the human tragedy of the conflict. However, the lists of the dead lend themselves most readily to collective, rather than to individual, analysis. For the military historian they can yield 'fatality calendars', highlighting those occasions when units went 'over the top' as well as quieter times in the trenches or behind the lines. For instance, of the total of 288 deaths suffered by soldiers of the 11th SWB, 63 occurred in July 1916, when the battalion was engaged in the battle for Mametz Wood, and a further 110 in July and August 1917, when it fought at Third Ypres.[20]

In assessing *SDGW*, it is important to note that there is no other source which consistently, from regiment to regiment and from battalion to battalion, gives such detailed information on the individual soldiers who served with these units. There are no detailed service-records for all of the 272,924 Welsh men who served in the conflict, no registers of even their most simple characteristics, such as date or place of birth. The stories of *individual* servicemen may be reconstructed, with luck, from various categories of documents: the 'burnt' and 'unburnt' documents in the National Archives, medal rolls, war diaries and so on.[21] But the survival of such data is uneven, and there is no way of drawing consistent generalizations about the bulk of the armed forces from such sources. *SDGW*, however, does provide some basic material on almost every soldier killed during the war.[22] It is acknowledged that to generalize about the whole army from this information is not an unproblematic step to take. One is forced to make the assumption that the hundreds, sometimes thousands, of dead from a particular battalion are a sufficiently representative sample of all those who served in the same battalion, and that the characteristics of the dead (in this essay, particularly the data on their birthplaces) can stand proxy for those of the survivors as well. Although it is important to acknowledge Ian Beckett's point that this method cannot provide 'a precise survey, since losses may have fallen disproportionately on sections within a unit', it is nonetheless accepted, by Beckett as well as by others, that the use of *SDGW* represents one of the most satisfactory methods of assessing the composition of individual units within a framework that allows comparative analysis from regiment to regiment over the course of the whole conflict.[23]

Birthplace is regarded here as the most reliable indication of an individual's nationality. It is accepted that this is neither a necessarily automatic correlation, nor is it the only indication of an individual's nationality that might be yielded by analysis of *SDGW*. In respect of the former, individuals may have been born overseas, in transit or simply in a place which they did not regard as 'home'. In the context of the regular army, where soldiers sometimes came from families of soldiers, they may have been born in garrison towns in India, the West Indies or the Mediterranean, yet would surely not have regarded themselves as Indian, Jamaican or Maltese. A more substantial problem, particularly with the 'citizen army' of the Great War, is that migration, especially internal migration, ensures that a good number of men born in England would have been living in Wales at the time of the war, and vice versa. According to the population census of 1911, 213,855, or 17.4 per cent, of males enumerated in Wales had been born in England, and 121,150, or 11.1 per cent, of males who had been born in Wales were enumerated in England.[24]

For the purposes of this analysis these complications will be set aside. As will be seen, the number of soldiers who both died while serving with Welsh regiments *and* had been born overseas was actually relatively small, at just 0.4 per cent of all those with recorded birthplaces. As for internal migration, this would be a more significant issue if contemporary notions had linked nationality more clearly to residence, rather than to birthplace. However, although the increased popularity of ideas of citizenship in recent decades has seen a greater acceptance of such a notion, there is little evidence from the late nineteenth and early twentieth centuries that internal migrants necessarily cast off any English or Welsh identity (insofar as they felt one or the other strongly at all) on crossing the border to live. The variety of emotions and attachments in this regard makes it unwise to attempt to rule decisively one way or the other on such an issue.[25]

Despite this qualification of the significance of data on residence, *SDGW* does, in theory, offer the possibility of analysing such data and, indeed, that on enlistment, as well as that on birthplace. However, as Table 6.1 reveals, the collection of residence information in *SDGW* was very uneven across the Welsh regiments, ranging from none at all for the Welsh Guards to over half for the Welsh Regiment. The total number of soldiers for whom residence is available is only just over a third of all the dead, which compares poorly with the recording of information on birthplace, which is available for 92.7 per cent. As for enlistment, a close reading of *SDGW* reveals the possibility that, where place of residence and place of enlistment were one and the same, sometimes place of residence was not entered. However, it is not safe to extrapolate from this that places of enlistment generally may stand surrogate for places of residence, as one needs only to notice the frequency with which the locations of army depots and camps occur as places of enlistment to realize that many soldiers travelled, sometimes long distances, to enlist. Such a pattern severs, in the absence of any further information in the pages of *SDGW*, any possible reliable link between residence and enlistment. One is left, therefore, with birthplace as the clearest and most consistent measure of the nationality of individual soldiers.

Table 6.1 Availability of data on residence, Welsh regiments.[26]

Regiment	Residence noted	Total dead	Percentage with residence data
Welsh Guards	0	819	0
Royal Welch Fusiliers	2805	9417	29.8
South Wales Borderers	1150	5436	21.2
Welsh Regiment	3992	7417	53.8
Monmouthshire Regiment	490	1499	32.7
TOTAL	8437	24588	34.3

Source: *Soldiers Died in the Great War 1914–19*

The analysis which follows is based on a quantitative assessment of the information contained in *SDGW*, particularly that relating to the Welsh regiments. It should be noted that it does not include officers. The publication *Officers Died in the Great War* (1919) does not provide information on place of birth. Furthermore, the territorial connection between officers and the units in which they served tended to be more tenuous than that between soldiers and their units. Robert Graves, for example, enlisted in the Royal Welch Fusiliers (hereinafter RWF) largely on the strength of a personal link via the secretary of the golf club at Harlech, where the Graves family had a holiday residence.[27] There is no evidence of even this level of connection in respect of other famous RWF officers, such as Siegfried Sassoon and Bernard Adams, both of whom were Englishmen educated at public school and Cambridge University.[28] Vivian de Sola Pinto (public school and Oxford) was invited to join the RWF because his father was friendly with an existing RWF officer, and Malcolm Trustram Eve, from Bedford and educated at public school and Oxford University, whose mother was Scottish and whose father English, joined the regiment because it happened to be billeted in Northampton.[29] Although, as the war progressed, Welsh-born officers became more and more common in Welsh regiments, at least initially the scarcity of suitably experienced personnel meant that New Army battalions often drew their officers from a wide range of other regiments. Graves explains that, when temporarily he joined the Welsh Regiment, all but three of the company officers were from other regiments, including the East Surreys, the Wiltshires, the Border Regiment, the King's Own Yorkshire Light Infantry and the Connaught Rangers.[30] Even when officers were Welsh, many of them possessed class and educational backgrounds that transcended any specific nationality. The 'Anglo-Welshmen of county families' whom Graves found in the regular battalions of the RWF were more likely to have things in common with their equivalents in other, non-Welsh, regiments, than they were to share interests and outlook with those in the ranks.[31] In due course this situation may well have changed: Wyn Griffith, for example, served as a subaltern in the 15th RWF, while his brother, Watcyn, killed at Mametz Wood on 10 July 1916, was a private soldier in the 17th RWF.[32] Nevertheless, any analysis of the characteristics of officers who died whilst serving with Welsh regiments would need to be conducted separately and to draw on a wider range of evidence than is utilized here.

The quantitative analysis of *SDGW* has been facilitated by the digitization of its data by the Naval and Military Press, which has produced a CD-ROM containing all the information from the eighty-one volumes.[33] This amounts to a relational database listing approximately 635,000 soldiers and 37,000 officers. The lists may be sorted electronically in a number of different ways, reducing the labour that would be involved in analysing the printed volumes alone. For much of the analysis that follows, the dead of each battalion were sorted by birthplace, and were totalled according to county of birth. As the design of the database preserves the original ordering of the data, whereby the specific parish, village, town or city precedes any county information in the same field, the totalling still has to be done by hand rather than electronically, but the researcher using the CD-ROM has the advantage that all those born in (for example) Cardiff will appear one after the other, rather than scattered throughout the list, as is the case with the original published version, in which the soldiers are listed alphabetically by surname. In many cases county data is not given, and in some cases is given incorrectly, and here the correct information has had to be added. When dealing with soldiers born in the London area one also faces the complication that whereas some lists consistently apply county data (usually Middlesex or Surrey), others content themselves simply with recording 'London'. These entries have not been rationalized in the tables that follow, but any assessment of soldiers' birthplaces in this area needs to bear this in mind. Relatively few soldiers were listed as born simply in 'England' or 'Wales', although in some cases, particularly those involving Welsh place-names, they have been so mangled by War Office clerks as to be unrecognizable, and have been assigned to the 'Wales not given' category! However, the numbers in both cases are so small (eighteen for England and fifteen for Wales) as to be insignificant. The further one moves away from England and Wales, however, the less specific the information tends to be, and there has been no attempt to generate county totals for those recorded as born in either Ireland or Scotland, much less for any from elsewhere in the world.

The results of the analysis are presented in a number of tables, and also in three maps. Of the 24,559 casualties listed for the Welsh regiments, places of birth were entered for 22,755, that is 92.7 per cent of the total.[34] Of those 22,755, 11,537 (50.7 per cent) were born in Wales, 10,679 (46.9 per cent) were born in England, 441 (1.9 per cent) were born in the remainder of the United Kingdom, and 98 (0.4 per cent) were born elsewhere in the world. Of the 11,537 born in Wales, their distribution across the counties of Wales is revealed in Table 6.2, and also represented in Map 6.1. The south-east of the country produced over half of all soldiers killed, with almost two-fifths from Glamorgan and almost one-fifth from Monmouthshire. The next most heavily represented counties were Denbighshire and Caernarfonshire.

To what extent do these figures reflect the balance of population across Welsh counties? Table 6.3 compares the geographical distribution of the dead taken from Table 6.2 with the geographical distribution of males aged between 15 and 44 recorded by the 1911 population census (that is, those who might well have been in the recruiting 'pool' during the war itself). This reveals that, although Glamorgan produced by far the greatest number of Welsh-born soldiers recorded in *SDGW*, in comparison with its male population of approximately military age it was actually under-represented amongst the dead (38.1 per cent as against 49 per cent, yielding a 'quota' of just 77.8 per cent). The only other counties to be under-represented were Carmarthenshire and Radnorshire. All other counties were over-represented, with the highest 'yields' being in Merioneth and Montgomeryshire.

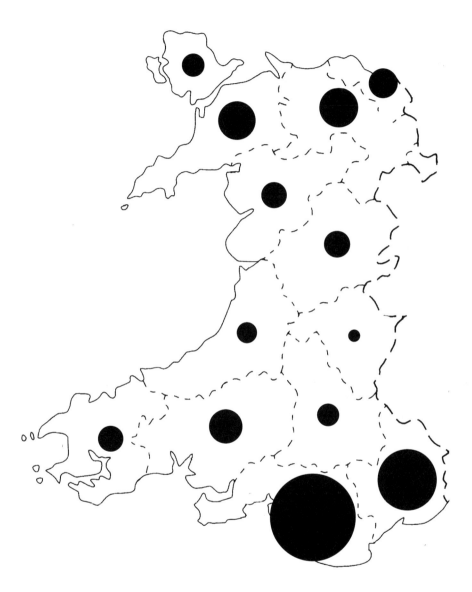

Map 6.1 Counties of birth, Welsh-born soldiers, Welsh regiments (based on Table 6.2). Circles are proportionate in area to the numbers of fatalities.

Table 6.2 Counties of birth, Welsh-born soldiers, Welsh regiments.[35]

County	Number	Percentage of all Welsh-born
Anglesey	305	2.6
Breconshire	288	2.5
Caernarfonshire	844	7.3
Cardiganshire	249	2.2
Carmarthenshire	666	5.8
Denbighshire	886	7.7
Flintshire	510	4.4
Glamorgan	4387	38.0
Merioneth	387	3.4
Monmouthshire	2144	18.6
Montgomeryshire	399	3.5
Pembrokeshire	382	3.3
Radnorshire	85	0.7
Wales not given	15	0.1
TOTAL	11537	100.1

Source: *Soldiers Died in the Great War 1914–19*

Table 6.3 Counties of birth, Welsh-born soldiers, Welsh regiments, and counties of enumeration, males 15–44, Wales, 1911 census.[36]

County	Percentage of dead, *SDGW*	Percentage of males (15–44), 1911 census	Under- or over-representation in *SDGW*
Anglesey	2.6	1.8	144.4
Breconshire	2.5	2.4	104.2
Caernarfonshire	7.3	4.5	162.2
Cardiganshire	2.2	1.9	115.8
Carmarthenshire	5.8	6.6	87.9
Denbighshire	7.7	5.6	137.5
Flintshire	4.4	3.5	125.7
Glamorgan[37]	38.1	49.0	77.8
Merioneth	3.4	1.6	212.5
Monmouthshire	18.6	17.1	108.8
Montgomeryshire	3.5	1.9	184.2
Pembrokeshire	3.3	3.3	100.0
Radnorshire	0.7	0.8	87.5
TOTAL	100.1	100.1	–

Source: *Soldiers Died in the Great War 1914–19*

Whilst this information is interesting, insofar as it helps to qualify impressions of under-recruitment in some areas of rural Wales and in some areas where the Welsh language remained strong, it has to be treated with extreme caution, for two reasons. First, the census figures being used are only an approximation of those males who would have been eligible for military service. By 1918 many who were not even teenagers in 1911 would have been in the ranks. Furthermore, there is plenty of evidence that men aged well over fifty and boys under eighteen served in the army during the Great War. My great-grandfather, William John Rogers (born West Dean, Gloucestershire, 1862), was fifty-three when he enlisted with the 11th SWB at Newport in May 1915, and thus would have fallen well outside the census category being used here. Robert Graves reflected that many in his first platoon in the Welsh Regiment were under- or over-age:

> Fred Prosser . . . who admitted to forty-eight, was really fifty-six. David Davies . . . who admitted to forty-two, and Thomas Clark, . . . who admitted to forty-five, were only one or two years junior to Prosser. James Burford . . . was even older than these [he was sixty-three]. William Bumford . . . who gave his age as eighteen, was really only fifteen.[38]

Second, and rather more crucially, recruiting in the industrial districts of south-east and north-east Wales would have been affected by the classification of many jobs in coal mining and in the iron and steel industries as reserved occupations. The impact of this undoubtedly fell most heavily on south-east Wales, and may help to account for the proportionate under-representation of men born in Glamorgan in the *SDGW* lists.

Rather more remarkable than the distribution of Welsh-born soldiers is the volume and distribution of English-born soldiers, displayed in Table 6.4 and Map 6.2. Representing almost 47 per cent of the total dead, the English-born are found to have come from every county in England, including Rutland. By far the largest contingent were from Lancashire, with other substantial groups from London, Cheshire, Gloucestershire and Staffordshire. There were more Lancastrians amongst the dead of the Welsh regiments than men from any county of Wales, with the exception of Glamorgan; more from Middlesex than from Merioneth, more from Herefordshire than from Anglesey, more from Surrey than from Cardiganshire. Of course, the population of many English counties was much bigger than that of most Welsh counties, but the fact remains that for every 100 Welsh-born soldiers killed in Welsh regiments, there were 93 English-born soldiers who had been killed alongside them.

Map 6.2 Counties of birth, English-born soldiers, Welsh regiments (based on Table 6.3). Circle are proportionate in area to the numbers of fatalities.

Table 6.4 Counties of birth, English-born soldiers, Welsh regiments.

County	Number	Percentage of all English-born
Bedfordshire	44	0.4
Berkshire	56	0.5
Buckinghamshire	36	0.3
Cambridgeshire	32	0.3
Cheshire	838	7.8
Cornwall	48	0.4
Cumberland	80	0.7
Derbyshire	106	1.0
Devonshire	214	2.0
Dorset	51	0.5
Durham	135	1.3
Essex	174	1.6
Gloucestershire	651	6.1
Hampshire	130	1.2
Herefordshire	329	3.1
Hertfordshire	43	0.4
Huntingdonshire	12	0.1
Kent	180	1.7
Lancashire	2396	22.4
Leicestershire	52	0.5
Lincolnshire	43	0.4
London	1140	10.7
Middlesex	393	3.7
Norfolk	55	0.5
Northamptonshire	63	0.6
Northumberland	59	0.6
Nottinghamshire	66	0.6
Oxfordshire	61	0.6
Rutland	2	0.0
Shropshire	412	3.9
Somerset	347	3.2
Staffordshire	649	6.1
Suffolk	58	0.5
Surrey	272	2.5
Sussex	70	0.7
Warwickshire	543	5.1
Westmorland	21	0.2
Wiltshire	135	1.3
Worcestershire	195	1.8
Yorkshire	472	4.4
England not given	18	0.2
TOTAL	10679	100.0

Source: *Soldiers Died in the Great War 1914–19*

A few other soldiers came from further afield still. Of the 441 born in the remainder of the United Kingdom, 269 had been born in Ireland, 143 in Scotland, 19 in the Isle of Man and 10 in the Channel Islands. Of the 98 born in more distant lands, 26 were from the USA, 19 from India, 16 from Canada, 9 from Australia, 6 each from New Zealand and the West Indies, 3 each from South Africa and Malta, 2 from Gibraltar, and 1 each from 'Arabia', Argentina, Denmark, Poland, St Helena, Singapore, 'South America' and Sweden. The Cheshire-born Saunders Lewis, who served as a signalling officer with the 12th (3rd Gwents) SWB, recalled that 'the majority of men were miners from Monmouthshire and South Wales, and in their midst a number of Irish, collected in one company under the leadership of an Irish officer'.[39] However, whilst not forgetting the presence in Welsh regiments of those born outside England and Wales, 97.6 per cent of the soldiers listed with a birthplace in *SDGW* were from those two countries, and it is on the Welsh/English dynamic that this chapter will focus.

Table 6.5 reveals that there were important differences between the types of battalion in terms of the birthplaces of those killed during the war. Throughout the Victorian and Edwardian eras Wales had not been fertile terrain for military recruitment. On the eve of the Great War Wales supplied just 1.4 per cent of the total personnel of the army, despite having 5.4 per cent of the population of Britain.[40] The 'Welsh' regiments of the regular army were used to relying on other regions of Britain to bring their establishments up to strength. The RWF were informally known as the 'Birmingham Fusiliers' because so many of their recruits came from the West Midlands.[41] Captain James Dunn calculated that, in 1914, only a tenth of the 2nd RWF were Welsh, and Graves suggested even fewer.[42] Table 6.5 indicates that, of the four different categories of battalion to be found in the Welsh infantry regiments, it was indeed the regular army battalions which had the lowest proportion (44.7 per cent) of Welsh-born soldiers who died over the course of the war as a whole. Of the 342 RWF soldiers killed in 1914, only 125, or 37 per cent, were born in Wales.[43] Although this covers all RWF battalions and not just regular battalions, 325 of those killed were serving with the regular battalions the 1st and 2nd RWF.[44] Such data suggests that Dunn and Graves may have exaggerated the non-Welsh nature of the regular battalions, but that, nonetheless, Welsh soldiers were certainly in a minority in their ranks. Gradually the balance was redressed somewhat, as drafts of volunteers and conscripts rendered regular battalions such as the 2nd RWF 'less English and more Welsh'.[45] Graves estimated that '[i]n the course of the war at least fifteen or twenty thousand men must have passed through each of the two line battalions, whose fighting strength was never more than eight hundred', and it seems likely that, overall, the new arrivals were more likely to be drawn from Wales than had been the pre-war regular soldiers, notwithstanding the occasional tendency, as noted by Dunn, to draft in men who had been recruited for the 'Cheshires, Shropshires and South Wales Borderers'.[46] By the summer of 1917 Dunn estimated that the 2nd RWF was 'about eighty-five per cent Welsh'.[47] As a consequence, the distinctions between regular army battalions and other battalions diminished as the conflict wore on. Frank Richards related that when the 2nd RWF was posted to the 38th (Welsh) Division in 1918 it was the only regular battalion 'yet with the exception of the transport we probably had more young soldiers with us than any of the others'.[48]

Table 6.5 Birthplaces, by battalion type, Welsh regiments (percentages in brackets).

Type of unit	Born in Wales	Born in England	Born elsewhere in the UK	Born overseas	Total given
Regular	3317 (44.7)	3882 (52.3)	181 (2.4)	44 (0.6)	7424 (100.0)
Territorial	2261 (65.4)	1152 (33.3)	35 (1.0)	10 (0.3)	3458 (100.0)
New Army	5737 (50.4)	5390 (47.4)	206 (1.8)	41 (0.4)	11374 (100.0)
Reserve	222 (44.5)	255 (51.1)	19 (3.8)	3 (0.6)	499 (100.0)

Source: *Soldiers Died in the Great War 1914–19*

By contrast, one might expect that territorial force battalions would, by their very nature, have drawn more heavily on their allotted recruiting areas, and this is borne out by Table 6.5. Vivian de Sola Pinto noted of the territorial 2nd/6th RWF that 'our men were chiefly farm labourers and quarrymen from North Wales and Anglesey. A fair proportion of them only spoke Welsh and a very large number were called Jones.'[49] Here again, however, the distinctions between territorial and other battalions diminished over time.[50]

The most dramatic transformation in the character of the British Army occasioned by the demands of the Great War was, of course, the raising of Kitchener's 'New Army', the citizen's army of 'pals' battalions', consisted initially of thousands of volunteers. As can be seen from Table 6.5, almost exactly half of all soldiers killed with Welsh regiments were killed serving with New Army battalions (11,374, as against a total of 11,381 serving with the other three types of battalion). All three Welsh regular army regiments in existence at the beginning of the war (that is the RWF, SWB and the Welsh Regiment, but neither the territorial Monmouthshire Regiment nor the Welsh Guards) were expanded massively to cope with the demands of the conflict. The SWB formed eight 'Service' (that is, 'active service') New Army battalions, the RWF ten and the Welsh Regiment twelve.[51] Of those killed with these units, just over half had been born in

Wales. We know from evidence other than *SDGW* that some battalions struggled to fill their ranks from their designated recruiting area alone. The 14th (Carnarvon and Anglesey) RWF managed to find only a third of its recruits from those two counties. Of the rest, a quarter came from other parts of north Wales, and a fifth each from south Wales and England. The 15th (Carmarthenshire) Welsh, 17th (2nd North Wales) and 19th RWF all included many recruits from Lancashire and the Midlands.[52] De Sola Pinto, on his transfer to the 19th RWF, found that his platoon 'consisted mainly of Lancashire and Staffordshire men with three Londoners and only one Welshman'.[53]

The differences in the recruiting areas allocated to each regiment shed some light on the results in Table 6.6. In terms of the birthplaces of soldiers who died, the 'most Welsh' of the five Welsh regiments was the territorial Monmouthshire Regiment, closely followed by the single-battalion Welsh Guards and then by the Welsh Regiment, which recruited in Glamorgan, Carmarthenshire, Pembrokeshire and Cardiganshire. Less than half of the RWF's dead were born in Wales, and just over two-fifths of those of the SWB. The RWF's recruiting area traditionally covered all of Wales, but it was only in the north, 'ordinarily the leanest recruiting district in the country', according to Dunn, that they experienced no direct competition from other regiments.[54] In assessing the composition of the SWB it is worth bearing in mind that, although its recruiting area covered Monmouthshire, Breconshire and Radnorshire, it contained no territorial battalions, as these were all organized in the Monmouthshire Regiment. If one adds the two regiments together, then 45.2 per cent of their dead were born in Wales, which still leaves it as the 'least Welsh' of all the Welsh regiments.

Table 6.6 Birthplaces, by regiment, Welsh regiments (percentages in brackets).

Regiment	Born in Wales	Born in England	Born elsewhere in the UK	Born overseas	Total given
Welsh Guards	478 (59.5)	313 (39.0)	11 (1.4)	1 (0.1)	803 (100.0)
Royal Welch Fusiliers	4170 (48.7)	4234 (49.5)	127 (1.5)	29 (0.3)	8560 (100.0)
South Wales Borderers	2152 (41.1)	2922 (55.8)	137 (2.6)	29 (0.6)	5240 (99.9)
Welsh Regiment	3964 (57.3)	2773 (40.1)	154 (2.2)	32 (0.5)	6923 (100.1)
Monmouthshire Regiment	773 (62.9)	437 (35.6)	12 (1.0)	7 (0.6)	1229 (100.1)

Source: *Soldiers Died in the Great War 1914–19*

Tables 6.7 and 6.8 yield additional insights into the regional nature of regimental recruitment. Whilst it should be no surprise that of those Welsh-born soldiers killed with the Monmouthshire Regiment, almost three-quarters were from Monmouthshire and over a sixth from Glamorgan, it is interesting to note that more than a fifth of its English-born dead came from Lancashire, which was much more highly represented than the contiguous English counties of Gloucestershire and Herefordshire. The SWB, on the other hand, drew more heavily than the Monmouthshire Regiment on both Glamorgan and Breconshire, and seems to have had more Londoners than Lancastrians in its ranks. The 'border counties' of Gloucestershire and Herefordshire were not as markedly represented in the SWB, but there were significant pockets of men from Cheshire, Yorkshire and Staffordshire. The Welsh Regiment depended substantially on Glamorgan, and less so on Carmarthenshire, Monmouthshire and Pembrokeshire. From England it drew heavily on Lancashire, Middlesex and Gloucestershire. Finally, the RWF appears to have been the most wide-ranging. The north-eastern counties of Denbighshire and Flintshire together were responsible for three-tenths of the regiment's Welsh-born dead, the north-west Wales counties of Anglesey, Caernarfonshire and Merioneth added a further three-tenths, and Glamorgan and Monmouthshire contributed over a quarter. In England the RWF drew heavily on Lancashire, London and Cheshire. Its tag of the 'Birmingham Fusiliers' was echoed in the 8 per cent totals found for both Staffordshire and Warwickshire.

Table 6.7 Soldiers born in Welsh counties (percentages), Welsh regiments, by regiment.

Welsh counties	Welsh Guards	Royal Welch Fusiliers	South Wales Borderers	Welsh Regiment	Monmouthshire Regiment
Anglesey	0.6	6.2	1.0	0.5	0.1
Breconshire	1.5	1.1	6.5	1.8	3.4
Caernarfonshire	4.6	16.2	3.1	1.9	0.5
Cardiganshire	3.2	1.5	2.6	2.9	0.0
Carmarthenshire	6.5	3.4	4.6	9.7	1.2
Denbighshire	6.1	18.1	2.4	1.3	0.4
Flintshire	3.6	10.6	1.4	0.5	0.3
Glamorgan	46.4	22.1	29.2	62.6	17.7
Merioneth	3.4	7.0	1.2	1.2	0.6
Monmouthshire	15.4	5.0	43.1	9.3	73.1
Montgomeryshire	2.7	7.0	2.1	1.1	0.9
Pembrokeshire	5.1	1.3	1.6	6.5	1.2
Radnorshire	0.8	0.5	1.3	0.7	0.6
TOTAL	99.9	100.0	100.1	100.0	100.0

Source: *Soldiers Died in the Great War 1914–19*

Table 6.8 Soldiers born in English counties (percentages), Welsh regiments, by regiment.

English counties	Welsh Guards	Royal Welch Fusiliers	South Wales Borderers	Welsh Regiment	Monmouthshire Regiment
Bedfordshire	–	0.3	0.6	0.5	0.2
Berkshire	0.6	0.4	0.7	0.5	0.7
Buckinghamshire	0.6	0.3	0.5	0.3	–
Cambridgeshire	1.3	0.3	0.1	0.4	0.2
Cheshire	2.9	10.8	6.3	6.0	5.7
Cornwall	–	0.3	0.4	0.8	0.2
Cumberland	–	0.9	1.0	0.5	0.2
Derbyshire	0.3	1.3	1.2	0.5	–
Devonshire	3.8	1.1	1.3	3.5	3.9
Dorsetshire	1.0	0.2	0.7	0.6	0.2
Durham	0.6	0.5	2.0	1.9	0.2
Essex	3.2	1.6	1.3	1.9	1.1
Gloucestershire	8.3	2.8	8.2	7.6	13.0
Hampshire	3.2	0.7	1.5	1.4	1.6
Herefordshire	2.6	1.2	4.2	3.5	11.4
Hertfordshire	–	0.3	0.3	0.7	0.7
Huntingdonshire	0.3	0.2	–	0.1	–
Kent	2.9	0.8	1.9	2.5	2.3
Lancashire	18.9	28.2	16.4	20.8	21.3
Leicestershire	2.6	0.5	0.5	0.3	0.2
Lincolnshire	0.6	0.4	0.5	0.4	0.2
London	2.9	12.5	16.9	3.2	4.6
Middlesex	4.2	1.5	1.6	9.5	0.9
Norfolk	0.6	0.4	0.5	0.7	0.5
Northamptonshire	0.6	0.5	0.8	0.5	–
Northumberland	3.5	0.3	0.7	0.5	–
Nottinghamshire	1.0	0.7	0.7	0.4	0.5
Oxfordshire	1.6	0.5	0.7	0.5	0.9
Rutland	–	–	–	–	–
Shropshire	1.9	5.1	2.9	3.1	4.6
Somersetshire	6.4	1.4	2.8	5.9	5.9
Staffordshire	4.5	8.0	6.0	3.7	4.8
Suffolk	1.3	0.4	0.5	0.8	–
Surrey	2.6	1.2	2.0	5.3	2.1
Sussex	1.6	0.3	0.8	1.0	0.2
Warwickshire	4.5	8.0	3.1	3.3	1.8
Westmorland	0.3	0.3	0.1	0.2	0.2
Wiltshire	1.3	0.5	1.4	1.9	3.2
Worcestershire	2.9	1.1	2.6	1.8	3.0
Yorkshire	4.5	4.2	6.2	3.1	3.2
TOTAL	100.1	100.0	99.9	100.1	99.9

Source: *Soldiers Died in the Great War 1914–19*

Table 6.9, the last to draw on the data available for the Welsh regiments, allows overall figures for regiments to be broken down by battalion. It can immediately be recognized that the gross figures for regiments, or indeed for types of battalion, mask significant variations within both categories. The 'most Welsh' regular army battalion was the Welsh Guards, the least the 2nd SWB, which also has the dubious distinction of having the highest total of casualties of any Welsh battalion. The much-documented 2nd RWF was not much 'more Welsh' than the 2nd SWB. Of territorial battalions, most show over 60 per cent of casualties as Welsh-born, but the 24th and 25th RWF deviate from this pattern, with fewer than half in this category. The 24th RWF had begun the war as the Denbighshire Yeomanry, the 2nd/1st battalion of which being only 27 per cent Welsh in 1914.[55] As for the New Army battalions, here there is enormous variation. According to the *SDGW* statistics, the 10th (1st Rhondda) Welsh was the most ethnically homogeneous of all these units, closely followed by other New Army battalions from the same regiment: the 16th (Cardiff City), 17th (1st Glamorgan), 14th (Swansea), 13th (2nd Rhondda), 11th and 9th.[56] The 'most-Welsh' of the RWF New Army battalions was the 17th, and of the SWB, the 11th. Those New Army battalions whose Welshness appears to have been heavily diluted include the 12th SWB (Saunders Lewis's battalion), the 15th (London Welsh) RWF and the 7th SWB.

Table 6.9 Soldiers born in Wales (percentages), Welsh battalions.[57]

Battalion	Type of battalion	Number with birthplace given	Percentage born in Wales
1st/4th Welsh Regiment	Territorial	225	79.1
6th Royal Welch Fusiliers	Territorial	191	79.1
7th Royal Welch Fusiliers	Territorial	290	72.4
1st/5th Welsh Regiment	Territorial	205	72.2
5th Royal Welch Fusiliers	Territorial	202	69.8
1st/6th Welsh Regiment	Territorial	219	67.6
10th Welsh Regiment	New Army	248	64.9
3rd Monmouthshire Regiment	Territorial	336	64.9
16th Welsh Regiment	New Army	379	63.9
2nd Monmouthshire Regiment	Territorial	386	63.7
24th Welsh Regiment	Territorial	192	63.5
17th Welsh Regiment	New Army	223	63.2
14th Welsh Regiment	New Army	508	62.2
1st Monmouthshire Regiment	Territorial	486	62.1
13th Welsh Regiment	New Army	472	61.9
11th Welsh Regiment	New Army	154	60.4
1st Welsh Guards	Regular	803	59.5

Table 6.9 *Contd.*

Battalion	Type of battalion	Number with birthplace given	Percentage born in Wales
9th Welsh Regiment	New Army	682	57.5
4th Royal Welch Fusiliers	Territorial	259	57.1
17th Royal Welch Fusiliers	New Army	529	54.4
11th Royal Welch Fusiliers	New Army	174	54.0
8th Welch Regiment	New Army	418	53.6
16th Royal Welch Fusiliers	New Army	607	52.2
14th Royal Welch Fusiliers	New Army	550	51.8
15th Welch Regiment	New Army	480	51.5
1st Welsh Regiment	Regular	507	51.3
2nd Welsh Regiment	Regular	1239	51.0
8th Royal Welch Fusiliers	New Army	453	50.6
10th Royal Welch Fusiliers	New Army	694	49.7
25th Royal Welch Fusiliers	Territorial	152	49.3
13th Royal Welch Fusiliers	New Army	542	48.5
11th South Wales Borderers	New Army	286	46.9
19th Welsh Regiment	New Army	163	45.4
5th South Wales Borderers	New Army	415	45.3
10th South Wales Borderers	New Army	438	45.2
9th Royal Welch Fusiliers	New Army	674	44.5
1st Royal Welch Fusiliers	Regular	1285	44.4
18th Welsh Regiment	New Army	406	44.3
24th Royal Welch Fusiliers	Territorial	150	44.0
4th South Wales Borderers	New Army	536	43.3
6th South Wales Borderers	New Army	374	42.2
1st South Wales Borderers	Regular	1181	41.7
2nd Royal Welch Fusiliers	Regular	1032	39.0
19th Royal Welch Fusiliers	New Army	222	36.5
7th South Wales Borderers	New Army	160	35.6
2nd South Wales Borderers	Regular	1377	34.9
15th Royal Welch Fusiliers	New Army	244	31.1
12th South Wales Borderers	New Army	218	28.0

Source: *Soldiers Died in the Great War 1914–19*

The poet and artist David Jones served with the 15th (London Welsh) RWF, and alluded directly to its ethnic heterogeneity in his poem *In Parenthesis*:

and the Royal Welsh sing:
Jesu
    lover of me soul . . . to *Aberystwyth*
But that was on the right with
the genuine Taffies
    but we are rash levied
from Islington and Hackney
and the purlieus of Walworth
flashers from Surbiton
men of the stock of Abraham
from Bromley-by-Bow
Anglo-Welsh from Queens Ferry
rosary-wallahs from Pembrey Dock[58]

Jones, though London-born himself, was of Welsh parentage, and thus was exactly the type of recruit the 15th RWF was designed to attract. Fellow volunteer W. A. Tucker enlisted in the same battalion only after having been discharged from the 10th County of London battalion, when it had been discovered that, at seventeen, he was underage. Tucker admitted that 'I had no Welsh connections of any kind. My new soldier comrades were real dyed-in-the-wool Welshmen who for various reasons had been living in London. Most of them spoke Welsh.'[59] Once at the training centre in Llandudno, however,

> it became obvious that the supply of real Welshmen exiled in London had run out and fell grievously below the number required for battalion strength. More and more non-Welshmen were therefore accepted, including a fair number of unmistakable London cockneys. Finally, pure Welshmen formed only the proud nucleus of the battalion.[60]

The last two tables drawn from *SDGW* have utilized the searchable facility of the CD-ROM to generate data that would have been irretrievable without immense labour, had one been able to use only the published volumes. Thus far, all analyses have been of those soldiers who died whilst serving with the Welsh regiments. Quite evidently, Welsh-born soldiers did not serve only in those units that were identifiably Welsh. Many joined units which had no specific regional base, such as the Royal Artillery, the Royal Engineers, the Royal Army Service Corps, the Royal Army Ordnance Corps and the Royal Army Medical Corps. Others joined infantry regiments which were simply not Welsh. The Welsh press in late 1914 and early 1915 reported that many Welsh soldiers were joining units as diverse as the Dublin Fusiliers, the Worcestershire Regiment, the Royal West Kents, the Munster Fusiliers and the East Lancashire Regiment.[61] Some Welsh-born men, of course, might have been living in England, and joined regiments such as the Cheshires, Herefordshires or King's Shropshire Light Infantry. Prior to the creation of the Welsh Guards in 1915, Wales was a designated recruiting area for the Grenadier Guards, so one would also have expected to find many Welsh soldiers in its ranks.[62] The motives for joining non-Welsh units no doubt varied widely. For some family ties or traditions may have been important, for others the glamour attached to a particular regiment. W. R. Owen, a Cardiff civil servant, attempted with a group of friends to join the 21st Lancers, only for one of the group to be below the required minimum height for the cavalry. They all joined the Rifle Brigade instead.[63] The army itself appears often to have exercised a major influence over the destination of volunteers as well as conscripts, Peter Simkins noting that 'it was not unusual for a recruit who met all the required standards to be persuaded to join the regiment of a county far removed from the place where he lived and worked'.[64] Drafts of Welsh volunteers were used to buoy up battalions in English regiments, such as the East Surreys and the Wiltshires, that were having trouble filling their ranks, and drafts of English soldiers were moved into the 38th (Welsh) Division when its supply of Welsh recruits began to peter out.[65] Wilfred George Bowden enlisted at Pontypridd in the 5th Welsh, only to be transferred with a batch of other recruits to the Cheshire Regiment, before moving again, this time to the 4th RWF.[66]

SDGW allows us to get some sense of the diversity of the service experience of Welsh recruits. Searching by town of birth, one can categorize the dead according to whether they served with a Welsh regiment, with a non-Welsh regiment with a distinctive regional identification (such as an English county regiment), or with a unit that ostensibly had no specific regional link (such as the Royal Artillery, Royal Engineers and so on). It should be noted that, frequently, units in the last category did recruit from Wales and were sometimes attached to Welsh formations, such as the 38th (Welsh) Division, but that the specific detachment in which they served is usually not recorded in *SDGW* and it is not possible to disentangle 'more Welsh' sub-units from the larger arm or corps.[67] A second caveat is that the earlier point about the disproportionate impact of casualties on different units is likely to apply with greater force to many of the service and support arms, making *SDGW* a less reliable indicator of overall patterns of service than of patterns of service between units of the same type (such as the infantry).

For this analysis thirty-four Welsh towns were selected from which to analyse the dead. The geographical location of these towns is shown in Map 6.3. The sample is a random one, with an attempt being made to include at least one settlement from each of the thirteen counties of Wales. The total number of the dead from each town varies widely, as may be seen

Map 6.3 Towns sampled.

from Table 6.10, from just 10, in the case of Hirwaun, to 204, in the case of Barry (both in Glamorgan). It would have been possible to undertake a complete survey of all Welsh-born dead recorded in *SDGW*, but as this would have involved working one's way through all 635,000 entries (it being impossible electronically to filter out the Welsh-born from the rest) it has not been attempted here. The purpose of this exercise is, then, simply to indicate the range of possible destinations for Welsh-born soldiers. A more rigorous analysis of the recruiting dynamics involved would need to pay greater attention to the available data on residence and place of enlistment, as well as to information (sometimes carried by *SDGW*) about transfers between units.

All that said, Table 6.10 reveals that, of the 1,614 Welsh-born dead sampled in this exercise, 53.5 per cent died serving with Welsh regiments, 27.5 per cent died serving with non-Welsh regiments, and 19 per cent died serving with units with no distinctive regional identity. The distribution across these three categories varies considerably from town to town, with the highest percentages of locally born dead in Welsh units to be found in Kidwelly (84 per cent), Machynlleth, Connah's Quay, Pwllheli, Brynmawr, Ystradgynlais, Cwmbrân, Llanidloes, Risca and Hirwaun. The lowest proportion of locally born dead is in Milford Haven (21.6 per cent), and other towns with fewer than four-tenths of their dead serving in Welsh regiments are Ammanford, Barry, Knighton and Rhayader.[68] A more extensive analysis might reveal a geographical pattern (such as an east–west divide, with proximity to the border being reflected in lower percentages in Welsh regiments) but this data can support no such hypothesis, with the most remote and inaccessible of all Welsh towns (Aberystwyth) returning a lower percentage of dead serving in Welsh regiments than the border town of Chepstow.

Table 6.10 Distribution by unit type, from towns sampled.

Town	Number of dead	Percentage in Welsh regiments	Percentage in non-Welsh regiments	Percentage in non-regional units
Aberystwyth	88	47.7	36.4	15.9
Amlwch	22	59.1	13.6	27.3
Ammanford	20	35.0	15.0	35.0
Bala	23	60.9	26.1	13.0
Barry	204	34.3	46.6	19.1
Beaumaris	23	56.5	30.4	13.0
Bridgend	76	44.7	28.9	26.3
Brynmawr	55	70.9	9.1	20.0
Caerphilly	40	40.0	35.0	25.0

Table 6.10 *Contd.*

Town	Number of dead	Percentage in Welsh regiments	Percentage in non-Welsh regiments	Percentage in non-regional units
Chepstow	78	55.1	28.2	16.7
Colwyn Bay	32	43.8	43.8	12.5
Connah's Quay	16	75.0	12.5	12.5
Cwmbrân[69]	84	70.2	11.9	17.9
Ffestiniog	66	69.7	15.2	15.2
Garw valley[70]	63	63.5	19.0	17.5
Harlech	13	69.2	23.1	7.7
Haverfordwest	82	52.4	19.5	28.0
Hirwaun	10	70.0	30.0	–
Holywell	66	42.4	34.8	22.7
Kidwelly	25	84.0	4.0	12.0
Knighton	55	30.9	52.7	16.4
Lampeter	27	48.1	29.6	22.2
Llanbrynmair	24	66.7	25.0	8.3
Llanidloes	47	70.2	21.3	8.5
Machynlleth	33	75.8	9.1	15.2
Milford Haven	37	21.6	37.8	40.5
Nelson	16	62.5	31.3	6.3
Pwllheli[71]	51	72.5	19.6	7.8
Rhayader	23	26.1	65.2	8.7
Risca	57	70.2	14.0	15.8
Ruthin	39	53.8	12.8	33.3
Tenby	46	54.3	23.9	21.7
Tonypandy	56	53.6	26.8	19.6
Ystradgynlais	17	70.6	11.8	17.6
TOTAL	1614	53.5	27.5	19.0

Source: *Soldiers Died in the Great War 1914–19*

Table 6.11 takes just a selection of the towns sampled to show which Welsh and non-Welsh infantry regiments were the most represented amongst the locally born dead. The identity of the Welsh regiments corresponds roughly to the nominal recruiting areas of those regiments, but whereas the identity of some of the non-Welsh regiments appears to follow a geographical logic (the connection of the King's Shropshire Light Infantry to Knighton and of the Gloucestershire Regiment to Chepstow being obvious examples), others (the links between the Devonshires and Tonypandy, or the Cheshires and Tenby) were probably generated by the army's decisions about the destination of particular groups of recruits.[72]

Table 6.11 Regiments with highest representation, from towns sampled.[73]

Town	Welsh regiment with highest representation	Non-Welsh regiment with highest representation
Aberystwyth	Royal Welch Fusiliers and Welsh Regiment	Cheshire Regiment
Barry	Welsh Regiment	Rifle Brigade
Brynmawr	South Wales Borderers	Gloucestershire Regiment
Chepstow	Monmouthshire Regiment	Gloucestershire Regiment
Colwyn Bay	Royal Welch Fusiliers	King's Liverpool Regiment
Ffestiniog	Royal Welch Fusiliers	King's Liverpool Regiment
Garw valley	Welsh Regiment	Duke of Cornwall's Light Infantry
Haverfordwest	Welsh Regiment	London Regiment
Knighton	South Wales Borderers	King's Shropshire Light Infantry
Llanidloes	Royal Welch Fusiliers	King's Shropshire Light Infantry
Milford Haven	Welsh Regiment	Royal Fusiliers
Rhayader	Royal Welch Fusiliers	Herefordshire Regiment
Tenby	Welsh Regiment	Cheshire Regiment
Tonypandy	Welsh Regiment	Devonshire Regiment

Source: *Soldiers Died in the Great War 1914–19*

To summarize the results of the analysis of *SDGW*, one may state with some confidence that Welsh-born soldiers in Welsh regiments were very likely to be serving alongside soldiers born outside Wales, particularly soldiers born in England. The proportions varied markedly from unit to unit, but ethnic heterogeneity was a marked feature of all Welsh regiments in the Great War. Furthermore, whilst many Welsh-born recruits served in Welsh regiments, almost as many may have served in other regiments, ranging from the Household Cavalry to the Argyll and Sutherland Highlanders, and from the Connaught Rangers to the Durham Light Infantry. Lewis Valentine, for example, served with the Royal Army Medical Corps, later writing that:

> I was sent to France to the first battles of the Somme. There, boys from the East End of London were my fellow-soldiers, the majority of them, – talented blasphemers, shameless fornicators, impudent thieves, and 'birds of crime' of all sorts, but I learnt to like them greatly, and I saw that God did not have his way with the best of men every time, nor the devil have his with the worst.[74]

Research undertaken by other scholars reveals that the Welsh regiments may have been considerably less ethnically homogeneous than their counterparts in both Ireland and Scotland. Using *SDGW*, Nick Perry has calculated that only 29 per cent of soldiers serving in Irish regiments during the Great

War were born outside Ireland (the comparable figure for Wales is 49.3 per cent). The 'most Irish' regiment was the Irish Guards, with 84 per cent of its dead Irish-born, the 'least Irish' the Royal Inniskilling Fusiliers, with 61 per cent of its dead Irish-born.[75] Perry has also examined the records for the Scots Guards and Cameron Highlanders, showing that the percentages of Scots-born dead in both cases were 58 and 88 respectively. As for the Somerset Light Infantry, although the proportion of dead born in Somerset was relatively low (40 per cent), the proportion of dead born in England was very high (95 per cent).[76] There is little doubt that some Scottish units were forced to recruit outside their nominal recruiting areas: most of the men in the 51st (Highland) Division were Scots, but not necessarily Highlanders, and as early as April 1915 the Division included a Lancashire Brigade. In 1917 the 16th Highland Light Infantry received a draft from Nottinghamshire, Derbyshire and Yorkshire depots, and there were so many Yorkshiremen in the 1st/4th (Ross and Cromarty) Seaforth Highlanders by the middle of 1917 that cricket matches were a popular recreational activity.[77] Undoubtedly more work is required, particularly on Scottish regiments, and on the regimental destinations of the Irish- and Scottish-born soldiers who died, before a conclusive comparative assessment may be made, but from the evidence presented here it appears that Welsh regiments suffered even more heavily than Irish and Scottish regiments from the steady erosion of their national identity, understood as reflected by the birthplaces of those in their ranks.

The impression given here of the diversity of Welsh regiments is one that has not been previously appreciated, in terms either of the range of that diversity or of the extent to which it characterized most Welsh regiments. In the remainder of this chapter a more speculative argument is explored, moving away from the specific investigation of statistical evidence for Welsh units and Welsh-born soldiers, to much broader studies of 'combat motivation': the impulses and beliefs which enabled men to carry on serving and fighting in very difficult and highly dangerous circumstances. After consideration of this material the discussion will revert to an examination of the relevant evidence for Welsh soldiers.

'Combat motivation theory', as it is sometimes termed, first developed out of studies of American soldiers conducted during the Second World War.[78] A substantial literature has grown up around this subject, some sociological, some psychological and a great deal historical.[79] Much of this scholarship, though not all, argues that, in the words of Hew Strachan, 'the small group – the rifle section, the platoon, at most the company – is the key to morale. Men fight not for their countries or even their regiments, but for their mates'.[80] A welter of historians of the British Army in the Great War have argued for the centrality of strong bonds ('love' is not an

Chris Williams

unknown term in this context) between front-line soldiers (the 'primary group') in explaining their doggedness, endurance and loyalty.[81] As John Baynes wrote in his study of the 2nd Scottish Rifles at Neuve Chapelle:

> Trust in the group is an essential part of the soldier's development. At the lowest levels the individual is dependent on his immediate fellows to an extraordinary degree. A private soldier in action finds that his section becomes the centre of his life. He finds his platoon and company important as well, and as far as reputation is concerned he thinks occasionally about the battalion and division he is in. But the small groups are the vital ones.[82]

The significance of the comradeship that evolves between the three central characters, Bourne, Shem and Martlow, is the powerful organizing theme of Frederic Manning's work, *Her Privates We*.[83] Manning (born Australia, 1882) fought with the King's Shropshire Light Infantry on the Western Front, and wrote that although his characters in his book were fictitious, 'the events described in it actually happened'.[84] At the end of the volume, after Shem has been wounded and taken away and Martlow killed, Bourne reflects that 'they had been three people without a single thing in common, and yet there was no bond stronger than that necessity which had bound them together'.[85] George Coppard, who served during the Great War with both the Royal West Surrey Regiment and the Machine Gun Corps, considered that morale amongst soldiers was based on 'trust and comradeship founded on the actual sharing of dangers together'.[86] This experience of 'sharing', of mutual interdependence and close loyalties in the tense circumstances of front-line service, appears to have had the potential to override the many social and cultural differences that marked men off from one another. Denis Winter considers that 'there was much more during the Great War to unite men than to divide them', and this argument has been extended to other Great War armies, most notably the French, German and the Russian.[87]

Such views have not gone wholly unchallenged, either at the level of the general argument, or of the specific instance of the British Army during the Great War. Omer Bartov has argued, with reference to the *Wehrmacht* on the Eastern Front during the Second World War, that the tremendous losses in combat and the rapid turnover of manpower amongst combat units meant that German forces could not rely on the 'primary group' for their cohesion.[88] Stéphane Audoin-Rouzeau, in his study of French trench journalism, concludes that 'the fraternity of the trenches was largely illusory', although much of the evidence he cites appears to point in the opposite direction.[89] In the case of the British Army during the Great War, recent work by Niall Ferguson and Joanna Bourke may mark an attempted revision of the importance of the 'primary group'. Ferguson suggests that the

152

importance of 'pals' should not be overstated, particularly as (he states) 'units often went into action shortly after being formed [and] friendships were so often terminated by death'. He prefers to see 'individualist, inward ways of coping' as counting for more.[90] The evidence on which Ferguson draws is, however, very slight, and it is certainly arguable, first, that many units did not go into action 'shortly after being formed', and second, that the prospect of violent death actually intensified feelings of friendship, rather than dissipated them. Joanna Bourke feels that 'comradeship' has become a cliché, and has made a sustained assault on the importance of 'male bonding' to the cohesion of British troops.[91] Yet her test of what would constitute effective 'bonding' is unrealistically high: 'It is axiomatic in the history of the First World War that servicemen "bonded" together, united by the gender-specific experiences of warfare. . . . It was sufficient to be "men": branch of service, rank and age meant little within the bond of shared military experiences.'[92] However, few of the authors already cited suggest that 'comradeship' easily crossed the divide between officers and other ranks, and to argue that '[a]lthough there was a certain amount of male bonding in wartime, such bonding was, however, contingent upon a wide range of conditions such as class and political identity' is hardly a dramatic qualification of the 'cliché'.[93] Furthermore, although she is right to point to tensions between front-line and rear-area troops, she overstates the degree of differentiation between 'Regular servicemen, Territorials and conscripted men'.[94]

Overall, although Ferguson and Bourke usefully caution against too ready an acceptance of the orthodoxy of 'comradeship', and remind us that we need to demonstrate, rather than assume, its relevance, their arguments are insufficiently substantial or well-rounded for the concept to be discarded. On the contrary, it may still be contended that such 'primary group loyalty' was a meaningful social force within the British Army during the Great War. 'Comradeship', born of necessity, brought many fighting men closer together. Perhaps this was only temporary and contextual, but while it lasted it could be profound and vivid.

Evidence from Welsh officers and soldiers, and from those serving with Welsh regiments, about comradeship and its potential to break down barriers between front-line servicemen, including those between Welsh and English troops, is not monolithic in the readings it offers. Llewelyn Wyn Griffith, born in Denbighshire, wrote in 1931 that the British army was 'an army of brothers', and 'there were two kinds of men in the world – those who had been in the trenches and the rest'.[95] Yet in a later essay, in 1968, he suggested that the Welsh language was an effective barrier to soldiers becoming totally absorbed in army culture:

English is the language of the Army, Welsh the language of friendship and companionship, 'ours' against 'theirs'. There is, inside you, a citadel which cannot be stormed by force, but which can be entered with the key of language. And when you find yourself in the company of your fellow countrymen, private soldiers with a private language with which to escape from this new world of drill and parade and discipline, a language belonging exclusively to a way of life in which you were nurtured and from which you are now exiled, companionship brings a new kind of intimacy. A new bond is created, a sense of being a community within a community, which intensifies the very meaning of comradeship.[96]

It would not be appropriate to discount this testimony altogether, but it is necessary to observe that Griffith's suggestion that his 'regiment, the Royal Welch Fusiliers, consisted mostly of Welsh-speaking Welshmen' is not borne out by the evidence drawn from *SDGW*, which, as has already been seen, suggests that under half of the RWF's dead were Welsh-born.[97] Emlyn Davies (also born in Denbighshire), who served with the 17th RWF, explained that whilst its infantrymen did not much like the Royal Engineers ('[t]hey did not fight'), there was 'comradeship always, a happy association' with the fellow foot-soldiers in the 55th West Lancashire Division.[98] Wilfred Bowden 'soon made new friends' on his transfer from the 5th Welsh to the Cheshire Regiment, but W. A. Tucker, the aforementioned Londoner who ended up in the 15th RWF, related that the Welshmen in the battalion initially 'accepted me in friendly and cultured fashion, but they quickly and outspokenly exposed that I was *not* Welsh'.[99] At the training centre in Llandudno there was occasional friction: 'As almost always happens among bodies of men drawn from various areas with different interests there were several partisan or sectarian disputes, a few of which ended in punch-ups.'[100] The most powerful testimony on this subject comes from the pen of David Jones, who captured the atmosphere of service and combat in a moving, human, non-polemical way.[101] The dedication of *In Parenthesis* sets the tone, being (*inter alia*) to:

No. 4 Working especially Pte R. A. Lewis – Gunner from Newport Monmouthshire killed In Action In The Boesinghe Sector NW of Ypres Some Time In The Winter 1916–17 And To The Bearded Infantry Who Exchanged Their Long Loaves With Us At A Sector's Barrier and To The Enemy Front-Fighters Who Shared Our Pains Against What We Found Ourselves By Misadventure[102]

When David Jones's central character, John Ball, names his friends, he names a group of ten.[103] When, later, a friend is relieved from the pre-parations for the attack on Mametz Wood, in order to serve as a runner for

HQ Company, his colleagues are upset '[f]or such breakings away and dissolving of comradeship and token of division are cause of great anguish when men sense how they stand so perilous and transitory in this world'.[104] Two nights before the attack John Ball snatches a brief meeting with two other friends from different companies:

> These three seldom met except for very brief periods out of the line – at Brigade rest perhaps – or if some accident of billeting threw them near together. These three loved each other, but the routine of their lives made chances of foregathering rare.
>   They talked of ordinary things. Of each one's friends at home; those friends unknown to either of the other two. Of the possible duration of the war. Of how they would meet and in what good places afterwards. Of the dissimilar merits of Welshmen and Cockneys.[105]

When the attack comes, John Ball finds himself in Mametz Wood, but the men of 'B' Company, with whom he had begun the attack, and from whose presence he had taken comfort and reassurance, could not be seen: 'You wished you could see people you knew better than the 'C' Company man on your right or the bloke from 'A' on your left, there were certainly a few of No. 8, but not a soul of your own – whichever way.'[106] Vividly, Jones's description of combat evokes the importance of 'mates'. And although cultural differences between 'Welshmen and Cockneys' are noted, the things that unite them cannot be left unsaid: 'the same jargon, the same prejudice against 'other arms' and against the Staff, the same discomforts, the same grievances, the same aims, the same deep fears, the same pathetic jokes'.[107]

If the qualitative evidence does not yield a clear impression one way or the other as to whether front-line service broke down barriers between Welsh and English soldiers serving alongside each other, neither do comparative studies emerge with a clear view. The Austro-Hungarian army has been considered a 'prison of the nations', its ethnic divisions a fundamental cause of its ineffectiveness, but it has also been argued that the Habsburg high command was successful in postponing the 'breakdown of its multinational forces until the closing stages of the conflict'.[108] Opinions are similarly divided on the French army. Audoin-Rouzeau considers that 'the diversity of geographical origins . . . constituted a considerable obstacle to individual rapprochement', yet Eugen Weber suggests that war carried soldiers 'all over a country they had recently learned about from books, forced them to "relearn French" in order to communicate with comrades and civilians, opened a door on unknown worlds, milieus, ways of life'.[109] Edward Spiers feels that comradeship developed between Scottish soldiers on the one hand and those, including Lancastrians, Gurkhas and Sikhs, 'with whom they were sharing the dangers and duties at the front', and Nick Perry considers that '[i]n general, non-Irish soldiers seem to have blended in well with the Irish troops' and that 'loyalty to their regiments, friends and comrades . . . kept the Irish troops going'.[110] John Bourne colourfully points out that, in the army, 'colonial pioneers, men who had travelled the world and tamed the wilderness, rubbed shoulders with Batley weavers who thought folk from Dewsbury had two heads'.[111] As for British and Empire forces more generally, J. G. Fuller in his study of troop morale and popular culture observes that:

> A striking feature of war memoirs is the rarity with which regional differences are alluded to, at least among English troops. As cross-drafting began the process of 'nationalizing' the various formations, men were confronted, often for the first time, by their countrymen from distant parts. The experience seems rarely to have been a surprising one. . . . men coming to a first-line Territorial battalion from outside might be struck by the narrowness of the men's viewpoint, by their shared local knowledge and intense suspicion of 'foreigners' from the nearest towns or counties, but they were not presented with an entirely unfamiliar welter of customs, attitudes, and recreations. Men played the same games, sang mainly the same songs, cherished like jokes and popular idols.[112]

Peter Simkins also suggests that, in the latter years of the war, as the 'highly localized character of early 1916 evaporated, the army increasingly became a "nationalized" force', closer to being 'a nation in arms' than ever before.[113] As with the French, the very business of training in different parts of Britain, of moving back and forth across the Channel, of coming into contact with fellow Britons hailing from diverse backgrounds and locations, could only widen horizons.[114] Of course, this was not always a positive experience: the 9th RWF were given a hostile reception in Weston-Super-Mare in January 1915 by locals, who believed them to be the 'wild and undesirable' Welsh miners who often visited the town during the summer season![115]

This chapter has explored connections between national identities and military service, using a range of qualitative and quantitative material in Welsh, British, European and imperial contexts. Particularly in relation to memoirs and war literature, there are narrative conventions that need further exploration than has been possible here. There are other, largely unpublished, sources, in both English and Welsh, that might shed further light on soldiers' views of their wartime experiences.[116] The records of *SDGW* could be subjected to further analysis, to qualify and to deepen the understanding provided thus far. That quantitative evidence points strongly towards ethnic heterogeneity as being a very common characteristic of Welsh regiments. It also suggests that Welsh-born men served in a wide range of units, well beyond the Welsh regiments themselves. What impact such experiences had no doubt varied from individual to individual. There was no universal experience of the trenches, and any process involving hundreds of thousands of men cannot be expected to produce a single consensus. Generalizing from the small number of memoirs is a necessarily speculative exercise, and the contextualization of Welsh material within broader debates about comradeship across a range of different armies and time periods has, it is hoped, performed a useful framing function. A tentative suggestion is that, all other things being equal and in the majority of cases, the dynamic loyalties of the 'primary group', the pressures towards comradeship, were probably sufficient to heighten a sense of shared experience and of common understanding between 'Welsh' soldiers, whether they were 'genuine Taffies' or not. David Jones's lines may thus provide an apposite ending: in 'the sudden violences and the long stillnesses' of the Western Front, '[m]en marched, they kept equal step . . . / Men marched, they had been nurtured together.'[117]

NOTES

[1] I should like to thank Andy Croll, Angela Gaffney, Martin Johnes, Major Nick Lock, Professor Keith Robbins, Colonel Richard Sinnett and Toby Thacker for specific comments on aspects of this research, as well as audiences at Aberystwyth, Bochum, Bryn Mawr (USA), Gregynog, London, Philadelphia and Pontypridd.

[2] John Davies, *A History of Wales* (London, 1994), p. 514.

[3] Erich Maria Remarque, *All Quiet on the Western Front* (St Albans, 1963; original edition 1929), p. 177.

[4] HMSO, *Statistics of the Military Effort of the British Empire During the Great War 1914–1920* (London, 1922), p. 363. All statistics relating to Wales in this chapter include Monmouthshire.

[5] Angela Gaffney, *Aftermath: Remembering the Great War in Wales* (Cardiff, 1998), p. 151; though note that, according to J. M. Winter, 'Britain's "lost generation" of the First World War', *Population Studies*, 31 (1977), 450–1, some 12.9 per cent of those serving in the British Army were killed during the conflict. If that proportion held true for Welsh enlistees, then the total dead would amount to 35,207.

[6] Peter Simkins, 'The four armies 1914–1918', in David Chandler and Ian Beckett (eds), *The Oxford Illustrated History of the British Army* (Oxford, 1994), p. 241.

[7] Anthony Smith, *National Identity* (Harmondsworth, 1992), p. 27.

[8] J. M. Winter, 'British national identity and the First World War', in S. J. D. Green and R. C. Whiting (eds), *The Boundaries of the State in Modern Britain* (Cambridge, 1996); J. H. Grainger, *Patriotisms: Britain 1900–1939* (London, 1986).

[9] Gerard De Groot, *Blighty: British Society in the Era of the Great War* (Harlow, 1996).

[10] Keith Robbins, *Nineteenth-Century Britain: England, Scotland, and Wales: The Making of a Nation* (Oxford, 1988).

[11] Ibid., pp. 175, 183.

[12] Ibid., pp. 174–5.

[13] Robbins, *Great Britain: Identities, Institutions and the Idea of Britishness* (Harlow, 1998).

[14] Gaffney, *Aftermath*; John S. Ellis, ' "Unity in diversity": ethnicity and British national identity, 1899–1918' (unpublished Ph.D., thesis, Boston College, 1997); Ellis, ' "The methods of barbarism" and the "rights of small nations": war propaganda and British pluralism', *Albion*, 30 (1998).

[15] Gervase Phillips, 'The Welsh soldier in the First World War' (unpublished M.Phil. thesis, University of Wales, Aberyshyth, 1991); Phillips, 'Dai bach y soldiwr: Welsh soldiers in the British army 1914–1918', *Llafur: Journal of Welsh Labour History*, 6, 2 (1993).

[16] Phillips, 'Dai bach y soldiwr', 94. Phillips drew on records of over 200 Welsh servicemen taken from the so-called 'unburnt documents' available at the National Archives, identifying 'Welsh' records by the problematic method of surnames. His evaluation of the apparently mutually exclusive options for 'Welsh characteristics' – 'submergence' by Britishness, or continued survival – ignores the possibility that national identities may be multiple, layered and situational.

[17] *Soldiers Died in the Great War 1914–19, Part 29: The South Wales Borderers* (repr. edn, Polstead, 1989), p. 51.

[18] *Free Press of Monmouthshire*, 11 Aug. 1916.

[19] His grave may be found at Flat Iron VI J8.

[20] For discussion of the potential of the source see Martin G. Staunton, '*Soldiers Died in the Great War 1914–19* as historical source material', *Stand To!*, 27, 6 (1989).

[21] See Simon Fowler, William Spencer and Stuart Tamblin, *Army Service Records of the First World War* (Richmond, 1996).

[22] There are exceptions, in the shape of those who were omitted from the original lists.

[23] Ian Beckett, 'The Territorial Force', in Ian F. W. Beckett and Keith Simpson (eds), *A Nation in Arms: A Social Study of the British Army in the First World War* (Manchester, 1985), p. 147. See also the important work of Nick Perry, 'Nationality in the Irish infantry regiments in the First World War', *War & Society*, 12 (1994), and 'Maintaining regimental identity in the Great War: the case of the Irish infantry regiments', *Stand To!*, 52 (1998).

[24] Dot Jones, *Statistical Evidence Relating to the Welsh Language 1801–1911* (Cardiff, 1998), pp. 145–6.

[25] Expatriate Welshmen, it was hoped at the time, would join Welsh regiments. According to Welsh Army Corps, 1914–1919, *Report of the Executive Committee* (Cardiff, 1921), p. 6, the ranks of the Corps were to be 'filled by residents of Wales, and, Welshmen throughout the Empire'; and J. E. Munby (ed.), *A History of the 38th (Welsh) Division* (London, 1920), p. 1, mentions the inclusion of 'Welshmen resident in London, Liverpool and Manchester'.

[26] The source for all tables and maps, except where otherwise stated, is *SDGW*.

27 Robert Graves, *Good-Bye To All That: An Autobiography* (Oxford, 1995 [1929]), p. 71.

28 Siegfried Sassoon, *Memoirs of a Fox-Hunting Man* (London, 1928); Sassoon, *Memoirs of an Infantry Officer* (London, 1930); Bernard Adams, *Nothing of Importance: A Record of Eight Months at the Front with a Welsh Battalion, October, 1915 to June, 1916* (London, 1917).

29 Vivian de Sola Pinto, *The City That Shone: An Autobiography (1895–1922)* (London, 1969), p. 141; Brigadier Lord Silsoe (Malcolm Trustram Eve), *Sixty Years a Welsh Territorial* (Llandysul, 1976), pp. 16–17.

30 Graves, *Good-Bye To All That*, p. 90.

31 Ibid., p. 80. See also Clive Hughes, 'Army recruitment in Gwynedd, 1914–1916' (unpublished MA thesis, University of Wales, Bangor, 1983), ch. 3.

32 Llewelyn Wyn Griffith, *Up To Mametz* (London, 1931). See also Graves, *Good-Bye To All That*, p. 160.

33 *Soldiers Died in the Great War 1914–19* (Naval and Military Press, Dallington, CD-ROM Version 1.1, 1998).

34 The discrepancy of 29 between the 24,588 dead recorded in Table 6.1 and the 24,559 recorded through the more detailed analysis of birthplaces is largely explicable through the elimination, in the latter analysis, of duplicate entries.

35 Percentage totals may not be exactly 100.0, owing to rounding.

36 Additional source, for census data: Jones, *Statistical Evidence*, pp. 242–9.

37 The figure for *SDGW* differs from that in Table 6.2 because of the removal from the calculation of 'Wales not given', and of changes produced by rounding.

38 Graves, *Good-Bye To All That*, pp. 91–2.

39 Saunders Lewis, 'Profiad Cymro yn y fyddin: 1. Yn Lloegr', *Y Cymro*, 5 (23 July 1919), reproduced in Gerwyn Wiliams, *Tir Neb: Rhyddiaith Gymraeg a'r Rhyfel Byd Cyntaf* (Cardiff, 1996), p. 290; (my translation); Lewis, 'Departmental committee on Welsh', Thomas Jones C. H. Papers, NLW, H21/7.

40 Ian Beckett, 'The nation in arms, 1914–18', in Beckett and Simpson, *Nation in Arms*, p. 11.

41 J. C. Dunn, *The War the Infantry Knew 1914–1919* (London, 1994 [1938]), pp. 429–30; Graves, *Good-Bye To All That*, p. 80.

42 Keith Simpson, 'Introduction' to Dunn, *War the Infantry Knew*, p. xxxviii; Graves, *Good-Bye To All That*, p. 80, estimated that the regular battalions of the regiment contained 'no more than one Welshman in fifty in the ranks'.

43 Perry, 'Nationality in the Irish infantry', 73.

44 *SDGW*.

45 Dunn, *War the Infantry Knew*, p. 246.

46 Graves, *Good-Bye To All That*, pp. 88–9; Dunn, *War the Infantry Knew*, p. 245. Dunn notes (p. 246) that '[w]hen a chance offered the Shropshires were bartered for half their number of RWF from a neighbouring division'.

47 Dunn, *War the Infantry Knew*, p. 430.

48 Frank Richards, *Old Soldiers Never Die* (Sleaford, 1994 [1933]), p. 274.

49 De Sola Pinto, *City That Shone*, p. 147. See also Silsoe, *Sixty Years a Welsh Territorial*, pp. 18–19.

50 Peter Simkins, *Kitchener's Army: The Raising of the New Armies, 1914–16* (Manchester, 1988), p. xv.

51 E. A. James, *British Regiments, 1914–18* (London, 1978).

52 Munby (ed.), *History of the 38ᵗʰ (Welsh) Division*, pp. 3–4; Thomas O. Marden, *The History of the Welch Regiment Part II: 1914–1918* (Cardiff, 1932), p. 285; Clive Hughes, 'The New Armies', in Beckett and Simpson, *Nation in Arms*, p. 116.

53 De Sola Pinto, *City That Shone*, p. 192.

54 Dunn, *War the Infantry Knew*, p. 246.

55 Beckett, 'Territorial Force', p. 146. Englishmen, surplus to requirements, had been drafted in from the 1st Lincolnshire Regiment: Hughes, 'Army recruitment', p. 85.

56 Of the 9th Welsh, M. St Helier Evans, who served with the battalion as an officer, noted that most of his men hailed from the Rhondda. *Going Across, or With the 9ᵗʰ Welch in the Butterfly Division: Being Extracts from the War Letters and Diary of Lieutenant M. St Helier Evans*, ed. Frank Delamain (Newport, 1952), extract reproduced in John Richards (ed.), *Wales on the Western Front* (Cardiff, 1994), p. 64.

57 Not all battalions have been included in this table. Excluded are all those with fewer than 100 soldiers who died with birthplace information, most of those being reserve or depot battalions.

58 London, 1963 [1937], p. 160.

59 W. A. Tucker, *The Lousier War* (London, 1974), pp. 12–13.

60 Tucker, *Lousier War*, p. 14. According to Emlyn Davies, *Taffy Went To War* (Knutsford, 1975), p. 3, the 17th RWF, also stationed at Llandudno, attracted 'Lancashire lads', who chose to enlist there as 'the North Wales resorts formed their favourite holiday spots'; they were also attracted by the prospect of 'a few months training by the sea'.

61 *Welsh Outlook*, 1, 10 (Oct. 1914) 417; *WM*, 29 Dec. 1914, 7 Jan. 1915.

62 Ivor Nicholson and Trevor Lloyd-Williams, *Wales: Its Part in the War* (London, 1919), pp. 33–5; Hughes, 'Army recruitment', pp. 154–5; *WM*, 1 Dec. 1914.

63 Simkins, *Kitchener's Army*, p. 180.

64 Ibid., p. 183.

65 Hughes, 'New Armies', p. 103; Joanna Bourke, *Dismembering the Male: Men's Bodies, Britain and the Great War* (London, 1999), p. 150; Perry, 'Nationality in the Irish infantry', 87. This became a matter for complaint in the *Welsh Outlook*, July 1916, 212–13, and Feb. 1917, 44–5.

66 Wilfred George Bowden, *Abercynon to Flanders – And Back: An Autobiography of a World War One (1914–18) Soldier from Abercynon in South Wales* (Risca, 1984), pp. 20, 26, 28–9. See also Dunn, *War the Infantry Knew*, p. 245.

67 Welsh Army Corps, *Report*, pp. 21–32; Colin Hughes, *Mametz: Lloyd George's 'Welsh Army' at the Battle of the Somme* (Guildford, 1990), p. 23. According to Munby (ed.), *History of the 38ᵗʰ (Welsh) Division*, p. 8, both the 123rd and 124th Field Companies of the Royal Engineers were drawn from recruits who had enlisted into the 13th Welsh.

68 An interesting comparison with *SDGW* data is afforded by the lists of Barry recruits, together with their regiments, that were printed in the *Barry Dock News* [*BDN*] from 26 May to 28 July 1916. The percentage of these recruits enlisting in Welsh regiments is similar to that yielded by *SDGW*: 32.9 per cent, as against 34.3 per cent; but there are significant discrepancies between the percentages for

non-Welsh regiments (31.6 per cent, as against 46.6 per cent) and non-regional units (35.5 per cent, as against 19.1 per cent). The fact that 64.5 per cent of the recruits listed in the *BDN* joined the infantry, as contrasted with 80.9 per cent of the Barry-born dead listed in *SDGW*, may reflect the better chances of survival in non-front-line units.

69 'Cwmbrân' also includes Croesyceiliog, Griffithstown, Pontnewydd and Sebastopol.

70 'Garw valley' includes Blaengarw, Llangeinor, Pantygog and Pontycymmer.

71 'Pwllheli' also includes Criccieth and Llanystumdwy.

72 Of the 930 total dead of the 9th Devonshire Regiment, 70 (that is 7.5 per cent) were Welsh-born, most of them from Glamorgan. Hughes, 'New Armies', p. 103, notes that the battalion attracted only 80 local men and was forced to fill its ranks mainly with recruits from London and the Midlands.

73 Only a selection of towns sampled are represented in this table. In other cases the numbers falling into one or other of the categories were so small as to make the exercise of little worth.

74 Cited by Wiliams, *Tir Neb*, p. 220 (my translation).

75 Perry, 'Nationality in the Irish infantry', 71. See also Keith Jeffery, *Ireland and the Great War* (Cambridge, 2000), pp. 33–5, 41, 59.

76 Perry, 'Nationality in the Irish infantry', 72–3.

77 J. G. Fuller, *Troop Morale and Popular Culture in the British and Dominion Armies 1914–1918* (Oxford, 1990), pp. 163–4; Edward Spiers, 'The Scottish soldier at war', in Hugh Cecil and Peter H. Liddle (eds), *Facing Armageddon: The First World War Experienced* (London, 1996), p. 316; Spiers, 'The regular army in 1914', in Beckett and Simpson, *Nation in Arms*, p. 53; Simkins, 'Four armies', p. 259; Ewen A. Cameron and Iain J. M. Robertson, 'Fighting and bleeding for the land: the Scottish Highlands and the Great War', in Catriona M. M. Macdonald and E. W. McFarland (eds), *Scotland and the Great War* (East Lothian, 1999), pp. 84–5; John Baynes, *Morale: A Study of Men and Courage: The Second Scottish Rifles at the Battle of Neuve Chapelle 1915* (London, 1967), p. 136; G. Urquhart, 'Negotiations for war: Highland identity under fire', in Bernard Taithe and Tim Thornton (eds), *War: Identities in Conflict 1300–2000* (Stroud, 1998).

78 Particularly S. L. A. Marshall, *Men Against Fire: The Problem of Battle Command in Future War* (New York, 1947). See also Arthur J. Vidich and Maurice R. Stein, 'The dissolved identity in military life', in Stein, Vidich and David Manning White (eds), *Identity and Anxiety: Survival of the Person in Mass Society* (Glencoe, IL, 1960), pp. 493–506; S. A. Stouffer et al., *The American Soldier: Combat and its Aftermath* (New York, 1965); Morris Janowitz and Edward A. Shils, 'Cohesion and disintegration in the Wehrmacht in World War II', in Janowitz, *Military Conflict: Essays in the Institutional Analysis of War and Peace* (Beverly Hills, 1975), pp. 177–220.

79 For a recent survey see John Keegan, 'Towards a theory of combat motivation', in Paul Addison and Angus Calder (eds), *Time to Kill: The Soldier's Experience of War in the West 1939–1945* (London, 1997), pp. 3–11.

80 Strachan, 'The soldier's experience in two world wars: some historiographical comparisons', in Addison and Calder, *Time to Kill*, p. 371. For similar arguments

see Christopher Coker, *War and the Twentieth Century: A Study of War and Modern Consciousness* (London, 1994), pp. 156–7; John Ellis, *The Sharp End of War: The Fighting Man in World War II* (Newton Abbot, 1980), pp. 328, 339, 341, 352; Richard Holmes, *Firing Line* (London, 1994), pp. 291–307; John Keegan, *The Face of Battle: A Study of Agincourt, Waterloo and the Somme* (Harmondsworth, 1978), p. 51; Eric J. Leed, *No Man's Land: Combat and Identity in World War I* (Cambridge, 1979), p. 24; John A. Lynn, *The Bayonets of the Republic: Motivation and Tactics in the Army of Revolutionary France, 1791–94* (Boulder, CO, 1996), pp. 31–2; George MacDonald Fraser, *Quartered Safe Out Here: A Recollection of the War in Burma* (London, 1992), p. 11; Mark Urban, *Rifles: Six Years with Wellington's Legendary Sharpshooters* (London, 2004), pp. 288–9.

[81] Tony Ashworth, *Trench Warfare 1914–1918: The Live and Let Live System* (Basingstoke, 1980), p. 155; J. M. Bourne, *Britain and the Great War 1914–1918* (London, 1989), p. 220; Bourne, 'The British working man at arms', in Cecil and Liddle, *Facing Armageddon*, pp. 345–6; John Ellis, *Eye-Deep in Hell: Trench Warfare in World War I* (New York, 1976), pp. 197, 202; Fuller, *Troop Morale*, pp. 21–3; Richard Holmes, *Tommy: The British Soldier on the Western Front 1914–1918* (London, 2005), pp. 531–2; Peter Liddle, 'British loyalties: the evidence of an archive', in Cecil and Liddle, *Facing Armageddon*, pp. 525–9; Denis Winter, *Death's Men: Soldiers of the Great War* (Harmondsworth, 1979), pp. 20–1, 45, 52, 54–6.

[82] Baynes, *Morale*, p. 102.

[83] Manning's novel was first published under the title *The Middle Parts of Fortune* in 1929. A fuller, if still expurgated, version was published as *Her Privates We* in 1930. The unexpurgated version was finally published in London in 1999, and it is from this edition that quotations are taken.

[84] Ibid., p. vii.

[85] Ibid., p. 232.

[86] George Coppard, *With a Machine Gun to Cambrai: The Tale of a Young Tommy in Kitchener's Army 1914–1918* (London, 1969), p. 77.

[87] Winter, *Death's Men*, pp. 20–1; Marc Ferro, 'Le soldat russe en 1917: indiscipline, patriotisme, pacifisme et révolution', *Annales: Économies, Sociétés, Civilisations*, 26 (1971), 37; Jacques Meyer, *Les Soldats de la Grande Guerre* (Paris, 1966), pp. 44–5; Antoine Prost, *In the Wake of War: 'Les Anciens Combattants' and French Society* (Oxford, 1992), p. 20; Hew Strachan, 'The morale of the German army, 1917–18', in Cecil and Liddle, *Facing Armageddon*, pp. 388–92; Eugen Weber, *Peasants into Frenchmen: The Modernization of Rural France 1870–1914* (London, 1979), p. 298.

[88] Omer Bartov, *Hitler's Army: Soldiers, Nazis, and War in the Third Reich* (Oxford, 1992), pp. 5, 30–58.

[89] Stéphane Audoin-Rouzeau, *Men at War 1914–1918: National Sentiment and Trench Journalism in France during the First World War* (Oxford, 1992), p. 52, but see, for example, pp. 46–7.

[90] Niall Ferguson, *The Pity of War* (London, 1999), p. 354.

[91] Joanna Bourke, *An Intimate History of Killing: Face-to-Face Killing*

in *Twentieth-Century Warfare* (London, 1999), pp. 141–2; and Bourke, *Dismembering the Male*, pp. 126–70. See also Ilana R. Bet-El, 'Men and soldiers; British conscripts, concepts of masculinity, and the Great War', in Billie Melman (ed.), *Borderlines: Genders and Identities in War and Peace 1870–1930* (London, 1998), pp. 86–8.

92 Bourke, *Dismembering the Male*, p. 126.

93 Ibid., pp. 144–5.

94 Ibid., pp. 145–6, 149. The latter formulation ignores the New Army altogether.

95 Griffith, *Up To Mametz*, pp. 180, 21.

96 Ll. Wyn Griffith, 'The pattern of one man's remembering', in George A. Panichas (ed.), *Promise of Greatness: The War of 1914–1918* (London, 1968), p. 287.

97 If one correlates the counties of birth of the Welsh dead of the RWF with the proportions of the male population between fifteen and forty-four recorded at the 1911 population census as being able to speak Welsh (an admittedly very approximate measure), then one might calculate that 58 per cent of the Welsh dead of the regiment as a whole would have been Welsh-speakers. The proportions of Welsh monoglots would respectively have been 12 and 13 per cent. Griffith's post-Second World War career as an influential Welsh public figure in the fields of culture and broadcasting may also have coloured his recollection. As he noted in 1968 (ibid., p. 293),

[t]he knowledge that the Somme and Passchendaele had more than decimated the youth of Wales, had almost destroyed a generation of my countrymen, may have brought me closer to my own country and helped to make me devote myself to playing a part in some kind of reconstruction of what we regarded as our national culture.

98 Davies, *Taffy Went To War*, p. 46.

99 Bowden, *Abercynon to Flanders*, p. 26; Tucker, *Lousier War*, p. 13.

100 Ibid., p. 14.

101 For a discussion of the extent to which *In Parenthesis* may be read as an authentic account of Jones's wartime experiences, see Colin Hughes, *David Jones: The Man who was On the Field. In Parenthesis as Straight Reporting* (Manchester, 1979). Hughes concludes (p. 22) that:

in writing *In Parenthesis* David Jones used a strictly historical account of the capture of Mametz Wood and of events leading up to it as a frame on which to weave his poetry, using as material his own observations and experiences. Sometimes – though not often – the experiences are transposed from other periods of the war, but only if they are typical of what would have been happening in the period to which they are assigned.

102 Jones, *In Parenthesis*, p. x.

103 Ibid., pp. 69–70.

104 Ibid., p. 136.

105 Ibid., p. 139.

106 Ibid., p. 171.

107 Ibid., p. x.

108 Geoffrey Wawro, 'Morale in the Austro-Hungarian Army: the evidence of Habsburg Army campaign reports and allied intelligence officers', in Cecil and Liddle, *Facing Armageddon*, pp. 409–10; David Englander, 'Mutinies and military morale', in Hew Strachan (ed.), *The Oxford Illustrated History of the First World War* (Oxford, 2000), p. 194.

109 Audoin-Rouzeau, *Men at War*, p. 50; see also Audoin-Rouzeau, 'The French soldier in the trenches', in Cecil and Liddle, *Facing Armageddon*, p. 222; Weber, *Peasants into Frenchmen*, p. 477.

110 Spiers, 'Scottish soldier at war', pp. 318–19; Perry, 'Nationality in the Irish infantry', 88–9.

111 Bourne, *Britain and the Great War*, p. 219.

112 Fuller, *Troop Morale and Popular Culture*, p. 160.

113 Simkins, 'Four armies', pp. 259, 262.

114 A point also made by Linda Colley, *Britons: Forging the Nation 1707–1837* (New Haven, CT, and London, 1992), p. 313, in relation to troop movements during the French and Napoleonic Wars.

115 Hughes, 'Army recruitment in Gwynedd', p. 79.

116 Particularly in the Imperial War Museum, the Liddle Collection at the University of Leeds, and in the National Library of Wales at Aberystwyth.

117 *In Parenthesis*, p. x, and title-page to Part I.

7

Christ and Caesar? Welsh Nonconformists and the State, 1914–1918

ROBERT POPE

O n 18 September 1914, the bill to disestablish the four dioceses of the Anglican Church in Wales received Royal Assent and, in effect, became law. At least on the surface it was a victory for the Welsh Nonconformists, whose faith in the freedom of the individual conscience and whose unwillingness to allow any external forces the right to interfere with personal conscience, especially in matters of religious conviction, appeared to have been vindicated. Even if its implementation would be delayed because of the Great War, which had broken out just over a month earlier, disestablishment appeared to reinforce Nonconformity's influence on Welsh public matters while also bearing witness to the strength, both political and moral, of its political ally, the Liberal Party. It was, after all, the Liberals who, in the nineteenth century, had made the stand for freedom of conscience over a Tory-dominated establishment and gradually repealed all the legislation which had effectively made second-class citizens of Nonconformists. Disestablishment, for Welsh Nonconformists, appeared to confirm that they were right to enter into partnership with the Liberal Party and that both (frequently overlapping) constituencies shared the same basic principle – that the individual should be free to follow the dictates of his or her conscience.

On 19 January 1916, the Military Service Act was passed, conscripting all single men between the ages of eighteen and forty-one into the army. The debate over conscription had rumbled on since at least the summer of 1915, when it had become clear that the war would not be over quickly and that the number of volunteers for the armed forces was insufficient to meet the need at the front. Even those Welsh Nonconformists who had supported the war opposed this new measure. Many of them remained silent, lest they have a detrimental effect on the war effort; others were vociferous in their opposition. This one move, more than any other, marked the end of both political Nonconformity and the Liberal Party. Conscription, for Welsh Nonconformists, was the issue which demonstrated that they had very little influence over government policy and that, when facing a national crisis, the government would act according to political necessity and even expediency, rather than in accordance with the highest (religious) ideals. As for the Liberal Party, it emerged from the war its reputation in tatters, its strength dissipated and its allies in disarray.

The disestablishment campaign and the opposition to conscription were two aspects of a far wider debate which, though rarely referred to directly in this period, was in fact an essential aspect of Nonconformist history and identity, namely the correct nature of the relationship between the Church and the State. Nonconformity had emerged because of a specific belief about how that relationship should be exercised. The national crisis which erupted in the summer of 1914 was, perhaps, the first occasion when Nonconformists considered a real compromise over that belief. This chapter discusses how the Welsh Nonconformists perceived their relationship with the State and how they tried to reconfigure it in the context of the pressures of the Great War.

ESTABLISHMENT AND DISESTABLISHMENT

Nonconformity's historical antecedents can be found among those groups which sought to keep separate what could be termed 'spiritual' authority from 'temporal' or 'civic' authority. Following the teaching of the Continental Reformers, particularly that of John Calvin, the sixteenth-century Puritans challenged the idea that the government or the monarch of the day could dictate to their citizens or subjects over matters of religion. Puritanism emerged in Britain particularly during Elizabethan times, when theology, rather than political expediency, caused its adherents to think both that the Henrician reforms had not gone far enough and that the Church had retained too much that pertained to Rome, while its Erastian basis contravened their understanding of faith, the ecclesiastical community and human character.

This was not to say that the Puritans and the Dissenters of the sixteenth and seventeenth centuries opposed the State per se. Instead, following Calvin (who was himself following the teaching of St Paul in Romans 13), they believed that the State (or the monarch) had a particular role in the divine economy. 'Let every person be subject to the governing authorities; for there is no authority except from God, and those authorities that exist have been instituted by God', said Paul (Rom. 13: 1). The upshot of the teaching in those few verses of the letter to the Romans is that those who hold temporal authority have been placed there by the divine will and that, consequently, they can claim the allegiance and obedience of their citizens. They are 'not a terror to good conduct, but to bad . . . the servant of God to execute wrath on the wrongdoer' (vv. 3, 4).

Calvin, building on the teaching of Scripture (and Augustine's interpretation of it)[1], claimed something similar. The governing authorities had been put in place by God and had to be obeyed, even if those who exercised authority were oppressive and heavy-handed in their government:

> We are not only subject to the authority of princes who perform their office toward us uprightly and faithfully as they ought, but also to the authority of all who, by whatever means, have got control of affairs, even though they perform not a whit of the princes' office . . . Indeed . . . those who rule for the public benefit are true patterns and evidences of this beneficence of his [that is, God's]; that they who rule unjustly and incompetently have been raised up by him to punish the wickedness of the people.[2]

Nevertheless, Calvin allowed two exceptions to this rule. When an unjust ruler is opposed, by a properly constituted authority (rather than by the arbitrary whim of the individual), in the name of justice, this may be interpreted as God's intervention. 'Here are revealed his goodness, his power, and his providence. For sometimes he raises up open avengers from among his servants, and arms them with his command to punish the wicked from miserable calamity.'[3] Secondly, though in similar fashion, obedience to the State is not required when it means disobedience to God's will.

> But in obedience which we have shown to be due the authority of rulers, we are always to make this exception, indeed, to observe it as primary, that such obedience is never to lead us away from obedience to him, to whose will the desires of all kings ought to be subject, to whose decrees all their commands ought to yield, to whose majesty their sceptres ought to be submitted. And how absurd would it be that in satisfying men you should incur the displeasure of him for whose sake you obey men themselves![4]

This teaching was adopted, with a degree of subtle reinterpretation, by the early Nonconformists: those who had rejected the State's right to interfere in religious practice but upheld the State's right to be the State. Both Robert Browne, the unstable pioneer of English Separatism, and Robert Harrison, a more convinced advocate of the Puritan way, had emphasized that Christ alone should be obeyed in the Church and that religion was not a matter over which the State should enforce allegiance. Yet both saw the State as fulfilling an important role. In Browne's case the State was to care for the Church; in Harrison's case the State was to promote reformation.[5] John

Smyth, a Fellow of Christ's College, Cambridge, and an early Separatist who helped to gather the church at Gainsborough in 1606, made the point clearly:

> The magistrate is not by virtue of his office to meddle with religion or matters of conscience, to force or compel men to this or that form of religion or doctrine; but to leave Christian religion free to every man's conscience, and to handle only civil transgressions . . . for Christ only is the King and Lawgiver of the Church and conscience.[6]

During the period of the Commonwealth those attracted to Puritanism in both its Independent (Congregational) and Presbyterian forms took a more compromising approach to the State, for they saw Cromwell's government, however mistakenly, as encapsulating their own highest principles. Nowhere was this better seen than in Wales. The government declared itself responsible for providing suitable preachers and ensured that Henry Walter, Walter Cradock and Richard Symonds all worked in south Wales, with £300 set aside for their stipend, while Ambrose Mostyn, Vavasor Powell and Morgan Llwyd were ordered to work in the north, with £350 set aside for them.[7] William Erbury, one of the most zealous of the early Welsh Puritans, and one who was convinced that individual conscience was supreme, refused to accept payment, on the grounds that the government should not interfere in religion, even if its interference was beneficial.[8] Morgan Llwyd was similarly convinced, and offered the advice 'neither seek to soften anyone else's conscience to your own opinion by force, but by reason, and allow everyone to speak his mind in peace, if he is peaceable'.[9] But he accepted his stipend after 1656.[10] Much of this was anomalous and, as R. Tudur Jones stated, recognized as such at the time: 'The compromises that were inherent in the attempt to reconcile a national State-supported church with the ideal of liberty of conscience were easily exposed by Anglican and Separatist alike.'[11]

Following the restoration of the monarchy in 1660, the Nonconformists were considered too dangerous to be allowed freedom to follow conscience in religious matters – they had, after all, executed the monarch. Legislation was introduced which reduced the rights of the Nonconformists as citizens, culminating in the Great Ejection of St Bartholomew's Day, 1662, which was the defining moment in the history of modern Nonconformity. While most Welsh Nonconformists had already left the Church (some 60 per cent of the identifiable Nonconformists left their livings in 1660),[12] 'Black Bartholomew' marked the point from which they were regarded as outsiders, disenfranchised and unable to take any real part in public life. This set the political nature of Nonconformity in Wales right up to the outbreak of war in 1914. Nonconformists sought the repeal of the discriminatory laws and the establishment in law of the principle of the liberty of individual conscience in matters of religion, both tasks being complicated by their exclusion from public life before the repeal of the Test and Corporation Acts in 1828. Following the extension of the franchise in 1868, they entered into a virtual partnership with the Liberal Party during the later nineteenth century.

By the beginning of the twentieth century, the modern Nonconformists had inherited a world-view which considered the Church and the State to be separate entities with separate responsibilities in the divine economy. They were not to interfere with each other unless ungodly policies were being pursued. Through their partnership with the Liberal Party, Nonconformists had ensured that all the discriminatory laws were repealed over the course of the nineteenth century, but the Anglican Church still retained its privileged position as part of the establishment. The Anglicans, who had followed the teaching of the seventeenth-century divine Richard Hooker, had promulgated a very different view of the relationship between the Church and the State. Hooker had made the case that: 'Church and State are one society, and this society is called the State because it lives under secular law . . . and Church because it possesses the spiritual law of Jesus Christ.'[13] The result was a concordat between the Church and State which secured rights and privileges for all those who subscribed to this view. The Nonconformists, being excluded from such privileges, gradually were persuaded that they should enter into a campaign to disestablish the Church of England in Wales.

Disestablishment came to the fore among Welsh Nonconformists shortly after the passing of the Reform Bill in 1832. By that time, and wearied by their treatment as second-class citizens, some Nonconformists considered disestablishment to be the panacea for all their ills. Samuel Roberts ('S.R.'), John Roberts ('J.R.') and Hugh Pugh were early spokesmen for disestablishment, and it is not insignificant that they were all Independents and spiritual descendants of Erbury, Cradock and Powell. The more conservative Calvinistic Methodists, who had separated from the Anglican Church in 1811, not for reasons of ecclesiology but in order to develop their own spirituality, were not convinced. Their patriarch, John Elias, endeavoured to dissociate himself from such radical views,[14] while the Association meeting at Bala in 1834 passed a resolution which repudiated the idea of 'divorcing the State Church from the Government'.[15] At least half a century would pass before they would join the campaign, by which time they had entered into closer relationships with other Nonconformists under the collective aegis of the 'Free Churches'.

After the 1851 census, which revealed the numerical superiority of the Nonconformists of Wales over the members of the Church of England, the disestablishment campaign gathered momentum – especially as Liberal and Nonconformist representation in the House of Commons increased. From

1865 onwards, more Liberals were returned for Welsh constituencies than Tories, and the meeting of Nonconformist grievances became inevitable.

The final disestablishment campaign, described by R. Tudur Jones as 'a sad affair, which bore all the hallmarks of a Greek tragedy',[16] was fought in two halves, the one occurring during the Liberal administrations of 1890–5, the other following the landslide Liberal victory in the 1906 election. The major hallmark of the campaign was its success in establishing the principle that Wales was a nation and ought to be treated as such. Those who supported the campaign for disestablishment during these years, Gladstone included, did so because the Anglican Church did not hold the allegiance of the vast majority of the religious population, a fact underlined by the evidence received by the Royal Commission on the Church of England and other Religious Bodies in Wales and Monmouthshire. However, it was not a victory for the 'Voluntary Principle', contrary to the beliefs of many Nonconformists. Had it been so, then the Church would also have had to be disestablished in England. While some Welsh Nonconformists believed that the State should be separate from the Church and that the State should not favour any particular group in society, in fact many of them agreed that it was more the superior status of Nonconformity in Wales that made the establishment of Anglicanism such an injustice. In fact, to all intents and purposes, it appears that many would have been satisfied with instituting a new, Nonconformist 'establishment' in Wales, in the same way as Morgan Llwyd had compromised with Cromwell's policies over two centuries before.

What was revealed in the disestablishment campaign was the idea that the State ought not be related to the Church in any governing sense, especially when the majority of religious practitioners had opted for a different form of religion. There can be little doubt that the campaign emerged from within a mindset established by Calvin's recognition that the two belonged to separate spheres of responsibility. But its fervour and potency – if not also its eventual success – relied far more on the sense of injustice that one group was the subject of undue privilege and that, in Wales, that group represented a minority within society. Any claim of victory, then, was more a victory for democracy (understood as following the will of the majority) than a victory for principle. That did not augur well when both the Church and the State were faced with the crisis of war.

NONCONFORMISTS AND THE WAR

Perhaps the most surprising fact about the churches' response to the outbreak of war was that support for armed action was virtually unanimous. Nonconformists, in particular, had been heavily embroiled in the movement for international peace and in criticism of other conflict for at least thirty years prior to 1914. The 'Nonconformist Conscience' had been active in opposing the Boer War and the build-up of militarism on the Continent. In fact, this was one way in which Nonconformists had revealed themselves to be independent of the political and social establishment. Yet, when war was declared in 1914, the vast majority of Free Church leaders, including the Baptist patriarch John Clifford, the Scottish Free Church minister and radical journalist Robertson Nicoll and the Congregationalist Campbell Morgan, as well as the Free Church journals, such as the *British Weekly*, supported the war and justified it with a righteous indignation which made much use of theological language. Robertson Nicoll put it thus:

> If we had not been Christians, we should not have been in this war. It is Christ . . . who has taught us to care for small nations and to protect the rights of the weak . . . the devil would have counselled neutrality but Christ has put the sword into our hands.[17]

The Nonconformists' almost total abandonment of the peace policy following the declaration of war was truly remarkable. Alan Wilkinson accounts for it by claiming that attempts for peace that preceded war were only temporary phenomena, a passing phase rather than a commitment to a new policy.[18] Be that as it may, it must be said that many of the Nonconformists, especially (though not exclusively) the Welsh ones, had fallen under the beguiling influence of their most famous son, David Lloyd George. The 'greatest Bible-thumping pagan of his generation' did not hesitate to utilize the pulpit rhetoric on which he had been raised in order to pursue the war and to persuade others of its propriety.[19] As he told a meeting in the City Temple: 'As the Lord liveth, we had entered into no conspiracy against Germany . . . We are in the war from motives of purest chivalry to defend the weak . . . [the] poor little neighbour [Belgium] whose home was broken into by a hulking bully.'[20] Through his mastery of religious rhetoric – particularly when in pursuit of his own goals – not to mention his understanding of the Nonconformist psyche, Lloyd George certainly played an important part in convincing Welsh Nonconformists to embrace the war as just, fought against an overbearing militarism which became, at least from the Allied powers' perspective, a virtual incarnation of evil. With the support of the religious establishment, he succeeded, according to Dewi Eirug Davies, 'in making a bloody war into a holy crusade'.[21] The result was that Nonconformists in England and Wales, almost entirely, supported the war effort.

In conformity to the tradition of the Just War, Welsh Nonconformists agreed that the qualifications of *jus ad bellum* had been met. There was no other option but to honour ancient treaties and go to war against a nation that had swept through 'little Belgium' and was, in the process, guilty of horrific atrocities. John Gwili Jenkins, the poet and radical Baptist preacher, claimed in his denomination's weekly *Seren Cymru* that the government could be trusted when it claimed that war had been inevitable.[22] H. M. Hughes, the highly regarded and influential Congregational minister of Ebeneser Chapel, Cardiff, also asserted that war had been inevitable, given the rise in German militarism, and that the British conscience could be clear for pursuing it,[23] but he warned against allowing the churches themselves to be involved in military activity.[24] The Calvinistic Methodists' *Goleuad* proclaimed, in September 1914, that militarism had to be opposed and the rape of the nations, which had begun with Belgium, simply had to be stopped.[25] For a number of years, the Wesleyan paper *Y Gwyliedydd Newydd* had been uncompromisingly pacifist, but even it joined in the call for war.[26] Although this appears to be the spiritual sanctioning of conflict, all these instances could be seen as falling into the traditional Calvinistic scheme (including *Y Gwyliedydd Newydd*), even though some of those mentioned (Gwili Jenkins, for example) were certainly not traditional Calvinists. Because war was a just option – it being fought to protect the weak – there could be no opposition to government policy. It remained a civil rather than a religious matter and, as such, it was not for the churches to interfere. The churches, then, were to allow the government to pursue the most appropriate policy, providing that policy was just.

The question remained, however, as to what extent, if the war was just, ministers and Church institutions should ensure a safe passage, and even active support, for government policy. Throughout the war, the denominations never deviated officially from total support for the war and righteousness of the cause. As Dewi Eurig Davies has commented:

> At the beginning of the War, all the denominational courts agreed that war was a barbaric policy, but for the sake of its own honour, Britain could not have behaved differently. Britain went to War with clean hands, and with true intent to bring an end to the warmongering spirit that made a lasting peace impossible.[27]

Support for the war varied from person to person, denomination to denomination, but many believed that the churches should act as recruiting agents for the war, and some acted as such, John Williams, Brynsiencyn, being most notorious among them.[28] As D. Densil Morgan has observed, the picture of Sir Henry Jones (the philosopher and former Welsh Calvinistic Methodist) and Lloyd George with the Reverend John Williams, Brynsiencyn, 'resplendent in clerical collar and the uniform of the 38th Welsh, standing in the garden of 11 Downing Street . . . illustrates the extent of Welsh

Nonconformity's compromise with the political establishment of the time'.[29]

The voices of protest were few and far between. Among the ordinary citizens, it is calculated that only about 1,000 professed conscientious objection to the conflict – and not all of those did so on religious grounds – while over 270,000 eventually served in the armed forces.[30] There was a general acknowledgement that war meant that the churches in Europe had failed in their responsibilities, and many voiced concern that the churches should not become media to wage the war and spread militarism. But on the whole the picture of Welsh Nonconformity that emerged was one of compromise and support for the government. The support was based on moral principle, a vital category for a Nonconformity profoundly influenced by Kantian philosophy. The need to honour historic agreements and the need to act in defence of the weak, small nations would override any concern about the morality of war.

Pacifism had yet to emerge as a developed policy, its 'principal intellectual weaknesses' being identified by D. Densil Morgan as 'an inability to face the implications of corporate responsibility and explicitly social ethics, and an idealism which had scant appreciation for the depths of human malignancy and evil'.[31] Nevertheless, there were those who opposed conflict in general, and this war in particular, on Christian and moral grounds. Among the more prominent were John Puleston Jones, the blind preacher of the Calvinistic Methodist Connexion; George M. Ll. Davies, also a Calvinistic Methodist and a man who would become famous for his work with the Fellowship of Reconciliation;[32] Herbert Morgan, the radical Baptist who spent much of his life as a tutor in the Extra-Mural Department at the University College of Wales, Aberystwyth; and Thomas Rees, the principal of Bala-Bangor Theological College, whose vociferous opposition resulted in vilification in the press and his ignominious and subsequently much-vaunted expulsion from Bangor Golf Club.[33]

Like others at the time, John Puleston Jones protested that the Church had been implicated in the growth of militarism by failing to condemn war down the centuries. If it had done so, he asserted, the present war might have been avoided.[34] His opposition to the war was based on a quasi-Calvinistic ecclesiology and a more modern Kantian moralism. For him, the Church was above the State; it was 'an inter-national institution . . . [consisting of] the redeemed of every tribe and language, and people and nation', and could not, therefore, simply endorse the policy of the nation in which it found itself. Its task was basically moralistic: the dissemination of the 'principles of Christ' so that those who adopted them could ensure their employment in whatever political party or other sphere in which they found themselves.[35] As a representative of the Church, it was the minister's task to instruct his congregation in these principles and this morality, rather than persuade them of the justice of government policy.[36] Alongside this, Puleston Jones also stressed a Hegelian evolutionism which allowed that war might have been permissible in more primitive times, but that enlightened modern human beings had come of age and ought to be able to discover other ways to resolve their disputes.[37] Similar arguments would be heard again and again from those who opposed the war.

From 1906 to 1912, Herbert Morgan was the minister at Castle Street Welsh Baptist Chapel, London, and, nominally at least, Lloyd George's pastor and spiritual guide. He had also adopted the pacifist position, basing his stance on the fact that war was inconsistent with Christ's teaching and the Kingdom of God. Morgan identified the problem as existing in the tension between Gospel demands on the one hand, and a contrary demand by the State on the other. This was causing great anxiety, but whenever Christ's law conflicted with British rights and interests the former always had to be obeyed.[38] Writing after the war, Morgan made the point, with his friend Nathaniel Micklem, that context and exigency could not determine whether or not an ideal should be followed.[39] This had implications for the individual's loyalty to the community. Only the community in which the highest ideal was manifest could demand loyalty, and then not because it was a community, but because the highest moral ideal dwelt within it.[40] No individual owed allegiance to any government or nation that pursued immorality. As a result, the State could be opposed in its pursuit of war because 'a moral end can only be served by means which are moral'.[41] Even if the motivation for war was just, war itself ought never be pursued. According to this argument, a government lost its legitimacy when it demanded that its citizens wage war.

For Thomas Rees, the government had acted illegitimately in pursuing the policy of war. His Kantianism was displayed in his deontological avowal that evil could not be defeated by engaging in evil methods. Alongside that, war itself was not a valid policy in trying to resolve disputes. But more, for Rees the cause for war had not been proven: instead, the moralistic cries of the government had hidden the true reason for conflict, namely the championing of British mercantile interests ahead of those of Germany.

These men had drunk deeply from the wells of Hegelian idealism and Kantian moralism. As a result, they believed that humankind was on an evolutionary path towards perfection and was governed by higher perceptions of values and principles. The war was a regression on this pathway, made all the worse because it was entered into consciously. This was not the way to solve international disputes in civilized, Christian societies.

In essence, the difference between the Nonconformists who supported the war and those who opposed it was not related to their understanding of the relationship between the Church and the State. They all saw the State as having its own role, which it should be left alone to fulfil. Nevertheless, those who supported the war believed that the State held the power of the sword (Rom. 13: 4) and had proved the justice of its cause, while those who opposed the war believed that force and violence should not be an option in resolving international disputes, owing to the evolution of history. For the former it was a matter of providential order which meant that the State's right to be the State in its own sphere ought to be upheld and given precedence, even when it was engaged in violent action. For the latter, it was a matter of morality and the overwhelming belief that part of the Church's mission was to ensure that, as well as individuals, public bodies, including the State, should act according to the highest principles, indeed the principles of Christ, at all times. Where the State truly overstepped the mark, however, was on the issue of conscription.

NONCONFORMISTS AND CONSCRIPTION

Conscription had been mooted as a distinct possibility throughout 1915. Robertson Nicoll, who had become a bellicose advocate of the government's war policy, supported it. In June 1915, Ellis Griffith, the MP for Anglesey, had suggested that conscription was a necessary evil, adopting a consequentialist ethic which argued that it would be better to lose freedom for a defined period rather than lose it for ever.[42] In support of conscription, W. R. Owen, a lay Congregationalist living in London, argued that the freedom championed by Nonconformity was, essentially, a *religious* freedom, which sought the right for the Church to regulate its own doctrine, worship and discipline without interference from external authorities and the State. The conviction of conscience could be paramount in matters of faith. But Nonconformists had never claimed that their adherents should not be obedient to the government's laws in matters of civil importance. War, and its legitimacy, were not the concerns of individuals and were not, either, the concerns of the Church, for they were civil rather than religious matters.[43] This was a rather weak argument for, in practice, it left the Church unable to make any real pronouncement on the State, even when the most profound moral principles were being flouted.

Of the Welsh Nonconformists, it is interesting to note that D. Miall Edwards, an otherwise sensitive soul and professor of systematic theology and the philosophy of religion at the Memorial College, the Independents' seminary in Brecon, was relatively nonchalant about conscription. Somewhat unexpectedly, his standpoint was not moralistic. The government had a certain role in God's providence, in the performance of which it could impose its decisions on its citizens. Conscription, then, was the result of the government exercising its God-given right to force its citizens to act in its defence. Edwards qualified his position only by claiming that conscription should not be adopted as a policy until all other options were exhausted.[44]

It has to be said that, despite his careful thought and impeccable theology (for he did, after all, have a point), the bestiality and inhumanity of war still caused 'a crisis of faith' for Miall Edwards.[45] Others did not suffer any such pangs of doubt, and the way in which some Nonconformists refused to stand above national policy did have the appearance of betraying their primary values. As D. Densil Morgan has commented: 'Rather than providing a moral code, a set of values and knowledge of God which could transcend temporal and merely national considerations, institutional Christianity appeared to have become a function of the imperial cause.'[46]

Miall Edwards was in many senses an exception. Welsh Nonconformists in general could not see the logic in fighting a war against militarism in the name of freedom and then allowing the State to introduce such a form of compulsion.[47] The journalist Beriah Gwynfe Evans made the point that militarism could not be defeated by militarism, and that it was for freedom of conscience that so many had enlisted and left so many parents mourning the loss of sons.[48] His colleague E. Morgan Humphreys believed that conscription was bringing a dangerous element into the government, for it attacked the much vaunted 'Voluntary Principle'.[49] Humphreys continued, in almost prophetic fashion, 'Nonconformity was built on the rights of conscience and once authority is granted to a State or an army or an official to trample those rights underfoot, the foundations of Nonconformity will crumble.'[50] It was, in fact, the adoption of the very policies which those Nonconformists who supported the war had hoped would be eradicated by the conflict. The Baptist Ungoed Thomas saw it as a degeneration in morals: 'The acknowledgement of the state's right to force its young citizens, against their own reason, conscience and inclination, to maim and kill their fellow men, indicates the extent to which the Kingdom's morals have deteriorated.'[51] H. M. Hughes also opposed conscription, though he believed that it ought not be opposed openly for fear of undermining the war effort,[52] while J. Gwili Jenkins expressed his disappointment that Lloyd George had chosen to support conscription, in a meeting in Conwy on 6 May 1916. 'Compulsion is every Liberal's *bête noire*', he said, but he made very little protest.[53] Herbert Morgan and Nathaniel Micklem opposed conscription in the name of liberty of conscience, adding that it was, furthermore, a logical contradiction as the war was being fought against 'the attempt on the part of Germany to make dominant and operative a view of the State's all-embracing sovereignty'. Conscription was the symbol of 'the absolute sovereign State which has a right to make an unlimited demand upon a man and to exact unquestioning obedience from him'.[54] But they wrote this after the armistice. As Dewi Eirug Davies has put it, 'the religious press agreed unanimously that compulsion was abhorrent but for the sake of the peace and unity of the country, personal wishes should be temporarily set aside'.[55]

There was an evident tension between standing up for the very principles for which the war was allegedly being fought, on the one hand, and destabilizing the national war effort, on the other. The Calvinistic Methodist General Assembly, meeting in May 1916 at Colwyn Bay, passed the resolution that while 'we as an Assembly promise to do what we can to support the government in its intention to bring this war to a swift and satisfactory conclusion' they would also 'stand by . . . convictions in the matter of peace and individual conscience'.[56] It was, prima facie, an ambiguous avoidance of the issue, but it did at least salve Methodist consciences and it gave a genuine rebuke to the government, as well as to Lloyd George for the way in which he, too, had ridden roughshod over Nonconformist convictions. Of course, the government took no notice; and this was the time when the 'Nonconformist Conscience' fizzled out as a force in British politics. Whether Calvinist or Erastian in viewpoint, the churches in fact had very little influence on government policy when they found themselves in opposition to it. The national crisis allowed political considerations to take precedence over religious ones. Even in a Calvinist system where the State and the Church have their own distinct spheres, with the Church able to criticize when God's will is being undermined, such a view allows politicians to do what they like, regardless of ecclesiastical consent or disapproval.

Thomas Rees was most uncompromising in his reaction to conscription. He opposed the right of the government to conscript men on the same grounds as those on which he had supported the disestablishment campaign. It was a matter of ideal and principle, rather than an attempt by the majority to achieve its goals:

That is the only spiritual power behind the disestablishment campaign, the conviction that the government of the land with its low ideals, its mixed motives and its unspiritual media should not presume to rule the Church of Christ, but the Church, because Christ dwells in it and speaks through it, should be a spiritual authority above the State on every matter of morality and religion.[57]

But instead of this, the Church in every Protestant nation had 'taken the standpoint of its governments and blessed the aims of their own land, with no word to say or mission to pursue which would rise above the limits of "Jew and Greek, barbarian and Scythian" '. He concluded, 'Both the Calvinists of Germany and the Calvinists of Wales have turned God's pulpits into Caesar's platform.'[58]

Rees recognized that governments had always used force to ensure that their policies were implemented. He was, in that sense, not surprised that the government of the day had turned to conscription. He regretted, however, that Nonconformist ministers, supposedly the champions of liberty of conscience and the highest principles, had acquiesced in government policy. Through conscription they had shown themselves to believe 'that the state's need is above principle, above conscience, and able to claim through compulsion and legislation the total obedience of every citizen'.[59] Having achieved disestablishment, he wrote in 1915, the Nonconformists were now turning into an established religion by adopting establishment principles: 'The test of the principle is not how many laws bind this or that denomination but is the church maintaining their [sic] spiritual principles and its Christian position independent of the government and above the state.'[60] In this argument, Rees betrayed his dependence on philosophical Idealism, in that he understood religion to be primarily concerned with the highest principles, and the Church to be entrusted with the mission of establishing those principles in public life. His claim that the Church ought to be independent of the State was based not so much on a Calvinistic criticism of an unjust policy, as on a Kantian sense that the highest moral values and principles should be allowed to dominate in political, as well as individual, life. Nevertheless, it must be said that his activity tended to suggest that the highest moral values could only be personal values and only be employed individually, rather than enshrined in institutions. This was evident in his courageous support of the conscientious objectors, who ought to have the right, he believed, to follow the prompting of their individual consciences, regardless of the social or consensus view. This resulted in his vilification in the press as a supporter of the Kaiser.[61]

At its most extreme, Rees's view – that the individual conscience always takes precedence over the social will – would make social life impossible. It seems that he was unaware of such a possibility, due to his unfailing belief, like Adam Smith, that the autonomous individual, if truly living according to conscience, would inevitably act for the good of others and not simply in self-preservation. There were those, especially on the Continent, for whom the war dispelled any lasting notion that the autonomous individual was anything more than a sinner, unable to redeem him or herself and certainly unable to act in society's best interests. Rees's view would not give rise to a renewed relationship between the Church and the State after the war, while the neo-orthodoxy of theologians such as Karl Barth and Emil Brunner gave at least a basis from which they could enter into a critique of politics – something which would be of some significance during the Second World War.

THE CHURCH AND THE STATE

Clearly, the period 1914 to 1918 was of signal importance for Non-conformists. Following disestablishment, they realized that they had to find a new identity, not least in their relationship with the State. They came to believe that they could no longer be the ally of any single political party, and certainly could not be the ally of the Liberal Party, which emerged from the war morally bankrupt. Thomas Rees was particularly scathing in this regard. The Great War had not affected his espousal of philosophical Idealism or theological liberalism. Instead, it had opened his eyes to a hypocrisy which was deeply embedded in the policy of the Liberal Party. For him, the Liberal Party had betrayed all its principles in order to win a war that was in itself evil, and should never have been fought:

> And however many diseased elements there were in our Liberalism before, it was the part which it played in the war that killed it. It was so contrary to all its previous professions and in the end it was driven to betray its basic principles. When Liberalism fails to protect personal freedom and the rights of every man's conscience, it loses the purpose of its existence.[62]

Rees believed that, during the war, the Liberals had disregarded the fundamental principle of personality, namely, the right of every individual to act according to his or her conscience. Writing in 1920, he noted that political involvement had resulted in the corruption of religion and in the betrayal of Nonconformity by its political allies.

> [Welsh Nonconformity] stood by and approved or tolerated the under-mining of its own foundations, the suspension of civic liberty, the imposition of military compulsion, the oppression of tender consciences and the betrayal of the principles for which its founders made their supreme sacrifices. Thousands of innocent men – let us suppose them mistaken or misguided – yet good and honest men, were imprisoned and cruelly used under the conscription Acts; dozens of them were done to death, and Welsh Nonconformity 'was standing by, and consenting, and keeping the garments of them that slew them.'[63]

Its long-standing preoccupation with politics had resulted in a crisis for Welsh Nonconformity after the war, as it sought to find an identity for itself and to rediscover a *raison d'être* in its fundamental principles. For Rees, this meant adopting a more 'spiritual' religion, which emphasized value and principle above all. This was the basis of his 'pure citizenship', which was his scheme for transforming society by individual commitment and perseverance.[64] While, on the one hand, Rees's ideas would lead to a politicization of the individual as he or she took civil responsibility seriously, it also depoliticized the Church as an institution and suggested a separation whereby the Church concentrated on its religious task and allowed the State freedom to concentrate on its political role. Only individuals were able to cross from one sphere into another. In practice, the Church and the State would live a kind of peaceful coexistence, but tend also to ignore each other. However, Rees's untimely death in 1926 meant that he never really placed his considerable intellect in the service of this 'spiritual' religion, neither did he live long enough to realize the implications this had for the relationship between the Church and the State.

Writing in 1921, Nathaniel Micklem and Herbert Morgan asserted that both Christ *and* Caesar, Church *and* State, were required in the attempt to rebuild the war-torn world. This was not a doctrine motivated by the need of the age; rather, it was based on a theological sense that both had divinely ordained tasks to fulfil for the benefit of humankind. Nevertheless, lessons had been learnt from the war, and they asserted that the Church must be over and above the State, and not subservient to it. Using political science and sociology, they justified this, in the German theologian Ernst Troeltsch's terms, by identifying the Church as a 'counter-cultural group' seeking 'by permeation and peaceful penetration to change the hearts of men and through this change of heart to affect the institutions and civilization'.[65] The implication of their work was, first, that society needed to be changed, second, that the Church's mission was to change it and, third, that change could occur only through the dedication of individuals. This set the tone for the Nonconformist social gospel in the 1920s and for such conferences as that on Christian Politics, Economics and Citizenship at Birmingham in 1924 and the International Conference on Life and Work held in Stockholm in 1925.[66] But again, it can be seen that Micklem and Morgan had very little sense of the Church as a corporate entity. They, like Rees, were left dependent on individuals, with the Church and State being little more than abstractions which, in reality, could not relate to each other because they did not exist apart from the individuals who constituted them.[67]

As well as lacking a clear ecclesiology, by the end of the Great War, Welsh Nonconformists were confused about the role of the State and the way in which they should relate to it. When embroiled in the disestablishment campaign, they knew that the State could be their enemy, especially when it interfered with the religious conscience, and that enemy was incarnate in the established Church. Once disestablishment had been accomplished, they failed to discern a more positive role for the State, especially because it was increasingly influential on the minds of the young through State-regulated education and because its wartime conscription policy was, with hindsight, justified by victory and accepted as such by a relieved and grieving populace.

Welsh Nonconformists would, in the 1920s, turn their attention to social renewal while also, somewhat paradoxically, advocating a withdrawal from direct political involvement. The only scheme remaining for them was to encourage individuals to live according to the highest ideals. What this shows is that, first, after the Great War they became somewhat ambivalent towards the State, perhaps owing to their disappointment at the State's behaviour during it, and, second, they had little sense of what it meant to be the 'Church', apart from a convenient association of individuals. Their Idealist philosophy and liberal confidence in human advance had been unaffected by the carnage wrought across Europe by militaristic rulers and politicians. Their subsequent withdrawal from politics and their dependence on godly individuals left them without an influencing voice through which they might have effected some of the changes they desired. Their depoliticization, and their unwavering faith in theological liberalism, in fact left the Nonconformists bereft of an identity and a mission in inter-war Wales. This would play a part in their mid twentieth-century decline.

NOTES

[1] Augustine reacted to the fall of Rome by writing *The City of God*, in which he identified two 'cities' which believers inhabited, the heavenly city and the earthly city. This distinguished religious from civil authority, but also showed that the same people inhabited the two cities simultaneously. This had major implications for how civil and religious authority should relate to each other.

[2] John Calvin, *Institutes of the Christian Religion*, book II, ed. J. T. McNeill (London, 1961), p. 1512.

[3] Ibid., p. 1517.

[4] Ibid., p. 1520.

[5] R. Tudur Jones, *Congregationalism in England, 1662–1962* (London, 1962), p. 16.

[6] Quoted in Nathaniel Micklem and Herbert Morgan, *Christ and Caesar* (London, 1921), p. 204n.

[7] R. Tudur Jones, *Hanes Annibynwyr Cymru* (Swansea, 1966), p. 47.

[8] *The Testimony of William Erbury Left Upon Record for the Saints of Succeeding Ages* (London, 1658), pp. 333–4.

[9] *Gweithiau Morgan Llwyd*, I, ed. T. I. Ellis (Bangor, 1899), p. 264.

[10] Jones, *Hanes Annibynwyr Cymru*, p. 65.

[11] Jones, *Congregationalism in England*, p. 32. Samuel Roberts ('S.R.'), in the nineteenth century, dismissed the Act of Propagation as 'completely opposed to the will of Christ and the spirit of the gospel' because it 'confounded the free action of the Voluntary Principle'; see S.R., 'Ychydig o hanes yr Eglwys

Gynulleidfaol yn Llanbrynmair', in *Hen Gapel Llanbrynmair*, ed. Iorwerth C. Peate (Llandysul, 1939), p. 40. This was, in part, the result of the Victorian obsession with the moral self. Individual conscience was to be nurtured and could be trusted, and thus it should not be interfered with by any external force. But it was, too, the recognition that in the Act of Propagation, Nonconformists had adopted the same policies as those they had previously opposed and of which they would later – in S.R.'s time – become victims.

[12] Jones, *Hanes Annibynwyr Cymru*, p. 73.

[13] John Keble (ed.), *The works of that learned and judicious divine, Mr. Richard Hooker, Laws of Ecclesiastical Polity*, VIII, I (Oxford, 1874), p. 4.

[14] *Y Dysgedydd*, 12 (1833), 145–9.

[15] E. Pan Jones, *Cofiant y Tri Brawd o Lanbrynmair a Conwy* (Bala, 1892), p. 233.

[16] R. Tudur Jones, *Ffydd ac Argyfwng Cenedl: Hanes Crefydd yng Nghymru 1890–1914, II: Dryswch a Diwygiad* (Swansea, 1982), p. 231.

[17] Cited in Alan Wilkinson, *Dissent or Conform? War, Peace and the English Churches 1900–1945* (London, 1986), p. 27.

[18] Ibid., pp. 22–3.

[19] It was his son, Richard, who coined the phrase. See Richard Lloyd George, *Lloyd George* (London, 1960), p. 10; cited in Adrian Hastings, *A History of English Christianity, 1920–1990* (London, 1991), p. 121.

[20] Cited in Wilkinson, *Dissent or Conform?*, p. 27.

[21] Dewi Eirug Davies, *Byddin y Brenin: Cymru a'i Chrefydd yn y Rhyfel Mawr* (Swansea, 1988), p. 35.

[22] *Seren Cymru*, 7 Aug. 1914.

[23] *Y Tyst*, 12 Aug. 1914.

[24] Ibid., 30 Sept. 1914.

[25] *Y Goleuad*, 4 Sept. 1914.

[26] *Y Gwyliedydd Newydd*, July 1915.

[27] Davies, *Byddin y Brenin*, p. 51. Author's translation.

[28] *WM*, 9 Oct. 1914.

[29] D. Densil Morgan, *The Span of the Cross: Religion and Society in Wales 1914–2000* (Cardiff, 1999), p. 44.

[30] Ibid., p. 64.

[31] Ibid., p. 63.

[32] See E. H. Griffiths, *Heddychwr Mawr Cymru* (Caernarfon, 1967); Griffiths, *Seraff yr Efengyl Seml* (Caernarfon, 1968).

[33] It seems that Bangor Golf Club was swift to act in expelling Rees, for J. Lewis Williams referred to it in his 'Yr eglwys a'r wladwriaeth', *Y Dysgedydd*, 94 (1915), 399.

[34] *Y Goleuad*, 11 Sept. 1914.

[35] R. W. Jones (ed.), *Ysgrifau Puleston* (Bala, 1926), p. 173.

[36] *Y Goleuad*, 18 July 1914.

[37] Ibid., 23 Oct. 1914.

[38] Herbert Morgan, 'The Church and the war', *Welsh Outlook*, 1 (1914), 499.

[39] Micklem and Morgan, *Christ and Caesar*, p. 150.

[40] Ibid., p. 153.

[41] Ibid., p. 171.

42 *Y Brython*, 17 June 1915.
43 W. R. Owen, 'Yr eglwys, y wladwriaeth, a'r rhyfel', *Y Dysgedydd*, 94 (1915), 346–50.
44 'D. M. E.', 'Oddiar y tŵr', *Y Dysgedydd*, 95 (1916), 33.
45 See T. Robin Chapman, 'Argyfwng ffydd Miall Edwards, 1916–1923', in *Y Traethodydd*, 137 (1982), 188–92.
46 Morgan, *Span of the Cross*, p. 46.
47 See *Y Brython*, 3 June 1915.
48 Davies, *Byddin y Brenin*, p. 106.
49 *Y Goleuad*, 7 Jan. 1916.
50 Ibid., 7 July 1916.
51 Ungoed Thomas, 'Trem ar fyd ac eglwys', *Seren Gomer*, 8, 2 (1916), 106.
52 *Y Tyst*, 19 Jan. 1916.
53 *Seren Cymru*, 12 May 1916.
54 Micklem and Morgan, *Christ and Caesar*, p. 142.
55 Davies, *Byddin y Brenin*, p. 108.
56 *Blwyddiadur y Methodistiaid Calfinaidd, am y Flwyddyn 1918* (Caernarfon, 1917), 29.
57 T. Rees, 'Yr eglwys a'r wladwriaeth', *Y Dysgedydd*, 94 (1915), 299. Author's translation.
58 Ibid., 300.
59 Ibid., 301.
60 Ibid., 302.
61 The following poem, for example, appeared in the *Western Mail*, 17 Oct. 1914:

Said Herr Professor von Rees
I've a plan my repute to increase
A nice little sermon
To back up the German
And the wheels of the enemy grease.

62 Thomas Rees, *Gwleidyddiaeth yng Nghymru*, Traethodau'r Deyrnas, 7, (Wrexham, 1924), p. 7.
63 Thomas Rees, 'The crisis of Welsh Nonconformity', *Welsh Outlook*, 6 (1920), 58.
64 Thomas Rees, *Dinasyddiaeth Bur* (Address given during the Gwynedd Temperance Association meeting in Bangor, 18 October 1923) (Liverpool, 1923).
65 Micklem and Morgan, *Christ and Caesar*, pp. 200–1.
66 See Robert Pope, *Seeking God's Kingdom: The Nonconformist Social Gospel in Wales, 1906–1939* (Cardiff, 1999).
67 Micklem and Morgan, *Christ and Caesar*, p. 100.

8

'The second Armageddon': remembering the Second World War in Wales

ANGELA GAFFNEY

On 27 April 1949, twenty-one years after the Welsh National Memorial to the Great War was unveiled, the people of Wales again remembered those who had died in a World War. The inscription 'MCMXXXIX–MCMXLV' was added to the memorial in Cardiff, and this marked the Welsh national commemoration of the fallen of the Second World War.[1] The memorial was rededicated by the Bishop of Llandaf and the ceremony was followed by a march-past, with contingents from the armed forces, the auxiliary forces including the women's services, civil defence associations, the British Legion and representatives of the police. The Cardiff-based daily newspaper the *Western Mail* reported that a 'great crowd' had gathered for the occasion and noted that many of them would have been present in 1928 when the memorial was first unveiled, by the Prince of Wales.[2] Yet the two events were fundamentally different. The ceremony in 1949 was low-key when compared to events in June 1928. Coverage in the self-styled 'national newspaper of Wales' was confined to less than half a page, accompanied by a small photograph, in stark contrast to the prolific reporting of the earlier ceremony, and the *Western Mail*'s editorial comment noted this difference:

> Though yesterday's ceremony commemorated a more perilous conflict than that of 1914–18, in which our gallant Service men proved themselves if possible even more heroic, it lacked inevitably something of the sombre grandeur of the original, of which it was really an extension represented by a plaque, expressing homage to those who gave their lives in the second Armageddon.[3]

The Order of Service for the ceremony mirrored the tone of the occasion, and looks plain in appearance and content when compared to the elaborate programme produced in 1928.[4] This quiet, almost restrained tribute to the fallen was reflected in other modes of commemoration. The Welsh National Book of Remembrance was not initiated until 1956 and was finally presented to the National Museum of Wales in 1966. Yet the Second World War had involved the men and women of Wales to a much greater extent than had the first, both on the battlefield and on the Home Front, and, as Mari Williams has pointed out,

> Few works on the British wartime experience have paid due attention to the distinctive nature of the Welsh situation, and Welsh historians have also failed to make any serious attempt to examine the impact of the Second World War upon the social and cultural life of Wales. Such studies are long overdue.[5]

Apart from a small number of Zeppelin raids, British soil remained inviolate during the Great War, but the threat and reality of air raids in 1940 literally brought war home to the civilian population. Violet Patricia (Pat) Cox, later Leversuch, lived in Cardiff throughout the war years, and her correspondence to family and friends provides a detailed insight into life in Cardiff during the Second World War.[6] In September 1939 public air-raid shelters were constructed at Cardiff Castle, and in November that year a mock air-raid was held in the city. The depiction of this period as the 'Phoney War' is borne out by Pat Cox's reaction to the news that the public were not required to wear gas-masks during the exercise, as no hand-rattles had been sounded to indicate the presence of gas. She commented that 'quite a number of women were glad of this . . . otherwise I am sure our hair would have been in a frightful mess'.[7] Even when heavy air-raids affected south Wales in early 1941, respondents to the Mass-Observation Survey recorded a similar reaction when it was noted that 'people were laughing and talking about not going to the shelters. During the daytime sirens very few people took cover and joked about "Here he is again".'[8] On 2 January 1941, however, Cardiff was subjected to its first large-scale air attack, resulting in fatalities and extensive structural damage.[9] The city endured thousands of incendiaries, together with high-explosive bombs and parachute mines, dropped by over 100 enemy aircraft. The eventual death toll was 165, with many more injured. An ARP (Air-Raid Precautions) warden on duty recalled his experience:

> After signing on at the Post we went out on patrol in pairs. The whole area was lit up with the artificial light of magnesium flares that had been dropped by the enemy . . . The searchlights were busy and the anti-aircraft guns of the ground forces had burst into life . . . During this time I

happened to walk down Westbourne Crescent towards The Parade where at that lookout point I could survey what was going on in Cardiff. When I got there the glare from the scattered fires in the city was clear and substantial damage could be surmised.[10]

The involvement of civilians was crucial to the war effort, and in Cardiff alone ninety-four ARP posts were continuously manned day and night from September 1939 to November 1944, with more than 4,000 voluntary part-time wardens.[11] The register of their activities contains many examples of residents being reprimanded for showing a light during black-out, as well as recording instances of courage and selflessness in often dangerous situations. The register also illustrates the humour that was so important in maintaining morale. In March 1940 two wardens were called to a house in Cardiff where fire was suspected. The report of the incident concluded: 'Investigation resulted in lady wearing hat which was smouldering. Fire promptly put out resulting in complete ruin of hat.'[12]

Mass-Observation reports provide a useful contemporary insight into the impact of war on the Home Front, but other documentary evidence exists, in the form of commissioned art.[13] Shortly after the outbreak of war, the War Artists Advisory Committee was established. Graham Sutherland was employed as an official war artist, and his first major commission was in south Wales during the summer of 1940 to make drawings of bomb damage. He visited Swansea once the air raids on cities began and recorded a variety of subjects, including farmhouses, offices, a public house and the Masonic Hall.[14] The aftermath of a raid in the town centre was also captured by the artist Mona Moore. She was part of a project initiated late in 1939 by the Ministry of Labour and National Service, with the help of the Pilgrim Trust, entitled 'Recording the Changing Face of Britain'. The aim was to make topographical drawings of places and buildings of national interest, particularly those exposed to the danger of destruction or industrial development.[15] Mona Moore had relatives in Swansea and on the Gower Peninsula, and chose to record that area. She arrived in Swansea early in 1941, just after the city had suffered three nights of heavy raids, and recalled that 'much of the dear old Swansea I was so fond of was devastated. I was the only artist at hand and with the backing of my Ministry of Information permit, I did a number of pen and wash drawings.'[16] Mass-Observation respondents reported that morale in Swansea after raids in February 1941 appeared to be good, owing to the efficiency of the emergency organizations. The fact that the centre of Swansea was cordoned off for fear of delayed-action time-bombs was deemed to have helped to conceal the extent of the damage.[17] The destruction of landmarks was often cited as adversely affecting morale, and a respondent in Swansea illustrated this when describing the bombing of a local church in February 1941: 'I mean to say, to me St Mary's was Swansea. Admittedly I use the car park more than the church – I've only been inside it once in my life, but still, it's Swansea.'[18]

The importance of good organization in maintaining morale and a stoic attitude to constant air-raid bombardment is evident in personal correspondence. Pat Cox commented in January 1941 on the heavy raids on Cardiff when

[a] good few land-mines, explosives and high incendiaries dropped very near where we lived. Some people are rather badly off, no homes, but we seem to have enough rest centres, with the help of people offering homes in safe areas to the poor people without, and they are taking it well.[19]

In Swansea it was noted that, since the civic centre was not damaged, the issue of ration books and food supplies continued, ensuring, at least, that some level of normal life would be maintained. Even when the impact was on a far more personal level, a similar response is apparent. After a heavy raid in April 1941 Pat Cox wrote:

I suppose you've noticed the change of address? The reason is that there is no more Five, Brook Street, because in the last blitz on Cardiff, Hirrell's street had some German property 'dropped' on it, and consequently all the houses in the street have been condemned, they have nearly all been pulled down now. I am glad to say that Hirrell, her mother and her two sisters escaped with nothing more than a few scratches and bruises; apart from that they were quite safe. I went round the morning after the Blitz to see how they were, and on that Wednesday morning the postman brought a letter along from you, he just put it in the shop as of course there was no door left; Mrs Davies was very upset, but everybody in the street were real bricks, they can certainly take it.[20]

The Leversuch correspondence documents the progress of the war, commenting on major events such as the invasion of France – which led to very little work being done 'as most of the time was spent in listening to the latest news flashes on the wireless . . . we really couldn't concentrate on work yesterday at all' – and offering sombre reflections on the losses at Arnhem and the advent of the 'doodlebug' bombs.[21] By September 1944 certain wartime restrictions were being eased to evident relief:

Good to know that this fire-watching lark will soon be all over too . . . Next thing I'm looking forward to is a big cut down on coupons required for the different types of clothing. Still, all will be back to normal peacetime standards soon I hope.[22]

Letters such as these allow a contemporary glimpse of everyday life for those on the Home Front as they coped with air-raids, rationing and the constant worrying about loved ones serving with the armed forces. A further collection of letters held at the Glamorgan Record Office provides a poignant example of the devastating impact of war on one family. John Baker lived in Cardiff and had two sons serving in the armed forces. One of his three daughters volunteered and worked as a Sergeant in the Auxiliary Territorial Service.[23] The volumes of correspondence compiled by John Baker consist of letters from his sons, giving insights both into their service life and into the experiences of living away from family and home during the war.[24] Ronald, the younger son, worked, as his father did, in the David Morgan department store in Cardiff, before volunteering for the RAF Volunteer Reserve in February 1940, at the age of eighteen. After training he was based in Lincolnshire and flew on ten operations over France, Germany and Italy. He was a Wireless Operator and Air Gunner in a Wellington bomber, and in February 1943 wrote to his father: 'I made another operational trip some days ago . . . The target was Lorient again. It was the usual show you know . . . That last trip was my 10th. Coming on eh Dad?'[25] Sergeant Ronald Baker and the rest of his crew were killed on his eleventh operational flight in February 1943. He was aged twenty-one.[26]

The telegram reporting Ronald Baker missing was received on 8 February 1943. The following day his father received a letter from Ronald's Wing Commander at RAF Ingham in Lincolnshire, stating that there was 'always the chance that your son may have escaped with his life and has been taken prisoner of war'.[27] This was entered in the scrapbook under the heading 'A little "Ray of Hope" remains', and the search for information began immediately. John Baker responded to the letter by asking specific questions about his son's last mission, including the target for the flight, whether any information was obtainable on how the aircraft was lost, such as being hit by flak, and whether anyone was seen descending by parachute. He concluded that he would 'rather know the worse now than live in false hope, only for those hopes to be shattered at a later date and have a repetition of the first severe shock over again'.[28] Predictably, little operational information was forthcoming, but one of his requests was more easily dealt with. A member of the crew, Barry Sullivan, was Australian, and John Baker had requested his home address so that he would be able 'to write his people a helpful sort of letter'.[29] This was provided, and the ensuing correspondence highlights the relationship that developed between the families of the missing crew after their sons had been reported missing. Sergeant David Pennycock from Dundee was the bomber's Front Gunner, and shortly after the news had been received his parents wrote:

Like yourself we share the anxiety for news of them. We hope and pray that they may have come down safely and been picked up. Should you have any news, will you please write us. We shall do likewise should we have any word. Trusting we all may soon have better news of our boys.[30]

Sadly, no such news was received, and in March 1943 John Baker received a telegram stating that his son was now reported missing, believed killed in action.[31] The exchange of letters appears to have provided a mutual support network for the families, and the correspondence reflects the anxiety and desperate search for news, yet also a continuing concern for each other. Sergeant Pilot Anthony Keeton's parents wrote in March 1943: 'We do hope and pray that you have better news of your boy and that at least he is a prisoner of war. We pray with all our hearts that your boy is safe.'[32] The letters also highlight the refusal to give up hope that their sons may have survived:

It would appear that they have come down in the sea and there may just be a possible chance of them being safe. David was a fairly good French and Spanish scholar and this asset may be of some assistance if they have been picked up.[33]

John Baker was not content to wait for confirmation of his worst fears and sought information from a variety of sources, including the Air Ministry and the British Red Cross Society. In August 1943 the Air Ministry confirmed Ronald's death, but were unable to provide details regarding his place of burial.[34] The lack of firm information led the families to hope their sons might have survived, as is evident in a letter from Anthony Keeton's mother:

It is all very heartbreaking about our dear boys, but I must say that until I get definite proof from the Red Cross where Tony is laid to rest I shall not give up hope entirely . . . Why details have not been forthcoming before this is beyond my comprehension as the majority of people hear within a few weeks of their dear boys being reported killed. I still feel there is something mysterious about the whole business.[35]

It was not until May 1944 that the long wait for news finally came to an end when the families received a letter from the Air Ministry, stating that the International Red Cross in Geneva had provided information that the crew were buried at a cemetery in Guidel, a village ten kilometres north-west of Lorient.[36] Six months later John Baker received a letter from a family friend, Marcel Alin, who was working in Pontivy, approximately sixty kilometres north-east of Guidel.[37] He visited the cemetery in July 1945 and was able to confirm that the graves were well cared for and adorned with flowers. He also confirmed that the bodies of the crew had been bought to Guidel for burial and that full military honours had been observed at the burial service.[38] John Baker passed this information to the families of the other crew members, and the response from Anthony Keeton's father was typical:

> At last after all this time we have something really authentic and I am sure to gain it you must have taken endless time and trouble, my wife and I thank you from our hearts. It is comforting to know where our lads rest and that their resting place is well cared for.[39]

Even when the last glimmer of hope had finally been extinguished, correspondence continued between the families and appeared to provide some degree of comfort. Photographs of the crew were also exchanged, and it is clear that such images were of great importance to the families. In April 1943 David Pennycock's parents enquired whether Ronald had ever sent his father any 'snaps' of the crew. They asked for copies 'so that we could see the Brave Boys' and, once these were supplied, commented in their letter of thanks that they felt 'drawn much closer to each other'.[40] They in turn sent a photo of their son, which could be 'placed alongside his other gallant pals'.[41] Anthony Keeton's mother sent a photograph of 'our dear son Tony and would appreciate very much a photograph of Ronald – I have forwarded one to all the parents of the crew'.[42] A particularly poignant image in the scrapbook shows Ronald standing outside the Mess at an RAF base. The negative for this had been found in the camera of his friend and crew-member, Barry Sullivan, when his personal effects were received at his home in Australia in October 1944. Sergeant Barry Sullivan had stayed with Ronald's family in Cardiff whilst on leave and is described in the scrapbook as 'Ron's Special Chum'.[43] Barry's father had the film developed and sent the photograph to John Baker. Catherine Moriarty has written eloquently about the emotional impact of photography in relation to the Great War, but her comments are equally appropriate for the later conflict. She suggests that the existence of photographs of a loved one, often in military uniform and perhaps taken shortly before the subject embarked for service, can become the most personal form of remembrance. The photograph has an added poignancy, as often this would be the most recent and also the last image, and can be contrasted with more formalized modes of commemoration that did not allow for individual grief:

> Amid the official communications and the censoring of letters the photograph assumed authenticity; incorruptible evidence of dearly loved faces. Thousands of similar photographs would have been destroyed in

battle or returned to families with service-men's 'effects', and in death the portraits of soldiers gained even greater value as the last portrait of an individual, and thus acquired a memorial function.[44]

For the family of Barry Sullivan in Australia the distances involved must have compounded their loss, as it may not have been possible for them to visit their son's grave. On receiving photographs from John Baker, Barry's father responded 'we do appreciate them as you were the last link between us and our lovely boy'.[45] The inclusion of photographs in John Baker's volume of correspondence somehow elevates it from a scrapbook into a personal act of remembrance, not only for his son, but for each member of the crew. The emotive impact and awareness of the sense of loss and grief are compounded by looking at slightly blurred images of smiling young men in uniform. It is rare within families for such images to be discarded, and photographs often remain as the last and most intimate form of personal commemoration.

Ronald Baker's name is included in the Welsh National Book of Remembrance, which lists 12,351 men and women from all arms of the Services. The idea for such a book was first suggested in 1956 by the Council of the British Legion in Wales, who were aware that a similar volume had been produced following the Great War and were concerned at the lack of its equivalent for those who had died during the Second World War. The criteria for inclusion mirrored that of the Great War, namely, those who died whilst serving with the regiments or units of Wales or who were of Welsh birth or parentage.[46] The campaign to produce the book was officially launched in Cardiff in May 1958 with the formation of a large committee, chaired by the Lord Mayor, including representatives of county, borough, urban and rural district councils, ex-service organizations, the armed forces and religious denominations from all parts of Wales. Local authorities were asked for their help in the compilation of names for inclusion. Discussions on who should be included or excluded were extensive, particularly with regard to whether or not to include civilians killed in the war.[47] At a committee meeting in February 1959 attention was drawn to the relative lack of donations to the campaign from north Wales. It was decided to give the initiative more publicity in local newspapers and to publish lists of the donors in the *Liverpool Daily Post*.[48] Problems were not confined to the north, however, as funds were not particularly forthcoming in south Wales. At a meeting of the Finance Committee of Cardiff City Council in July 1960 a request for a contribution to the Book Appeal was considered, but the Town Clerk replied 'that he had been unable to discover any legal power enabling the Corporation to make a contribution'.[49] By October 1960 nearly 18,000 pro formas requesting information on those killed in the war had been distributed throughout Wales, but fewer than half had been returned. The position in Pembrokeshire was described as 'delicate', as it transpired that a Roll of Honour was being compiled for Pembrokeshire alone and, as a result, they were unwilling to provide information for inclusion in the book.[50] Despite the slow progress, work began on preparing the all-Wales volume and attention turned to finding a suitable location to house it. In March 1965 the committee were asked to choose between the Temple of Peace and, the National Museum of Wales, or to suggest some other location.[51] The United Nations Association suggested that as the Great War Book of Remembrance lay in the crypt of the Temple of Peace it would be appropriate to house the new book alongside the old.[52] It was finally decided to place the volume in the National Museum and a site was selected just inside the museum entrance, close to where the Great War Book of Remembrance was originally located, before it was moved to the Temple of Peace.[53]

The Welsh National Book of Remembrance for the Second World War was dedicated by the Archbishop of Wales at a ceremony in Llandaff Cathedral in June 1966, in the presence of the Queen Mother.[54] After the dedication ceremony she laid a wreath at the Welsh National War Memorial on behalf of the ex-servicemen and women of Wales, and presented the book to the Marquess of Anglesey for display in the National Museum of Wales.[55] It was to be displayed in the main hall of the museum in a specially designed steel, glass and granite casket.[56] This was finally completed later than planned, and dedicated in a religious ceremony at the museum in March 1968.[57] The Book of Remembrance remains at the National Museum Cardiff, and is now housed in the Prints and Drawings Study Room within the Art Department. It is available to view by appointment but is essentially out of the public domain. The original location of both the casket and book in the main hall of the National Museum presented a highly visible symbol of Welsh involvement in, and remembrance of, the Second World War. At the dedication ceremony in 1966 the Queen Mother noted that, 'It was fitting that the book would be kept in the museum for those who lived in freedom would be reminded of the debt they owed – a debt that could only be repaid by grateful remembrance of their sacrifice.'[58] Even though the form of commemoration had been the subject of debate, even controversy, the need to remember the dead had rarely been disputed. However, the subsequent destruction of the casket and removal of the book from permanent public display in the museum may suggest a waning of the commemorative impulse.[59] Inherent in the need to remember is the fear of forgetting, and as the years pass it seems that 'Lest we forget' has become a warning, rather than an exhortation.

Unlike after the Great War, a valuable source of contemporary opinion exists on the debates that took place over the most appropriate way to remember the dead of the Second World War. In November 1944 the Mass-Observation Survey recruited a national panel of observers who were asked their views on the form that war memorials should take after the end of the war.[60] The panel members were not a cross-section of the public but were 'more-than-averagely thoughtful people . . . with all sorts of beliefs and in all sorts of jobs'.[61] A common theme ran through the responses, articulated by the plea of one respondent for 'Anything but monuments'. The panel was unanimous in its view that memorials commemorating the Second World War should not echo those built after the First and should 'be useful or give pleasure to those who outlive the war'.[62] Typical comments rejecting stone memorials included:

'Whatever shape memorials take it should not take the form of useless monuments. We are fighting for posterity, so let the memorials be for the use of posterity – libraries, drama schools, playing fields, village halls, they would all serve a useful purpose' (Schoolmistress); 'Certainly not stone monoliths or plaques. Something useful to the community. Memorial halls, clinics, Homes for invalids and distressed – anything useful, but spare us grey stone memorials' (Nurseryman); 'The only point on which my mind is fully made up is that they should not take the form of stone monstrosities on every street corner and village green and not one penny would I willingly contribute to any scheme to erect any such' (Chemist).[63]

The main body of suggestions concerned improving facilities and amenities for the living as the best means of perpetuating the memory of those who had fallen but, as Nick Hewitt has argued: 'Objection to traditional memorials on aesthetic grounds was coupled with an underlying cynicism about the values and the faith in the future which they represented.'[64] The cynicism noted by Hewitt is clearly demonstrable in the comments of one contributor to the *Mass Observation Bulletin*:

I would suggest that on each memorial there should be placed a neat plaque saying – 'This Sacrifice was not enough. Another was called for – and was made.' Care should be taken to leave room for the plaque that will be necessary about thirty years hence.[65]

The change of nomenclature from the Great War to the First World War itself highlighted the perceived failure of society to prevent further conflict, and this may also have influenced responses to the survey.[66] The major difference, of course, between the two conflicts on the Home Front was the extent of material damage inflicted by enemy bombing raids. By the end of 1942 two and a half million people occupied bombed houses which had received only temporary repairs.[67] There was an evident need to rebuild Britain, and it was perhaps appropriate that commemoration should be seen to serve a practical, rather than symbolic, purpose. New housing and hospitals were frequently suggested by contributors to the Survey. Others suggested that funds raised in memory of the fallen should be used for the wounded or their dependants, or for scholarships, either for local children or specifically for the children of ex-servicemen. The views of the national panel were on occasions reflected at a local level in Wales. A public meeting was held in Haverfordwest in October 1946 to discuss whether to proceed with a Pembrokeshire County Memorial to the 500 who had died, and to decide what form the memorial should take. An ambitious scheme was suggested to build small houses in every part of the county for the parents of those who had fallen. Each house would have a plate inset in the wall, inscribed to the memory of one who had lost his or her life. Money for this scheme would be raised via a 'Salute the War Heroes' week. It was also suggested that a capital sum should be invested for the purpose of awarding scholarships throughout the county for the children of the fallen.[68] Lack of finance prevented these elaborate plans from being carried through but also affected smaller schemes in Wales, such as at Caerwent in Monmouthshire, where a meeting was held in November 1946 to discuss a suitable memorial. The first choice was a playing field with a garden of remembrance, although by the following month it had been decided that this was beyond the committee's financial means.[69]

The trend towards utilitarian memorials was recognized before the end of the war, when the Royal Society of Arts set up a War Memorials Sub-Committee, which produced a report in November 1944. Whilst initially seeming to favour symbolic sculptural memorials, the bulk of the report is devoted to advocating utilitarian forms of commemoration, such as gardens, parks and hospitals, under the umbrella heading 'Projects of Social Service'.[70] It seems likely that, as Hewitt has suggested, the artistic establishment was merely trying to catch up with popular opinion, and that the concept of utilitarianism was well rooted in Britain by the end of November 1944.[71] Yet, adding names to existing memorials remained the most popular form of commemoration across the United Kingdom. It was the most practical and, perhaps more important, often the cheapest option. In a direct parallel with the Great War, it appears that finance, or lack of it, dictated the eventual form of memorial. The obvious difference after 1945 was that in most communities, memorials of some description already existed and provided an instant and relatively inexpensive solution. A survey conducted recently by the National Inventory of War Memorials has concluded that boards, plaques and tablets were the most popular type of memorial after the Second World War, and that 'in many instances, erecting another memorial was considered unnecessary'.[72] At the Pembrokeshire village of Lampeter Velfrey in September 1948 a ceremony was held at the Great War memorial to unveil a plaque in memory of four local men who lost their lives in the war, whilst at Rudry in Glamorgan in July 1952 a new inscription was added to the Great War monument, in memory of six local men.[73] Regional and national forms of commemoration persisted but could be perceived as remote, with little intrinsic meaning or relevance to the bereaved. However, the addition of names to a local war memorial provided family and friends with an immediate, daily reminder of their loved ones. As with the Great War, the war memorial in town or village, church or chapel, urban or rural location signalled a very local contribution to the war, echoing Edna Longley's comment: 'Commemorations are as selective as sympathies. They honour *our* dead, not your dead.'[74]

It is clear that the experience of remembering the Great War – when commemoration was driven by local needs, rather than being shaped or directed by national administrative, artistic or political opinions – was repeated in Wales and throughout Britain in the years after 1945.[75] A further parallel is that, whilst an individual may have fought and died as a Welsh man or woman, he or she was commemorated as a British citizen. This duality so evident in the commemoration process after 1918 and in the ceremonies after 1945 appears to support Gwyn A. Williams's opinion:

> What is immediately clear, from even a cursory survey of our broken-backed history, is that the tiny Welsh people, for we were always very thin on the ground, have survived by being British. Welsh identity has constantly renewed itself by anchoring itself in variant forms of Britishness.[76]

It probably seemed less complicated in 1939, when the threat from a formidable external enemy was real and immediate. In November 1939 Hirrell Davies wrote: 'I remember when War was declared I thought it strange that practically everything went on as usual, you know milk-man, baker, fish-man all coming to the door as usual. Yet I guess if we didn't it wouldn't be British would it?'[77]

Recent years have witnessed a number of new memorials commissioned to commemorate the Second World War. These include the national memorial to Civilian Workers unveiled in Coventry Cathedral in November 1999. In April 2004 planning permission was granted for a Civilians Remembered memorial at Hermitage Wharf in Wapping, London. In the same month the National Heritage Memorial Fund awarded nearly £1m to construct a memorial to honour the seven million service- and civilian women who contributed to the war effort. The bronze sculpture depicting images of hats, gas-masks, uniforms and overalls is sited near the Cenotaph in Whitehall and was unveiled in July 2005. As the years pass, it seems as if those who took part in the war are belatedly seeking recognition of their efforts, to ensure that they and their dead comrades are not forgotten.

The National Inventory of War Memorials notes that the number of memorials for the Second World War is lower than that for the First and that a contributory factor to this was the lower casualty numbers.[78] Whilst British military casualty figures from the Second World War are less than half those from the Great War, the blunt comparison of statistics reveals little of the individual pain of loss. Whether a community lost five or five hundred the priority was to remember the individual, and that remained the key to commemoration in 1918 and also in 1945, even if the process and outcome were more subdued after the Second World War. Ceremonies in the 1920s to unveil war memorials were often described as the highlight of the local year and given prolific press coverage, whilst those held after 1945 barely merit a mention in Welsh newspapers. Even the report of the unveiling of the additional inscription on the Welsh National War Memorial in 1949 was relegated to an inside page of the *Western Mail*. Jay Winter has suggested that 'both the political character of the Second World War and some of its horrific consequences . . . helped to put an end to the rich set of traditional languages of commemoration and mourning which flourished after the Great War'.[79] The irony of having to inscribe additional names on memorials to an earlier war which had so blatantly failed to prevent further conflict would not have been lost on communities, yet local memorials remained the focus of private and collective grief. They had fulfilled this purpose for at least two decades, so seeking additional forms of commemoration may simply have been considered unnecessary. Even allowing for the financial dimension to commemoration, the frequency with which names were added perhaps implies tacit agreement with the sentiments of pride and sacrifice that adorn most memorials. Yet it would be unwise to dismiss such languages of mourning as outmoded and inappropriate, as they may have provided a degree of solace and even justification for the bereaved, as they struggled to come to terms with their grief.

Each name inscribed on a war memorial or recorded on a Roll of Honour, whether after 1918 or after 1945, represented a personal family tragedy. The danger is that the sheer scale of death subsumes individual stories under a collective narrative. The languages of remembrance insist that '*They* shall not be forgotten' and 'At the going down of the sun we will remember *them*'. Personal loss is often presented as a statistic, another casualty of war. Ronald Baker is commemorated on his local war memorial and, as noted earlier, his name also appears in the Welsh National Book of Remembrance.

It is one name amongst thousands. When visiting the battlefields of France and Flanders the sense of loss is overwhelming, whilst the immaculately maintained cemeteries worldwide tell a more recent story of bravery and sacrifice.[80] Contemporary correspondence can provide a personal insight into the human experience of war and the pain of bereavement, which was often compounded by a lack of information. During the Second World War families of missing servicemen and women clung to the hope that in the absence of a body, their loved one was still alive and a prisoner of war. The families of Ronald Baker's crew followed similar paths to those followed by many thousands of bereaved families after the Great War, when the search for information often became an obsession. Extant photographs, letters and family scrapbooks often remain as testimonies of private grief which endure beyond the building of monuments and halls. John Baker must have been comforted by letters from his elder son, Brian, once news of Ronald's death had been confirmed. In May 1943 Brian wrote to his father:

> I have seen enough of this world to realise what home means. No Pop, I'm going to settle down at some job or other, and see if we cannot make up a little of the loss of Ron to each other. I would like to take up golf, and perhaps we can manage a little car between us . . . we could have some grand times eh?[81]

Brian Baker died whilst still serving with the armed forces in November 1945 aged twenty-six, and his name, together with that of his brother, is inscribed on the war memorial in Whitchurch, Cardiff.[82]

NOTES

[1] The ceremony to unveil the inscription was performed by the Duke of Beaufort. The inscription '1939–45' was added to the Cenotaph in London. The Land Fund, originally intended for reconstruction, was created from surplus war funds in 1946 as a memorial to the dead of both World Wars.

[2] *Western Mail* (hereafter *WM*), 28 Apr. 1949. The parade later proceeded through the centre of Cardiff. For coverage of the ceremony to unveil the Welsh National Memorial to the Great War, see *WM*, 13 June 1928.

[3] *WM*, 28 Apr. 1949.

[4] The Orders of Service for both 1928 and 1949 are held at the Glamorgan Record Office.

[5] Mari A. Williams, *A Forgotten Army: Female Munitions Workers of South Wales, 1939–1945* (Cardiff, 2002), p. 4. The sixtieth anniversary of the end of hostilities prompted a number of publications in Wales, including John O'Sullivan, *When Wales Went To War 1939–45* (Stroud, 2004), and Phil Carradice, *Wales at War* (Llandysul, 2003). See also Leigh Verrill-Rhys and

Deidre Beddoe (eds), *Parachutes and Petticoats: Welsh Women Writing on the Second World War* (Dinas Powys, 1992); Fay Swain, *Wales and the Second World War: Women* (Bridgend, 1989); and Philip Tapper and Susan Hawthorne, *Wales and the Second World War* (Bridgend, 1991). Articles on the subject have appeared in a number of local history journals, for example, Gwyn Davies, 'Ceredigion in the Second World War', in *Ceredigion*, 13 (2000). For a contemporary article, see Isobel Wylie Hutchison, 'Wales in wartime', in *National Geographic*, 85, 6 (June 1944).

[6] The Leversuch correspondence is held in the Glamorgan Record Office (GRO). The main series of letters was written between 1939 and 1946 by Violet Patricia Cox (Pat) to L. A. C. John W. Leversuch, who was serving abroad with the RAF. The collection also contains correspondence from their parents, siblings and friends, and provides not only an invaluable primary source on life on the Home Front, but also information on national and international events during the war years.

[7] GRO, Leversuch correspondence, letter of 22 Nov. 1939. For an overview of this period, see Angus Calder, *The People's War: Britain 1939–45* (London, 1971).

[8] Mass-Observation Archive (hereafter M-O A), FR 602 (Mar. 1941). The social research organization Mass-Observation was founded in 1937. Teams of observers and volunteer writers were recruited, with the aim of studying the everyday lives of 'ordinary' people in Britain. The original work continued until the early 1950s. The Archive is held at the University of Sussex. A particularly useful study was carried out in Blaina, Monmouthshire. See M-O A, FR 1196 and 1498, 'Blaina: a study of a coal mining town', Apr. and Nov. 1942. See also Brian Roberts, 'A mining town in wartime: the fears for the future', *Llafur: Journal of Welsh Labour History*, 6, 1 (1992); Roberts, 'The "budgie train": women and wartime munitions work in a mining valley', *Llafur: Journal of Welsh Labour History*, 7, 3–4 (1998–9).

[9] For a detailed account of the air-attacks on Cardiff see O'Sullivan, *When Wales Went To War*, pp. 4–38. See also Dennis Morgan, *Cardiff: A City at War* (Cardiff, 1998), pp. 44–70. The severity of the raids on Cardiff and Swansea was noted at the time. See Vere Hodgson, *Few Eggs and No Oranges: The Diaries of Vere Hodgson 1940–45* (London, 2002) pp. 108, 129, 132. Mass-Observation respondents noted a slightly different response in the Tiger Bay district of Cardiff, where it was recorded that 'nowhere have we recorded less war talk, and a lower degree of war interest . . . As the barmaid of the Ship & Pilot put it: "We don't seem to notice the war much down here" ' (M-O A, FR 788 (July 1941)).

[10] GRO, World War II, ARP Sector 18 B.I.D. (Whitchurch, Cardiff) Records, 3 Jan. 1941. It was during this raid that Llandaff Cathedral suffered extensive damage.

[11] Information contained in an *Open Letter to All Wardens in the City of Cardiff* (GRO, Cardiff Air Raid Wardens' Organisation Records), 30 June 1945.

[12] GRO, World War II, ARP Sector 18. Warden's Post No. 18B, 4 Mar. 1940.

[13] Angus Calder has described the diaries kept for Mass-Observation as the 'most veridical documentation we have on the Home Front . . . Filed month by month, these were subject neither to official censorship nor to retrospective self-censorship. Here one can find immediate representation of experience and the earliest stages

of memory-formation.' Angus Calder, *Disaster and Heroes: On War, Memory and Representation* (Cardiff, 2004), p. viii.

[14] Sutherland worked as a war artist from 1940 to 1945. He returned to Wales later in the war but also worked in London, Cornwall and France. The Sutherland Archive is held at the National Museum Cardiff. It includes the war drawings and contemporary photographs of subject areas used for the drawings. The archive also contains correspondence between Graham and Kathleen Sutherland and Kenneth Clark concerning the artist's war work. For more details on Sutherland's war work, see Roger Berthoud, *Graham Sutherland: A Biography* (London, 1982), pp. 94–117; Ronald Alley, *Graham Sutherland* (London, 1982), pp. 92–104. The War Artists' Archive is held at the Imperial War Museum.

[15] The *Recording Britain* series was published between 1946 and 1949 by Oxford University Press. A total of seventy-six watercolours were painted in Wales.

[16] Interview with artist, 9 June 1997. Mona Moore's watercolour entitled 'Castle Street Swansea shortly after a raid' is held at the National Museum Cardiff. For details of the blitz on Swansea, see O'Sullivan, *When Wales Went To War*, pp. 39–52.

[17] M-O A, FR 591 (Feb. 1941), FR 595 (Mar. 1941).

[18] M-O A, FR 595 (Mar. 1941). St Mary's Church was destroyed by enemy bombing on 21 February 1941. In May 1959 the Queen Mother unveiled a stone at the church to commemorate the rebuilding. Derek Boorman, *For Your Tomorrow: British Second World War Memorials* (York, 1995), p. 67.

[19] GRO, Leversuch correspondence, letter of 8 Jan. 1941.

[20] Ibid., letter of 22 May 1941. Presumably this refers to the raid of 30 April 1941, when parachute mines caused many fatalities and extensive structural damage. The Riverside and Cathays areas of the city were particularly badly affected. The 'Five, Brook Street' referred to by Pat Cox was in Riverside. For details of this raid, see O'Sullivan, *When Wales Went To War*, pp. 21–5.

[21] GRO, Leversuch correspondence, letters of 7 June, 8 Sept., 1 Oct. 1944.

[22] Ibid., letter of 11 Sept. 1944.

[23] John Baker and his three brothers had all fought in the Great War. One brother was killed at Gallipoli and another at Ypres.

[24] John Baker's elder son, Brian Harold, volunteered for the armed forces in April/May 1939 and entered the Royal Corps of Signals. His duties included dispatch riding and acting as a courier. He was stationed in the Middle East from December 1941 but had a motorcycle accident, requiring hospital treatment, in March 1943. He was then posted to Sicily, but had a further accident in August 1943. On recovery he returned to the Middle East Forces and later joined a Signals Unit in the Central Mediterranean. The letters from Brian finish in March 1945. He died in November 1945, aged twenty-six, and is buried in Cathays Cemetery, Cardiff.

[25] GRO, Baker family Second World War correspondence, letter of 4 Feb. 1943.

[26] The target was once again the U-boat base at Lorient, France. The scrapbook appears to have been compiled by John Baker after Ronald's death, as it starts with a telegram of condolence from the King and photographs of Ronald and other members of his aircrew.

[27] GRO, Baker correspondence, letter of 9 Feb. 1943. A similar letter was sent by the RAF Record Office at Gloucester on 12 Feb. 1943.

[28] Ibid., letter of 12 Feb. 1943.

[29] Ibid. By coincidence the mother of another member of the crew, Flight Lieutenant Ken Powell, also lived in Cardiff and asked to be included in John Baker's enquiries.

[30] Ibid., letter of 24 Feb. 1943. Mr and Mrs Pennycock also passed on the family address of a further crew member.

[31] Ibid., telegram from the RAF Records Office, Gloucester, 19 Mar. 1943. This stated that information had been received from the International Red Cross, quoting German sources. A letter confirming the telegram was received the following day. This was noted in the scrapbook as 'The letter of awful confirmation'. Ronald Baker's obituary was published in the *South Wales Echo* hereafter *SWE*) on 23 March 1943.

[32] GRO, Baker correspondence, letter of 20 Mar. 1943. Sergeant Pilot Anthony Keeton was killed on his first operational trip, which was taken with Ronald Baker's crew to gain the necessary experience before taking on his own plane.

[33] Ibid., letter of 22 Mar. 1943.

[34] Ibid., letter of 4 Aug. 1943.

[35] Ibid., letter of 22 Oct. 1943.

[36] Ibid., letter of 18 May 1944. The Red Cross supplied further information on the graves in Jan. 1945.

[37] Ibid., letter of 5 Nov. 1944. Marcel had been friendly with John's daughter, Marjorie, and had visited Cardiff in 1935. He had subsequently mislaid Marjorie's address and asked for his letter to be forwarded. By April 1945 Marcel was in charge of the American Red Cross in Pontivy.

[38] Ibid., letter of 7 July 1945. The cemetery at Guidel lies two kilometres off the Lorient–Quimperle road. There are over 100 casualties from the 1939–45 war commemorated at this site.

[39] Ibid., letter of 3 Aug. 1945.

[40] Ibid., letter of 29 Apr. 1943.

[41] Ibid., letter of 20 Aug. 1943.

[42] Ibid., letter of 22 Oct. 1943.

[43] Ibid., letter of 5 Oct. 1944. Barry Sullivan visited Cardiff in October 1942 and January 1943.

[44] Catherine Moriarty, ' "Though in a picture only": portrait photography and the commemoration of the First World War', in Gail Braybon (ed.), *Evidence, History and the Great War* (Oxford, 2003), p. 37.

[45] GRO, Baker correspondence, letter undated.

[46] The cover of the book also refers to 'others who gave their lives in the war of 1939–1945'.

[47] GRO, Welsh National Book of Remembrance Memorial Committee Minute Books, meetings of 21 Nov. 1957 and 2 May 1958. The Book does not record the names of civilians killed but does include those who died from the Home Guard, Fire Service, Air–Raid Wardens and police. It was also decided not to include the names of those who died in the Korean War.

[48] GRO, Memorial Committee meeting, 23 Feb. 1959. Virtually the same problem had been encountered nearly forty years earlier when attempting to raise funds for the Great War Book of Remembrance; see Angela Gaffney, *Aftermath: Remembering the Great War in Wales* (Cardiff, 1998), pp. 44–57.

[49] GRO, Finance (Staff and General Purposes) Sub-Committee meeting, 13 July 1960.

[50] GRO, Memorial Committee meeting, 24 Oct. 1960. The Pembrokeshire Book of Remembrance for the Second World War is located in the north transept in St David's Cathedral. A page is turned every day.

[51] Ibid., 12 Mar. 1965.

[52] Ibid., 14 May 1965. The opposite argument was put forward four months later, when the United Nations Association was asked to consider permitting the Great War Book of Remembrance to lie alongside its 'sister' volume at the National Museum of Wales. GRO, Memorial Committee meeting, 30 Sept. 1965. No response is documented, and the Great War volume remains at the Temple of Peace.

[53] The Welsh National Book of Remembrance commemorating those who died in the Great War was presented to the National Museum of Wales 'for permanent custody' on the occasion of the unveiling of the memorial in Cathays Park in June 1928. The Book was transferred to the Temple of Peace when the building opened in November 1938. For a history of the Temple of Peace, see W. R. Davies, *The Temple of Peace & Health 1938–1998* (Cardiff, 1998). See also W. R. Davies, 'Laying the foundations: the contribution of Lord Davies of Llandinam', in Davies (ed.), *The United Nations at Fifty: The Welsh Contribution* (Cardiff, 1995).

[54] *WM*, 9 June 1966; *SWE*, 8 June 1966.

[55] The Marquess of Anglesey was President of the National Museum of Wales. Replicas of the book were presented by the Queen Mother to representatives of county boroughs and councils. The volume presented to Glamorgan County Council is still displayed in the main foyer of the former Glamorgan County Hall in Cathays Park, Cardiff. A further copy is held in the Pembrokeshire Record Office.

[56] The Memorial Committee held a competition to design a casket to house the book and offered a cash prize for the winning design. This was awarded to Ceri Jones, an architect from Swansea.

[57] *SWE*, 2 Mar. 1968; *WM*, 4 Mar. 1968.

[58] *WM*, 9 June 1966.

[59] The casket was destroyed during refurbishment of the main hall of the National Museum in the mid 1990s.

[60] *Mass-Observation Bulletin P.B.6*, Nov. 1944.

[61] Ibid.

[62] Ibid.

[63] Ibid.

[64] Nick Hewitt, 'A sceptical generation? War memorials and the collective memory of the Second World War in Britain, 1945–2000', in Dominik Geppert (ed.), *The Postwar Challenge: Cultural, Social and Political Change in Western Europe, 1945–58* (Oxford, 2003), p.82.

[65] *Mass-Observation Bulletin P.B.6*, Nov. 1944.

[66] The Roll of Honour for Cowbridge Grammar School is entitled '2nd Great War', but it is rare for the Second World War to be described in this way.

[67] I. C. B. Dear and M. R. D. Foot (eds), *The Oxford Companion to the Second World War* (Oxford, 2001), p. 88.

[68] Pembrokeshire Record Office, Minutes of a public meeting held at the Shire Hall, Haverfordwest, 5 Oct. 1946.

[69] Gwent Record Office, Minutes of Caerwent War Memorial Committee, Nov. and Dec. 1946. A monument was erected to commemorate both wars, with names from each conflict inscribed. It was unveiled in January 1948. Even the addition of names to an existing memorial could cause financial problems, as in Rudry, when a collection was taken during the unveiling ceremony 'to defray the cost of inscribing the memorial'. Gwent Record Office, Order of Service for the unveiling and dedication of the addition to the Rudry War Memorial, 27 July 1952.

[70] *War Memorials: A Survey made by a Committee of the Royal Society of Arts and published by the War Memorials Advisory Council* (London, 1944).

[71] Hewitt, 'A sceptical generation?', p. 87.

[72] Jane Furlong, Lorraine Knight and Simon Slocombe, ' "They shall grow not old": an analysis of trends in memorialisation based on information held by the UK National Inventory of War Memorials', *Cultural Trends*, 45 (2002): 13. The National Inventory of War Memorials at the Imperial War Museum records details of memorials throughout the United Kingdom and I am grateful for their help with the preparation of this chapter.

[73] The addition of names to existing memorials occurred in many communities in Wales. Examples include Denbigh, Waen, Lampeter, St Asaph, Solva, Llechryd, Neyland, Borth, Llangadog, Taliaris, Overton, Whitland, Llandudno, Bangor, Pwllheli, Miskin, Berriew, Llandegfan and Cemmaes (Montgomeryshire). An inscription was added to Llandaff War Memorial in 1989. There was no room on the memorial for the additional names, but a Roll of Honour was compiled and placed in Llandaff Cathedral (*SWE*, 6 Sept. 1989).

[74] Edna Longley, 'The Rising, the Somme and Irish memory', in Mairin Ni Dhonnchadha and Theo Dorgan (eds), *Revising the Rising* (Londonderry, 1991), p. 29 (italics in original).

[75] This helps to explain why the names of civilians killed in the war are included on some memorials and not on others. The decisions on which names to include or exclude were always made locally.

[76] Gwyn A. Williams, 'When was Wales?', in Williams, *The Welsh in Their History* (Beckenham, 1982), p. 194. Unveiling ceremonies after 1945 frequently utilized both national anthems and flags, with hymns and prayers in Welsh and English. See, for example, the Order of Service for the ceremony at the National War Memorial of Wales 1939–1945 in April 1949 (GRO).

[77] GRO, Leversuch correspondence, letter 3 Nov. 1939.

[78] Furlong, Knight and Slocombe, ' "They shall grow not old" ', 13. See also Commonwealth War Graves Commission, *Annual Report 2002–2003*. Numbers for war dead for the United Kingdom and its former colonies (not including the self-governing Dominions) were 918,507 for the Great War and 351,112 for the Second World War. The names of 67,075 civilians of the Commonwealth whose deaths were due to enemy action in the Second World War are commemorated on the Civilian War Dead Roll of Honour located near St George's Chapel in Westminster Abbey, London. UK civilian and civil-defence casualties at 31 July 1945 (killed and missing, believed killed) totalled 60,595. Half of the civilian deaths occurred in London. Dear and Foot (eds), *Oxford Companion to the Second World War*, p. 886.

[79] Jay Winter, *Sites of Memory, Sites of Mourning: The Great War in European Cultural History* (Cambridge, 1995), p. 9.

[80] For the policy of the Commonwealth War Graves Commission after 1945, see Philip Longworth, *The Unending Vigil: A History of the Commonwealth War Graves Commission, 1917–1984* (London, 1984), pp. 187–213.

[81] GRO, Baker correspondence letter of 28 May 1943.

[82] For information on Brian Baker, see above, n. 24.

9

Don't mention the war? Interpreting and contextualizing the 1982 Falklands/Malvinas War[1]

GERWYN WILIAMS

The Falklands/Malvinas War was a brief conflict between British and Argentinian forces that lasted for two and a half months, from 1 April until 14 June 1982. But despite its brevity, it represents a significant historic moment. It was a battle fought three years after the debacle of the referendum campaign to decentralize power from Whitehall to Wales and Scotland, legislative measures that represented an attempt to modernize the British constitution during the crisis-ridden finale to James Callaghan's Labour administration. Elected in its place on 6 May 1979 was the right-wing centralizing government of Margaret Thatcher, which grasped the opportunity inherent in the Falklands/Malvinas War to boast British might as an imperialist power to be reckoned with. It is needless to say that the 1982 conflict poured further salt into the wounds of those Welsh men and women who had supported the constitutional reforms on offer in 1979: not only was the authority of London government confirmed by the war, the British status quo was reinforced, and Margaret Thatcher was carried like a modern-day Boadicea on a wave of insular and isolated nationalism. Added to this was another factor related to the Falklands/Malvinas War and one that had a specific Welsh importance and significance, namely the special relationship between Wales and Patagonia, the Argentinian province where a Welsh colony had been established in 1865.[2] This raised the possibility of Welsh servicemen from the Welsh Guards fighting face to face with soldiers of Welsh descent conscripted into the Argentinian armed forces. On a number of fronts, therefore, it appeared as though Welsh identity was under vicious attack, at the very time when it was struggling to recompose and redefine itself following the near fatal body-blow some felt it had suffered on St David's Day 1979.

This essay aims to consider Welsh literary interpretations – as represented by fictional accounts written by civilians and more recent autobiographical evidence by members of the armed forces and their families – of the Falklands/Malvinas War. It concentrates primarily, although not exclusively, on Welsh-language material. The chapter also attempts to provide a context for those interpretations and to consider what they suggest about Welsh identity. For numerous reasons, it has not always been easy for Welsh people to deal with the experience of war during the twentieth century; this war, in particular, posed various challenges, and is in danger of being considered a forgotten war. It is, however, true that the Welsh were not the only ones who found it hard to face up to the reality of this war: Paul Greengrass, who produced the film *Resurrected* (1989),[3] states that it also created a dilemma for those on the left wing of English politics:

> There has been, I think, a conspiracy of sorts to bury the Falklands ex-perience . . . a national conspiracy born of shame which presents us from confronting the realities of that war, and the fact that, like a junkie, Britain took a lethal fix of jingoism and xenophobia in 1982.[4]

But at least these words come from the foreword to *Framing the Falklands*, a multidisciplinary volume of essays on nationhood, culture and identity that appeared in 1992, and which lists in its bibliography over 200 separate items, both factual and fictional, dealing with the war. On 10 November 2004, the Google Internet search engine listed 145,000 references to 'Falklands War', 178 titles resulted from the same enquiry on the Amazon.co.uk website, and the British Library online catalogue came up with 57 books containing the exact phrase in their titles. The Welsh reticence regarding this war is more funda-mental, and makes one wonder what it suggests. Is it a sense of awkwardness and nervousness regarding the war, a feeling of embarrassment and shame, which not only makes it easier not to talk about it – 'Don't mention the war!' – but verges on denial? Is it merely a coincidence that only in the twenty-first century, over twenty years after the war came to an end, and in an Assembly-governed Wales which, despite its shortcomings, has helped resurrect a sense of Welsh pride, that the author Ioan Roberts has published such a mature and confident book as *Rhyfel Ni: Profiadau Cymreig o Ddwy Ochr Rhyfel y Falklands/Malvinas*?[5]

THE WAR

> The world did not stop for the Falklands war. It hesitated, perhaps, for five or ten minutes each day as people switched on for the latest bulletin. The war changed the lives of the people who went down to the South Atlantic, it changed the lives of the families of those who are buried down there, but the world kept right on moving.[6]

Those are the balanced and measured words of Simon Weston as he calls to mind the war in which he fought, and from which he was to escape by the skin of his teeth. I count myself among the daily audience he mentioned, one of those who hesitated for five or ten minutes each day, and can clearly recall the whole saga developing in television and press coverage: the ill-fated attempts by the American Secretary of State, Alexander Haig, at shuttle diplomacy; the emotional departure of British forces on board the *QE2* in a riot of Union flags at the outset of their 8,000-mile voyage to defend the islands and their 1,800 inhabitants in the South Atlantic; Rod Stewart's haunting anthem, 'Sailing', previously popularized as the theme song for the BBC documentary series *Sailor* (1976), following the exploits of servicemen on board HMS *Ark Royal*;[7] Margaret Thatcher in her most Churchillian mode commanding journalists to 'Rejoice, rejoice!' when South Georgia was recaptured by British forces;[8] the *Sun*'s infamous 'GOTCHA' headline when the Argentinian cruiser *General Belgrano* was sunk, together with over 300 servicemen on board;[9] and the aforementioned Simon Weston, the working-class Welsh Guardsman from Nelson, Mid Glamorgan, who suffered 46 per cent body burns when the Argentinian air-force attacked the *Sir Galahad* and whose physical and emotional rehabilitation was recorded in a remarkable series of documentary programmes on BBC television.[10]

The Falklands/Malvinas War proved to be a physical, messy conflict, fought at close range and in sharp contrast to the high-tech images and the long-range bombing associated with the 1991 Gulf War and the 2003 Iraq War. The impression one gets from reading *Rhyfel Ni* is of a concentrated affair, a conflict with something approaching a communal feel, indeed, a microcosm of war, where major and minor players were in touch with one another: one civilian, Vali James de Irianni, describes 'the Malvinas' as 'our own *little* war'[11] – my emphasis – and since it was a comparatively small affair, names familiar in grander contexts are mentioned casually in passing: a Patagonian, Milton Rhys, for instance, worked as an interpreter for the head of the Argentinian army, General Menendez, supplied him with cups of tea and darned his socks, as well as sharing living quarters with him in the home of the ousted British Governor, Rex Hunt. Ultimately – at least according to official figures[12] – more than 900 people were killed in the Falklands/Malvinas War, 655 from Argentina and 255 from Britain. They did so in a war considered needless by many: 'Nott and Galtieri: two bald men squabbling over a comb'[13] was the graffiti daubed on the wall of the field hospital in Ajax Bay to which Simon Weston refers, and he himself, following the transmission of *Simon's Heroes* in 2002, received a letter from John Nott, the Defence Secretary during the conflict, referring in retrospect to the war as a needless one.[14]

This essay is not concerned primarily with the political confrontation between Argentina and Britain which led to the Falklands/Malvinas War, or with its military history: those are matters discussed by, for example, Max Hastings and Simon Jenkins from a British perspective in *The Battle for the Falklands* (1983), and Martin Middlebrook from an Argentinian perspective in *The Fight for the 'Malvinas'* (1989);[15] Anthony Barnett in *Iron Britannia* (1982) also provides a highly readable analysis of the political culture and climate that resulted in Britain going to war.[16] Sovereignty of the islands located 350 miles off the southern tip of Argentina had been a matter of political contention since their existence had been formally recorded in the seventeenth century: they had been ruled by Britain since 1833, but Argentina asserted her claim as part of the old Spanish Empire. In retrospect, General Galtieri's decision to invade the islands in April 1982 may be regarded as a desperate attempt by his unpopular military junta to hang on to power; Margaret Thatcher's response, in sending a taskforce to reclaim the islands for the inhabitants of British descent, was a factor that helped ensure a second parliamentary term for her Conservative administration.

Margaret Thatcher's first term in office had proved to be particularly problematic and unpopular: Value Added Tax was more or less doubled in her first budget, and taxes increased in 1981 whilst Britain was experiencing a recession. In the words of John Sergeant, who as a political correspondent had a bird's-eye view of current events: 'What she needed to guarantee success in the next election was a good war.'[17] And that's exactly what the Falklands/Malvinas War proved to be for Margaret Thatcher: a good war that contributed greatly to defining her as a resolute and single-minded states-woman who experienced an unrivalled series of electoral successes,[18] a foreign war that would soon provide her with the confidence to conduct what might be considered a civil war against working-class communities, such as those of the south Wales coalfield.[19] In a speech delivered to the Conservative party faithful in a rally held at Cheltenham racecourse on 3 July 1982, she could be heard celebrating her victory in the South Atlantic campaign, as well as making political profit from it.[20] She related the lessons of war – the 'Falklands Factor', in her own words – to Britain at large. Yes, Britain had fought with the support of the international community – the UN Security Council, the Commonwealth, the European Community and the USA – but Britain had also fought alone for her own people and her own sovereign territory. Sceptics had long assumed that British might was in terminal decline after the Second World War, 'that Britain was no longer the nation that had built an Empire and ruled a quarter of the world'.[21] Britons had at last proved themselves to themselves: 'The faltering and the self-doubt has given way to achievement and pride. We have the confidence and we must use it.'[22] There was an undeniably Churchillian ring to her rhetoric, and it is therefore not surprising to hear her quoting directly from a speech delivered by Winston Churchill himself following the Second World War. In drawing such a blatant comparison between the two wars, she appeared to be claiming a global significance for what was in essence a rather parochial affair. However hollow and hypocritical her words may have sounded later, owing to the social division caused by her monetarist policies, she could claim that Britons had joined forces during the war to strive towards a common aim and had therefore rediscovered their true character: 'we rejoice that Britain has re-kindled that spirit which has fired her for generations past and which today has begun to burn as brightly as before. Britain found herself again in the South Atlantic and will not look back from the victory she has won.'[23]

From a Welsh perspective, part of the difficulty in confronting this war is that it is one thing to dissociate oneself from the British nationalism that interpreted the defeat over the Argentinians in imperialist terms, but quite another thing altogether to protest against such a brand of Britishness by identifying with the Patagonians. Galtieri's campaign was, after all, an eleventh-hour attempt by his military dictatorship to hang on to power: it was hardly an honourable campaign, as he cynically exploited for his own political ends the natural allegiance of the Argentinian people to the Falklands/Malvinas cause. As stated by Anthony Barnett as early as August 1982:

> Internal control and military expansionism – the Junta's real *raison d'être* for invading the Falklands – had nothing to do with the sentiment of Argentina's population about sovereignty over the Malvinas. On the contrary, the invasion was an attempt to exploit the reasonableness of the country's claim so as to mobilize the issue for other, utterly ignoble aims.[24]

The collapse of the Argentinian armed forces in the Falklands/Malvinas – and those who survived the war were to pay a long and bitter price for such a national disgrace – prefigured the collapse of Galtieri himself: in 1983, his government was defeated and democracy reinstated in the country.

CIVILIAN IMAGES

The event that has captured the imagination of Welsh writers most often is the bombing of the landing ship *Sir Galahad* whilst anchored at Bluff Cove: the attack represented the largest single loss for British forces throughout the war when forty-eight servicemen were killed, thirty-one of them members of the Welsh Guards. This controversial tragedy, and the military blunder associated with it, has grown to symbolize the perennial slaughter and sorrow of war and has led to responses as varied as the Socialist Workers' Party member Greg Cullen's powerful stage and radio play, *Taken Out* (1986),[25] and Llwybr Llaethog's anti-Thatcherite song 'Rhywbeth Bach yn Poeni Pawb' (1986).[26] The feature of the war that has most excited a response among Welsh writers has been the special relationship between Wales and Patagonia, a feature which ensured an ironic and uniquely Welsh dimension to the conflict. The major Welsh-language reflection on the war came just over a year later, during the 1983 National Eisteddfod, in the form of Eluned Phillips's Crown-winning long poem, 'Clymau', and Myrddin ap Dafydd and Geraint Løvgreen's theatrical review, *Tros Ryddid?* (1983).[27] Reading newspaper reports from this period one gets a strong impression of the anti-militaristic context within which both creative works operated: three headlines from the 16 August 1983 issue of *Y Cymro* – the Welsh-language weekly newspaper – are 'Galw am bleidlais ar Cruise' ('Calling for a vote on Cruise'), which referred to the protests against locating American Cruise missiles in Britain, 'Cerdded dros yr hawl i fyw mewn hedd' ('Walking for the right to live in peace'), which referred to the campaign by Greenham Common women against the stationing of those missiles on a military base at Newbury, in Berkshire, and 'Y Fali'n fygythiad' ('Valley is a threat'), which referred to the fears of CND members regarding the RAF base located on Anglesey.

It hardly needs stating that the National Eisteddfod is more than a competitive gathering: it is also an annual forum for cultural and political debate and, by means of the Crown and Chair competitions in particular, gives major prominence to the role and status of the poet within Welsh public life. It is not unusual for poems containing contemporary social comment to gain the top honours, as though there is an unwritten expectation for the poet to give artistic expression to the voice of Welsh-speaking Wales.[28] Such an expectation was certainly satisfied in 1983: 'It was high time that somebody declared the feeling of the Welsh regarding the unecessary Malvinas war', stated Nesta Wyn Jones, one of the adjudicators in that year's Crown competition.[29] Eluned Phillips's 'Clymau' is divided into two main sections, the first section portraying the tenants of Pant Glas farm sailing forth to Patagonia on board the *Mimosa* in 1865 in search of religious and political freedom, as well as material wealth; the second section introduces a member of the same farm a century later seeking employment in the army and fighting in the Falklands/Malvinas. The final subsection sees two wounded soldiers meeting up in a temporary hospital in San Carlos: the Welshman from Pant Glas, who has been seriously injured on board the *Sir Galahad*, and a soldier from Patagonia; the two of them acknowledge their Celtic ties and recognize their common inheritance. There was certainly an element of risk involved in such an ending. Its chance meeting is reminiscent of much Victorian and Great War popular verse, whereby two Welsh soldiers co-incidentally come across each other on a foreign field and this conveniently ties in with the death of one of them. However, this part of the poem is potentially the most creatively exciting and, keeping in mind the emphasis on the smallness of this war, was rooted in possibility: the nurse on whom the nurse in the poem is based, Bronwen Williams, has described the hospital in Port Stanley as divided in two by a curtain, with British casualties on one side and Argentinian casualties on the other.[30] And nine years after the war, as he prepared to return to the Falklands/Malvinas and meet the pilot of the Argentinian Skyhawk that attacked the *Sir Galahad*, this scenario also presented itself to Simon Weston: 'maybe he was from Patagonia, from one of those pioneering sheep-breeding families who had moved from Wales a century ago. Maybe we had ancestors in common. Now there was a strange thought.'[31] But ultimately the poem fails to face up to the complexity and the contradiction signified by the relationship between the two servicemen on different sides of the war, and what is offered instead is a tidy and idealized vision of mutual understanding and reconciliation between them. The parting message is uncontroversially pacifist: 'I am totally opposed to war and opposed to every war throughout the ages', stated Eluned Phillips when interviewed soon after winning her Crown.[32]

'Clymau' as a whole represents a dignified and restrained response to the war, yet it is essentially a third-person response that cannot convey first-person subjective and emotional turmoil. The Crown competition is often seen as a showcase for poems in *vers libre*, and the decision in 1983 to request a poem in regular rhyme and metre proved a controversial one. In a development deemed progressive by some and retrograde by others, Eluned Phillips managed to add a further layer of traditionalism to her poem by employing the *Pedwar Mesur ar Hugain*, the Twenty-four Metres classified in the first half of the fourteenth century, but the poem was free from *cynghanedd*.[33] On the one hand, this adds a semblance of agelessness and antiquity to the treatment of war and locates it within a distinguished lineage of war poems, central to the Welsh bardic tradition; on the other hand, this artificial formality tends to undermine the fundamentally messy subject-matter of the poem. In comparison, a poem which makes more successful use of tradition while interpreting the same war is Tony Conran's 'Elegy for the Welsh dead in the Falkland Islands, 1982'. As translator of *The Penguin Book of Welsh Verse*,[34] the highly regarded anthology of Welsh-language poetry throughout the ages, the elegy was written by one of those most consciously steeped in the Welsh literary tradition among Welsh poets writing through the medium of English. It was first performed on BBC Radio 3, published in *Blodeuwedd* (1988) and republished in *Eros Proposes a Toast: Collected Public Poems and Gifts* (1998),[35] and the reference to public poems as well as the radio broadcast is again faithful to the traditionally public nature of Welsh poetry. Tony Conran's viewpoint is unambivalently anti-imperialist: 'Figment of empire, whore's honour, held them./Forty-three at Catraeth died for our dregs'.[36] However, as the allusion to Catraeth suggests, the sea voyage and later death of the Welsh soldiers is presented as a modern-day campaign by the men of the Gododdin tribe:[37] 'Men went to Catraeth. The luxury liner / For three weeks feasted them'.[38] In addition to honouring the individual humanity of those elegized by employing proper nouns, according to a pattern set out in *Canu Aneirin* and R. Williams Parry's elegies for victims of the Great War[39] – 'Malcolm Wigley of Connah's Quay; Clifford Elley of Pontypridd; Phillip Sweet of Cwmbach; Russell Carlisle of Rhuthun; Tony Jones of Carmarthen'[40] – Tony Conran manages to exploit creatively the powerful juxtaposition which is central to this long poem dating from the seventh century: *Y Gododdin* is a eulogy, but it is simultaneously an elegy for men who lost a battle. Tony Conran is thus able to pay fitting homage to the fallen, while dissociating himself at the same time from the British and Thatcherite reading of the war as a military and political success. This complexity of perspective guarantees a poem with both intellectual rigour and imaginative stimulus.

Tros Ryddid? was a stage show originally produced and published in book form during the 1983 National Eisteddfod. The script contains a combination of monologues and dialogues, songs, documentary evidence and recruiting material, and it argued unambiguously that Wales had been used throughout the ages to fight England's battles. Three characters – or, perhaps, caricatures – are employed to represent three historical periods, namely the wars between England and Scotland during the Middle Ages, the Great War and the Falklands/Malvinas War. The most resonant song and the one which contained the most obvious relevance at the time was 'Yn Dewach Na Dŵr', which focused on the alleged meeting between a Welsh-speaking nurse and a Welsh-speaking Patagonian soldier.[41] In line with the two soldiers portrayed by Eluned Phillips, both these characters are aware of the irony surrounding their situation:

> Rwyt yn siarad fy iaith, iaith mam a fy nhad,
> Er hynny yn ymladd rhai o fechgyn fy ngwlad,
> Pa fath o ddynion yw'r rheini a fynn
> Roi dau o'r un teulu mewn congl fel hyn?
>
> Arfogi un brawd yn erbyn ei frawd,
> Gan feddwl bod lifrai yn cuddio pob cnawd,
> A dyma ni'n dau dan ormes dau rym,
> Nad yw hil a pherthynas yn cyfri fawr ddim.[42]

This song was based on an actual meeting that has become increasingly caught up in mythology and gained iconic status in the memory of the war. This is how it is presented in *Tros Ryddid?*:

> During the Malvinas War a nurse from Powys came across a soldier in an Argentinian uniform crying in a wooden church in Port Stanley while British ships and aeroplanes attacked the town. On approaching him, she realized that his language was Welsh, and that he was a child of *Y Wladfa*.[43]

As part of his research for *Taken Out*, Greg Cullen interviewed members of the Welsh Guards who survived the war. Once the Argentinians had surrendered Port Stanley, the men served on board the troop-ship *Canberra*, escorting Argentinians home. Cullen refers to conversations between them: 'None were more poetic than the Welsh-speaking Argentinians meeting Welsh-speaking Guardsmen or the Welsh nurse who cried with a wounded Argentinian when he asked for help in Welsh.'[44] What can really be detected here is a mythologizing process in action, transporting the original nurse via folklore and urban legend from the mainland on to the ship, and therefore providing a meeting more steeped in drama and emotion than that described in *Tros Ryddid?* Ioan Roberts maintains that the meeting has been 'over-romanticised',[45] and one of the services rendered by *Rhyfel Ni* has been to track down the nurse and the soldier – the original authors rather than the secondary actors, as it were – and separate fact from fiction. Bronwen Williams, who was stationed as a nurse on the islands, had a Nonconformist background in Wales; her grandparents came from Blaenau Ffestiniog and her grandfather had served as a minister in Welshpool; her father had been born in Montgomeryshire but spent most of his life in London, where he worked as a dentist; her parents had returned to mid Wales when they retired; she did not speak Welsh, and has since returned to live on the islands, after getting married. As she explains, she first met the Argentinian soldier from Patagonia, Milton Rhys, when he came to worship in Port Stanley's Anglican church:

> It was an awfully strange feeling. Such a coincidence. And I could not help but wonder whether this was the kind of contact between people that would help heal wounds after wars and promote international peace. I felt as though we were in a far more significant situation, and one with far wider consequences than those directly facing us in that community.[46]

Milton Rhys's experience also contains a warning against overemphasizing the Welshness of the Falklands/Malvinas War: 'Throughout the war, Milton did not come across any soldiers, on either side, who spoke Welsh. His only contact with Wales was meeting Bronwen in church.'[47] The meeting in question has been demythologized, deromanticized and desentimentalized by Ioan Roberts. However, what remains apparent is the personal significance of their meeting to both involved: in the words of Milton Rhys, 'Meeting Bronwen made me realize how absurd our situation was during the war.'[48]

In contrast to 'Clymau', *Tros Ryddid?* does not attempt to dignify the experience of the Falklands/Malvinas War or tidy up its essential messiness, and it is more true to the nature of the war as a consequence. The anti-British political subtext more or less takes over on the cover of *Tros Ryddid?*, with its unambiguous image of a Union flag dripping blood. The same image was also used by the folk-singer Tecwyn Ifan the same year, on the cover of *Herio'r Oriau Du*, his cassette and LP which contained the song 'John Bull', with its critical references to the war.[49] *Tros Ryddid?* is far less reverent and reticent than 'Clymau', far more angry and argumentative, but one should not forget its genre: it was, after all, an example of campaigning agitprop theatre – described by one reviewer as a 'didactic, nearly Brechtian document'[50] – constructed unapologetically to score political points in front of a live audience, and, as a result, tended to peddle a simplified, stereotypical and predictably biased interpretation of events. Although it wore its Nationalist stance on its sleeve – and Plaid Cymru was the only political party officially to oppose the war[51] – in their foreword to *Tros Ryddid?* the authors encouraged more research into the matter, and it is a tribute to Myrddin ap Dafydd's magnanimity that his own publishing house, Gwasg Carreg Gwalch, published twenty years later *Rhyfel Ni*, which established the reality, as opposed to the legend on which the song 'Yn Dewach na Dŵr' was based.

It hardly needs stating that the Falklands/Malvinas war remains a potentially explosive subject. The Chair in the 1983 Powys Provincial Eisteddfod Powys was won by Peredur Lynch with an *awdl* about the war that proved controversial:[52] although he did not understand Welsh, a Methodist minister from Welshpool felt confident enough to complain that it was nonsense to suggest that this had been an English imperialist war, but he retracted his criticism after receiving a translation of the poem, suggesting instead that the *awdl* in question read like a Great War poem by Wilfred Owen.[53] It therefore appeared acceptable to interpret the war as a symbol of war's age-old futility, and that seems to characterize the way in which Welsh writers have since then responded to the conflict: following the fairly early reactions, only occasionally have they touched upon the subject by concentrating on its human consequences and avoiding its wider political, though non-partisan, significance. 'Gwraig ifanc â'i gŵr wedi dychwelyd o'r Falklands gydag anafiadau difrifol'[54] by Angharad Jones was originally a television monologue, and 'Sgrech Rhyfel' a short story written from the point of view of a survivor of the *Sir Galahad* disaster who still suffers from post-traumatic stress disorder (PTSD) years later.[55] *The Mimosa Boys*, an English-language television play, was broadcast by the BBC in 1985: written by Ewart Alexander and directed by John Hefin, it dealt with the experience of a company of Welsh soldiers who took part in the war.[56] The fate of a young Welsh soldier from a working-class background serving in Northern Ireland is depicted in the hard-hitting and graphic *Boy Soldier* in 1986: directed by Karl Francis, the film was described as 'powerful and sometimes disturbing' and as centring 'on a young Welsh soldier's struggle for his own identity within the British Army'.[57] Although that film touched upon themes associated with the Falklands/Malvinas War, adding to its contemporary relevance, the conflict was not directly revisited in an extended searching and challenging creative project[58] – a state-of-the-nation novel, for instance[59] – and a translation into Welsh in 1996 of Tony Marchant's 1983 stage play, *Welcome Home*, was left to fill part of the void.[60] But for over twenty years a mainly unbridged gap remained between the images and interpretations of war by civilian authors which appeared soon after the war ended and the direct testimony, recorded in interviews, of those who took part in the war and were immediately affected by it, which appeared in *Rhyfel Ni* in 2003.[61]

MILITARY EXPERIENCES

Besides the obvious contrasts in scale and degree, another factor that sets the Falklands/Malvinas War apart from the two world wars of the twentieth century is the fact that professional members of the armed service, rather than conscripted servicemen, fought in it. Since civilians – such as Cynan and W. J. Gruffydd during the Great War and Elwyn Evans and Alun Llywelyn-Williams during the Second World War – had encountered military life at first hand, we are left with a body of creative work based on their experiences.[62] The Falklands/Malvinas War was fought by a professional army during 'peace time', and therefore nothing comparable is available in Welsh to counterbalance the inexperienced civilian images – such as those already cited in the previous section – of the Falklands/Malvinas War. The unfortunate, if unintentional, result of this is that there is a danger that civilian words speak patronizingly and presumptuously for those who have taken part in the war. That is one gap that is finally filled by *Rhyfel Ni*, for, in addition to providing a platform for parents and journalists, the book provides a voice for some of the soldiers and their families, on both sides of the Atlantic, who experienced the war directly. The book serves a function similar to the one Tim Wilcox refers to when discussing the art therapy engaged in by some of the survivors of the war suffering from PTSD: 'these images seize back the representation of the war from the cultural milieu of those who proposed to speak on behalf of those who fought'.[63] What these eyewitness accounts provide is a new perspective on the war through the medium of Welsh.

Were these Welsh soldiers concerned at all by the possibility that they could be going into face-to-face battle with Patagonians whose families originated from Wales? If they sailed to fight the enemy, did the fact that the enemy might actually speak Welsh worry them in the slightest? This is an extract from the testimony of Michael John Griffith from Sarn Mellteyrn on the Llŷn Peninsula, outside whose home a Welsh Dragon flies on a mast:

> I knew some of the history of the Welsh in Patagonia but didn't realize at the time that Patagonia was part of Argentina . . . But had I known that there were Welsh-speaking boys on the other side, it wouldn't have made any difference. I was eighteen at the time, but everyone who has been in a war would say the same. There's no point you being there if you're going to start thinking 'I suppose that lad has got a brother or a sister somewhere, or perhaps he's got a wife at home who's just had a baby'. And in the same way, there's no point thinking his great-grandfather might have come from Wales. It was war, and that's that.[64]

Wil Howarth from Amlwch in Anglesey was one of the last three members of the Welsh Guards to come off the *Sir Galahad* alive, and he provides a similar perspective:

> They told us on the ship on the way over that it was a possibility [that 'there could be Welsh on the other side']. And I could remember learning in school about Patagonia, about them going from Anglesey and similar places because they had been ill-treated by the English and this and the other. It was a funny thing to consider on the way over, what if you met some of these people, and they talked the same language? Perhaps you would kill a relative of yours, you never know. But the thing is, when you're at war you can't afford to allow anything weak to stay on your mind, you've got no choice but to carry on. If you're a jockey in the Grand National you've got to win, got to win. There are no ifs, buts, maybes, you've got to carry on.
>
> [. . .]
>
> In any war, if you give a nineteen-year-old boy a gun, all he has to do is pull the trigger. It doesn't matter who the enemy is, you don't stop and think how old he is or who he is before killing him. You don't think about it, because you'd be the dead one if you did. 'Ours not to reason why, just to do or die.' You can't afford a conscience when you're going into war.[65]

215

This represents one of the most honest reactions in Welsh, certainly during the late modern period, relating to the plain truth about the soldier's vocation. The soldier's duty is to act – act in accordance with orders – rather than analyse and question the justification for and morality of the war in which he is involved. Grahame Davies also expressed the plain truth in a review of *Rhyfel Ni* when he said of the war, 'Although there was a Welsh aspect to it, it was not a stage for a surrogate battle for Welsh identity', and that the 'Welsh connections' were 'quite marginal for those touched by the war'; basically, 'both sides were fighting dutifully and with conviction despite the Welsh connections'.[66]

As already suggested, the Welsh did not necessarily find the experience of war during the twentieth century an easy one to digest and discuss, and such a difficulty partly explains why some memoirs of war have been so late appearing. Again in generalized terms, one senses an undercurrent of regret in some of those memoirs, as if the narrator were in the confessional seeking understanding and forgiveness, not necessarily for the sins he committed during the war, but for the basic sin he committed in participating in war at all. In this sense, the veterans of war still seem to be battling – battling with ethical, cultural and political arguments: was there a tension between their Welshness and Britishness? Was there an inconsistency between the pacifist teaching of the chapel and the experience of going into war? Not all combatants could explain their motive for joining the armed services during the Second World War with the clarity displayed by D. Gwyn Jones, in an episode of the documentary series *Cymru 2000* (Ffilmiau'r Bont for S4C) broadcast in 1999:

> I didn't want anything to happen to Cilfynydd as had happened to the small villages in the Netherlands and France and so on. As far as I was concerned, he – Hitler – wouldn't be allowed to come there. It was in a sense a personal matter.

Perhaps this is an indication of the cultural assimilation intensified by the experience of two world wars, but there is nothing regretful or apologetic about the wartime reminiscences of the servicemen interviewed in *Rhyfel Ni* who refer to combat during the latter stages of the twentieth century; their words provide first-hand evidence of the reality of modern war faced by the professional soldier. Wil Howarth insisted on swearing his oath of allegiance to the Queen in Welsh when he first joined the Welsh Guards as a twenty-one-year-old recruit, and he took pride in the fact that his grandfather and later his uncle had won military honours during both world wars. He therefore regarded himself as being part of a succession, a link within a tradition, and he assumed multi-identities as a Welshman, a Briton and a soldier. And his strong suggestion was that considerations pertaining to identity – amid a war directly triggered by unresolved arguments pertaining to identity and territory – were not a relevant matter for him as a common soldier whilst engaged in the pragmatic business of fighting.

The most famous Welshman identified with the Falklands/Malvinas War is Simon Weston: his damaged face is probably one of the primary images that comes to mind when one recalls the conflict. He has come to symbolize and embody the war, and in the three autobiographical books that he has penned, published between 1989 and 2003, he expresses pride in Nelson, his hometown, and in Wales, his country. His first volume, *Walking Tall* (1989), is illustrated with a series of photographs, among them one taken on board the *QE2* during the voyage to the South Atlantic and showing him in the company of three of his best friends in the army. Of the group of four, he alone survived the attack on the *Sir Galahad*, and he has referred on various occasions to the sense of guilt that has plagued him ever since. What all four display, with the same pride that characterizes any Welsh rugby team or choir on tour abroad, is a Welsh Dragon flag, with the place-name 'Bangor' emblazoned across its lower half. Who would dare doubt the substance or authenticity of their Welshness? Simon Weston has not for a second suggested any inconsistency between his patriotism and his membership of the army: on the contrary, he has taken real pride in his membership of the Welsh Guards, which has provided him with discipline, challenge and adventure. In terms of identity and nationhood, he, too, considered himself a Welshman, a Briton and a monarchist. Recounting his thoughts in 1982 regarding the war in which he would soon be engaged, he referred to a clear sense of duty:

> We were sailing south in the belief that it was only fair and right to protect the freedom of British subjects. If we didn't stand by them in their hour of need, we would be failing them. If we believed in freedom ourselves, we had no choice.
>
> [. . .]
>
> I had joined the Army and had signed on the dotted line. I had to obey orders. I had never thought that I would actually go to war – but then, who had?[67]

No doubts lingered in his mind, at least as to whether or not his comrades' blood was lost for freedom. In the first two volumes of his autobiography, *Walking Tall* and *Going Back* (1992), he remained convinced that the war he took part in was a just war; not until *Moving On*, published in 2003 on the twenty-first anniversary of the war, did he come to view it as an unnecessary war and express total disillusionment with Margaret Thatcher. But although his scarred body is a daily reminder of the price he paid because of the war, he has fought hard to fend off the image of himself as a victim and has striven to see himself instead as a survivor: 'Instead of seeing myself as a victim, I began to see myself as somebody who was lucky.'[68]

It is therefore clear that the images these three servicemen possess of themselves is at odds with the images constructed by civilian writers of victims caught up in a war that conflicted with their Welshness; the evidence appears to challenge the rather tidy and comforting interpretation behind civilian images.

Rhaid i Bopeth Newid is a first novel, published in 2004 by the poet and journalist Grahame Davies. It adopts an ambitious structure, juxtaposing the life of the socialist philosopher Simone Weil in France between the two World Wars with the life of Meinwen Jones, an imaginary language-activist in twenty-first-century Wales. This is Assembly-led Wales, the new Wales that forces Meinwen and her fellow-campaigners fundamentally to reconsider their strategies and tactics, and insists that they become politically astute. This loaded quotation is particularly striking:

> This was the version of Welsh history that was believed as gospel by the people whom Meinwen spent her life almost exclusively in their company, a version where every labourite, conservative, soldier or royalist was quietly sidelined, where world statesmen like Lloyd George and Aneurin Bevan were less than dust in the scales, and where a figure such as Saunders Lewis bestrode the world like a colossus. The piquant and complex mixture of the nation's real history was filtered through the narrow mesh of nonconformity, pacifism and nationalism until it had been distilled into a clear, colourless, anodyne and alcohol-free liquid – an elixir which kept people like Meinwen eternally youthful and eternally hopeful for the coming day when nationalism would sweep the country and when the old language would once again be enthroned at the heart of Welsh life. In Meinwen's mental republic, only the language was accorded anything so royal as a throne.[69]

So potent is this 'version of Welsh history' that it does not acknowledge the inconsistencies or tensions within it, for example, the fact that Saunders Lewis converted from Nonconformism to Catholicism, and that he was anything but a pacifist![70] Grahame Davies has sketched what is admittedly a caricature, an exaggerated cartoon image, and yet, what one senses in contrasting the literary interpretations of civilian writers of the Falklands/Malvinas War with the evidence of those who actually experienced that war for themselves, is how potentially partial and selective some images of Wales and Welshness can be. The suggestion in *Rhyfel Ni* that 'identity is not always black and white',[71] is clearly an example of understatement, yet must the complexity suggested about Welsh identity and nationhood inevitably be seen as a potential threat, rather than a source of nourishment for the Welsh mind and imagination?

THE SPECIAL RELATIONSHIP

Russell Isaac was a Welsh-speaking Welshman who found himself in a unique position during the war, a journalist with HTV who spoke Spanish after spending time in Patagonia studying for a postgraduate degree. In an interview for *Rhyfel Ni*, he explained what he attempted to do by means of his 'independent' news broadcasts, which at the time represented 'nearly the only daily material that took a slightly different viewpoint compared to the British spin that featured in the whole affair':[72]

> Trying to show that we the Welsh had a very, very special attachment down there and that these people felt the same; that they saw Wales as being apart from England, apart from Britain, and they sought to uphold their culture and Welshness because of this historical link . . . that there were people who thought in a different way, beyond the propaganda, beyond the rhetoric, beyond the jingoism.[73]

But how did the people themselves respond, those caught in the middle of war? A positive reaction from a professional soldier who fought in the war is hardly surprising and when Julio Oscar Gibbon of Esquel was asked whether it had been worth his while to fight for the islands, his answer came loud and clear: '*Sí, sí, sí*. I went there to represent my country, to defend my country and my flag. I went there to offer up my life.'[74] This response earned him praise from the interpreter, who used to teach him at primary level: 'Well done, son, I taught you that at school!'[75] Benja and Lila Lewis's son was keen to fight in the war: educated in a military college, he came originally from Comodoro Rivadavia, where military recruits were trained for the battle ahead, and, as suggested by his answer – so reminiscent of an emotionally charged Great War recruiting poster[76] – it was first and foremost a matter of pride in his case: 'What shall I tell my children when they ask "Where were you Dad during the Malvinas war?" '[77] However, the response of the Argentinians was not completely uniform and one-sided, and British soldiers were not the only ones unsure about the location of the islands: Milton Rhys referred to some of the raw recruits born and bred on the prairie as real innocents:

> [They had] never seen the sea nor travelled on a boat or an aeroplane, they had hardly any education and some could not even write their name. And all of a sudden they were at war. Against whom? British? Europeans? Fighting for what? The Malvinas? Where was that? They had never heard of the place before.[78]

Even a civilian such as Iris Sbannaus, who believed passionately that the islands belonged to Argentina – 'we feel that we own the Malvinas. That's what we've been taught and that's what we believe to be right' – occasionally wondered whether they were worth all the bother: 'sometimes I wonder why we need the blinking islands, they're ugly and it's so windy there'.[79] Carlos Eduardo ap Iwan, a nineteen-year-old conscript in 1982, felt in retrospect that he had been misled and betrayed: 'It was such an awful experience, and so much suffering for nothing.'[80] Since the war, according to Milton Rhys, over 300 Argentinian soldiers have either committed suicide or died as a result of excessive drinking brought on by the war, and he has been highly critical of the lack of care available to those who served in the war. This has also been a familiar theme in the memoirs of Simon Weston: despite the obstacles that he himself has overcome, he referred in *Moving On* to the fact that more British survivors of the war have committed suicide since the end of it than were killed during the conflict itself, and also to the failed attempts by veterans to get compensation for the suffering they endured during the war.[81] Horacio Jose Kent from Trelew has referred to the sub-standard conditions suffered by Argentine soldiers during the war itself: he has mentioned the lack of food, the deaths from botulism, the inadequate footwear worn by Argentinians and the fact that a substantial number of soldiers were untrained recruits. As recently as 7 October 2004, an item on the Antiwar.com website contained a newspaper report by Marcela Valente, 'Argentina finally recognizes veterans of Falklands War', which referred to the substantial increase in pension to the veterans of a war that continued to cause suffering and death twenty-two years later.[82] Despite the obvious distinctions between the two conflicts, the Falklands/Malvinas War has come to haunt the Argentinian psyche, as the Vietnam War has haunted the American psyche.

Referring to the general support that the war attracted among Argentinians, Lila Lewis has stated that they had later learnt that 'it was all lies. There's something soft in the Argentino. He believes *politicos* and he believes the military. But they aren't people you can believe.'[83] Has there not been a similar element of naivety and gullibility in the Welsh response to the special relationship between Wales and Patagonia? Was there not at the time a retreat into the mythology of that relationship, in an attempt to ensure some sort of counterpoint to the imperialistic Britishness that had been released by the conflict? Is not this the type of easy and unthinking response satirized by the novelist Aled Islwyn in *Cadw'r Chwedlau'n Fyw*, in 1984?[84] And although the historian Prys Morgan took that novel as the starting point for an article in which he argued that it was essential that, post-1979, Wales sought to redefine herself and live through the medium of her legends and myths, I somehow doubt whether the type of response generated by the Falklands/Malvinas War was what he had in mind.[85] I also doubt whether this rather defensive and predictable response represented the type of new relevance and reality in Welsh literature which two young critics, Wiliam Owen Roberts and Iwan Llwyd Williams, called for at the time.[86]

The relationship between Wales and Patagonia has long been regarded as something of a sacred cow.[87] That relationship was put under immense pressure during the 1982 crisis, as suggested by a forthright letter that appeared in January 1983 in *Y Cymro* and which was quoted in *Tros Ryddid?* Glyn Ceiriog Hughes of Trelew reprimanded the Welsh for taking part in what he described as:

> pilfering and greedy Great Britain's imperialist war . . . After the Malvinas war, the people of Argentina consider the Welsh in exactly the same terms as the Gurkhas, since they travelled to the islands on the same ship. There's no difference, they're all hired murderers.[88]

The reference to the Nepalese mercenary soldiers, renowned for their bravery in war, was particularly revealing. John Benjamin Lewis, who moved from the Gaiman to Comodoro Rivadavia during the 1950s in search of employment, experienced many conflicting feelings:

> The awful thing was thinking about a young boy, the son of Welsh people over here, going to war and knowing that there were also young boys from Wales coming to fight on the other side. It's a very sad thing for us on both sides. We worried for ourselves and the Malvinas, and also worried for the people on the other side. I found it all very painful.[89]

Perhaps what accounts for some of the relative failure to interpret the Falklands/Malvinas experience intellectually and imaginatively, the lack of creative ambition, has been the sense of guilt and shame surrounding it – guilt and shame born of the fact that the Welsh had been caught up in a war against those of similar descent. But how much sentiment, as opposed to reality, characterized that special relationship by the start of the 1980s? Those who have written about the war have tended to confirm uncritically the bonds of attachment, and there is only one Welsh author, the aforementioned Wiliam Owen Roberts, who has proved brave enough to probe beyond the superficial perception. Published in 1990, 'Saludos de Patagonia' was a short story constructed as a series of letters between two friends, one from Patagonia and the other from Wales.[90] It was set in 1979, around the time of the referendum on devolution, and it revealed the lack of perspective and the failure of imagination which prevented a representative of a Welsh bourgeois democracy – and a right-wing and reactionary representative at that – from seeing beyond the constitutional defeat of the pro-devolution campaign in order to realize the far more sinister fate of the disappeared in the military dictatorship of Argentina.

It is appropriate to draw this chapter to a close with the words of Simon Weston, which provide a wise perspective on the particular war in question:

> We did not take part in a holocaust. It was not a war that will be remembered for ever. It was just another conflict, and now is just another already half-forgotten story, a more and more distant memory of Union Jacks [*sic*] and cheers and glory . . . My story, like those of other Falklands veterans, is not going to be recorded alongside histories of the two World Wars or the American Civil War, wars that raged for years and years and cost hundreds of thousands of lives, and in a way, I am glad. The Falklands war will die a natural death.[91]

But before we all rush off to its funeral, surely the act of remembering this war is a step in the process of beginning to understand it, of facing up to it honestly and maturely, whilst acknowledging at the same time some of the complexity and variety which characterize our Welsh identities.

NOTES

[1] This is an extended and annotated version of an article commissioned by Geraint H. Jenkins for the *Cof Cenedl* series of historical essays: 'Cofio rhyfel anghofiedig: dehongli a chyd-destunoli Rhyfel y Falklands/Malvinas 1982', *Cof Cenedl*, 21 (2006), 159–91. Since a Welsh version is publicly available, I have chosen to present the majority of Welsh quotations solely through the medium of authorial translations into English; relevant titles are translated.

[2] Of the titles listed at the end of the entry on 'Patagonia' in Meic Stephens (ed.), *The New Companion to the Literature of Wales* (Cardiff, 1998), pp. 571–2, probably the most analytical and objective approach to the Patagonian experience is provided by Glyn Williams, *The Desert and the Dream: A Study of Welsh Colonization in Chubut, 1865–1915* (Cardiff, 1975), and Williams, *The Welsh in Patagonia: The State and the Ethnic Community* (Cardiff, 1991). Robert Owen Jones investigates the linguistic situation in 'The Welsh language in Patagonia', in Geraint H. Jenkins (ed.), *Language and Community in the Nineteenth Century* (Cardiff, 1998).

[3] Discussed by Jeffrey Walsh, ' "There'll always be an England": the Falklands conflict on film', in James Aulich (ed.), *Framing the Falklands War: Nationhood, Culture and Identity* (Milton Keynes and Philadelphia, 1992), pp. 42–4.

[4] Cited in 'Foreword', in Aulich (ed.), *Framing the Falklands War*, pp. ix–x.

[5] Ioan Roberts, *Rhyfel Ni: Profiadau Cymreig o Ddwy Ochr Rhyfel y Falklands/Malvinas* ('Our War: Welsh Experiences on Both Sides of the

Falklands/Malvinas War') (Llanrwst, 2003). It was deservedly included in the Welsh-language long-list for the Welsh Arts Council Book of the Year award in 2004; translation into English and Spanish would provide a valuable service, and both are urgently required.

[6] Simon Weston, *Walking Tall: An Autobiography* (London, 1989), p. 183.

[7] See Jeff Evans, 'Sailor', *The Penguin TV Companion* (Harmondsworth, 2001), p. 524.

[8] As can be seen in Elizabeth Knowles (ed.), *The Oxford Dictionary of Quotations* (Oxford, 1999), p. 769, her actual words outside Downing Street on 25 April 1982 were 'Just rejoice at the news and congratulate our armed forces and the Marines. Rejoice!', but they are usually quoted as 'Rejoice, rejoice!'

[9] The headline appeared on the front page of the 4 May 1982 issue of the *Sun* and was followed by a smaller headline: 'Our lads sink gunboat and hole cruiser'.

[10] The three programmes were *Simon's War* (1983), *Simon's Peace* (1985) and *Simon's Triumph* (1989); they are critically discussed by John Taylor in 'Touched with glory: heroes and human interest in the news', in Aulich (ed.), *Framing the Falklands War*, pp. 26–31.

[11] Roberts, *Rhyfel Ni*, p. 174.

[12] See Simon Weston with John Mann, *Going Back: Return to the Falklands* (London, 1992), p. 91, where it is suggested during a meeting between Argentinian and British veterans of the war that 'thousands', rather than hundreds, of Argentinian soldiers actually died. A cover-up is suggested, an attempt to hide the real scale of Argentina's defeat, and members of the armed forces portrayed as scapegoats:

> the government had constantly sought to blame the Army for the defeat. Documentaries and articles always harped on about the inadequacy of the soldiers. No one looked at the politics of the defeat, the failure to look after the troops during the war, the lack of information, the terrible reception the men had when they returned. The truth was constantly covered up. (p. 90)

[13] Simon Weston, *Moving On* (London, 2003), p. 160. *The Oxford Dictionary of Quotations*, p. 143, attributes the quotation to the Argentinian writer, Jorge Luis Borges in *Time* (14 February 1983): 'The Falklands thing was a fight between two bald men over a comb.'

[14] Quoted in Weston, *Moving On*, p. 156.

[15] Max Hastings and Simon Jenkins, *The Battle for the Falklands* (London, 1983); Martin Middlebrook, *The Fight for the 'Malvinas': The Argentine Forces in the Falklands War* (London, 1989). A wealth of material is also easily available online, e.g. *www.yendor.com/vanished/falklands-war.html*, *www.news.bbc.co.uk/hi/english/static/in_depth/uk/2002/falklands/*, *www.channel4.com/history/microsites/F/falklands/*.

[16] Anthony Barnett, *Iron Britannia: Why Parliament Waged its Falklands War* (London, 1982).

[17] John Sergeant, *Give Me Ten Seconds* (London, 2001), p. 219.

[18] The following comments by Hastings and Jenkins, *Battle for the Falklands* (London, 1997 edn), p. 155, underline familiar characteristics of her public persona: 'Her constant supportive remarks to the fleet staff made a deep impression. The simplicity of her objectives and her total determination to see them achieved

came as a welcome change to men used to regarding politicians as hedgers and
doubters.'

[19] See Barnett, *Iron Britannia*, p. 131, who highlights the irony that 'Thatcher, who
has destroyed community upon community in Britain itself has decided that the
Kelper's way of life must be preserved at all costs'.

[20] The full text of the speech is contained in an appendix to Barnett, *Iron Britannia*,
pp. 149–53, and can also be found on the Margaret Thatcher Foundation website,
*www.margaretthatcher.org/Speeches/displaydocument.asp?docid=104989&doc
type=1*.

[21] Cited in Barnett, *Iron Britannia*, p. 150.

[22] Ibid.

[23] Ibid., p. 153.

[24] Ibid., pp. 110–11.

[25] *Taken Out* was originally performed by Theatr Powys in 1985 and broadcast on
BBC Radio 4 on 3 March 1986. Both a stage performance and the radio production
are reviewed in Hazel Walford Davies (ed.), *State of Play: Four Playwrights of
Wales* (Llandysul, 1998), pp. 376–8; the author himself discusses his research for
the play in Greg Cullen, 'The real war', *Planet: The Welsh Internationalist*, 58
(Aug./Sept. 1986).

[26] Llwybr Llaethog, 'Rhywbeth Bach yn Poeni Pawb' ('Something Small Worries Us
All') (1986). Craig Owen Jones discusses the song in ' "Beatbox Taffia": Welsh
underground music', *Hanes Cerddoriaeth Cymru/Welsh Music History*, 6 (2004),
232–3. Thanks to Sally Harper, School of Music, University of Wales Bangor, for
this information and to Craig Jones for his assistance.

[27] Eluned Phillips, 'Clymau' ('Ties'), in T. M. Bassett (ed.), *Cyfansoddiadau a
Beirniadaethau Eisteddfod Genedlaethol Frenhinol Cymru 1983* (Llandysul, 1983);
republished in Eluned Phillips, *Cerddi Glyn-y-Mêl* (Llandysul, 1985). The poem was
translated by Gillian Clarke as 'Ties', in Menna Elfyn and John Rowlands (eds),
*The Bloodaxe Book of Modern Welsh Poetry: 20th-century Welsh-language
Poetry in Translation* (Northumberland, 2003). Myrddin ap Dafydd and Geraint
Løvgreen, *Tros Ryddid?* ('For Freedom?') (Llanrwst, 1983).

[28] An interesting case in point is the strong response provoked by the winning
poem in the 2002 competition for the Crown. Written by possibly the most
exciting playwright currently working in Welsh, Aled Jones Williams, 'Awelon'
('Breezes') is a prose poem which makes abundant use of stream-of-
consciousness and employs highly personal and private imagery. The feelings
aroused by this most uncompromising of poems, one that made no transparent
attempt to voice public sentiments, verged on expressions of anger and betrayal.
See Aled Jones Williams, 'Awelon', in J. Elwyn Hughes (ed.), *Cyfansoddiadau a
Beirniadaethau Eisteddfod Genedlaethol Cymru Sir Benfro, Tyddewi 2002*
(Llandybïe, 2002). For a cross-section of opinion regarding the poem, see the
various contributions to *Barddas*, 269 (Sept./Oct./Nov. 2002); Aled Jones
Williams's own comments in *Barddas*, 270 (Dec. 2002/Jan. 2003); 'Cloriannu
cerdd y Goron', *Taliesin*, 117 (Winter 2002), and Emyr Lewis, 'Tacsi i'r
Tywyllwch', *Taliesin*, 117 (Winter 2002); Vaughan Hughes, 'Eisteddfod
Gwynedd', *Barn*, 476 (Sept. 2002).

[29] Nesta Wyn Jones, in Bassett (ed.), *Cyfansoddiadau*, p. 44.

[30] Roberts, *Rhyfel Ni*, p. 32.

[31] Weston, *Going Back*, p. 39.

[32] *Y Cymro*, 9 Aug. 1983. See also 'Holi Eluned Phillips' ('Interviewing Eluned Phillips'), *Barddas*, 80 (Dec. 1983).

[33] For critical responses to the poem, see for example the comments made by Vaughan Hughes, 'Y 'steddfod yn ei lle', *Y Faner*, 19 Aug. 1983; and Gwyn Thomas, 'Gwyn Thomas yn ateb cwestiynau Gerwyn Williams (21.9.83)', *Y Traethodydd*, 139 (1984). For 'The twenty-four metres' and 'Cynghanedd', see Stephens (ed.), *New Companion to the Literature of Wales*, pp. 742, 139–40. For alternative responses to 'Clymau', see Menna Elfyn, 'Bardd ffrwythlon y tir diffaith', *Y Faner*, 26 Aug. 1983; Moses Glyn Jones, 'Fy marn am gynhaeaf Môn', *Barddas*, 77 (Sept. 1983); Donald Evans, 'Pryddest prifwyl Môn', *Barn*, 248 (Sept. 1983); and Rhydwen Williams, 'Gorau barn . . . gorau chwedl', *Barn*, 248 (Sept. 1983).

[34] *The Penguin Book of Welsh Verse* (Harmondsworth, 1967), republished as *Welsh Verse* (Bridgend, 1986).

[35] Tony Conran, 'Elegy for the Welsh dead, in the Falkland Islands, 1982', *Eros Proposes a Toast: Collected Public Poems and Gifts* (Bridgend, 1998). The poet provides a detailed discussion of the poem in his *Visions and Praying Mantids: The Angelological Notebooks* (Llandysul, 1997), pp. 163–74; textual notes are also supplied in his *The Shape of My Country: Selected Poems and Extracts* (Llanrwst, 2004), pp. 116–18.

[36] Conran, 'Elegy for the Welsh dead', p. 82.

[37] *Canu Aneirin* (Caerdydd, 1938) was edited by Ifor Williams; Kenneth Jackson provides a translation into English in *The Gododdin: the Oldest Scottish Poem* (Edinburgh, 1969), as does A. O. H. Jarman in *Y Gododdin* (Llandysul, 1988).

[38] Conran, 'Elegy for the Welsh dead', p. 81.

[39] For a discussion of the war poems of R. Williams Parry, see Gerwyn Wiliams, 'The literature of the First World War', in Dafydd Johnston (ed.), *A Guide to Welsh Literature c. 1900–1996* (Cardiff, 1998), pp. 27–9. Bedwyr Lewis Jones discusses the poems in *Robert Williams Parry* (Cardiff, 1972), pp. 30–6. Joseph P. Clancy provides some translations in *Twentieth Century Welsh Poems* (Llandysul, 1982), pp. 46–7, and in Elfyn and Rowlands (eds), *Bloodaxe Book of Modern Welsh Poetry*, pp. 60–1.

[40] Conran, 'Elegy for the Welsh dead'. As Conran explains in *Visions and Praying Mantids*, p. 165, the five names belong to actual casualties:

> It was then that I heard that forty-three Welsh soldiers had been killed when an Argentine air-born missile damaged a British ship offshore. In the Welsh weekly newspaper, *Y Cymro* there was a preliminary list of nine soldiers who had died in the incident . . .

[41] 'Yn Dewach Na Dŵr' ('Thicker Than Water'), Dafydd and Løvgreen, *Tros Ryddid?*, pp. 72–3.

[42] Dafydd and Lovgreen, *Tros Ryddid?*, p. 73. This is a literal translation:

> You speak my language, the language of my mother and father,
> And yet you are fighting against boys from my country.
> What sort of men are those who insist on putting
> Two from the same family in a predicament like this?

> One brother enarmoured against the other,
> Assuming that an uniform hides all flesh,
> And here are the two of us oppressed by two powers
> For whom race and belonging barely count.

[43] Ibid., p. 72.

[44] Cullen, 'Real war', p. 39.

[45] Roberts, *Rhyfel Ni*, p. 28.

[46] Ibid., p. 36.

[47] Ibid., p. 46.

[48] Ibid., p. 47.

[49] *Herio'r Oriau Du* ('Challenging the Dark Hours') was released in 1983 by Sain record company.

[50] Richard Morris Jones, review of *Tros Ryddid?*, *Llais Llyfrau* (Winter 1983), 20. See also the feature 'Oferedd rhyfel yn amlwg yn y brifwyl: marciau llawn i Wasg Carreg Gwalch' ('The futility of war obvious in the Eisteddfod: full marks to Gwasg Carreg Gwalch'), *Y Cymro*, 16 Aug. 1983.

[51] Barnett, *Iron Britannia*, p. 154, note 6: 'Two Plaid Cymru MPs also voted against the assault; their party was the only one to oppose the fighting officially.'

[52] Peredur Lynch, 'Gorwelion (i'r milwyr o Gymru a laddwyd yn rhyfel y Falklands)' ('Horizons (for the soldiers from Wales who were killed in the Falklands war)'), *Barddas*, 81 (Jan. 1984), 3.

[53] *Y Cymro*, 8 Nov. 1983.

[54] Angharad Jones, 'Gwraig ifanc â'i gŵr wedi dychwelyd o'r Falklands gydag anafiadau difrifol' ('A young wife whose husband has returned from the Falklands with severe wounds'), broadcast on the youth programme *Heno, Heno* (HTV for S4C) and later published in the short-lived literary journal, *A5*, 2 (Summer 1986), 72–3.

[55] Martin Huws, 'Sgrech Rhyfel' ('The Scream of War'), *Sgrech Rhyfel* (Llanrwst, 2001), pp. 10–16.

[56] *The Mimosa Boys* was first broadcast on 19 June 1985. Writing in the *Paumanock Review*, 1/2 (Spring 2000), *http://www.etext.org/Fiction/Paumanok/1.2/feature.html*, Tim Rees describes his role as military adviser in the making of the play:

> A few months after joining the BBC Wales Film Unit the then Head of Drama, John Hefin, approached me with a proposal to make a film based on my view of the Falkland Islands War where I'd fought with the 1st Battalion Welsh Guards. My specialisation in the army was intelligence, so I had a pretty good grasp of the facts. The resulting drama was broadcast as a primetime *Play For Today* titled *Mimosa Boys* after the ship 'Mimosa' that had sailed from Liverpool to Argentina in 1865 with the Welsh men and women who colonised the area in Argentina that came to be known as Patagonia.

[57] Cited in *http://www.s4c.co.uk/festivals/e_milwrbychan.shtml*. Released four years after the Falklands/Malvinas War, the following description further suggests resonant themes: 'The film is a powerful, claustrophobic work examining the teenager's increased alienation from an army which makes him a scapegoat – and his affinity and identification with Celts subjugated by the occupying British forces.'

⁵⁷ Interestingly, Cullen contends that the war had a merely temporary significance:

> I write for my immediate community, and from that specific hope something universal will arise. It doesn't always, and doesn't always have to. Sometimes you have a piece of theatre that has an immediate impact and is gone. Take *Taken Out*, for example. Who now wants a play about the *Sir Galahad*? But it served the bereaved families at the time, and the soldiers whose stories were suppressed by the Ministry of Defence.

Quoted in 'Discovering a theatrical landscape: Greg Cullen is interviewed by Hazel Walford Davies', 1 Jan. 1997, *http://www.theatre-wales.co.uk/features/features_detail.asp?profilesID=12*; ultimately published in *New Welsh Review*, 39 (Winter 1997–8).

⁵⁹ Although untimately unsuccessful, an ambitious-sounding novel was sent to the competition for the Daniel Owen Memorial Prize in the 2003 National Eisteddfod. A competitor writing under the pseudonym 'Fflur' submitted a novel charting a family's history over three generations: the narrator's husband died during the First World War, her son died in the Second World War, and her grandson died in the Falklands/Malvinas War. The adjudicators were Sioned Davies, Marion Eames and Gwerfyl Pierce Jones, and their comments can be read in 'Gwobr Goffa Daniel Owen: nofel heb ei chyhoeddi', in J. Elwyn Hughes (ed.), *Cyfansoddiadau a Beirnadaethau Eisteddfod Genedlaethol Cymru Maldwyn a'r Gororau 2003* (Llandybïe), p. 115.

⁶⁰ *Croeso Nôl* (Aberystwyth, 1996) was translated by John A. Owen and first performed by Dalier Sylw drama company on 26 February 1996.

⁶¹ The images of Welsh Guards that appear in the war memoirs of English soldiers tend to be clichéd, if not contentious. In his uncompromising account of the conflict, *A Soldier's Song: True Stories from the Falklands* (London, 1999 [1993]), Ken Lukowiak portrays a survivor of the *Sir Galahad* as a thief: see pp. 116–21. And in *Falklands Commando* (London, 2002 [1984]), pp. 222–3, Sandhurst-educated captain, Hugh McManners, paints Welsh soldiers in a negative light – ill-prepared for battle, ineffective and also larcenists:

> military equipment and personal belongings went missing. One of my friends complained to the Welsh Guards hierarchy after their military stores were raided, to be told there was little that could be done. A senior officer said ruefully: 'Taffy is [a] Welshman, Taffy is a thief.'

The description is listed as part of a traditional rhyme dating from *c.*1780 in Meic Stephens (ed.), *A Most Peculiar People: Quotations about Wales and the Welsh* (Cardiff, 1992), p. 30.

⁶² On Welsh literature of the Great War, see Wiliams, 'Literature of the First World War'. Elwyn Evans himself provides an introduction to the work of his friend and former colleague in *Alun Llywelyn-Williams* (Cardiff, 1991). See also *The Light in the Gloom: Poems and Prose* (Denbigh, 1998), a selection of Alun Llywelyn-Williams's work translated into English by Joseph P. Clancy, in addition to Gerwyn Wiliams, 'Occupying new territory: Alun Llywelyn-Williams and Welsh-language poetry of the Second World War', in Tim Kendall (ed.), *The Oxford Handbook of British and Irish War Poetry* (Oxford, 2007), pp. 340–61.

[63] Tim Wilcox, ' "We are all Falklanders now": art, war and national identity', in Aulich (ed.), *Framing The Falklands War*, p. 82.

[64] Roberts, *Rhyfel Ni*, pp. 56–7.

[65] Ibid., pp. 121–2.

[66] Grahame Davies, review of *Rhyfel Ni*, published in *Llais Llên*, BBC Cymru Cymru'r Byd website, *http://www.bbc.co.uk/cymru/adloniant/llyfrau/adolygiadau/352-rhyfel-ni.shtml*.

[67] Weston, *Walking Tall*, p. 175.

[68] Weston, *Moving On*, p. 15.

[69] Grahame Davies, *Rhaid i Bopeth Newid* ('Everything Must Change') (Llandysul, 2004), pp. 126–7. I am grateful to the author for providing me with his own translation.

[70] As the military historian Ian Miller revealed on the BBC documentary *Aderyn Dieithr* (BBC for S4C, 2002), Saunders Lewis appealed against the fact that he was to lose his military rank of Lieutenant, gained during the Great War, after being convicted guilty of arson at the Penrhos bombing-range in 1936.

[71] Roberts, *Rhyfel Ni*, p. 17.

[72] Ibid., p. 162.

[73] Ibid., pp. 161–2.

[74] Ibid., p. 141.

[75] Ibid., p. 142.

[76] A copy of the British recruiting poster, 'Daddy, what did YOU do in the Great War?', may be seen at *www.firstworldwar.com/posters/uk.htm*.

[77] Roberts, *Rhyfel Ni*, p. 186.

[78] Ibid., p. 45.

[79] Ibid., p. 173.

[80] Ibid., p. 109.

[81] See Weston, *Moving On*, pp. 163–73.

[82] See *www.antiwar.com/ips/valente.php?articleid=3722*.

[83] Roberts, *Rhyfel Ni*, p. 186.

[84] Aled Islwyn, *Cadw'r Chwedlau'n Fyw* ('Keeping the Legends Alive') (Caerdydd, 1984).

[85] See Prys Morgan, 'Keeping the legends alive', in Tony Curtis (ed.), *Wales: The Imagined Nation – Studies in Cultural and National Identity* (Bridgend, 1986). Mythology is not an unfamiliar component of the Falklands/ Malvinas story: in his introduction to *The Argentine Fight for the Falklands* (Barnsley, 2003), Martin Middlebrook states: 'The difficulty of dealing with wartime myths was my greatest problem, both when interviewing in Argentina and in the subsequent writing of this book' (p. xi).

[86] Wiliam Owen Roberts and Iwan Llwyd Williams, 'Myth y traddodiad dethol' ('The myth of the selective tradition'), *Llais Llyfrau* (Autumn 1982), 10–11; and 'Mae'n bwrw glaw yn Torremolinos – ac yn bryd ailddiffinio ein "traddodiad" llenyddol' ('It's raining in Torremolinos – and time to redefine our literary "tradition" '), *Y Faner*, 14 Dec. 1984.

[87] As recently as August 2005, the decision by prize-winning novelist Siân Eirian Rees Davies to adopt historically factual names but fictitious personalities for a company of Welsh pioneers who ventured to Patagonia in the 1860s proved controversial. In an attempt to convey an unromanticized portrayal of the early

settlers and demythologize their actions, the less-than-complimentary depiction of their characters and activities in *I Fyd Sy Well* ('To a Better World') which won the Daniel Owen Memorial Prize in the 2005 National Eisteddfod was criticized by some descendants. See 'Nofel Daniel Owen – "ffug" ddim yn ddigon' ('Daniel Owen novel – "fiction" not sufficient'), *Golwg*, 17, 48 (11 Aug. 2005), 6, and also the online discussion at *http://maes-e.com/viewtopic.php?t=13953*. In the same Eisteddfod, a competitor bearing the pseudonym 'Llwch yr Heli' submitted a novel in the competition for the Prose Medal which, according to Catrin Stevens in her online adjudication, presented a

> soldier from a middle-class background who finds himself in Belfast and the Malvinas . . . and the descriptions of his nightmarish experiences having witnessed an unprincipled officer murdering an innocent civilian, the effect of dumdum bullets on his enemy's body or the valour of face-to-face combat in the trenches of the Falklands.

See *http://www.eisteddfod.org.uk/uploads/MediaRoot/CY_484_Beirniadaeth% 20Catrin%20Stevens%20–20%20Ryddiaith.doc*.

88 Dafydd and Løvgreen, *Tros Ryddid?*, p. 39.
89 Roberts, *Rhyfel Ni*, p. 186.
90 Wiliam Owen Roberts, 'Saludos de Patagonia', *Hunangofiant (1973–1987): Cyfrol 1 – Y Blynyddoedd Glas* ('Autobiography (1973–1987): Volume 1 – The Blue Years') (Caernarfon, 1990).
91 Weston, *Walking Tall*, p. 184.

Selected further reading

WORKS OF WELSH HISTORY

Brereton, J. M., *A History of the Royal Regiment of Wales (24th/41st Foot) and Its Predecessors* (Cardiff, 1989).

Cragoe, Matthew, *Culture, Politics and National Identity in Wales, 1832–86* (Oxford, 2004).

Davies, D. Hywel, *The Welsh Nationalist Party, 1925–1945: A Call to Nationhood* (Cardiff, 1983).

Davies, Dewi Eirug, *Byddin y Brenin: Cymru a'i Chrefydd yn y Rhyfel Mawr* (Swansea, 1988).

Evans, Gwynfor, *Nonviolent Nationalism* (New Malden, 1973).

Gaffney, Angela, *Aftermath: Remembering the Great War in Wales* (Cardiff, 1998).

Glover, Michael, *That Astonishing Infantry: Three Hundred Years of the History of the Royal Welch Fusiliers (23rd Regiment of Foot) 1689–1989* (London, 1989).

Hughes, Colin, *Mametz: Lloyd George's 'Welsh Army' at the Battle of the Somme* (Norwich, 1990).

Hughes, R. R., *Y Parchedig John Williams, D.D. Brynsiencyn* (Caernarfon, 1929).

Jones, Aled Gruffydd, *Press, Politics and Society: A History of Journalism in Wales* (Cardiff, 1993).

Jones, Goronwy J., *Wales and the Quest for Peace* (Cardiff, 1969).

Jones, Ieuan Gwynedd, *Henry Richard: Apostle of Peace, 1812–1888* (Llandysul, 1988).

——, *Mid-Victorian Wales: The Observers and the Observed* (Cardiff, 1992).

Lord, Peter, *The Visual Culture of Wales: Industrial Society* (Cardiff, 1998).

——, *The Visual Culture of Wales: Imaging the Nation* (Cardiff, 2000).

Millward, E. G., *Cenedl o Bobl Ddewrion: Agweddau ar Lenyddiaeth Oes Victoria* (Llandysul, 1991).

Morgan, D. Densil, *The Span of the Cross: Religion and Society in Wales 1914–2000* (Cardiff, 1999).

——, *Cedyrn Canrif: Crefydd a Chymdeithas yng Nghymru'r Ugeinfed Ganrif* (Cardiff, 2001).

Morgan, Herbert, and Nathaniel Micklem, *Christ and Caesar* (London, 1921).

Morgan, Kenneth O., *Wales in British Politics, 1868–1922* (Cardiff, 1980).

——, *Rebirth of a Nation: Wales, 1880–1980* (Oxford and Cardiff, 1981).

——, *Modern Wales: Politics, Places and People* (Cardiff, 1995).

Munby J. E., (ed.), *A History of the 38th (Welsh) Division* (London, 1920).

O'Sullivan, John, *When Wales Went To War 1939–45* (Stroud, 2004).

Owen, Bryn, *History of Welsh Militia and Volunteer Corps, 1757–1908: Anglesey and Caernarfonshire* (Caernarfon, 1989).

——, *History of Welsh Militia and Volunteer Corps, 1757–1908: The Glamorgan Regiments of Militia* (Caernarfon, 1990).

——, *Owen Roscomyl and the Welsh Horse* (Caernarfon, 1990).

——, *History of Welsh Militia and Volunteer Corps, 1757–1908: Carmarthenshire, Pembrokeshire and Cardiganshire Regiments of Militia* (Wrexham, 1995).

——, *Welsh Militia and Volunteer Corps, 1757–1908: Denbighshire and Flintshire Regiments of Militia* (Wrexham, 1997).

——, *History of Welsh Militia and Volunteer Corps, 1757–1908: Montgomeryshire Regiments of Militia, Volunteers and Yeomanry Cavalry* (Wrexham, 2000).

Peate, Iorwerth C., *Y Traddodiad Heddwch yng Nghymru* (Dinbych, 1963).

Pope, Robert, *Building Jerusalem: Nonconformity, Labour and the Social Question, 1906–1939* (Cardiff, 1998).

——, *Seeking God's Kingdom: The Nonconformist Social Gospel in Wales, 1906–1939* (Cardiff, 1999).

Retallack, John, *The Welsh Guards* (London, 1981).

Richards John, (ed.), *Wales on the Western Front* (Cardiff, 1994).

Roberts, Ioan, *Rhyfel Ni: Profiadau Cymreig o Ddwy Ochr Rhyfel y Falklands/Malvinas* (Llanrwst, 2003).

Royle, Trevor, *Anatomy of a Regiment: Ceremony and Soldiering in the Welsh Guards* (London, 1990).

Wallace, Ryland, *Organise! Organise! Organise!: A Study of Reform Agitations in Wales, 1840–1886* (Cardiff, 1991).

Weston, Simon, *Walking Tall: An Autobiography* (London, 1989).

——, with John Mann, *Going Back: Return to the Falklands* (London, 1992).

——, *Moving On* (London, 2003).

Wiliams, Gerwyn, *Y Rhwyg: Arolwg o Farddoniaeth Gymraeg ynghylch y Rhyfel Byd Cyntaf* (Llandysul, 1993).

——, *Tir Neb: Rhyddiaith Gymraeg a'r Rhyfel Byd Cyntaf* (Cardiff, 1996).

——, *Tir Newydd: Agweddau ar Lenyddiaeth Gymraeg a'r Ail Ryfel Byd* (Cardiff, 2005).

Williams, Mari A., *A Forgotten Army: Female Munitions Workers of South Wales, 1939–1945* (Cardiff, 2002).

Selected further reading

WORKS OF BRITISH HISTORY

Arthur, Max, (in association with the Imperial War Museum), *Forgotten Voices of the Second World War* (London, 2004).

Aulich, James, (ed.), *Framing the Falklands War: Nationhood, Culture and Identity* (Milton Keynes and Philadelphia, 1992).

Barnett, Anthony, *Iron Britannia; Why Parliament Waged its Falklands War* (London, 1982).

Beckett, Ian F. W., *The Amateur Military Tradition, 1558–1945* (Manchester, 1991).

—— and Keith Simpson (eds), *A Nation in Arms: A Social Study of the British Army in the First World War* (Manchester, 1985).

Boorman, Derek, *For Your Tomorrow: British Second World War Memorials* (York, 1995).

Brand, C. P., *Italy and the English Romantics: The Italianate Fashion in Early Nineteenth-Century England* (Cambridge, 1957).

Braybon, Gail, (ed.), *Evidence, History and the Great War* (Oxford, 2003).

Brock, Peter, *Freedom From War: Nonsectarian Pacifism, 1814–1914* (Toronto, 1991).

Brown, Malcolm, *Tommy Goes To War* (Stroud, 1999).

Calder, Angus, *The People's War: Britain 1939–45* (London, 1971).

——, *Disaster and Heroes: On War, Memory and Representation* (Cardiff, 2004).

Ceadel, Martin, *Semi-Detached Idealists: The British Peace Movement and International Relations, 1854–1945* (Oxford, 2000).

Cecil, Hugh, and Peter H. Liddle (eds), *Facing Armageddon: The First World War Experienced* (London, 1996).

Chandler, David, and Ian Beckett (eds), *The Oxford Illustrated History of the British Army* (Oxford, 1994).

Colley, Linda, *Britons: Forging the Nation, 1707–1837* (New Haven, CT, and London, 1992).

Cunningham, Hugh, *The Volunteer Force: A Social and Political History, 1859–1908* (London, 1975).

Dear, I. C. B., and M. R. D. Foot (eds), *The Oxford Companion to the Second World War* (Oxford, 2001).

De Groot, Gerard J., *Blighty: British Society in the Era of the Great War* (Harlow, 1996).

Evans, Martin, and Ken Lunn (eds), *War and Memory in the Twentieth Century* (Oxford, 1997).

Fuller, J. G., *Troop Morale and Popular Culture in the British and Dominion Armies 1914–1918* (Oxford, 1990).

Gardiner, Juliet, *Wartime: Britain 1939–1945* (London, 2004).

Hastings, Max, and Simon Jenkins, *The Battle for the Falklands* (London, 1983).

Hennessy, Peter, *Never Again: Britain, 1945–1951* (London, 1992).

Selected further reading

Holmes, Richard, *Tommy: The British Soldier on the Western Front 1914–1918* (London, 2005).

Keegan, John, *The Face of Battle: A Study of Agincourt, Waterloo and the Somme* (Harmondsworth, 1978).

Middlebrook, Martin, *The Fight for the 'Malvinas': The Argentine Forces in the Falklands War* (London, 1989).

Simkins, Peter, *Kitchener's Army: The Raising of the New Armies, 1914–16* (Manchester, 1988).

Strachan, Hew, (ed.), *The Oxford Illustrated History of the First World War* (Oxford, 2000).

Wilkinson, Alan, *Dissent or Conform? War, Peace and the English Churches, 1900–1945* (London, 1986).

Winter, Jay, *Sites of Memory, Sites of Mourning: The Great War in European Cultural History* (Cambridge, 1995).

Index

Aberafan 41, 47
Aberdare 94
Abergavenny 47
Abergele 107
Aberystwyth 41, 42, 148, 150
Adams, Bernard 131
Admiralty 46
Afghan War (1838–42) 58
Afghanistan 1
Africa 103
Agincourt, battle of (1415) 2,
   17, 18, 25
Air Ministry 189
Air-Raid Precautions 185, 186
Ajax Bay 206
Alexander, Ewart 214
Alexander of Denmark,
   Princess 93
Alexandria 103
Alin, Marcel 189
Allen, J. Davies 111
Alma, battle of (1854) 41
America 75, 111, 118
   see also United States of
   America
American Civil War (1861–5)
   7, 222
American soldiers 151
American War of Independence
   (1775–83) 75
Amlwch 148, 215
Ammanford 148
Amserau, Yr 7, 64, 85
Anglesey 23, 41, 42, 49, 71, 134,
   135, 139, 141, 175, 209
Anglesey, Marquis of 192
Anglesey Rifle Volunteers 69,
   70

Anglican Church 19, 86, 169, 170
   see also Church of England
   and Established Church
Anglican Establishment 24
Anglicanism 170
Anglicans 42
Anglicisation 15, 32
Anglo-Saxon materialism 22
Arabia 138
Archbishop of Wales 192
Argentina 138, 207, 215, 222
Argentinian forces 204
Argentinians 208, 219
Argyll and Sutherland
   Highlanders 150
Ark Royal 206
Arnhem, battle of (1944) 187
Arnold, Matthew 22, 25
Arthur 17, 25, 26
Artillery Corps 69
Aspromonte, battle of (1862) 88
Asquith, H. H. 28
Assheton-Smith, George
   William Duff 109
Atlantic 214
Audoin-Rouzeau, Stéphane
   152, 155
Australia 138, 152, 190, 191
Austria 87
Austro-Hungarian army 155
Auxiliary Territorial Service 188

Baker (family) 5
Baker, Brian 197
Baker, John 188, 189, 191, 197
Baker, Ronald 188, 190, 196,
   197
Baker, Stanley 8

Bala 148, 169
Bala-Bangor Theological
   College 28, 173
Baner ac Amserau Cymru 83,
   90, 91
Baner Cymru 8, 64, 71
Balaclava, battle of (1854) 64
Bangor 107, 108, 109
Bangor, Bishop of 111
Bangor Golf Club 173
Bardsey 30
Barnett, Anthony 207, 208
Barry 148, 150
Barry Conservatives 108
Barry Docks 108
Barth, Karl 178
Bartov, Omer 152
Batley 156
Bavarians 50
Baynes, John 152
BBC Radio 3 210
Beales, Derek 87
Beales, Edmund 95
Beaumaris 148
Beckett, Ian 129
Bedford 87, 131
Bedfordshire 137, 142
Belgian refugees 53
Belgium 53, 55, 171, 172
Berkshire 137, 142, 209
Bethesda 48
Bevan, Aneurin 218
Bible 84, 90, 171
Bible Society 91
Birkenhead 45
Birmingham 180
Black Bartholomew 168
Black Mountains 11

Index

Blaenau Ffestiniog 52, 212
Blitz 187
Blue Books *see* Treason of the
    Blue Books
Bluff Cove 208
Boadicea or Buddug 17, 27, 204
Board of Trade 118
Boer Commando 110
Boer Republics 105
Boer War (1899–1902) 1, 4, 5,
    8, 11, 42, 44, 45, 72, 78,
    101, 107, 108, 110, 114,
    120, 171
    see also Chapter 5
Boers 105, 106, 110
Boesinghe Sector 154
Border Regiment 131
Bosworth, battle of (1485) 18, 56
Bottomley, Horatio 115
Bourke, Joanna 152
Bourne, John 156
Bowden, William George 146,
    154
Brace, William 48
Bradley, A. G. 44, 45
Bramley-by-Bow 145
Brecht, Bertolt 213
Brecon 43
Brecon Beacons 11
Brecon Memorial Collge 175
Breconshire 44, 72, 77, 134, 140
Bridgend 148
Bright, John 38
Bristol 115
Britannia 116
British Army 2, 18, 19, 38, 42,
    104, 126, 139, 151, 152,
    214
British Cape Colony 110
British Empire 1, 9, 2, 4, 32, 38,
    39, 42, 101, 102, 105, 106,
    107, 108, 109, 112, 114,
    115, 118, 207
British Library 205
British Lion 117
British Navy 104
British Red Cross Society 189
British State 3, 4, 38, 57
British Volunteers 75
British Weekly 171
Britishness 3
Briton Ferry 48
Brown, Thomas (ironmaster)
    70, 71
Browne, Robert 167
Bruce, Henry Austin 66
Brunner, Emil 178
Bryant-Quinn, M. Paul 8
Brynmawr 70, 73, 148, 150
Buckinghamshire 137, 142
Buddug *see* Boadicea
Builth Rifle Volunteers 77

Bulkeley, Sir Richard 41
Bumford, William 135
Burford, James 135
Bute (family) 108
Bute, Marquis of 45, 69

Caernarfon 30, 32, 58, 112, 211
Caernarfonshire 49, 69, 72,
    111, 132, 134, 141
Caerphilly 148
Caerwent 194
Caesar 178
Caine, Michael 8
Caldicot Levels 51, 119, 120
Caledfryn *see* Williams,
    William
Callaghan, James 204
Calvin, Jean 166, 167, 170, 177
Calvinistic Methodist
    Connexion 173
Calvinistic Methodist General
    Assembly (1916) 177
Calvinistic Methodists 42, 169,
    172
Calvinists 172, 177, 178
Cambrian Collieries 48
Cambrian Combine Strike
    (1910–11) 48
Cambrian News 21
Cambrian Railway Company
    70
Cambridge University 130
Cambridgeshire 137, 142
Cameron Highlanders 151
Campaign for Nuclear
    Disarmament 10
Canada 138
Canberra 212
Cape Parliament 115
Cape Town 103
Caprera 83, 93
Cardiff 5, 25, 44, 45, 49, 50, 68,
    69, 74, 75, 101, 107, 114,
    115, 116, 117, 118, 120,
    131, 184, 185, 186, 187,
    190, 191
Cardiff, Mayor of 47
Cardiff Boroughs 4, 105
Cardiff Castle 185
Cardiff City Council 191
Cardiff Conservatism 108
Cardiff People's Corps 7, 70,
    76
Cardiff People's Rifle Corps 68
Cardigan 107
Cardiganshire 41, 72, 134, 135,
    140
Cardwell Reforms (1868–74)
    23
Carlisle, Russell 211
Carlyle, Thomas 86
Carmarthen 111

Carmarthen Journal 106, 108,
    111
Carmarthenshire 41, 52, 72, 74,
    107, 132, 134, 140, 141
*Carnarvon and Denbigh
    Herald* 50, 111
Carnarvonshire Constitutional
    Association 104
Carr, Lascelles 109
Castle Street Welsh Baptist
    Chapel, London 174
Cathays ward, Cardiff 118
Catraeth 211
Cavell, Edith 58
Celtic forebears of the Welsh
    16
Celticism 22
Celts 22, 25
Cenotaph, Whitehall 196
Census (1851) 19, 169
Chair competition 209
Chamberlain, Neville 112
Chancellor of the Exchequer 50
Channel Islands 138
Chappell, Edgar Leyshon 1
Charge of the Light Brigade
    (1854) 64
Charing Cross 93
Chartism 70
Chartists 64, 65
Cheltenham 207
Chepstow 148, 149, 150
Cheshire 135, 137, 141, 142
Cheshire regiment 139, 146,
    149, 150, 154
Chester 40
Chester castle 75
Christ 88, 167, 168, 169, 171,
    173, 174, 177
Christ's College, Cambridge
    168
Christendom 87
Christianity 2, 29, 103, 176
Church of England 42
    see also Anglican Church
    and Established Church
Churchill, Winston 208
Cilfynydd 216
Civil Wars 38
Clark, G. T. 70
Clifford, John 171
Cobden, Richard 38
Cold War 10
Colwyn Bay 47, 149, 150, 177
Commonwealth 88, 168, 207
Commonwealth War Graves
    Commission 128
Comodoro Rivadavia 219, 221
Compensation Act 119
Conference on Christian
    Politics, Economics and
    Citizenship (1924) 180

Index

Congregationalism 168
Congregationalists *see*
    Independents
Connah's Quay 148, 149, 211
Connaught Rangers 131, 150
Conran, Tony 210, 211
Conservative Central Office 115
Conservative Clubs 119
Conservative militarism 106
Conservative newspapers 116
Conservative Party 5, 114, 117
Conservative press 41
    see also Tory press
Conservative working-men's
    clubs 4
Conservatives 8, 11, 103, 104,
    109, 111, 115, 116, 118,
    120
    see also Tories and
    Unionists
Contagious Diseases Acts
    (1864, 1866, 1869) 39
Continental Reformers 166
Convention of Pretoria (1881)
    110
Conway or Conwy 55, 171
Conwy *see* Conway
Coppard, George 152
Cornwall 137, 142
Cornwallis-West, Patsy 55
Council of the British Legion
    in Wales 191
County of London Battalion
    145
Coventry Cathedral 195
Cowbridge 105
Cox, Violet Patricia 185, 187
Cradock, Walter 168, 169
Cragoe, Matthew 4, 8
Crecy, battle of (1346) 2, 17,
    18, 25, 26
Criccieth 50
Crimean War (1853–56) 3, 7,
    20, 39, 41, 58, 64, 65, 66
Cromwell, Oliver 41, 51, 56,
    170
Cronicl, Y 20, 92
Crown competition 209, 210
Cruise missiles 209
Crumlin Burrows 74
Crystal Palace 90
Cuban Missile Crisis (1962) 10
Cullen, Greg 209, 212
Cumberland 137, 142
Cwmbach 211
Cwmbrân 148, 149
Cymro, Y 209, 221
Cymru Fydd 50
Cynan *see* Evans-Jones, Albert

Dafydd, Myrddin ap 209, 213
Dame Wales 47

Danes 26
Daniels, J. (fancy goods dealer)
    52
Dante 85, 86
Darwin, Charles 24
Daunton, Martin 118
David 32
David Morgan department
    store, Cardiff 188
Davies, David (editor) 105
Davies, David (soldier) 135
Davies, Dewi Eirug 171, 172,
    177
Davies, George M. Ll. 173
Davies, Grahame 216, 218
Davies, Hirrell 195
Davies, John (historian) 127
Deacon, S. W. 115
Dean of Canterbury 87
DeGroot, Gerard J. 127
Denbigh 54, 83
Denbigh Boroughs 112
Denbighshire 43, 52, 66, 72,
    107, 132, 134, 141, 142
Denbighshire Volunteers 66
Denbighshire Yeomanry 143
Denmark 138
Derbyshire 137
Devonshire 137
Devonshire Regiment 137, 149
Dewsbury 156
Deyrnas, Y 28, 29
Dickens, Charles 95
Dillwyn, (Major) Lewis
    Llywelyn 67
Director General of Recruiting
    39
Disestablishment of the
    Anglican Church in
    Wales 165, 166, 169,
    177, 179
Disraeli, Benjamin 106
Dissenters 90, 166
Dodd, T. R. 113
Dolgellau 23, 107
Dorsetshire 137, 142
Dowlais 75
Dowlais Ironworks 70
Drake, T. O. 112
Drummond, Mr 118
Dublin Fusiliers 145
Dublin Steam Packet
    Company 69
Duke of Cornwall's Light
    Infantry 150
Dundee 188
Dunn, James 138, 140
Durham 137, 142
Durham Light Infantry 150

East Denbighshire 112
East End of London 150

East Lancashire Regiment 145
East Surrey Regiment 131, 146
Eastern Front 152
Ebbw Vale 70, 76
Ebeneser Chapel, Cardiff 172
Edward the Black Prince 18
Edwardian era 138
Edwards, D. Miall 175, 176
Edwards, Robert Jones 54
Edwards, Wynne 49
Egerton, Alan Tatton 107
Egypt 103
Elias, John 169
Elizabeth I (Queen) 216
Elizabethan times 166
Elley, Clifford 211
Ellis, John S. 2, 4, 6, 7, 127
Ellis, T. E. 57
Ellis-Nanney, Sir Hugh 109
England 20, 27, 39, 43, 46, 51,
    53, 84, 96, 106, 114, 119,
    126, 129, 132, 135, 137,
    150
English Channel 156
English people 16, 54
English Princes of Wales 18
English Separatism (religious)
    167, 168
English soldiers 155
Enlightenment 84
Erastian doctrine 166, 177
Erbury, William 168, 169
Essex 137, 142
Established Church 38
    see also Anglican Church
    and Church of England
Esquel 219
European Community 207
Evans, Beriah Gwynfe 176
Evans, (Captain) Evan 74
Evans, Elwyn 214
Evans, Evan (brewer) 70
Evans, Gwynfor 15, 30, 31, 32
Evans, Neil 2, 3
Evans, Wynne 112
Evans-Jones, Albert (Cynan)
    214
Eve, Malcolm Trustram 131

Fair Trade 1, 120
Falklands War (1982) 1, 6, 11
    see also Chapter 9
Far Eastern campaign 9
Fascist parties 9
Fellowship of Reconciliation
    173
Fenians 75, 93
Ferdinand, Franz (Archduke)
    7

Ferguson, Niall 152
Ffestiniog 149, 150

Index

Finland 111
Finsbury 95
Fisher, Hayes 103
Flanders 197
Flannery, Sir Fortescue 118
Flat Iron Copse Cemetery 128
Flint 41
Flintshire 43, 72, 134, 141
Flintshire Rifles 70
Fluellen 18
France 51, 53, 66, 111, 150, 187, 188, 197
France and Flanders 128
Francis, Karl 214
Free Church leaders 171
Free Churches 42, 169
Free Press of Monmouthshire 1
Free Wales Army 2, 11
French (people) 17, 64
French Army 152
French Revolution (1789) 38
Freud, Sigmund 5
Fuller, J. G. 156
Furlong, R. S. J. 107

Gaffney, Angela 5, 127
Gaiman 221
Gainsborough 168
Galtieri, (General) Leopoldo 206, 207, 208
Garibaldi, Guiseppe 3, 75
  see also Chapter 4
Garrison Towns Acts *see* Contagious Diseases Acts
Garw Valley 149, 150
General Belgrano 206
Geneva 189
George 111, 93
German Army 152
German militarism 54, 172
German states 75
Germans 8, 9, 30, 46, 54
Germany 55, 106, 171, 176, 178, 188
Gibbon, Julio Oscar 219
Gibraltar 138
Giraldus Cambrensis 16
Gladstone, William Ewart 86, 87, 96, 106, 170
Gladstonian Liberals 57
Glamorgan 41, 48, 49, 72, 132, 134, 135, 195, 140, 141
Glamorgan Aldermen 108
Glamorgan Record Office 188
Glamorganshire Bute Volunteers 69
Glamorganshire Rifle Volunteers 67, 70
Glasgow 52
Glendower 26
Gloucester Volunteer Reserve 69

Gloucestershire 74, 135, 137, 141, 142
Gloucestershire Regiment 149, 150
God 88, 89, 91, 166, 167, 174, 176
Gododdin 211
Gohebydd, Y *see* Griffith, John
Goleuad, Y 172
Google Internet 205
Gordon, (General) Charles 8, 106, 108
Gower branch of the Primrose League 107
Gower peninsula 107, 186
Grainger, J. H. 127
Grand National race 215
Graves, Robert 22, 27, 130, 131, 135, 138
Great Ejection (1662) 168
Great Famine (1845–8) 66, 87
Great War Book of Remembrance 192
Greeks 177
Green, Ewen 104
Greengrass, Paul 205
Greenham Common 209
Grenadier Guards 146
Griffith, Ellis 175
Griffith, John (Y Gohebydd) 3, 7, 83, 90, 93, 95, 96
Griffith, Llewelyn Wyn 131
Griffith, Michael John 215
Griffith, Owen (Ywain Meirion) 65
Griffith, T. Gwynfor 82
Griffith, Watcyn 131
Gruffydd, W. J. 214
Guidel 189, 190
Gulf War (1991) 206
Gurkhas 17, 156, 221
Gwasg Carreg Gwalch 213
Gwilym Hiraethog *see* Rees, William
Gwyliedydd, Y 172
Gwynedd 52

Hackney 145
Haig, Alexander 206
Hamilton, (Lord) George 116
Hampshire 142
Harcourt, F. C. Vernon 116
Harlech 49, 130, 149
Harlech Castle 19
Harlech Television 219
Harries, (the Reverend) J. 113
Harris, Howell 51
Harris, Rutherfoord 102, 103, 104, 109, 112, 114, 115, 116, 117, 119, 120
Harrison, Robert 167
Hartshorn, Vernon 46, 48

Hastings, Max 207
Haverfordwest 41, 149, 150, 194
Hefin, John 214
Hegelian evolutionism 174
Hegelian idealism 174
Henry V, (King) 51
Henry Tudor 18, 19, 43
Herbert, (Sir) Ivor 49
Herbert of Cherbury, (Lord) 19, 43
Herefordshire 135, 137, 141, 142
Herefordshire Regiment 146, 150
Hermitage Wharf, Wapping 195
Hertfordshire 137
Hewitt, Nick 193, 194
High Church 87
Highland Light Infantry 151
Highland regiments 18, 44
Hind, C. Lewis 83
Hirwaun 148, 149
Hitler, Adolf 9, 10
Holyhead 69
Holywell 41, 149
Home Front 9, 185, 186, 188, 193
Hooker, Richard 169
House of Commons 169
Household Cavalry 150
Howard, Colonel 42
Howarth, Wil 215, 216
Hughes, Glyn Ceiriog 221
Hughes, H. M. 172, 176
Humphreys, E. Morgan 176
Hun 54
Hundred Years War 5, 17, 18, 38
Hunt, George W. 111
Hunt, Rex 206
Huntingdonshire 137, 142
Hutchinson, (Major-General) 69

Ifan, Tecwyn 213
Illustrated London News 75
Imperial South African Association 111
Independents 91, 169
India 103, 105, 116, 129, 138
Indian Mutiny (1857–8) 93
Ingram, (Colonel) 104
International Conference on Life and Work (1925) 180
International Red Cross 189
Inverness 127
Investiture of the Prince of Wales (1969) 32
Iraq War 206
Ireland 9, 11, 12, 39, 40, 43, 126, 132, 151
Irianni, Vali James de 206

Index

Irish Guards 151
Irish (people) 19, 22, 25, 75, 87
Irish People, The 93
Irish regiments 23, 150
Irish Republican Army 11
Irish soldiers 138, 151, 156
Isaac, Russell 219
Isandhlwana 43
Islamists 11
Isle of Man 138
Islington 145
Islwyn, Aled 220
Italophobia 86, 87
Italy 3, 4, 9, 83, 86, 87, 88, 87, 90, 120
Ivor Bach 26
Iwan, Carlos Eduardo ap 220

Jacobin rhetoric 96
Jager 90
Jameson Raid 110
Janus 15
Japan 9, 10, 93
Japanese people 12
Jeffrey, James 108
Jenkins, John (MAC) 32
Jenkins, John Gwili 172, 176
Jenkins, Simon 207
Jenkins, Tim 47
Jeremiah 87
Jerusalem 85
Jews 177
Job 32
Johannesburg 113
Jones, Angharad 213
Jones, David 144, 145, 155, 157
Jones, D. Gwyn 216
Jones, Goronwy 1
Jones, (Mr) H. 107
Jones, (Sir) Henry
Jones, Ieuan Gwynedd 95
Jones, John (Talhaiarn) 64
Jones, John Puleston 173, 174
Jones, Major 104
Jones, Meinwen 218
Jones, Nesta Wyn 209
Jones, R. Tudur 168, 170
Jones, Tony 211
J. R. *see* Roberts, John
Just War 171
Justice, (Colonel) J. F. 104

Kant, Immanuel 173, 174, 178
Keeton, Anthony 189, 190
Kent 137, 142
Kent, Horacio Jose 220
Kenyon, George 112
Khaki election (1900) 4, 8
Khartoum 8, 108
Kidwelly 148, 149
Killingback, Henry 128
Kimberley 110, 114

King's Liverpool Regiment 131, 150
King's Own Yorkshire Light Infantry 131
King's Shropshire Light Infantry 146, 149, 150, 152
Kinmel Park 55
Kirk 66
Kitchener, (Lord) Horatio Herbert 108, 139
Kitchener's Army 4, 48
Knighton 148, 149, 150
Korea 10
Kruger, S. J. P. 110, 112, 116

Labouchere, Henry 116
Labour Exchanges 56
Labour movement 9
Ladysmith 110, 114
Lambeth 82
Lampeter 149
Lampeter Velfrey 195
Lancashire 49, 118, 135, 137, 140, 141, 142
Lancashire Brigade 151
Lancaster 115
Lancastrians 156
Lancers 146
Lawrence, (Alderman) James 102, 109, 117, 119, 120
Lawrence, William 95
Leicestershire 137, 142
Leversuch, Violet Patricia *see* Cox, Violet Patricia
Levi, (the Reverend) Thomas 42
Lewis, Benja and Lila 219
Lewis, John Benjamin 221
Lewis, Lila 220
Lewis, Saunders 29, 30, 138, 143, 218
Liberal Association 118
Liberal newspapers 51, 92, 94
Liberal Party 3, 87, 165, 169, 179
Liberalism 3, 23, 40, 43, 50, 179
Liberals 11, 42, 101, 112, 114, 169, 170
Liberation Society 94, 95
Lincolnshire 137, 142, 188
Liverpool 87
Liverpool Daily Post 191
Liverpool Mercury 87
Llanbedr 56
Llanbrynmair 149
Llandaf, Bishop of 184
Llandaf Cathedral 44
Llandeilo 107
Llandudno 49, 145
Llanelli 44
Llanfair, Merioneth 57
Llangibby Castle 115, 119
Llangollen 23

Llanhilleth 128
Llanidloes 148, 149, 150
Llewelyn, Leonard 48
Lleyn peninsula 29, 30, 215
Lloyd, D. Tecwyn 15
Lloyd George, David 1, 2, 4, 26, 27, 28, 29, 42, 49, 50, 51, 63, 67, 77, 78, 111, 171, 174, 176, 177, 218
Llwybr Llaethog 209
Llwyd, Morgan 51, 168, 170
Llywelyn the Last Prince 17, 25, 27, 32
Llywelyn, J. T. D. 105
Llywelyn-Williams, Alun 214
Lobengula 103
London 82, 84, 89, 92, 93, 118, 132, 135, 137, 142, 145, 212
London and North Wales Railway Company 69
London Daily Chronicle 112
London Irish 67
London Regiment 150
London Scottish 67
London Welsh Volunteer Corps 67
Londoners 140
Longley, Edna 195
Lord, Peter 116
Lords Lieutenant 47
Lorient 189
Løvgreen, Geraint 209
Luftwaffe 6
Lusitania 54, 55
Lutzow 90
Lynch, Peredur 213
Lyne, Colonel 104
Lyons, Isaac 115

Machine Gun Corps 152
Machynlleth 148, 149
Mackenzie, John 101
Maclean, John 115
Madagascar 111
Mafeking 4, 45, 110, 113, 114, 117
Majuba Hill 105, 106
Malta 138
Malvinas War *see* Falklands War
Mametz Wood 128, 131
Manchester 75, 115
Manning, Frederic 152
Marchant, Tony 214
Marshall, Colonel 104
Masonic Hall, Swansea 186
Mass Observation Bulletin 193
Mass-Observation Survey 185, 186, 193, 194
Massey, Gerald 88
Matabele 103

Index

Mathias, T. P. 113
Mazzini, Giuseppe 82, 85, 87, 88, 94, 95
Mediterranean 129
Meibion Glyndŵr 11, 32
Menendez, General 206
Merioneth 132, 134, 141
Merionethshire Herald 84
Merthyr Tydfil 44, 47, 64, 66, 68, 75
Miall, Edward 95
Micklem, Nathaniel 174, 176, 180
Middlebrook, Martin 207
Middlesex 95, 132, 135, 137, 141, 142
Military Service Act (1916) 165
Milford Haven 148, 149, 150
Milner, Alfred 110
Mimosa 209
Ministry of Information 186
Ministry of Labour and National Service 186
Monmouth 17, 22, 66, 71, 113, 135
Monmouth Boroughs 4, 101, 109, 114, 115, 116, 119, 120
Monmouthshire 43, 48, 49, 70, 107, 126, 132, 134, 138, 141, 194
Monmouthshire Regiment 130, 139, 140, 141, 143, 150
Montgomery County constituency 105
Montgomeryshire 9, 47, 71, 132, 134, 141, 212
Montgomeryshire Rifle Corps 69
Moore, Mona 186
Morgan, Campbell 171
Morgan, David Watts 48
Morgan, D. Densil 172, 173, 176
Morgan, Godfrey 68
Morgan, Herbert 173, 176
Morgan, Kenneth O. 4, 109, 117, 118, 120
Morgan, Prys 220
Moriarty, Catherine 190
Morley, John 112
Moses 30
Mostyn, Ambrose 168
Mountain Ash 73
Mudiad Amddiffyn Cymru 32
Mumbles Fort 73
Munster Fusiliers 145
Mynydd Epynt 11

Naples 90, 91
Napoleonic era 58
Napoleonic Wars (1803–15) 64

National Archives 128
National Assembly for Wales 205, 218
National Eisteddfod 209
National Eisteddfod (1918) 23, 27
National Eisteddfod (1983) 209, 211
National Heritage Memorial Fund 195
National Inventory of War Memorials 194, 196
National Memorial to Civilian Workers, Coventry 195
National Museum of Wales 185, 192
National Service 9
Nationalism 24
Naval and Military Press 131
Neath Steel and Galvanising Works 47
Nelson, Horatio (Viscount) 47, 105, 149, 206, 217
Nepalese mercenaries 221
Neuve Chapelle 152
New Army 131, 139, 143
New Empire Music Hall, Newport 113
New Model Army 56
New Testament 88
New Zealand 138
Newbury 209
Newcastle 115
Newport 47, 74, 76, 103, 112, 113, 114, 115, 117, 120, 128, 135
Newport, Mayor of 43
Newport Rising (1839) 19
Newport Volunteers 73
Nicholas I, Tsar 65
Nicoll, Robertson 171, 175
Nile 93
Nine Elms station 92
Ninian Park, Cardiff 43
Nonconformist chapels 7
Nonconformist conscience 32, 119, 171, 177
Nonconformist culture 8
Nonconformist faith 1, 29
Nonconformist leaders 82
Nonconformist ministers 5, 21, 22, 25, 27, 42, 44, 48, 178
Nonconformists 2, 23, 38, 55, 57, 63, 77, 87, 94, 111, 167, 168, 174, 176
Nonconformity 2, 5, 7, 15, 19, 38, 40, 41, 43, 58, 165, 166, 173, 179, 218
Norfolk 137, 142
Normans 17, 26, 51
North Wales Chronicle 84, 108, 109, 112

North Wales Chronicle Company 109
Northamptonshire 131, 137, 142
Northern Ireland 214
Nott, John 206
Nott, (General) Sir William 58
Nottinghamshire 137

Offa's Dyke 84
O'Leary, Paul 3, 4, 11
Owain Lawgoch 51
Owain Glyndŵr 17, 19, 27, 28, 32, 43
Owen, Wilfred 213
Owen, W. R. 146, 175
Oxford 85
Oxford University 9, 131
Oxfordshire 137, 142

Palmerston, (Viscount) Henry John Temple 95
Pals' Battalions 139
Pantecelyn 27
Papacy 85
Paradise 85
Parliamentary Recruiting Committee 52
Patagonia 6, 204, 209, 212, 215, 219, 221, 226
Patagonians 208
Patriotic Front 32
Peace of Vereeniging (1902) 111
Peace Society 3, 21, 40, 63, 64, 92
Pembrey Dock 145
Pembroke Dock 44, 72
Pembrokeshire 67, 72, 134, 140, 141, 192, 195
Pembrokeshire County Memorial 194
Penarth 105
Pendine 11
Pennant, John 10
Pennant, (Major) S. G. D. 69
Pennant slate quarries 69
Pennycock, David 188, 190
Penrhyn Estate 50
Penrhyn, Lord 109
Penyberth 29
People's Corps 69
Perry, Nick 150, 151, 156
Philippines 111
Phillips, Eluned 21, 209, 210
Phillips, Gervase 127
Phoney War 185
Picton, Thomas 58
Pilgrim Trust 186
Pius IX 88
Plaid Cymru 1, 2, 6, 10, 29, 30, 31, 32, 213

see also Plaid Genedlaethol
  Cymru
Plaid Genedlaethol Cymru 5
  see also Plaid Cymru
Platt, Colonel 104
Plymouth 44, 127
Poland 138
Pontivy 189
Pontymister 128
Pontypool 94
Pontypridd 47, 146, 211
Pope, Robert 4, 5
Port Stanley 210, 212
Porth Neigwl 30
Porthmadog 67
Powell, Vavasor 168
Powys 212
Powys Provincial Eisteddfod
  (1983) 213
Prebble, John 43
Presbyterianism 168
Prescott, Mr 115
Prestatyn 46
Pretoria 110, 112, 117
Pretoria Convention 105
Price, Richard 101, 117, 121
Price, Thomas 3, 93, 95, 96
Price-Yearsley, Mr 104
Primrose League 4, 103, 106,
  107, 108
Prince and Princess of Wales 44
Prince of Wales 93, 184
Prince of Wales Light Horse 42
Prince of Wales Relief Fund
  47, 53, 93
Prison-Made Goods Act (1897)
  120
Prosser, Fred 135
Protestant ethic 57
Prussia 106
Pugh, Hugh 169
Pugh, Martin 101, 102, 104,
  106, 107
Punch 22
Punch Cymraeg, Y 89
Puritanism 21, 168
Puritans 166
Pwllheli 148, 149

Quakerism 57
Quay Workers' Society 119
Queen Mother 192
Queens Ferry 145
Queenstown 54

Radnorshire 68, 72, 132, 134,
  140, 141
Radnorshire Volunteers 68
Railway Clerks' Association 118
Railway Herald 118
Railway Rifles *see*
  Montgomeryshire

Rifle Corps
Readman, Paul 101, 117, 121
Rebecca Riots (1839–44) 19
Red Dragon (flag) 17, 25
  see also Welsh Dragon
Reed, Sir Edward 101, 116,
  117, 118
Rees, Thomas (Principal) 28,
  173, 174, 177, 178, 179,
  180
Rees, William (Gwilym
  Hiraethog) 7, 20, 28, 82,
  84, 85, 86, 87, 89, 93, 94,
  95, 96
Reform Act (1867) 70
Reform Bill (1832) 169
Reform League 95
Regular Army 67, 71, 75, 77,
  139
Religious Census *see* Census
  (1851)
Remarque, Erich Maria 126
Renan, Ernest 22
Restoration of the Monarchy
  (1660) 168
Rhayader 148, 149, 150
Rhodes, Cecil 109, 110, 115
Rhodesia 104, 112
Rhondda 48, 107
Rhymney 73
Rhymney Valley 48
Rhys, Milton 206, 212, 213,
  219, 220
Richard, Henry 1, 3, 17, 20, 21,
  28, 38, 63, 64, 105
Richards, Edward Priest 45
Richards, Frank 139
Risca 148, 149
Risorgimento 85, 87
Robbins, Keith 127
Roberts, Bryn 111, 112
Roberts, Gwyneth Tyson 20
Roberts, Ioan 205, 212, 213
Roberts, John (J. R.) 92, 93, 169
Roberts, (Lord) Frederick
  Sleigh 110
Roberts, Samuel (S. R.) 20, 28,
  38, 63, 64, 92, 169
Roberts, T. J. 55
Roberts, William Owen 221
Roden, Captain 70
Rogers, William John 135
Roman Catholic hierarchy 87,
  88
Roman Catholicism 29, 43, 87,
  218
Roman Republic 85
Romans 2, 16, 17
Rome 85, 87, 166
Rorke's Drift (1879) 23, 43
Royal Air Force 11, 25, 209
Royal Air Force Ingham 188

Royal Air Force Volunteer
  Reserve 188
Royal Army Medical Corps
  145, 150
Royal Army Ordnance Corps
  145
Royal Army Service Corps 145
Royal Artillery 113, 145, 146
Royal Commission on the
  Church of England and
  Other Religious Bodies
  in Wales and
  Monmouthshire 170
Royal Engineers 145, 146
Royal Gulf Club 56
Royal Inniskilling Fusiliers 151
Royal Navy 11
Royal Society of Arts 194
Royal Welsh Fusiliers 18, 22,
  43, 52, 113, 130, 131,
  138, 139, 140, 141, 143,
  145, 150, 156
Birmingham Fusiliers 43
Royal West Kents 145
Royal West Surrey Regiment
  152
Rudry 195
Russell, D. (Colonel) 40
Russell, John 86
Russia 64, 86, 111
Russian Army 152
Ruthin 3, 52, 53, 54, 57, 58, 147
Ruthin Castle 55
Rutland 135, 137, 142

St Asaph 56
St Asaph, Bishop of 42
St Clears 48
St David's, Bishop of 43
St David's Day 17, 18
St David's Day (1979) 204
St Helena 138
St Mary's Church, Swansea 187
St Paul 166
St Peter's Square, Rhuthun 52
Salisbury, (Lord) Robert
  Arthur Talbot
  Gascoyne-Cecil 101, 105, 107,
  108, 110
Salvation Army 50
San Carlos 209
Sarajevo 7
Sarn Mellteyrn 215
Sassoon, Siegfried 131
Saxons 17, 25, 26, 50, 51, 89, 92
Sbannaus, Iris 220
Scotland 1, 9, 27, 39, 46, 66,
  71, 72, 114, 126, 132,
  138, 150, 204, 211
Scots (people) 17, 19, 22, 25
Scots Guards 157
Scottish Free Church 171

Scottish Highlanders 40
Scottish regiments 23
Scottish Rifles 152
Scottish soldiers 151, 155
Scriptures 84
Scythians 177
Seaforth Highlanders 151
Sebastopol, battle of (1855) 65
Second Reform Act (1867) 84, 94
Seren Cymru 94, 95, 96, 172
Seren Gomer 65
Scrgeant, John 207
Sermon on the Mount 23
Seven Years War (1756–63) 51
Shaen, William 85, 95
Shakespeare, William 17, 18
Shrewsbury 39
Shropshire 137, 142
Shropshire Regiment 139
Sikhs 156
Simkins, Peter 146, 156
Simmel, Georg 45
Sinclair, J. D. 86
Singapore 138
Sir Galahad 1, 6, 206, 208, 209, 210, 213, 215, 217
Snowdonia 51
Socialist Workers' Party 209
Somerset Light Infantry 151
Somersetshire 137, 142
Smith, Adam 178
Smith, Anthony 126
Smyth, John 167
Sola Pinto, Vivian de 131, 139, 140
Soldiers' and Sailors' Rest Homes 50
Somme, battle of the (1916) 150
South Africa 42, 43, 101, 103, 105, 111, 112, 115, 119, 120, 138
South African League 113
South African War *see* Boer War
South America 138
South Atlantic 6, 70, 205, 206, 207, 208
South East Asia 30
South Georgia 206
South Glamorgan 105
South Wales Argus 109
South Wales Borderers 23, 29, 43, 128, 130, 135, 138, 140, 141, 143, 150
South Wales Daily Post 108, 109
South Wales Miners' Federation 46, 50
South Wales Telegraph 109, 111, 114, 119
Southampton 82

Spanish Civil War (1936–39) 9
Spectator, The 89
Speke, Captain [John Hanning] 93
Spicer, Albert 101, 117, 120
S. R. *see* Roberts, Samuel
Stacey Hall, Cardiff 118
Staffordshire 135, 137, 140, 141, 142
Staniforth, Joseph Morewood 47, 50, 116
Stanley, Henry Morton 8
Stanton, Charles 46, 48
Statham, Mr 112
Stewart, (Captain) N. P. 104
Stewart, Rod 206
Stockdale, J. Box 68
Stockholm 180
Strachan, Hew 151
Sudan 106, 108
Suffolk 137, 142
Sullivan, A. M. 93
Sullivan, Barry 188, 190, 191
Summers, Anne 104
Sun, The 206
Sunday Closing 115
Sunday School 20, 23
Surbiton 145
Surrey 132, 135, 137, 142
Sussex 137, 142
Sutherland, Duke of 94
Sutherland, Graham 186
Swansea 44, 49, 67, 73, 72, 75, 186
Sweden 138
Sweet, Phillip 211
Symonds, Richard 168

Taff Vale Railway 120
Taffs and Taffies 22, 126, 127, 157
Taliesin 89
Taylor, Peter Alfred (Jnr.) 85, 95
Temple of Peace, Cardiff 192
Tenby 149, 150
Territorial Army 11, 42, 139
Teutons 26
Thatcher, Margaret 6, 204, 206, 207, 211, 217
Third Reform Act (1885) 109
Thomas, D. A. 109
Thomas, (Lieutenant-General) Owen 27, 42
Thomas, Ungoed 176
Times, The 53, 65, 73, 90, 94
Tonypandy 149, 150
Tories 58, 101, 111, 113, 117, 120, 170
see also Coservatives and Unionists
Tory press 41
see also Conservative press

Town Improvements Association, Prestatyn 45
Trafalgar, battle of (1805) 105
Transvaal 105, 110, 111, 116
Treason of the Blue Books (1847) 19, 20, 86, 94
Treason of the Long Knives 92
Tredegar 48, 70, 103, 108
Tredegar Hall, Newport 104, 105, 106, 115, 117
Tredegar Park 76
Tregaron 21
Trelew 221
Troedrhiwfuwch 48
Troeltsch, Ernst 180
Troubles, The (Northern Ireland) 11
Tucker, W. A. 145, 154
Tudors 18
Twenty-four Metres (Welsh prosody) 210
Tylorstown Silver Band 51
Tyst, Y 28

Uitlanders 110, 111
Unionists 101, 107
see also Conservatives and Tories Unitarians 83, 85
United Kingdom 104, 132, 194
United Nations Association 192
United Nations Security Council 207
United States of America 120, 138, 207
see also America
University College of Wales, Aberystwyth 173
Usk 115

Vale of Clwyd 52, 56
Vale of Neath Brewery 70
Valente, Marcela 220
Valentine, Lewis 29, 30, 150
Value Added Tax 207
Vatican 88
Vaughan, (Colonel A. O.) 45
Victoria (Queen) 103
Victorian era 138
Vietnam War (1954–75) 10, 220
Virgil 85
Voluntary Artillery 69
Volunteer Force 66, 71
see also Chapter 3
Volunteer movements 3, 39, 57

Wallis, (Colonel) C. T. 104
Walter, Henry 168
Walthamstow 120
Walworth 145
War Artists Advisory Committee 186
War Office 3, 43, 44, 132

Index

Warwickshire 137, 141, 142
Warwickshire Regiment 23
Waterloo, battle of (1815) 23, 51, 64, 105
Wawr, Y 28, 29
Weber, Eugen 155
Weber, Max 38
Weil, Simone 218
Wehrmacht 152
Welch Regiment 43, 44, 51
Wellington, (Duke) Arthur Wellesley 51, 64, 82, 105
Wellington bomber 188
Welsh Army 55
Welsh Army Corps 4, 25, 50, 51
Welsh Division 4, 128, 138
Welsh Dragon (flag) 215, 217
    see also Red Dragon
Welsh Guards 130, 139, 140, 143, 146, 204, 208, 212, 215, 216
Welsh Horse (regiment) 47
Welsh Liberal Party 5
Welsh Liberals 57, 115
Welsh National Book of Remembrance 185, 191, 196
Welsh National Memorial to the Great War 184, 192, 196
Welsh Nonconformity 24, 51, 58
    see also Chapter 7
Welsh Puritans 168
Welsh Regiment 130, 135, 140, 143, 150
Welsh Republican Movement 32
Welsh Rifles *see* London Welsh Volunteer Corps
Welsh Tories 4, 107

Welsh Toryism 50, 107
Welshpool 212, 213
Welshpool Conservative Workingmen's Club 104
Wesleyans 172
West Dean 135
West Indies 129, 138
West Lancashire Division 154
West Midlands 138
Western Front 152, 157
Western Mail 10, 44, 46, 47, 50, 108, 109, 116, 119, 184, 196
Westminster 82
Westmorland 137, 142
Weston, Simon 6, 206, 210, 217, 220, 222
Weston-super-mare 156
Weyman, Stanley J. 53
Whigs 96
Whitchurch, Cardiff 197
White Island 89
Whitehall 204
Whitehead Steel and Iron Company 50
Wigley, Malcolm 211
Wilcox, Tim 214
Wiliams, Gerwyn 6, 10, 11
Wilkinson, Alan 171
Williams, Bronwen 210, 212, 213
Williams, Chris 4, 11
Williams, Christopher 51
Williams, David (editor) 109
Williams, D. J. 29, 30
Williams, Gwyn A. 195
Williams, Iwan Llwyd 221
Williams, John (of Brynsiencyn) 172

Williams, Llewelyn 21
Williams, Mari 185
Williams, William (Caledfryn) 20, 64
Williams Parry, Robert 211
Williams-Wynn, Robert 105
Williams-Wynn, (Sir) Watkins 66
Wiltshire 137
Wiltshire Regiment 131, 146
Windland, Kees 3, 7
Winter, Denis 152
Winter, J. M. [Jay] 126, 96
Worcestershire 137, 142
Worcestershire Regiment 145
Working Men's Committee 95
Working Men's Reception Committee 94, 95
Workmen's Compensation Act (1897) 12
Wrexham 23, 43, 56, 112, 113
Wrexham, Mayor of 43
Wurtemburgers 50
Wyndham, George 116, 117
Wyndham-Quinn, Major 103, 105, 106
Wynn Finch, Colonel 104

Yorath, Councillor 119
Yorkshire 137, 141, 142
Ystradgynlais 148, 149
Ypres 128
Ywain Meirion *see* Griffith, Owen

Zeppelin raids 185
Zulu (1964) 31, 43
Zulu Wars 8